COMPLETE OUR SURVEY AND LET US KNOW WHAT YOU THINK!

☐ Please do NOT send me information about VIZ and SHONEN JUMP products, news and events, special offers, or other information.

☐ Please do NOT send me information from VIZ's trusted business partners.

Name: _____

Address: _____

City:_____ State:_____ Zip:_____

E-mail: _____

☐ Male ☐ Female Date of Birth (mm/dd/yyyy): ___ / ___ / ___ (Under 13? Parental consent required)

1 Do you purchase SHONEN JUMP Magazine?

☐ Yes   ☐ No (if no, skip the next two questions)

If **YES**, do you subscribe?

☐ Yes   ☐ No

If **NO**, how often do you purchase SHONEN JUMP Magazine?

☐ 1-3 issues a year

☐ 4-6 issues a year

☐ more than 7 issues a year

2 Which SHONEN JUMP Graphic Novel did you purchase? (please check one)

☐ Beet the Vandel Buster   ☐ Bleach   ☐ Dragon Ball
☐ Dragon Ball Z   ☐ Dr. Slump   ☐ Eyeshield 21
☐ Hikaru no Go   ☐ Hunter x Hunter   ☐ I"s
☐ Knights of the Zodiac   ☐ Legendz   ☐ Naruto
☐ One Piece   ☐ Rurouni Kenshin   ☐ Shaman King
☐ The Prince of Tennis   ☐ Ultimate Muscle   ☐ Whistle!
☐ Yu-Gi-Oh!   ☐ Yu-Gi-Oh!: Duelist ☐ YuYu Hakusho
☐ Other _____

Will you purchase subsequent volumes?

☐ Yes   ☐ No

3 How did you learn about this title? (check all that apply)

☐ Favorite title   ☐ Advertisement   ☐ Article
☐ Gift   ☐ Read excerpt in SHONEN JUMP Magazine
☐ Recommendation   ☐ Special offer   ☐ Through TV animation
☐ Website   ☐ Other _____

4 Of the titles that are serialized in SHONEN JUMP Magazine, have you purchased the Graphic Novels?

☐ Yes ☐ No

If **YES**, which ones have you purchased? (check all that apply)

☐ Dragon Ball Z ☐ Hikaru no Go ☐ Naruto ☐ One Piece
☐ Shaman King ☐ Yu-Gi-Oh! ☐ YuYu Hakusho

If **YES**, what were your reasons for purchasing? (please pick up to 3)

☐ A favorite title ☐ A favorite creator/artist ☐ I want to read it in one go
☐ I want to read it over and over again ☐ There are extras that aren't in the magazine
☐ The quality of printing is better than the magazine ☐ Recommendation
☐ Special offer ☐ Other

If **NO**, why did/would you not purchase it?

☐ I'm happy just reading it in the magazine ☐ It's not worth buying the graphic novel
☐ All the manga pages are in black and white unlike the magazine
☐ There are other graphic novels that I prefer ☐ There are too many to collect for each title
☐ It's too small ☐ Other ______________________

5 Of the titles NOT serialized in the Magazine, which ones have you purchased?
(check all that apply)

☐ Beet the Vandel Buster ☐ Bleach ☐ Dragon Ball ☐ Dr. Slump
☐ Eyeshield 21 ☐ Hunter x Hunter ☐ I"s ☐ Knights of the Zodiac
☐ Legendz ☐ The Prince of Tennis ☐ Rurouni Kenshin ☐ Whistle!
☐ Yu-Gi-Oh!: Duelist ☐ None ☐ Other ______________

If you did purchase any of the above, what were your reasons for purchase?

☐ A favorite title ☐ A favorite creator/artist
☐ Read a preview in SHONEN JUMP Magazine and wanted to read the rest of the story
☐ Recommendation ☐ Other

Will you purchase subsequent volumes?

☐ Yes ☐ No

6 What race/ethnicity do you consider yourself? (please check one)

☐ Asian/Pacific Islander ☐ Black/African American ☐ Hispanic/Latino
☐ Native American/Alaskan Native ☐ White/Caucasian ☐ Other

THANK YOU! Please send the completed form to:

VIZ Survey
42 Catharine St.
Poughkeepsie, NY 12601

All information provided will be used for internal purposes only. We promise not to sell or otherwise divulge your information.

鳥 山 明

I don't know how many times I've said it—I hate the cold and I hate winter! I wish I could hibernate like a bear. I often get invited to go skiing, but there's no way I would go. Why would I go out of my way to go someplace that's so cold? But on the other hand, I love it when it's hot, in the summertime! I get so excited! That's why it's mostly summer in my manga. I love the summer! Now if only there weren't any mosquitoes...

—*Akira Toriyama, 1989*

Artist/writer Akira Toriyama burst onto the manga scene in 1980 with the wildly popular **Dr. Slump**, a science fiction comedy about the adventures of a mad scientist and his android "daughter." In 1984 he created his hit series **Dragon Ball**, which ran until 1995 in Shueisha's best-selling magazine **Weekly Shonen Jump**, and was translated into foreign languages around the world. Since **Dragon Ball**, he has worked on a variety of short series, including **Cowa!**, **Kajika**, **SandLand**, and **Neko Majin**, as well as a children's book, **Toccio the Angel**. He is also known for his design work on video games, particularly the **Dragon Warrior** RPG series. He lives with his family in Japan.

DRAGON BALL Z VOL. 2
The SHONEN JUMP Graphic Novel Edition

This graphic novel is number 18 in a series of 42.

STORY AND ART BY
AKIRA TORIYAMA

English Adaptation/Gerard Jones
Translation/Lillian Olsen
Touch-Up Art & Lettering/Wayne Truman
Cover Design/Izumi Evers & Dan Ziegler
Graphics & Design/Sean Lee
Original Editor/Trish Ledoux
Editor/Jason Thompson

Managing Editor/Elizabeth Kawasaki
Director of Production/Noboru Watanabe
Vice President of Publishing/Alvin Lu
Vice President & Editor-in-Chief/Yumi Hoashi
Sr. Director of Acquisitions/Rika Inouye
Vice President of Sales and Marketing/Liza Coppola
Publisher/Hyoe Narita

In the original Japanese edition, DRAGON BALL and DRAGON
BALL Z are known collectively as the 42-volume series DRAGON
BALL. The English DRAGON BALL Z was originally volumes 17-42
of the Japanese DRAGON BALL.

Published by VIZ Media, LLC
P.O. Box 77010 • San Francisco, CA 94107

SHONEN JUMP Graphic Novel Edition
10 9 8 7 6 5 4
First printing, March 2003
Second printing, July 2003
Third printing, October 2004
Fourth printing, May 2005

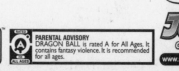

THE WORLD'S
MOST POPULAR MANGA

SHONEN JUMP

GRAPHIC NOVEL

www.shonenjump.com

www.viz.com

PARENTAL ADVISORY
DRAGON BALL is rated A for All Ages. It
contains fantasy violence. It is recommended
for all ages.

SHONEN JUMP GRAPHIC NOVEL

DRAGON BALL Z

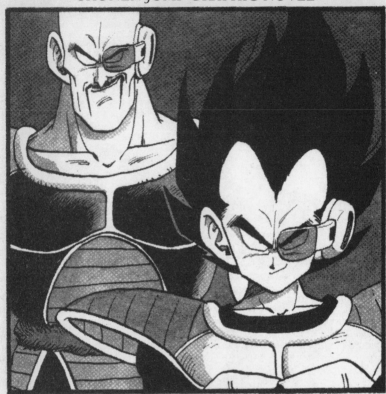

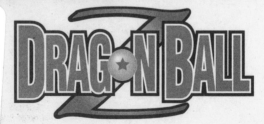

Vol. 2

DB: 18 of 42

STORY AND ART BY
AKIRA TORIYAMA

THE MAIN CHARACTERS

Son Gohan

Goku's four-year-old son. As a half-human, half-Saiyan, he may be even stronger than a regular Saiyan!

Son Goku

The greatest martial artist on Earth. Although he looks human, he's actually one of the alien Saiyans. Unlike most Saiyans, he does not have a monkey's tail, as it was cut off several years ago.

Bulma

Goku's oldest friend, Bulma is a scientific genius. She met Goku while on a quest for the seven magical Dragon Balls which, when gathered together, can grant any wish.

Tenshinhan

Three-eyed Tenshinhan is one of Goku's former rivals.

Kuririn

Goku's former martial arts schoolmate under Kame-Sen'nin.

Yamcha

A former bandit and martial artist, Yamcha is Bulma's ex-boyfriend.

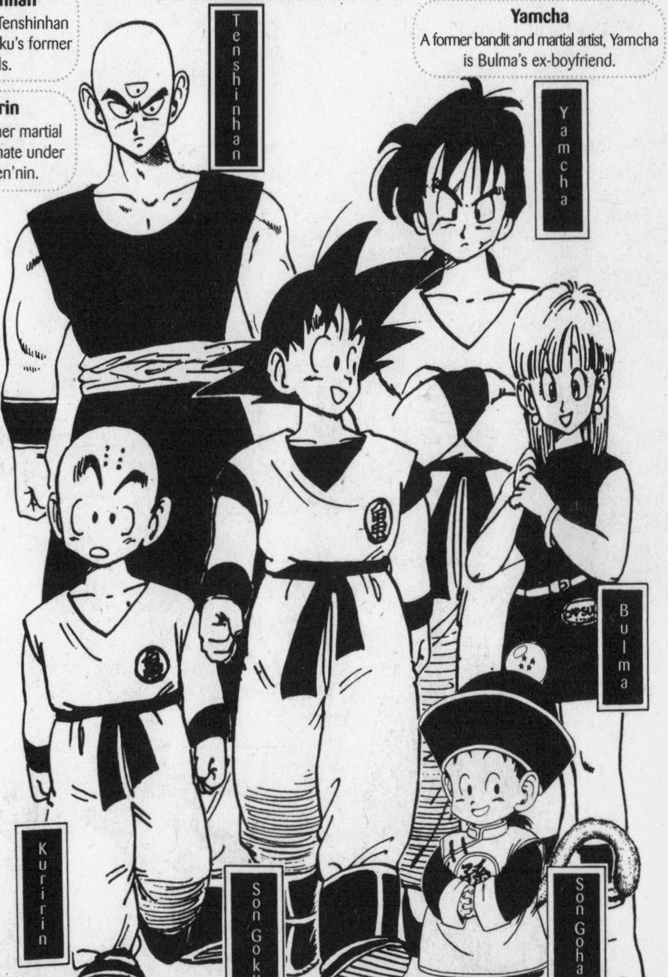
Tenshinhan
Yamcha
Bulma
Kuririn
Son Goku
Son Gohan

Son Goku was Earth's greatest hero, but no one knew where he got his strength…until a stranger came from outer space bearing the news that Goku was an alien! The shocking news turned worse when the stranger, Goku's brother Raditz, proved to be a ruthless killer. By teaming up with his old enemy Piccolo, Goku was able to defeat his extraodinarily powerful brother…only to die in the process. Now, Goku has gone to the afterlife, and Earth is in even more trouble…in one year, Raditz's partners will arrive to steal the Dragon Balls and wipe out all life on Earth!!

Piccolo
Goku's arch-enemy, Piccolo *Daimaô* ("Piccolo the Great Demon King") once tried to become ruler of the world.

Kami-sama
The deity who watches over the Earth, Kami-sama is the good side to Piccolo's evil. He is assisted by Mr. Popo.

Vegeta & Nappa
The two Saiyan warriors who will arrive on Earth in one year.

Kame-Sen'nin
Kame-Sen'nin, also known as the "Turtle Hermit" or *Muten-Rôshi* (the "Invincible Old Master"), helped train Goku and Kuririn in the martial arts.

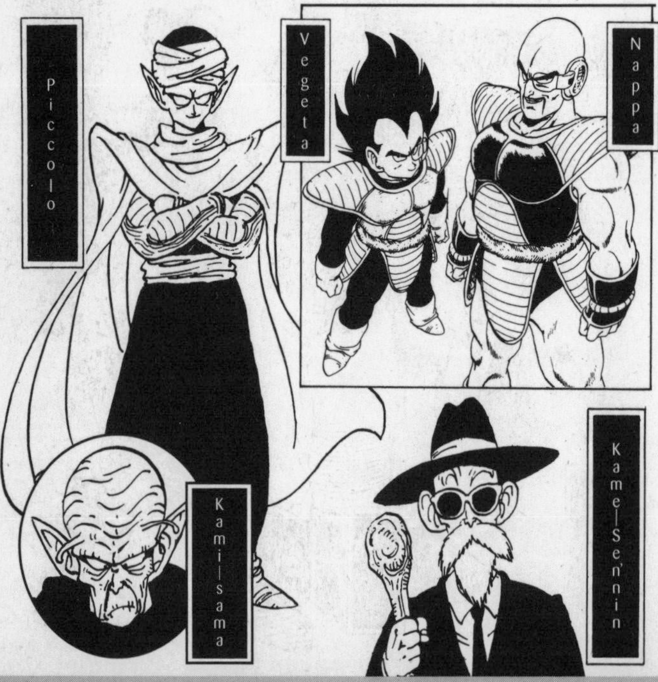
Nappa
Vegeta
Piccolo
Kame-Sen'nin
Kami-sama

DRAGON BALL Z 2

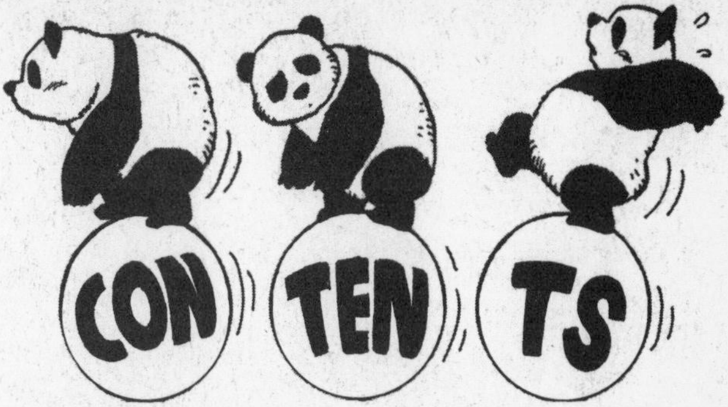
CON
TEN
TS

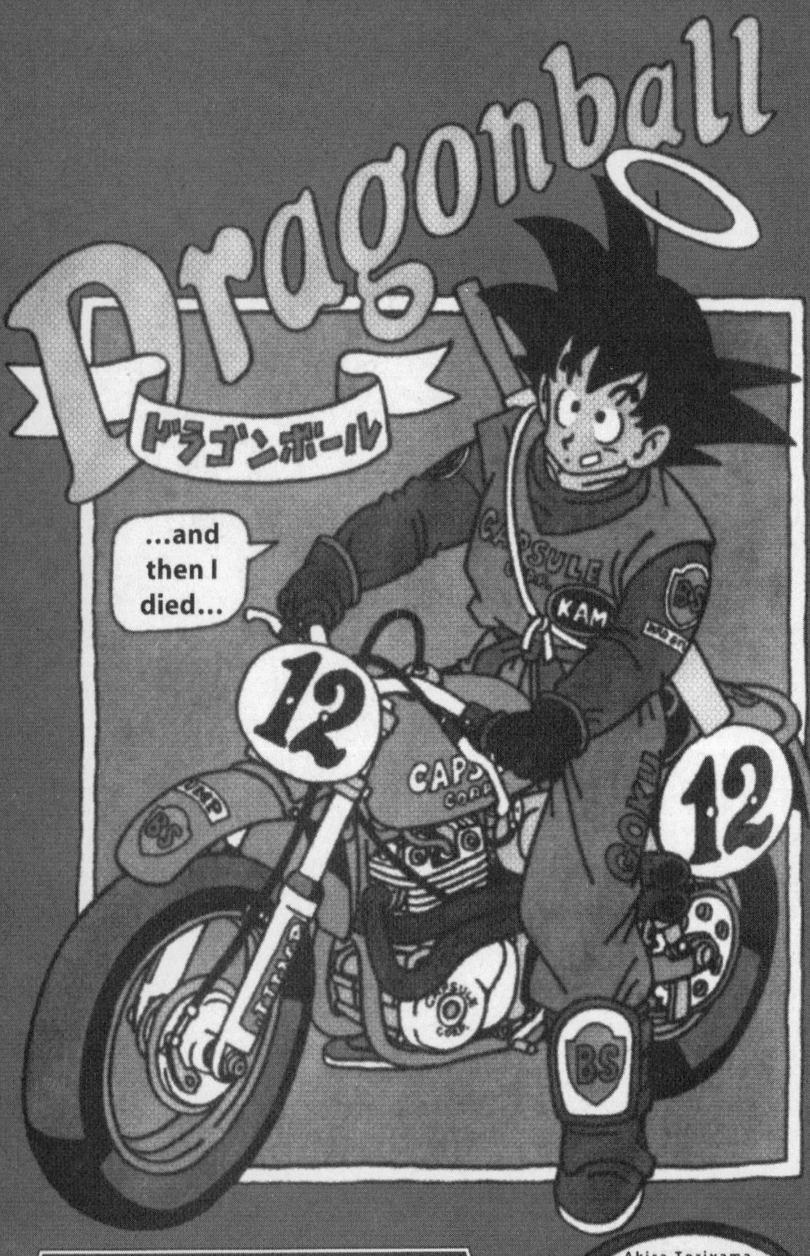
Dragonball
ドラゴンボール
...and then I died...
CAPSULE
KAM
12
CAPSULE CORP.
BS
GOKU
12
Akira Toriyama
鳥山明
BIRD STUDIO

DBZ:11
A Warrior in Hell

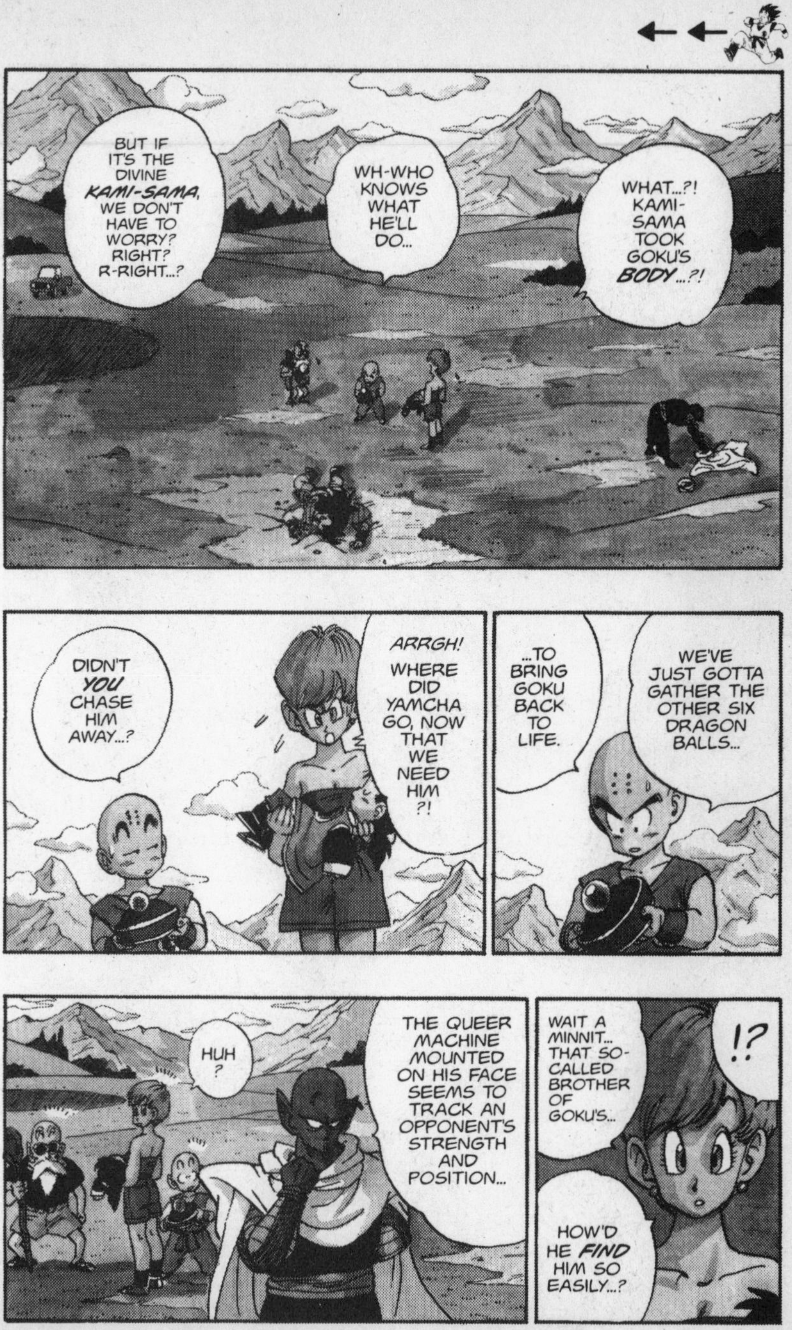
WHAT...?! KAMI-SAMA TOOK GOKU'S *BODY*...?!
WH-WHO KNOWS WHAT HE'LL DO...
BUT IF IT'S THE DIVINE *KAMI-SAMA*, WE DON'T HAVE TO WORRY? RIGHT? R-RIGHT...?
WE'VE JUST GOTTA GATHER THE OTHER SIX DRAGON BALLS...
...TO BRING GOKU BACK TO LIFE.
ARRGH! WHERE DID YAMCHA GO, NOW THAT WE NEED HIM?!
DIDN'T *YOU* CHASE HIM AWAY...?
!?
WAIT A MINNIT... THAT SO-CALLED BROTHER OF GOKU'S...
HOW'D HE *FIND* HIM SO EASILY...?
THE QUEER MACHINE MOUNTED ON HIS FACE SEEMS TO TRACK AN OPPONENT'S STRENGTH AND POSITION...
HUH?

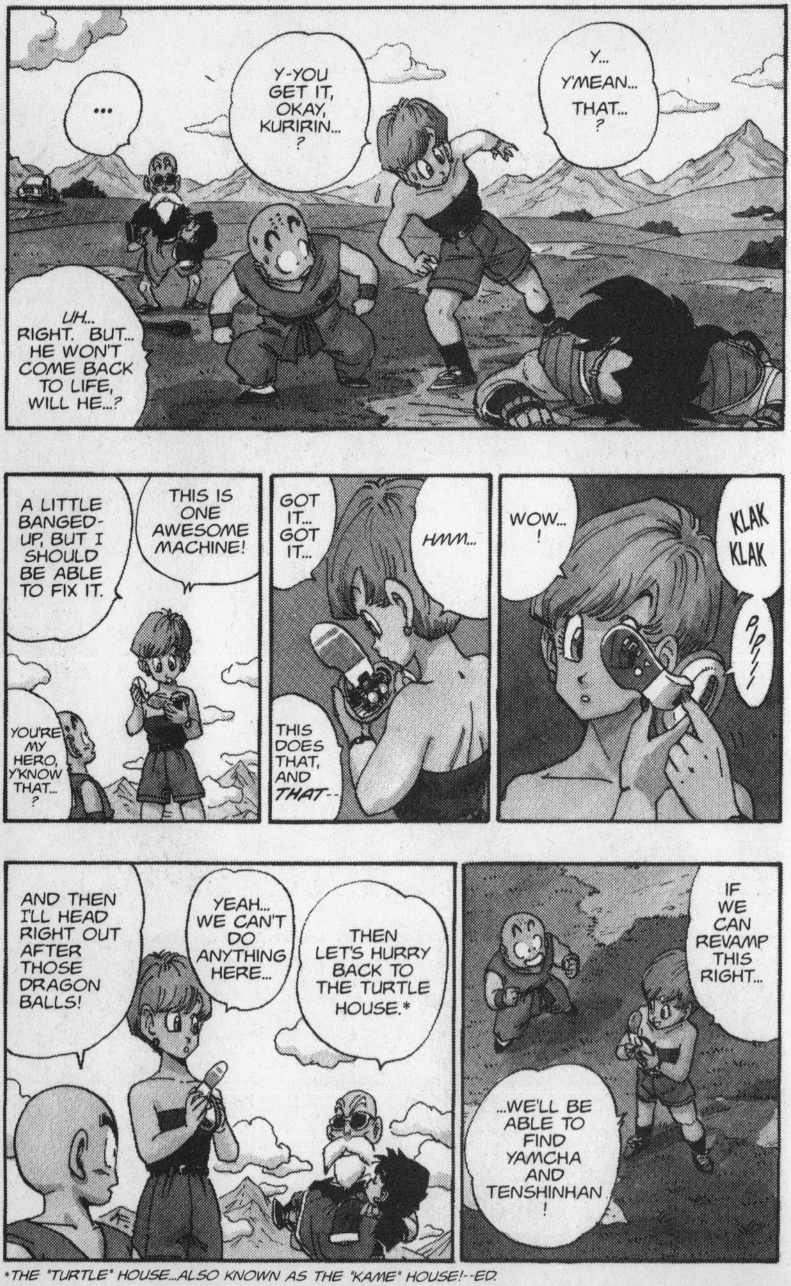
Y... Y'MEAN... THAT...?
Y-YOU GET IT, OKAY, KURIRIN...?
...
UH... RIGHT. BUT... HE WON'T COME BACK TO LIFE, WILL HE...?
WOW...!
KLAK KLAK
PIPI
HMM...
GOT IT... GOT IT...
THIS DOES THAT, AND *THAT*--
THIS IS ONE AWESOME MACHINE!
A LITTLE BANGED-UP, BUT I SHOULD BE ABLE TO FIX IT.
YOU'RE MY HERO, Y'KNOW THAT...?
IF WE CAN REVAMP THIS RIGHT...
...WE'LL BE ABLE TO FIND YAMCHA AND TENSHINHAN!
THEN LET'S HURRY BACK TO THE TURTLE HOUSE.*
YEAH... WE CAN'T DO ANYTHING HERE...
AND THEN I'LL HEAD RIGHT OUT AFTER THOSE DRAGON BALLS!

*THE "TURTLE" HOUSE...ALSO KNOWN AS THE "KAME" HOUSE!--ED.

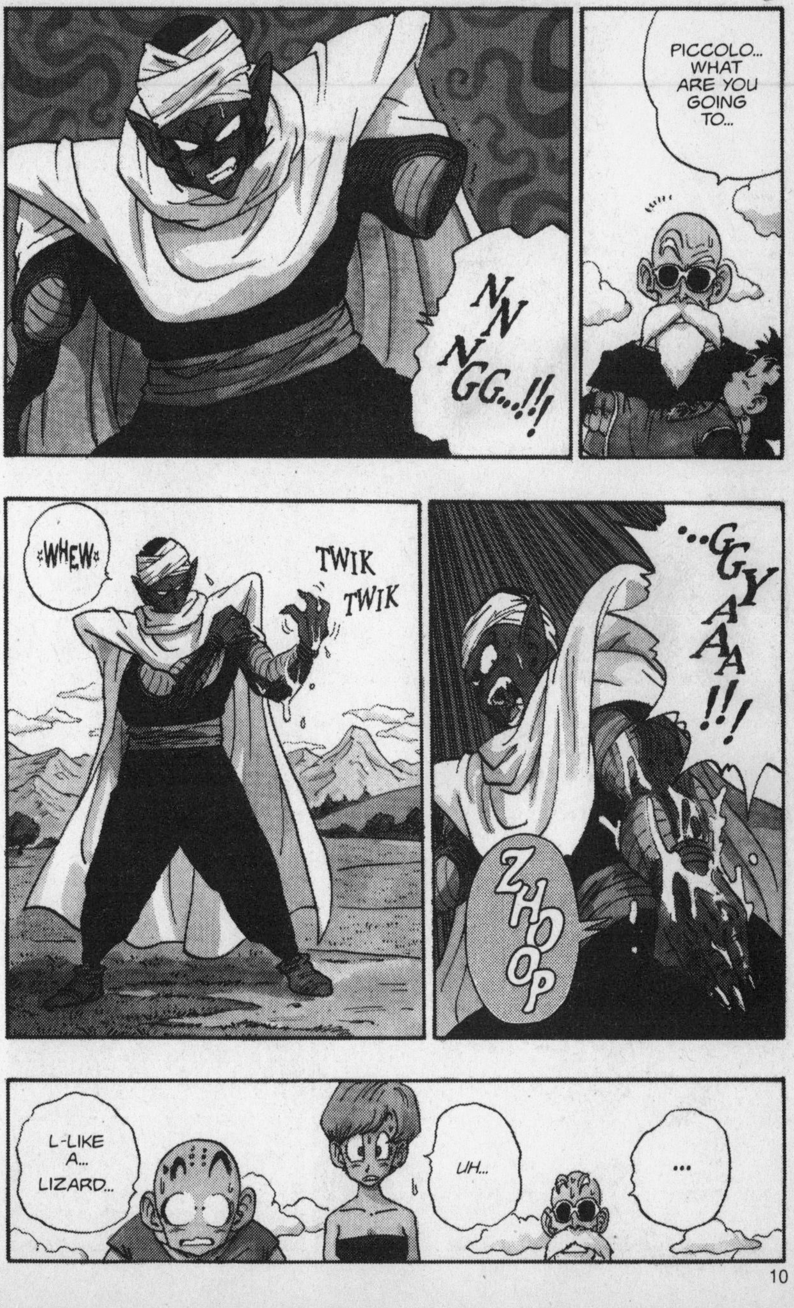
PICCOLO... WHAT ARE YOU GOING TO...
NNNGG...!!!
...GGYAAA!!!
ZHOOP
WHEW
TWIK TWIK
...
UH...
L-LIKE A... LIZARD...

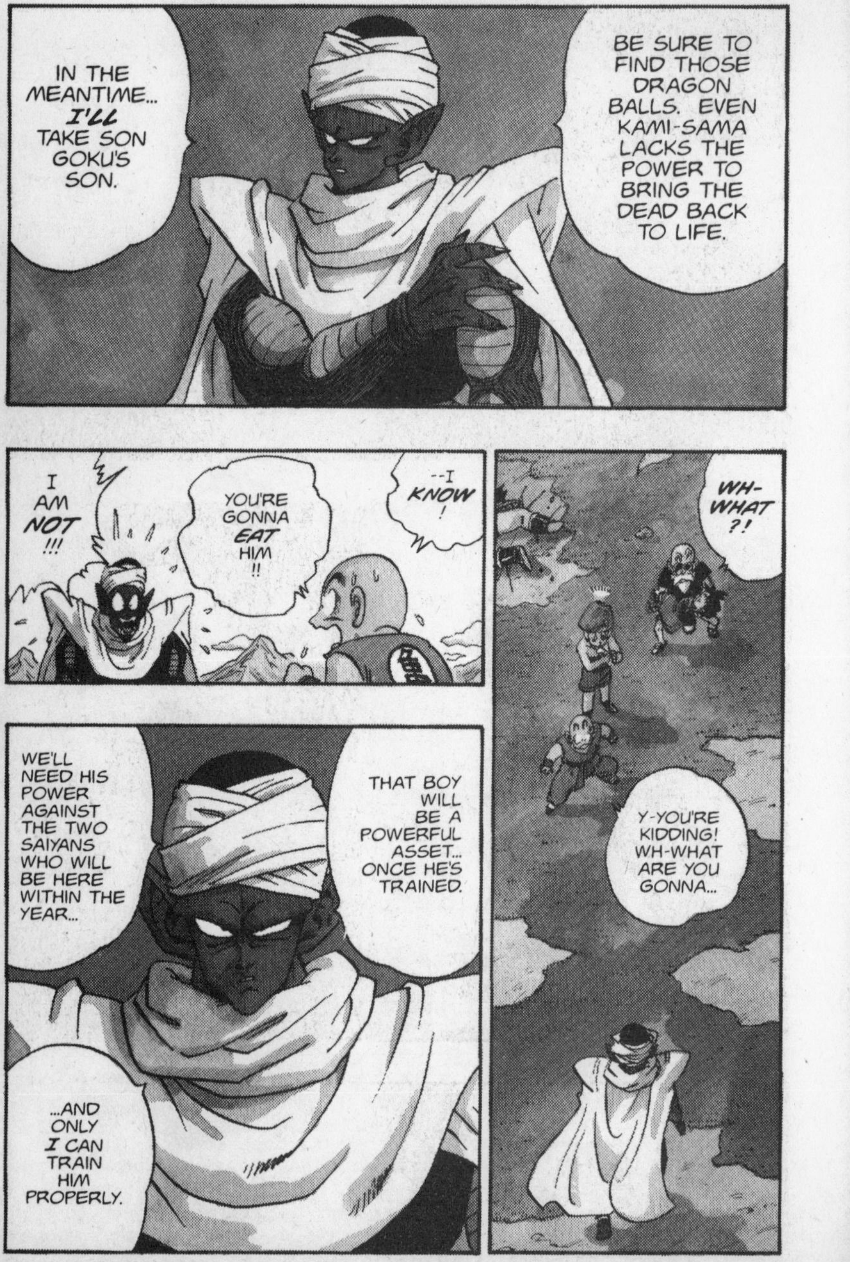
BE SURE TO FIND THOSE DRAGON BALLS. EVEN KAMI-SAMA LACKS THE POWER TO BRING THE DEAD BACK TO LIFE.
IN THE MEANTIME... *I'LL* TAKE SON GOKU'S SON.
WH-WHAT ?!
Y-YOU'RE KIDDING! WH-WHAT ARE YOU GONNA...
--I *KNOW* !
YOU'RE GONNA *EAT* HIM !!
I AM *NOT* !!!
THAT BOY WILL BE A POWERFUL ASSET... ONCE HE'S TRAINED.
WE'LL NEED HIS POWER AGAINST THE TWO SAIYANS WHO WILL BE HERE WITHIN THE YEAR...
...AND ONLY *I* CAN TRAIN HIM PROPERLY.

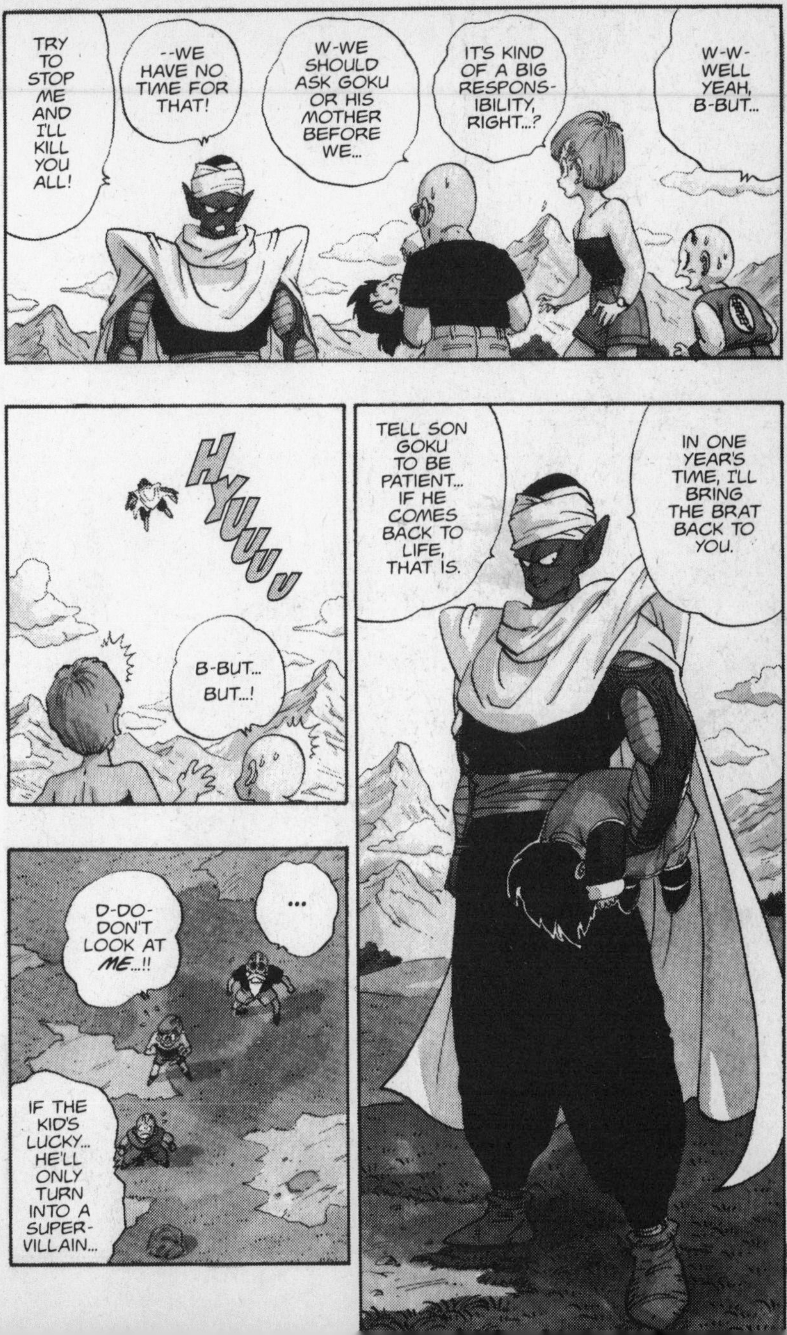
W-W-WELL YEAH, B-BUT...
IT'S KIND OF A BIG RESPONSIBILITY, RIGHT...?
W-WE SHOULD ASK GOKU OR HIS MOTHER BEFORE WE...
--WE HAVE NO TIME FOR THAT!
TRY TO STOP ME AND I'LL KILL YOU ALL!
IN ONE YEAR'S TIME, I'LL BRING THE BRAT BACK TO YOU.
TELL SON GOKU TO BE PATIENT... IF HE COMES BACK TO LIFE, THAT IS.
HYUUUU
B-BUT... BUT...!
...
D-DO-DON'T LOOK AT *ME*...!!
IF THE KID'S LUCKY... HE'LL ONLY TURN INTO A SUPER-VILLAIN...

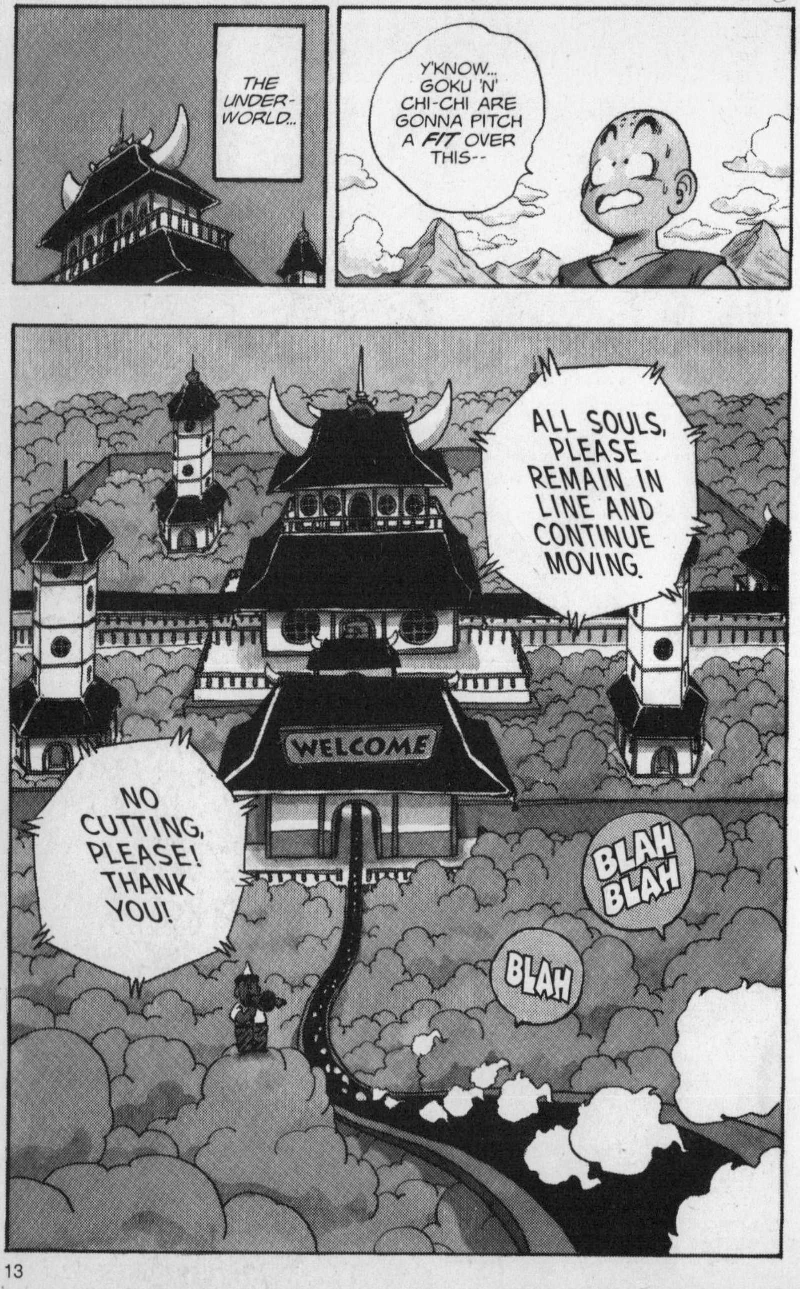
Y'KNOW... GOKU 'N' CHI-CHI ARE GONNA PITCH A FIT OVER THIS--
THE UNDER-WORLD...
ALL SOULS, PLEASE REMAIN IN LINE AND CONTINUE MOVING.
WELCOME
NO CUTTING, PLEASE! THANK YOU!
BLAH BLAH
BLAH

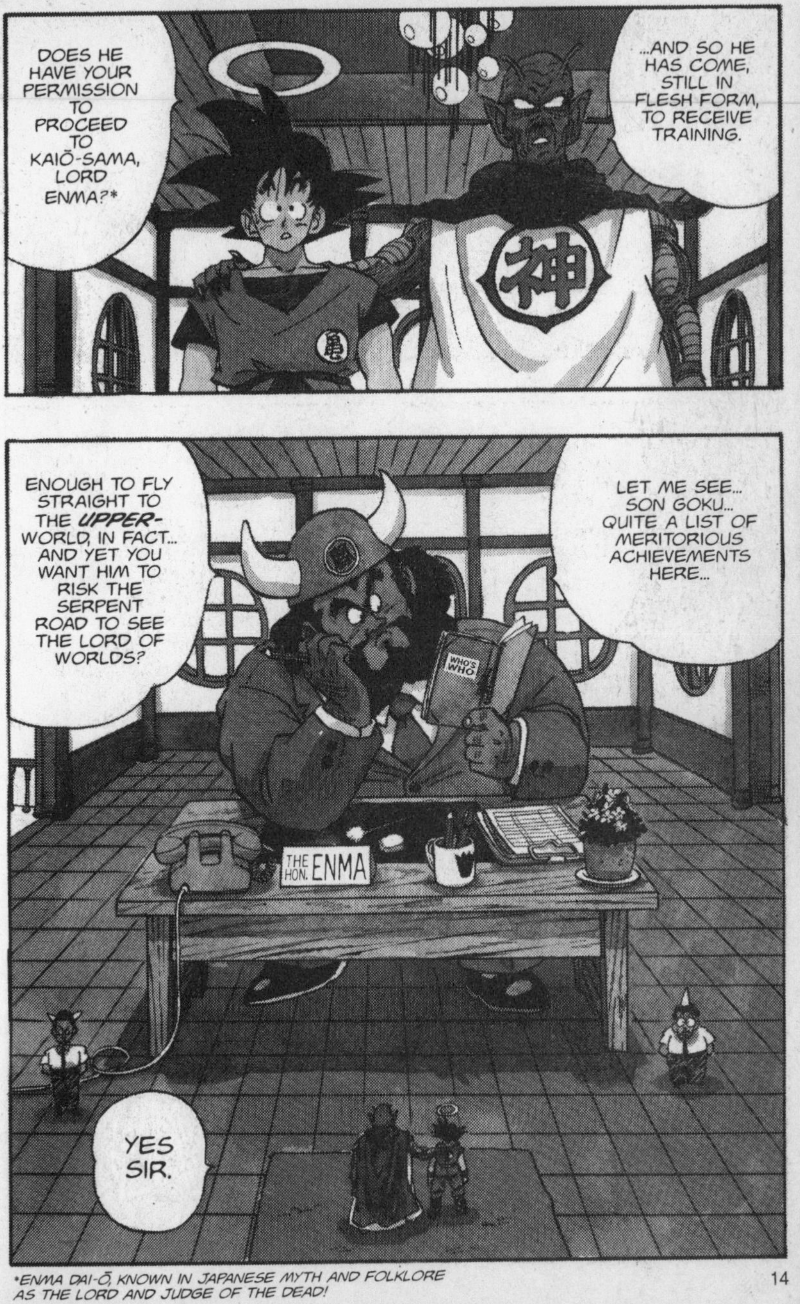
...AND SO HE HAS COME, STILL IN FLESH FORM, TO RECEIVE TRAINING.
DOES HE HAVE YOUR PERMISSION TO PROCEED TO KAIŌ-SAMA, LORD ENMA?*
LET ME SEE... SON GOKU... QUITE A LIST OF MERITORIOUS ACHIEVEMENTS HERE...
WHO'S WHO
ENOUGH TO FLY STRAIGHT TO THE *UPPER*-WORLD, IN FACT... AND YET YOU WANT HIM TO RISK THE SERPENT ROAD TO SEE THE LORD OF WORLDS?
THE HON. ENMA
YES SIR.

**ENMA DAI-Ō, KNOWN IN JAPANESE MYTH AND FOLKLORE AS THE LORD AND JUDGE OF THE DEAD!*

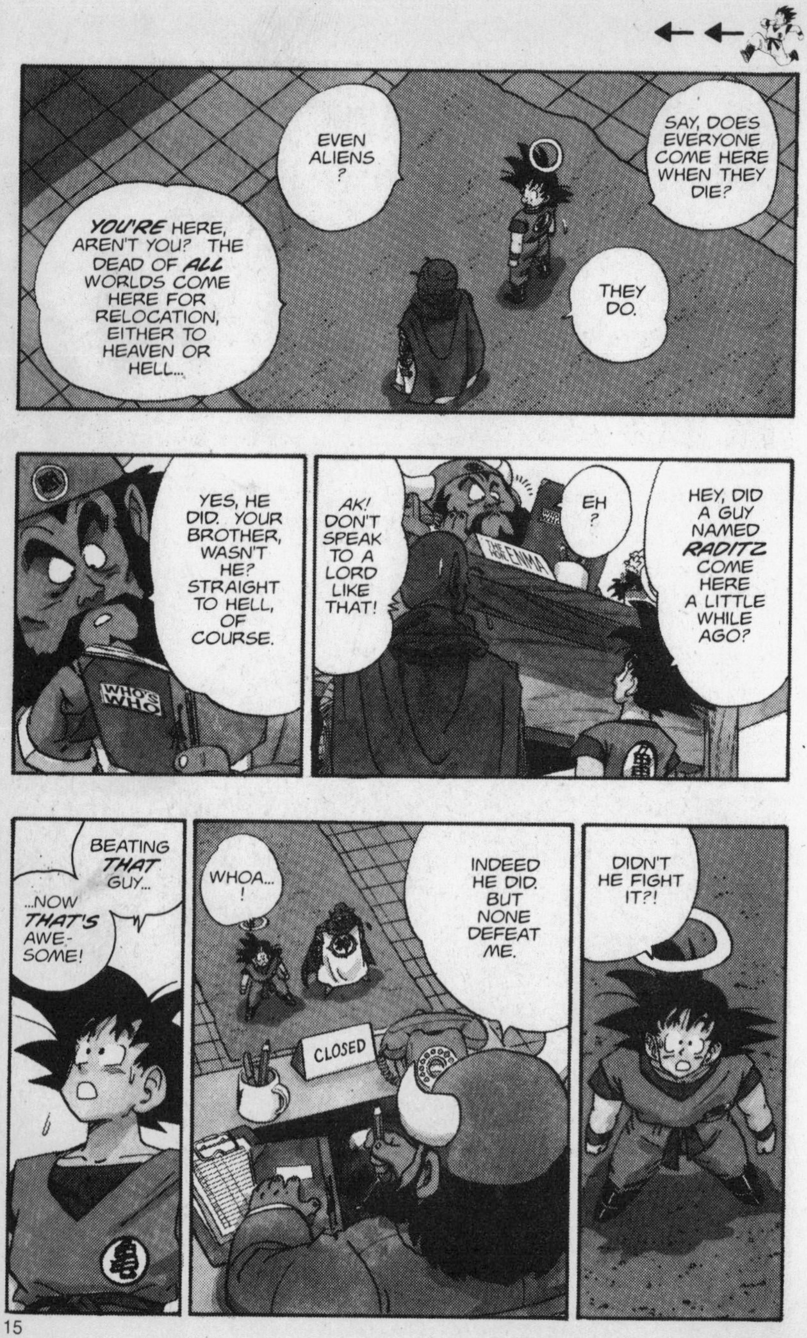

SAY, DOES EVERYONE COME HERE WHEN THEY DIE?
THEY DO.
EVEN ALIENS?
YOU'RE HERE, AREN'T YOU? THE DEAD OF ALL WORLDS COME HERE FOR RELOCATION, EITHER TO HEAVEN OR HELL...
HEY, DID A GUY NAMED RADITZ COME HERE A LITTLE WHILE AGO?
EH?
ENMA
AK! DON'T SPEAK TO A LORD LIKE THAT!
YES, HE DID. YOUR BROTHER, WASN'T HE? STRAIGHT TO HELL, OF COURSE.
WHO'S WHO
DIDN'T HE FIGHT IT?!
INDEED HE DID. BUT NONE DEFEAT ME.
WHOA...!
CLOSED
BEATING THAT GUY...
...NOW THAT'S AWESOME!

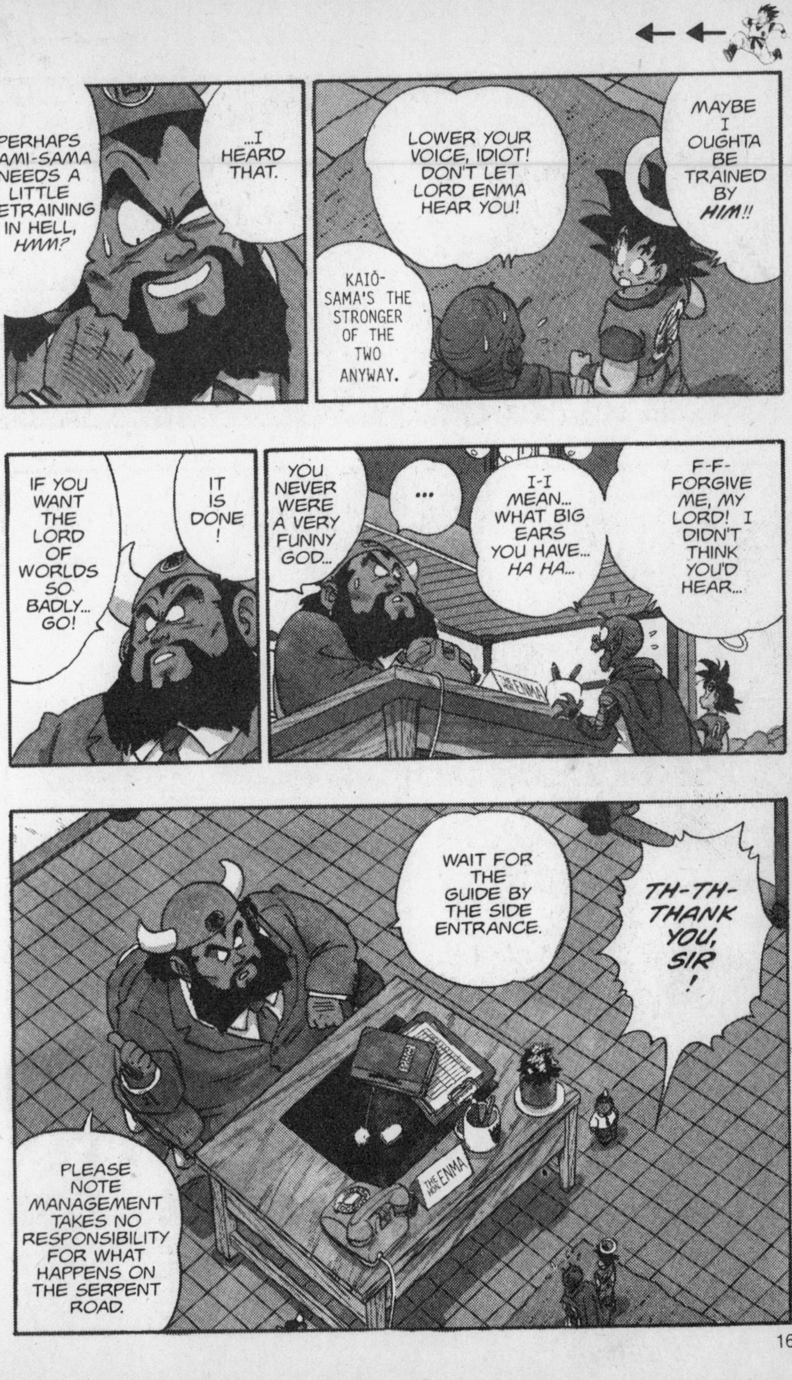
MAYBE I OUGHTA BE TRAINED BY *HIM*!!
LOWER YOUR VOICE, IDIOT! DON'T LET LORD ENMA HEAR YOU!
KAIÔ-SAMA'S THE STRONGER OF THE TWO ANYWAY.
...I HEARD THAT.
PERHAPS KAMI-SAMA NEEDS A LITTLE RETRAINING IN HELL, *HMM?*
F-F-FORGIVE ME, MY LORD! I DIDN'T THINK YOU'D HEAR...
I-I MEAN... WHAT BIG EARS YOU HAVE... *HA HA...*
...
YOU NEVER WERE A VERY FUNNY GOD...
IT IS DONE!
IF YOU WANT THE LORD OF WORLDS SO BADLY... GO!
WAIT FOR THE GUIDE BY THE SIDE ENTRANCE.
TH-TH-THANK YOU, SIR!
PLEASE NOTE MANAGEMENT TAKES NO RESPONSIBILITY FOR WHAT HAPPENS ON THE SERPENT ROAD.

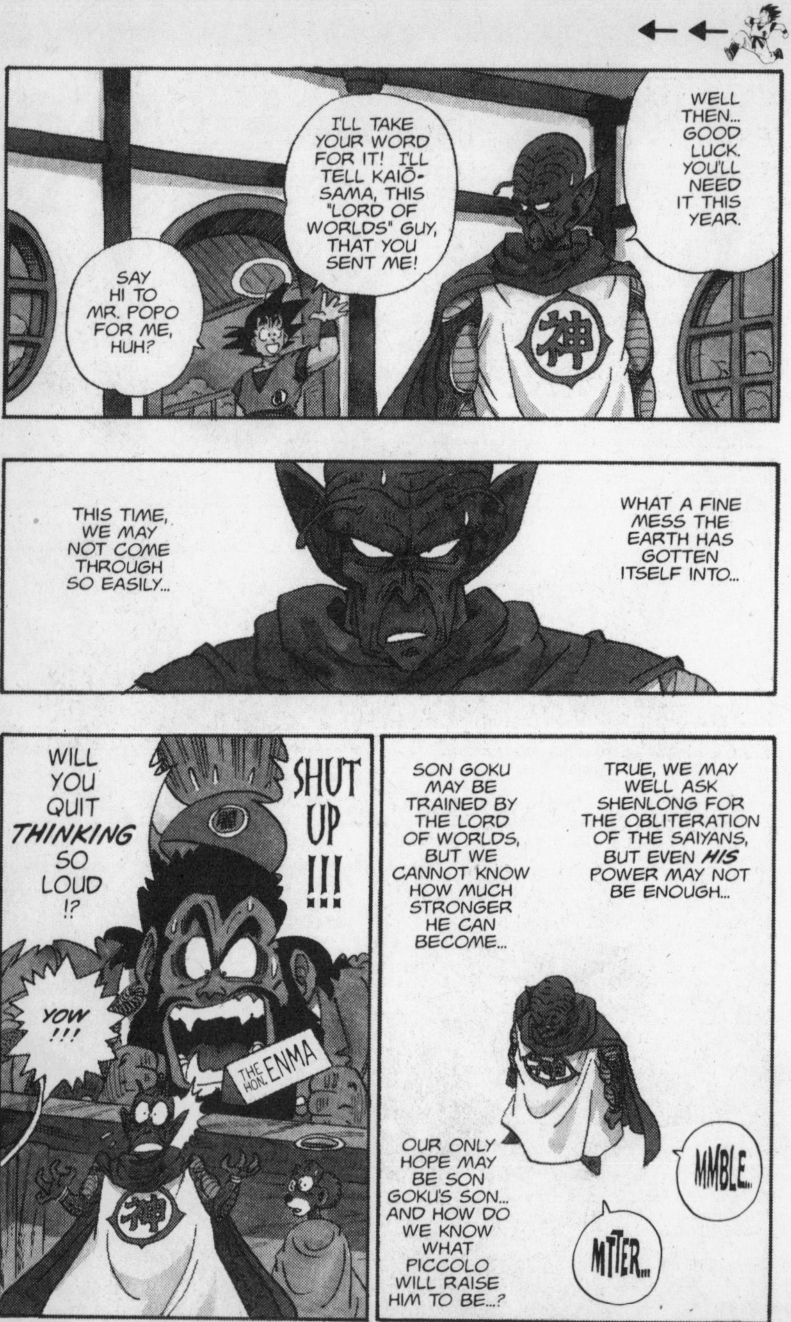
WELL THEN... GOOD LUCK. YOU'LL NEED IT THIS YEAR.
I'LL TAKE YOUR WORD FOR IT! I'LL TELL KAIŌ-SAMA, THIS "LORD OF WORLDS" GUY, THAT YOU SENT ME!
SAY HI TO MR. POPO FOR ME, HUH?
WHAT A FINE MESS THE EARTH HAS GOTTEN ITSELF INTO...
THIS TIME, WE MAY NOT COME THROUGH SO EASILY...
TRUE, WE MAY WELL ASK SHENLONG FOR THE OBLITERATION OF THE SAIYANS, BUT EVEN *HIS* POWER MAY NOT BE ENOUGH...
SON GOKU MAY BE TRAINED BY THE LORD OF WORLDS, BUT WE CANNOT KNOW HOW MUCH STRONGER HE CAN BECOME...
MMBLE...
OUR ONLY HOPE MAY BE SON GOKU'S SON... AND HOW DO WE KNOW WHAT PICCOLO WILL RAISE HIM TO BE...?
MTTER...
SHUT UP !!!
WILL YOU QUIT *THINKING* SO LOUD !?
YOW !!!
THE HON. ENMA

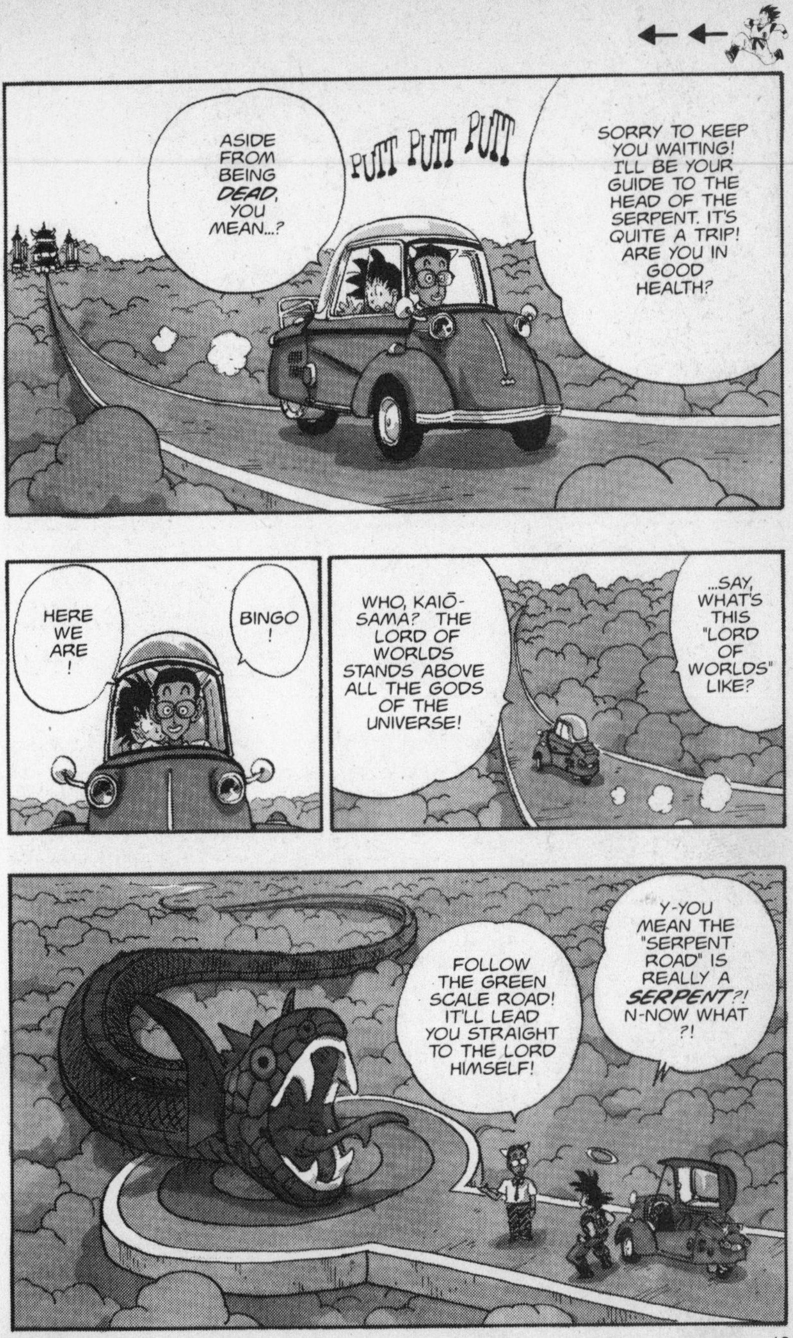
SORRY TO KEEP YOU WAITING! I'LL BE YOUR GUIDE TO THE HEAD OF THE SERPENT. IT'S QUITE A TRIP! ARE YOU IN GOOD HEALTH?
PUTT PUTT PUTT
ASIDE FROM BEING *DEAD*, YOU MEAN...?
...SAY, WHAT'S THIS "LORD OF WORLDS" LIKE?
WHO, KAIŌ-SAMA? THE LORD OF WORLDS STANDS ABOVE ALL THE GODS OF THE UNIVERSE!
BINGO!
HERE WE ARE!
Y-YOU MEAN THE "SERPENT ROAD" IS REALLY A *SERPENT*?! N-NOW WHAT?!
FOLLOW THE GREEN SCALE ROAD! IT'LL LEAD YOU STRAIGHT TO THE LORD HIMSELF!

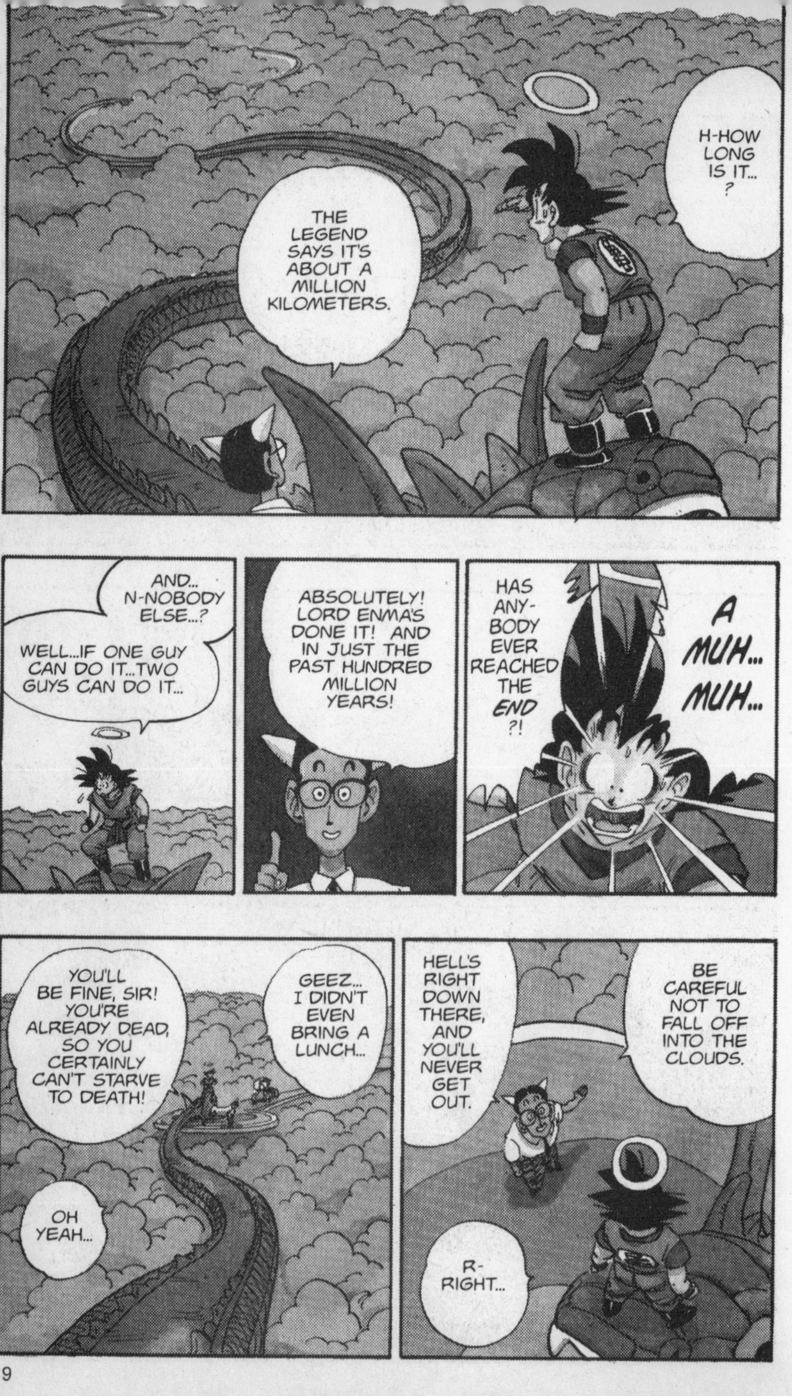
H-HOW LONG IS IT...?
THE LEGEND SAYS IT'S ABOUT A MILLION KILOMETERS.
HAS ANYBODY EVER REACHED THE *END*?!
A MUH... MUH...
ABSOLUTELY! LORD ENMA'S DONE IT! AND IN JUST THE PAST HUNDRED MILLION YEARS!
AND... N-NOBODY ELSE...?
WELL...IF ONE GUY CAN DO IT...TWO GUYS CAN DO IT...
BE CAREFUL NOT TO FALL OFF INTO THE CLOUDS.
HELL'S RIGHT DOWN THERE, AND YOU'LL NEVER GET OUT.
R-RIGHT...
GEEZ... I DIDN'T EVEN BRING A LUNCH...
YOU'LL BE FINE, SIR! YOU'RE ALREADY DEAD, SO YOU CERTAINLY CAN'T STARVE TO DEATH!
OH YEAH...

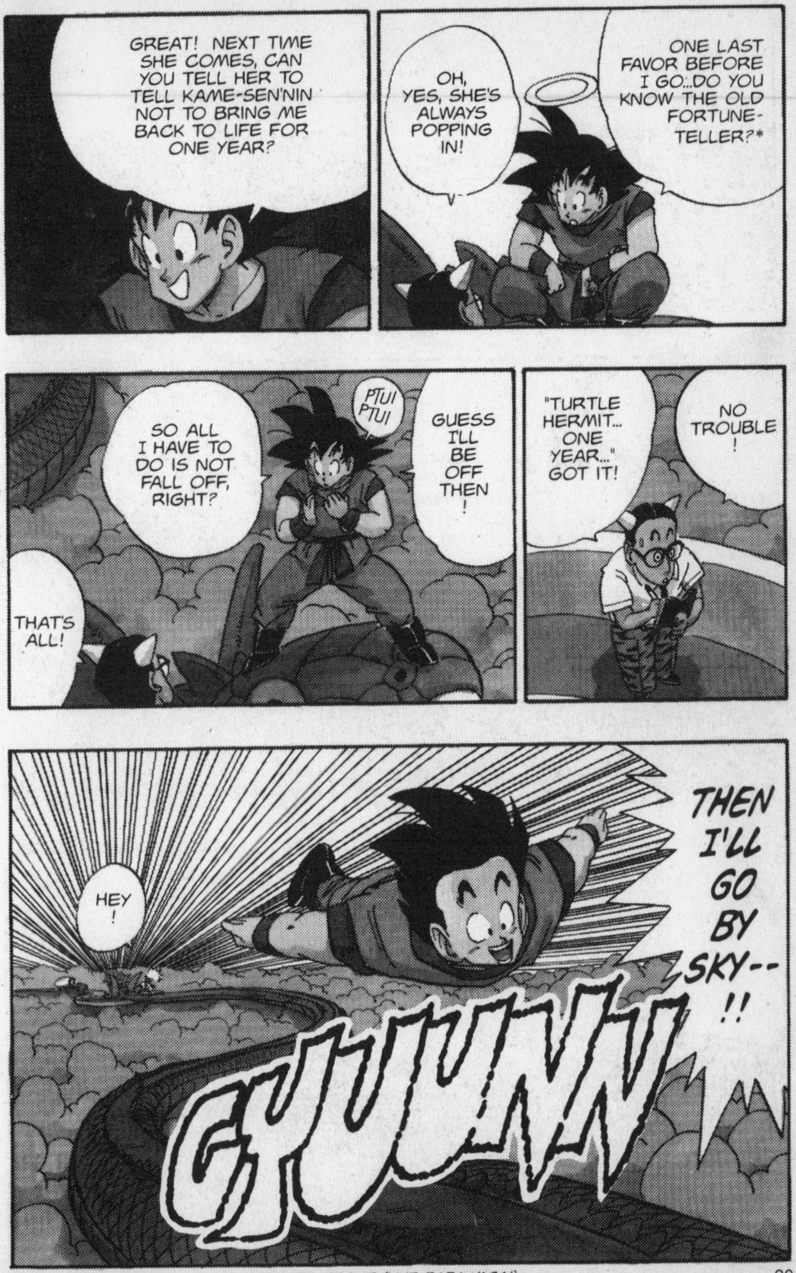
ONE LAST FAVOR BEFORE I GO...DO YOU KNOW THE OLD FORTUNE-TELLER?*
OH, YES, SHE'S ALWAYS POPPING IN!
GREAT! NEXT TIME SHE COMES, CAN YOU TELL HER TO TELL KAME-SEN'NIN NOT TO BRING ME BACK TO LIFE FOR ONE YEAR?
NO TROUBLE!
"TURTLE HERMIT... ONE YEAR..." GOT IT!
GUESS I'LL BE OFF THEN!
PTUI PTUI
SO ALL I HAVE TO DO IS NOT FALL OFF, RIGHT?
THAT'S ALL!
THEN I'LL GO BY SKY--!!
HEY!
GYUNN

*A.K.A. "BABA URANAI," A WISE, WIZENED CRONE (LIKE BABA YAGA!) FIRST MET BY GOKU & CO. IN EARLIER ***DRAGON BALL*** STORIES.

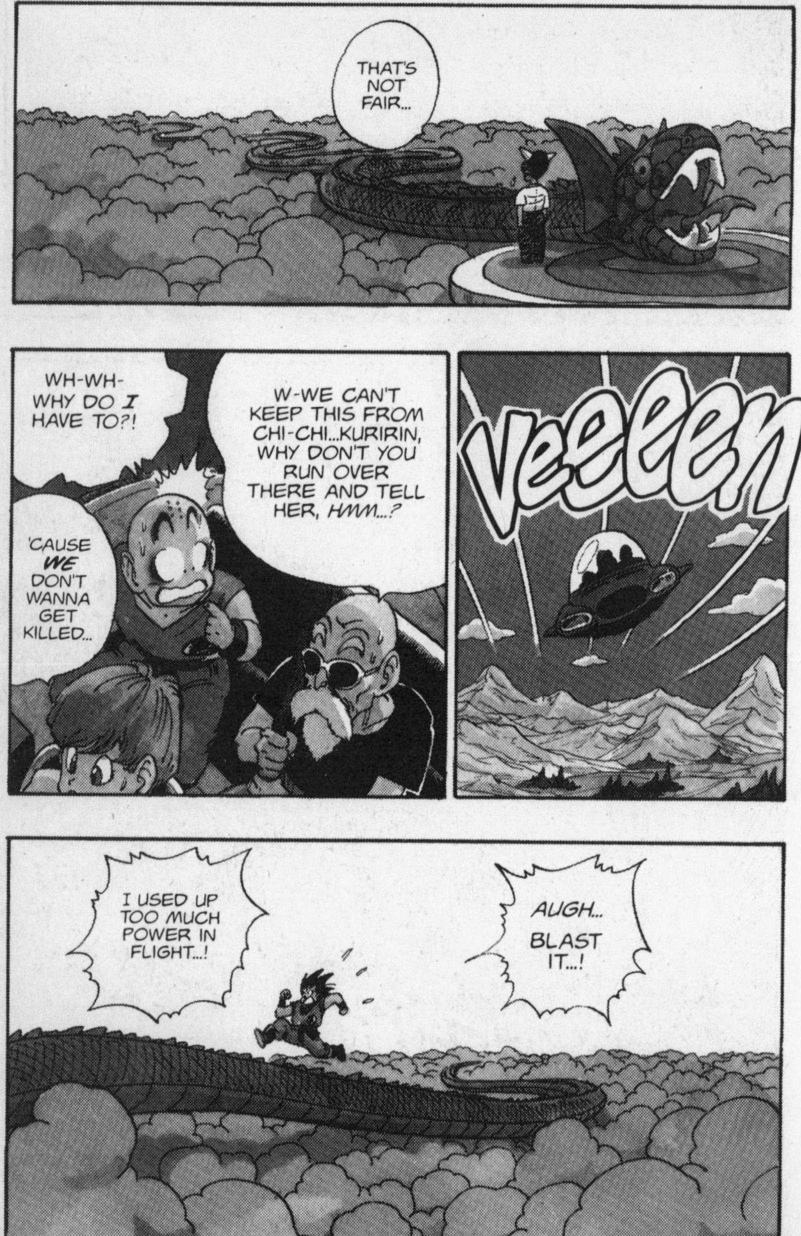
THAT'S NOT FAIR...
VEEEEN
W-WE CAN'T KEEP THIS FROM CHI-CHI...KURIRIN, WHY DON'T YOU RUN OVER THERE AND TELL HER, *HMM...?*
WH-WH- WHY DO *I* HAVE TO?!
'CAUSE ***WE*** DON'T WANNA GET KILLED...
AUGH... BLAST IT...!
I USED UP TOO MUCH POWER IN FLIGHT...!

NEXT: A STERN TASKMASTER

DBZ : 12 • Gohan and Piccolo

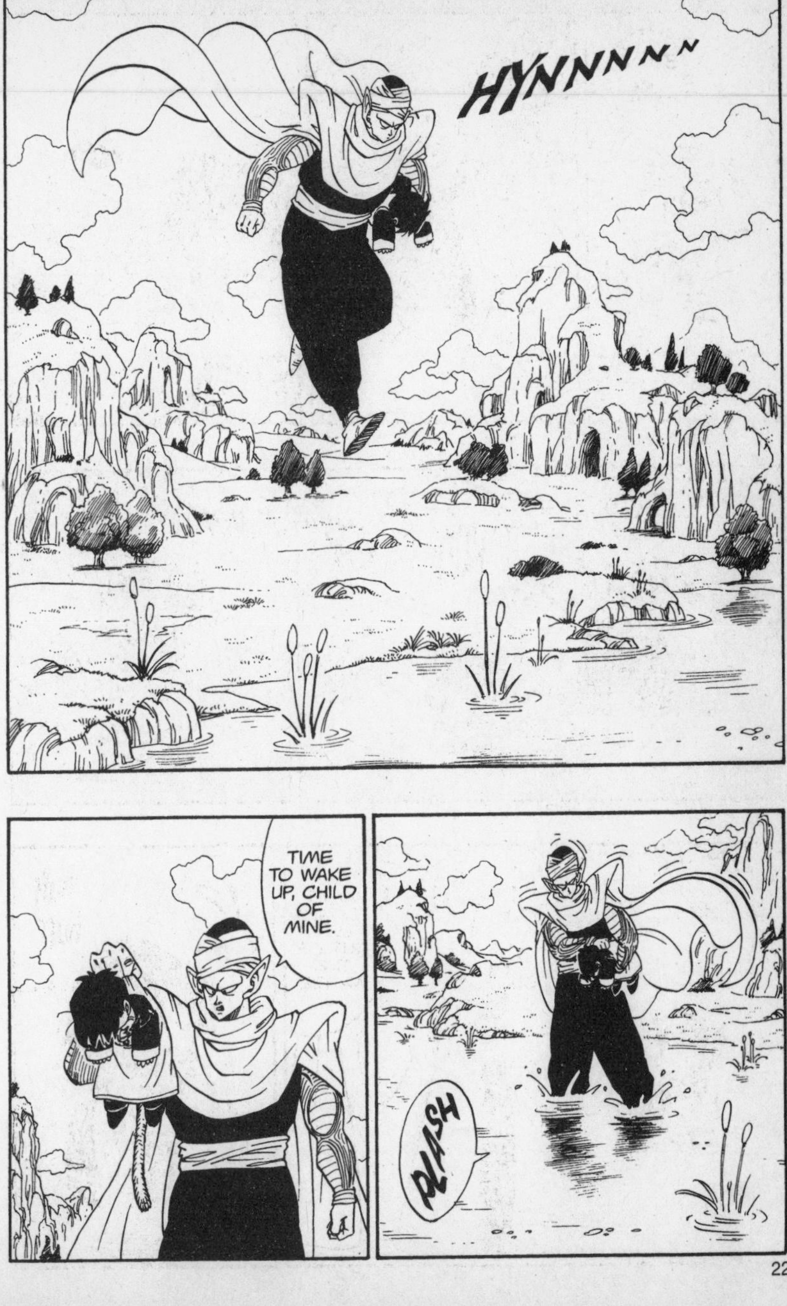
HYNNNNNN
PLASH
TIME TO WAKE UP, CHILD OF MINE.

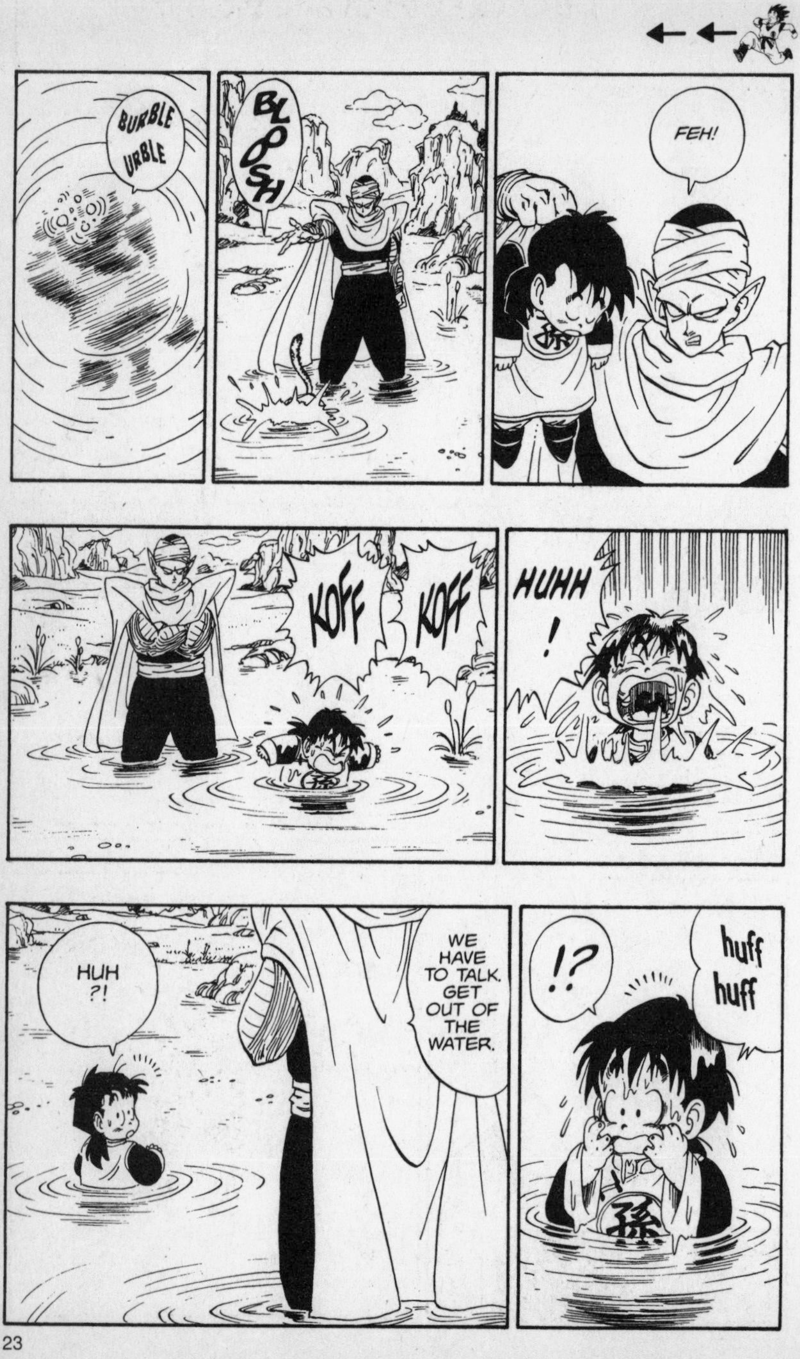
FEH!
BLOSH
BURBLE URBLE
HUHH!
KOFF KOFF
!?
huff huff
WE HAVE TO TALK. GET OUT OF THE WATER.
HUH ?!

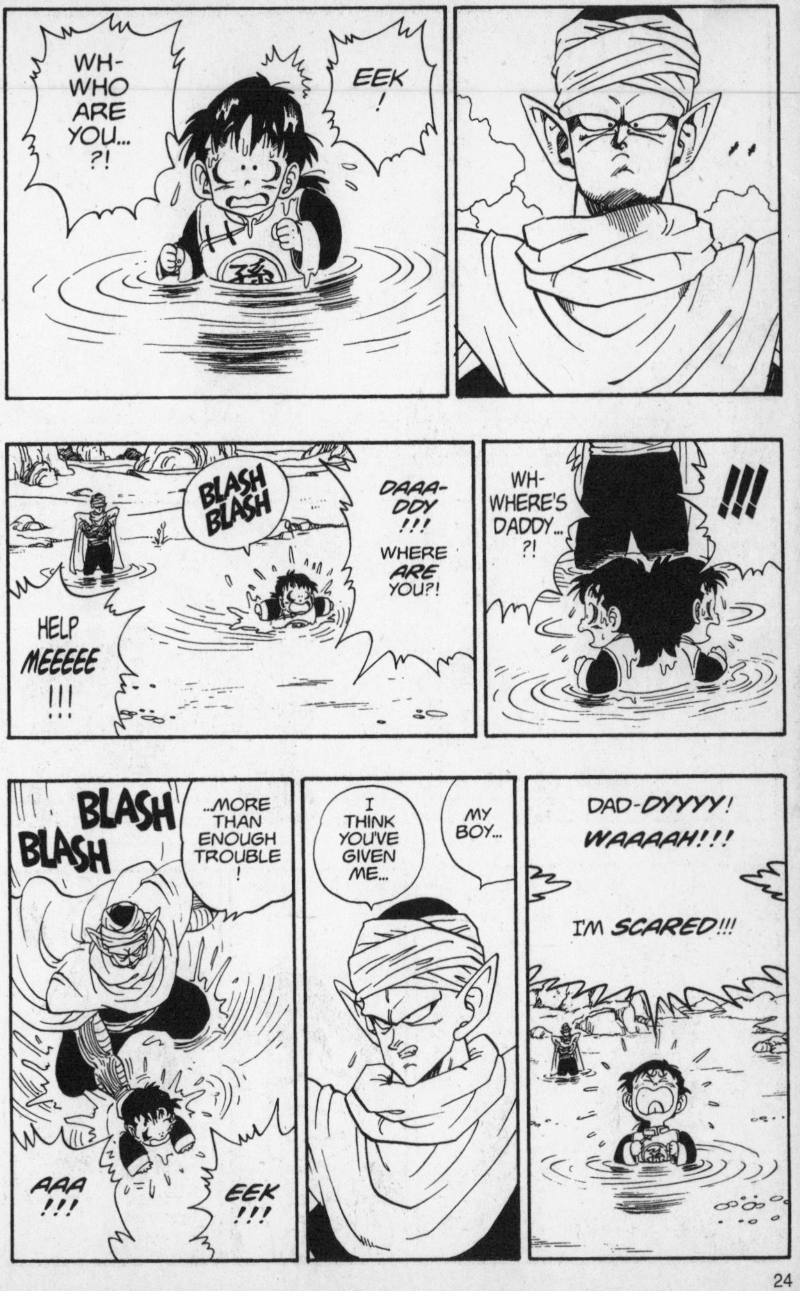
EEK!
WH- WHO ARE YOU...?!
!!!
WH- WHERE'S DADDY...?!
DAAA-DDY!!! WHERE ARE YOU?!
BLASH BLASH
HELP MEEEEE!!!
DAD-DYYYY! WAAAAH!!!
I'M SCARED!!!
MY BOY...
I THINK YOU'VE GIVEN ME...
...MORE THAN ENOUGH TROUBLE!
BLASH
BLASH
EEK!!!
AAA!!!

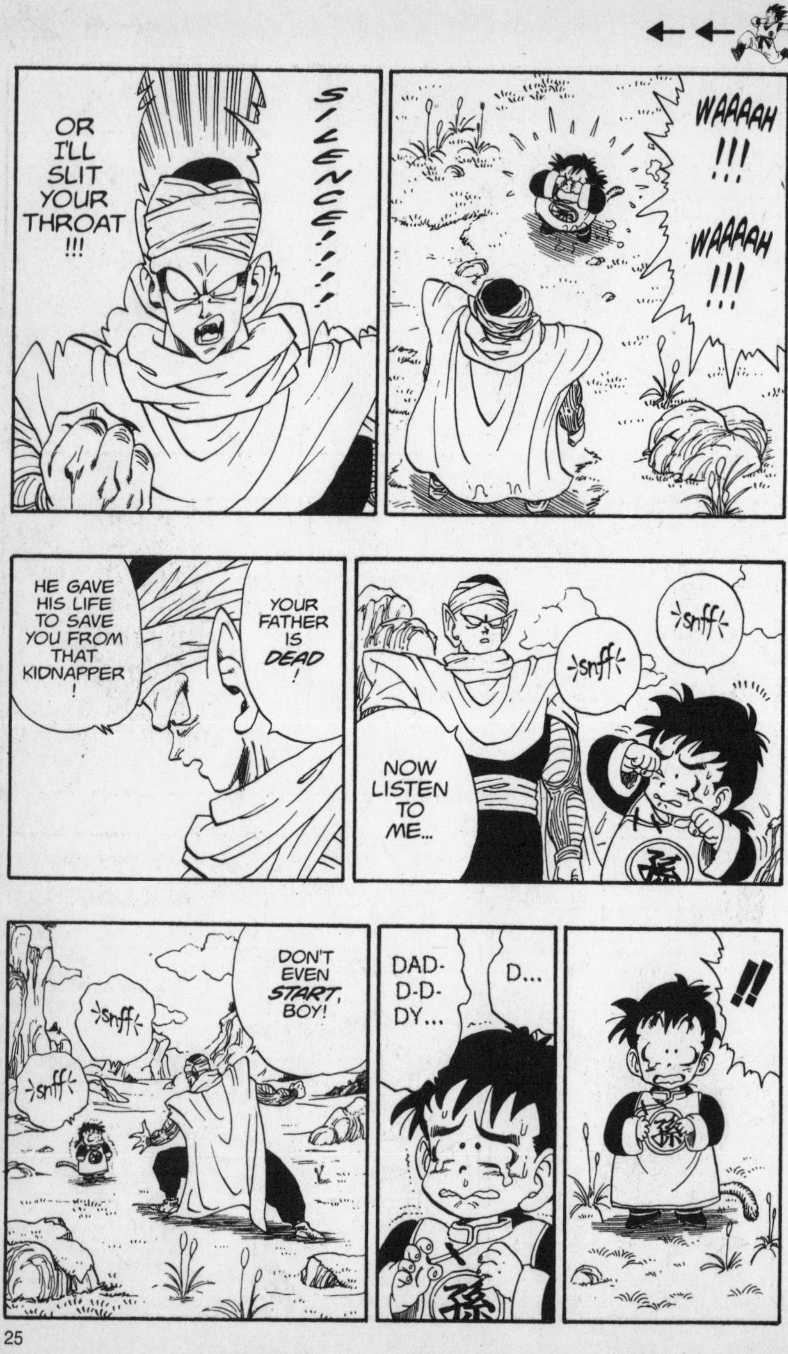
WAAAAH !!!
WAAAAH !!!
SILENCE!!!!!
OR I'LL SLIT YOUR THROAT !!!
snff
snff
NOW LISTEN TO ME...
YOUR FATHER IS DEAD!
HE GAVE HIS LIFE TO SAVE YOU FROM THAT KIDNAPPER!
!!
D...
DAD-D-D-DY...
DON'T EVEN START, BOY!
snff
snff

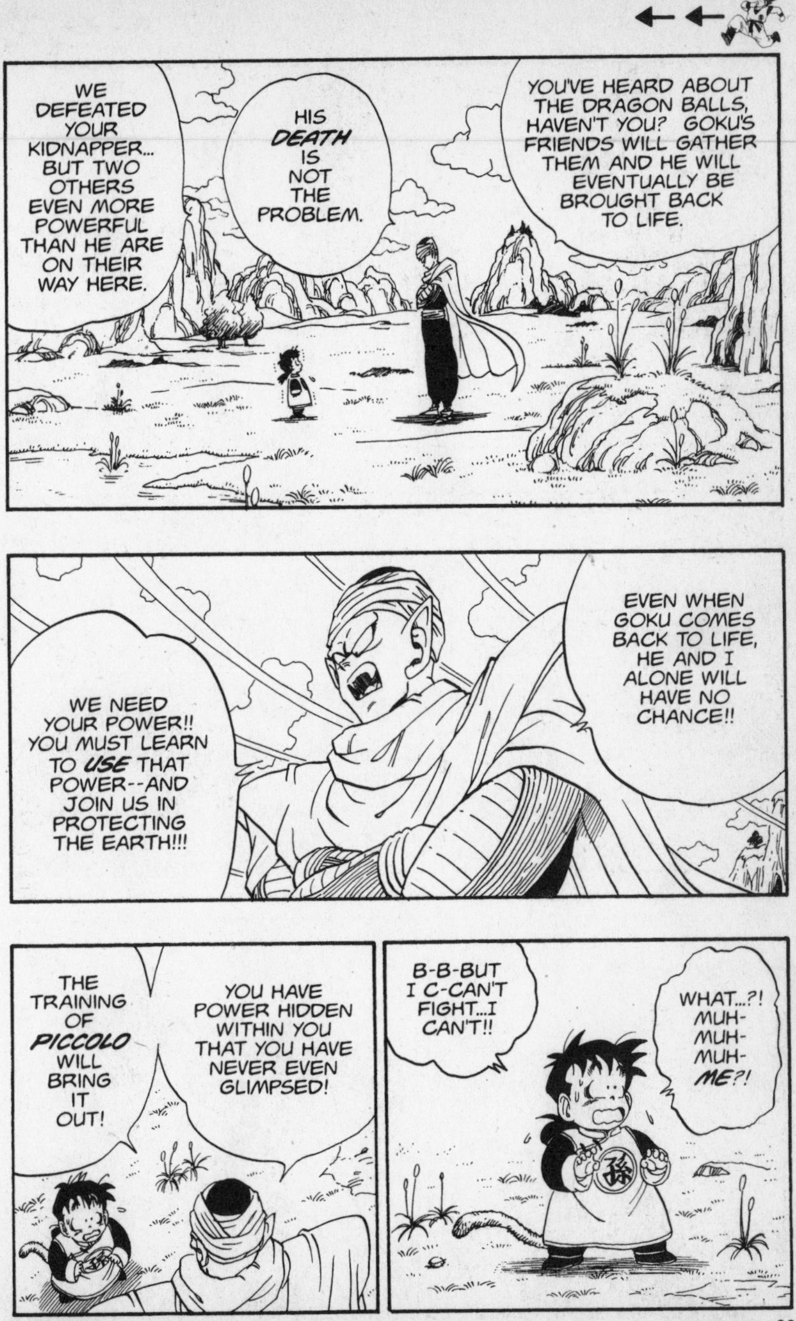
YOU'VE HEARD ABOUT THE DRAGON BALLS, HAVEN'T YOU? GOKU'S FRIENDS WILL GATHER THEM AND HE WILL EVENTUALLY BE BROUGHT BACK TO LIFE.
HIS *DEATH* IS NOT THE PROBLEM.
WE DEFEATED YOUR KIDNAPPER... BUT TWO OTHERS EVEN MORE POWERFUL THAN HE ARE ON THEIR WAY HERE.
EVEN WHEN GOKU COMES BACK TO LIFE, HE AND I ALONE WILL HAVE NO CHANCE!!
WE NEED YOUR POWER!! YOU MUST LEARN TO *USE* THAT POWER--AND JOIN US IN PROTECTING THE EARTH!!!
WHAT...?! MUH-MUH-MUH-*ME*?!
B-B-BUT I C-CAN'T FIGHT...I CAN'T!!
YOU HAVE POWER HIDDEN WITHIN YOU THAT YOU HAVE NEVER EVEN GLIMPSED!
THE TRAINING OF *PICCOLO* WILL BRING IT OUT!

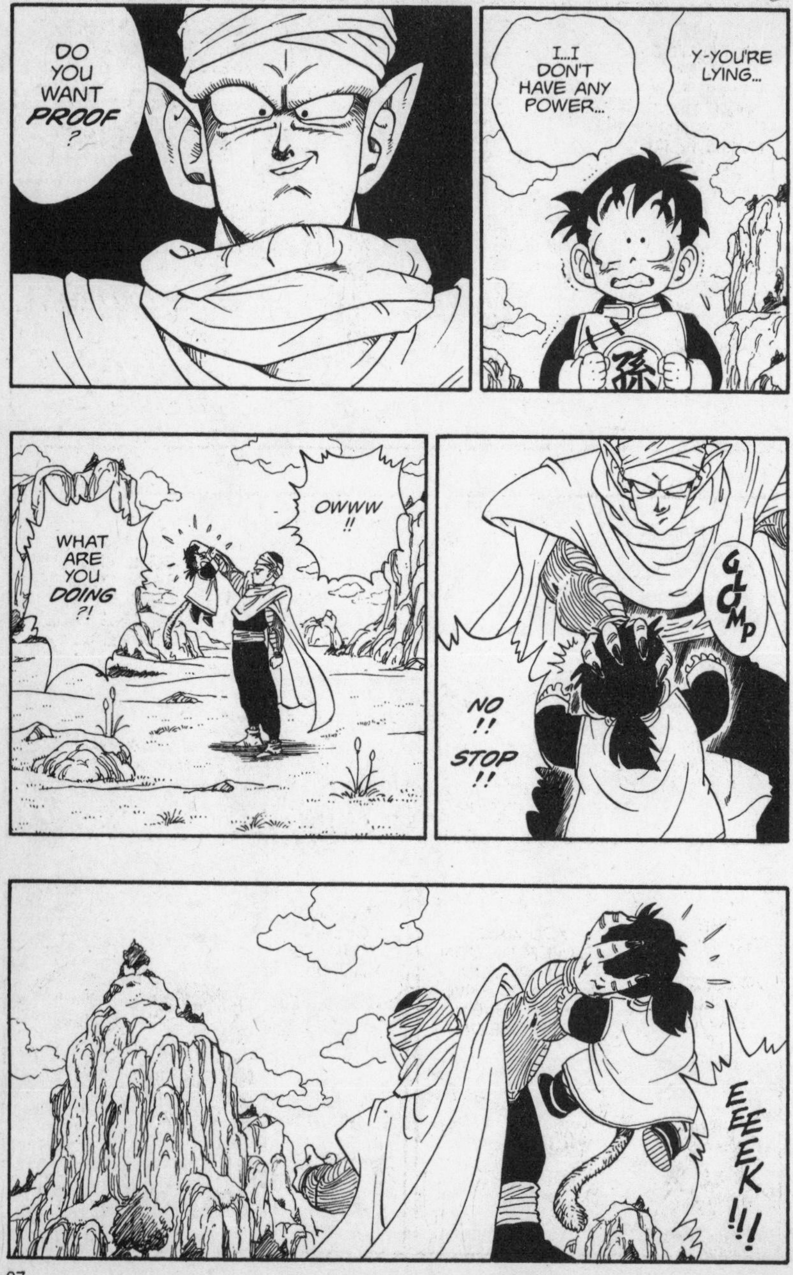

Y-YOU'RE LYING...
I...I DON'T HAVE ANY POWER...
DO YOU WANT *PROOF* ?
GLOMP
NO!! STOP!!
OWWW!!
WHAT ARE YOU *DOING* ?!
EEEEK!!!

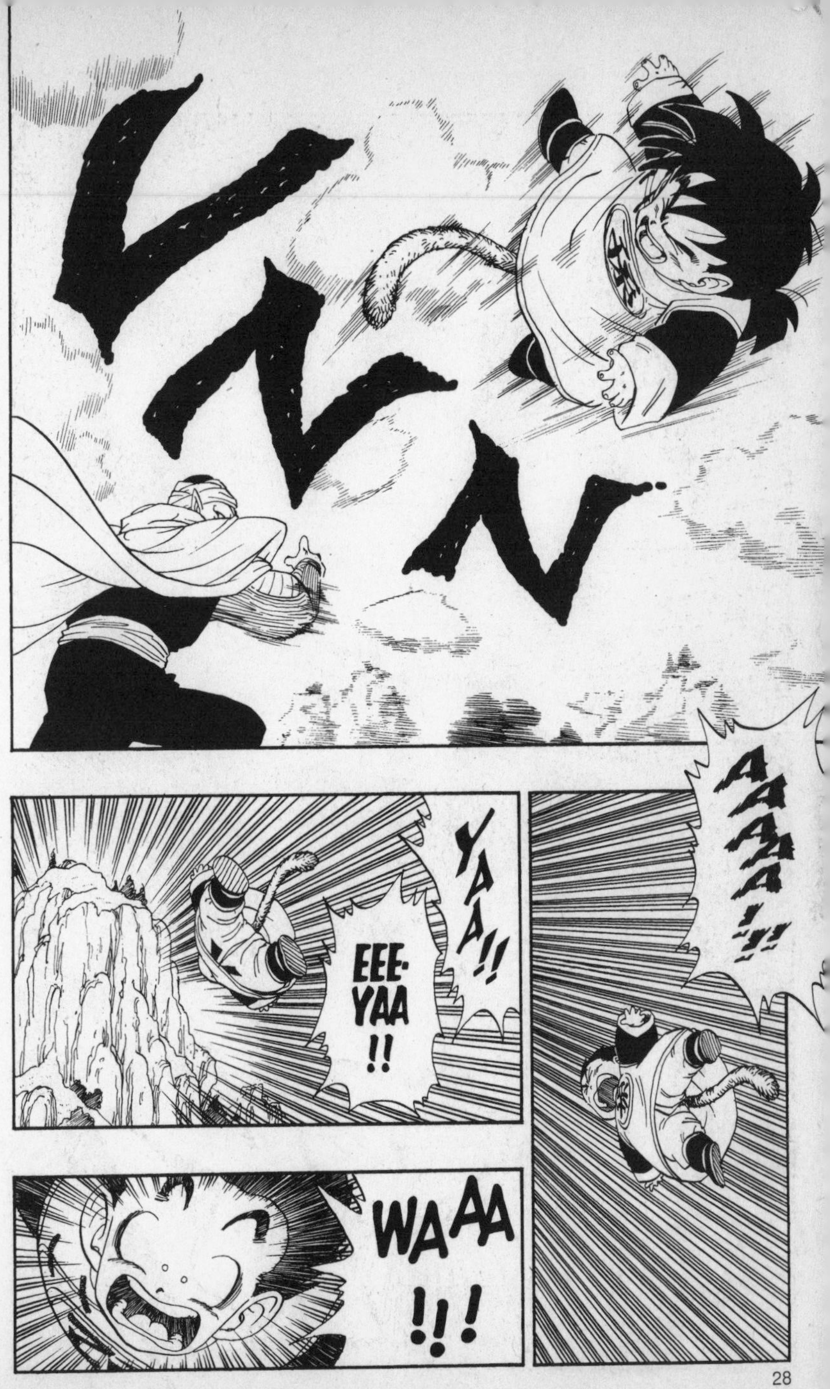
AAAA!!!
YAA!!
EEE-YAA!!
WAAA!!!

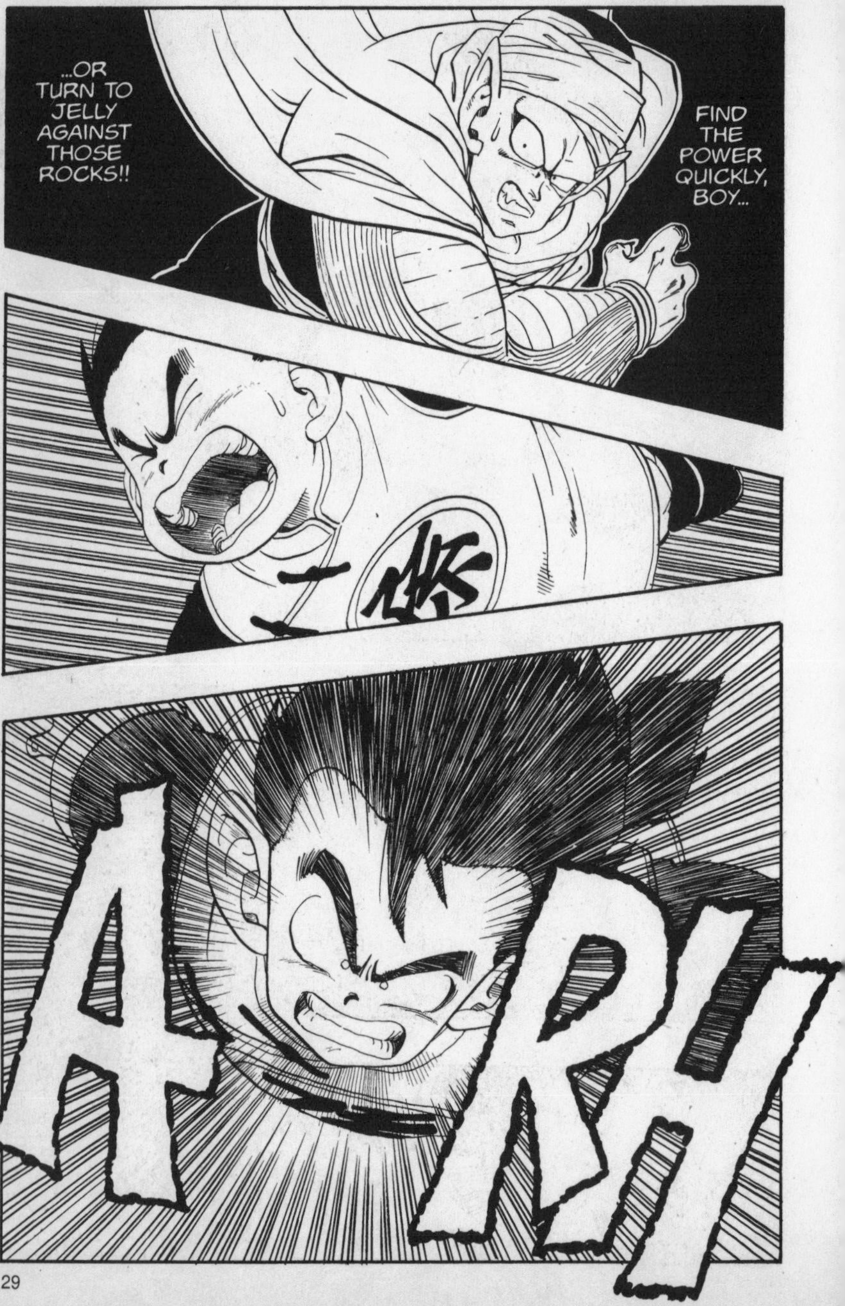
FIND THE POWER QUICKLY, BOY...
...OR TURN TO JELLY AGAINST THOSE ROCKS!!
ARH

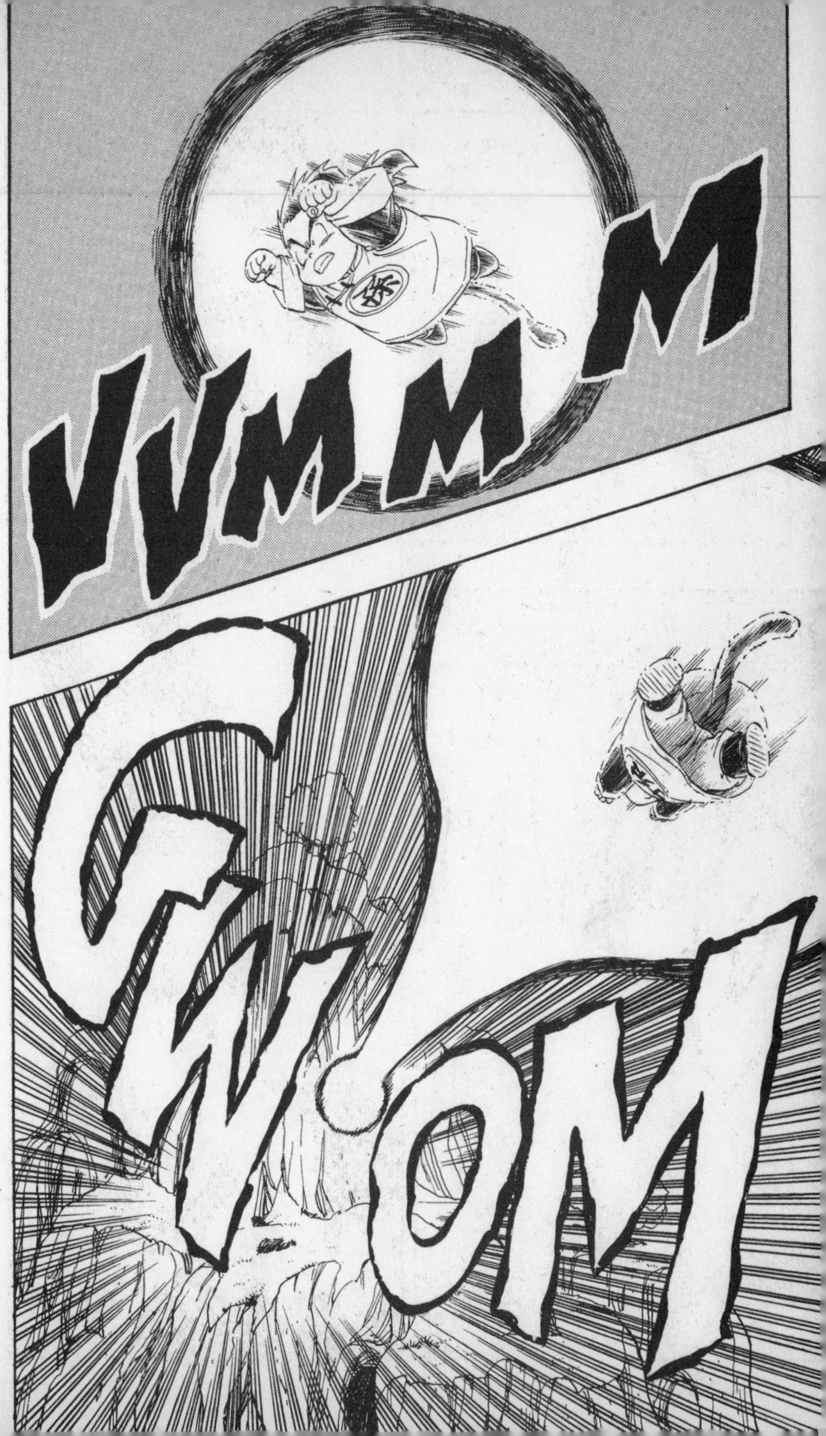
VMMM
CHOOM

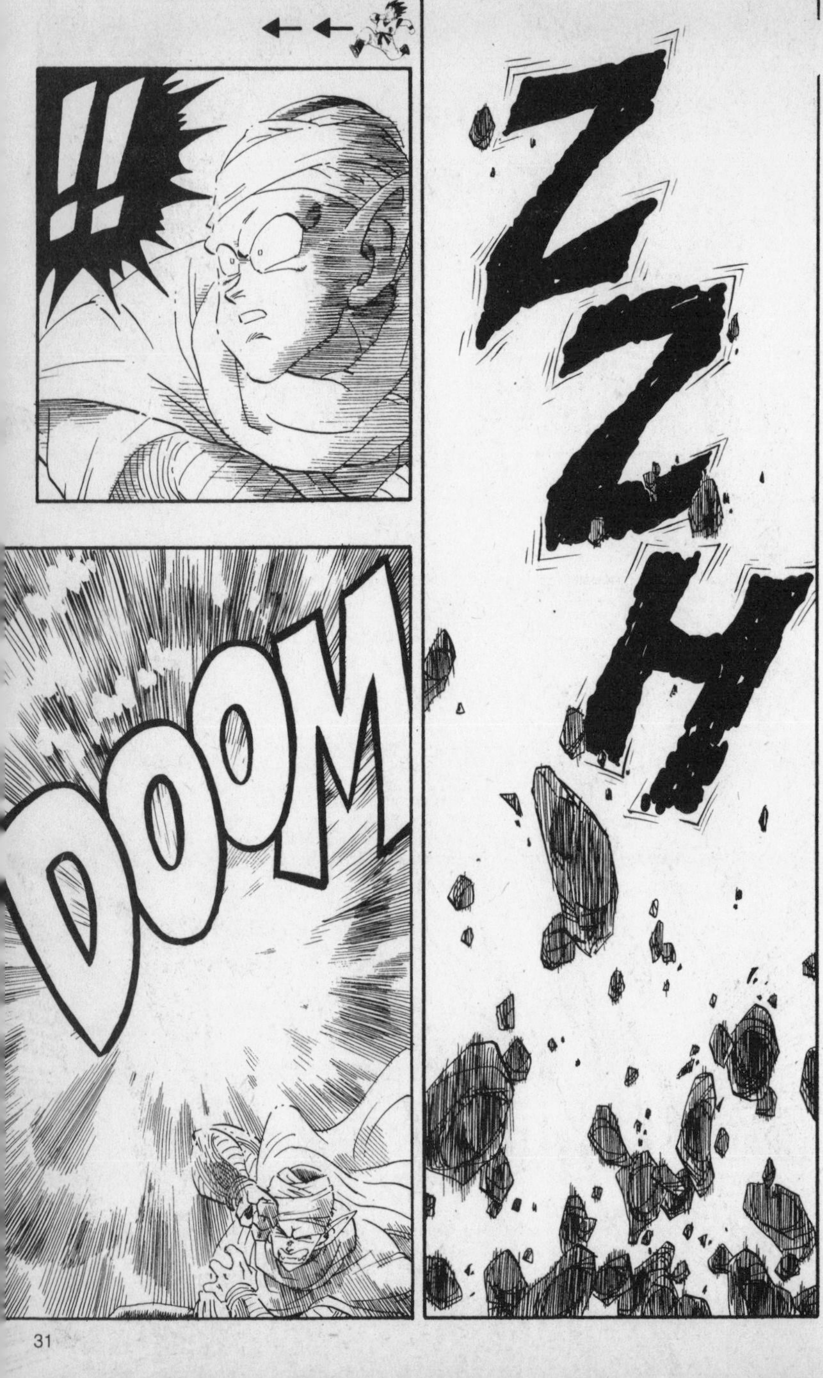
ZZZH
!!
DOOM

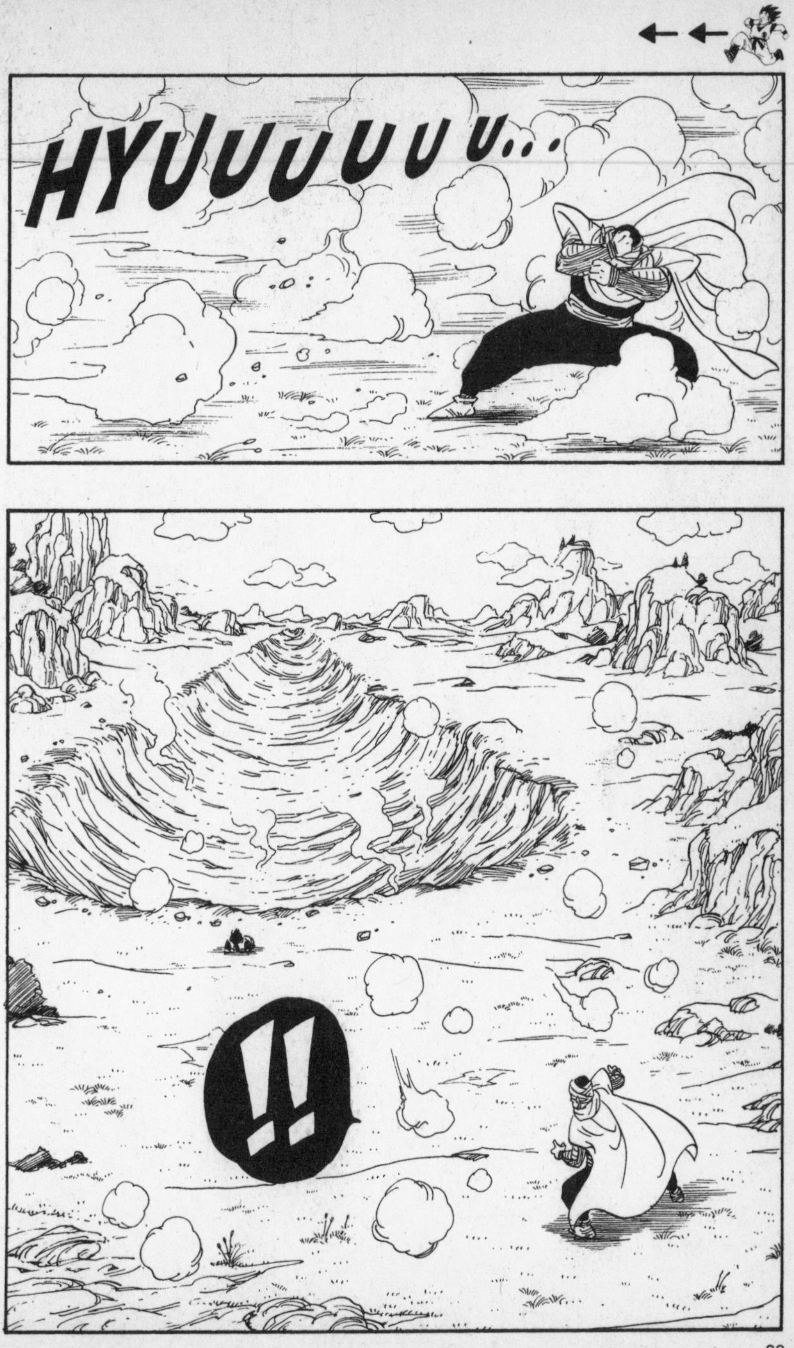
HYUUUUUUU...
!!

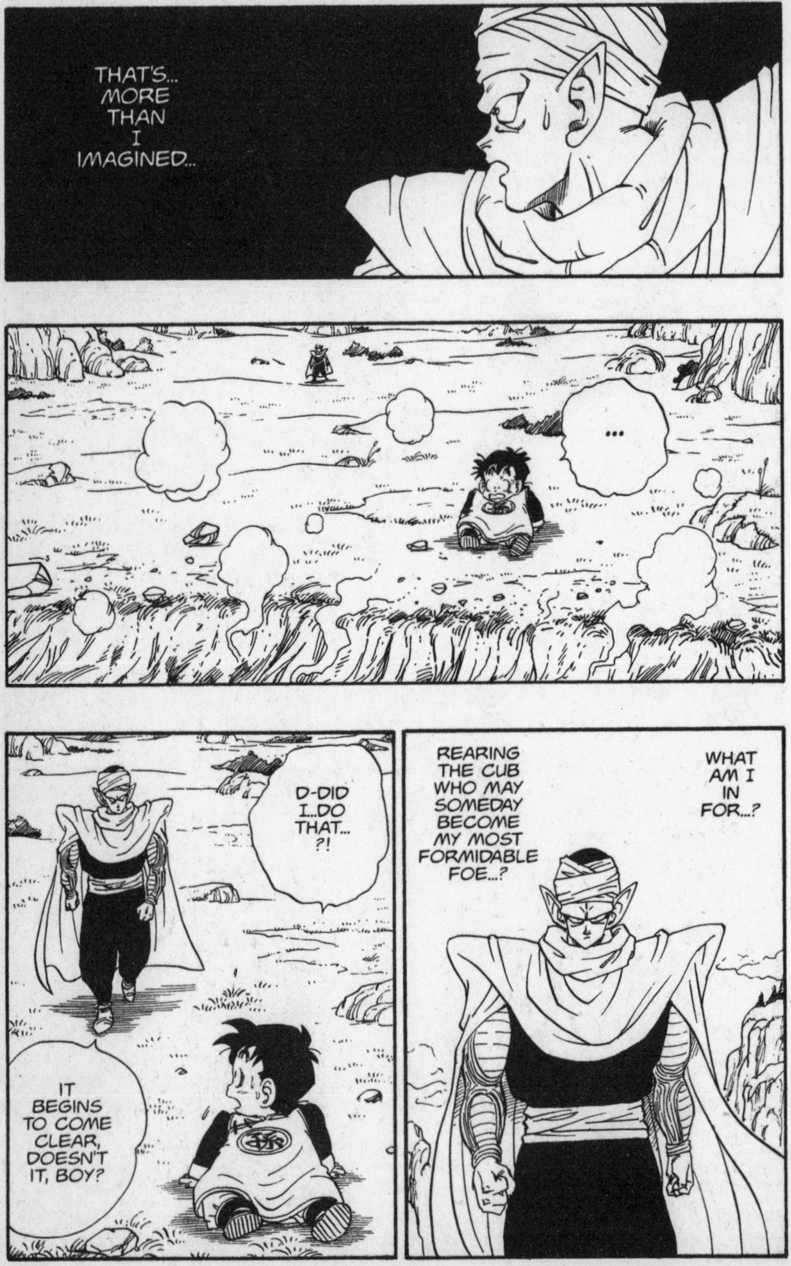
THAT'S... MORE THAN I IMAGINED...
...
WHAT AM I IN FOR...?
REARING THE CUB WHO MAY SOMEDAY BECOME MY MOST FORMIDABLE FOE...?
D-DID I...DO THAT...?!
IT BEGINS TO COME CLEAR, DOESN'T IT, BOY?

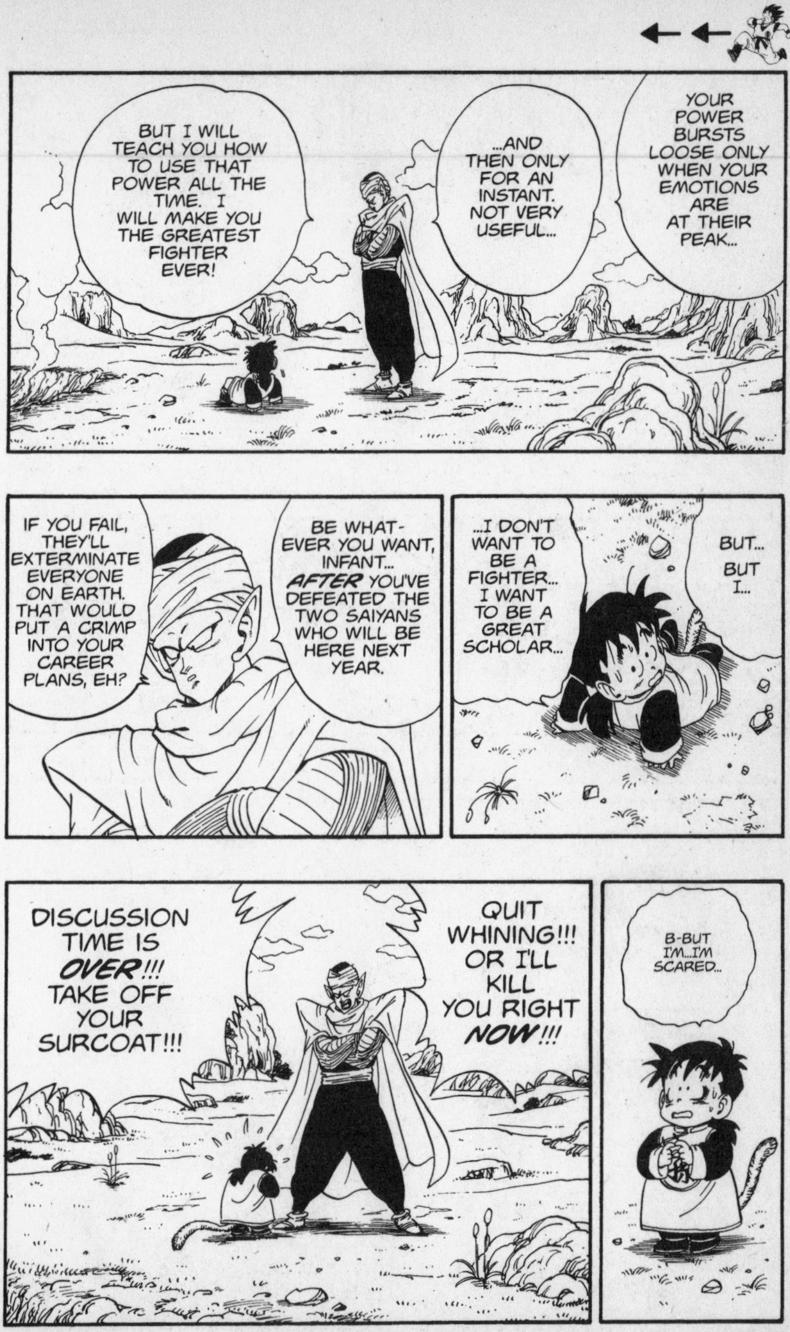
YOUR POWER BURSTS LOOSE ONLY WHEN YOUR EMOTIONS ARE AT THEIR PEAK...
...AND THEN ONLY FOR AN INSTANT. NOT VERY USEFUL...
BUT I WILL TEACH YOU HOW TO USE THAT POWER ALL THE TIME. I WILL MAKE YOU THE GREATEST FIGHTER EVER!
BUT... BUT I...
...I DON'T WANT TO BE A FIGHTER... I WANT TO BE A GREAT SCHOLAR...
BE WHAT-EVER YOU WANT, INFANT... AFTER YOU'VE DEFEATED THE TWO SAIYANS WHO WILL BE HERE NEXT YEAR.
IF YOU FAIL, THEY'LL EXTERMINATE EVERYONE ON EARTH. THAT WOULD PUT A CRIMP INTO YOUR CAREER PLANS, EH?
B-BUT I'M...I'M SCARED...
QUIT WHINING!!! OR I'LL KILL YOU RIGHT NOW!!!
DISCUSSION TIME IS OVER!!! TAKE OFF YOUR SURCOAT!!!

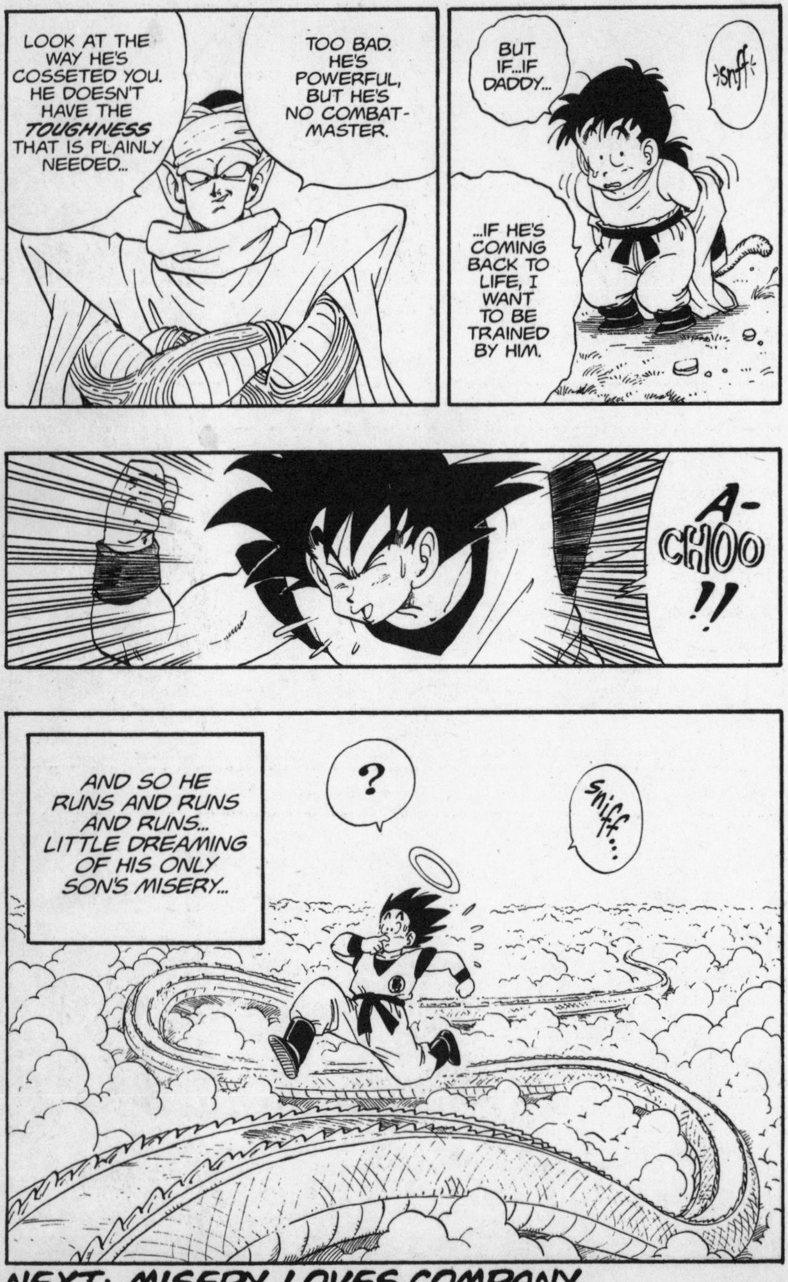

snff
BUT IF...IF DADDY...
...IF HE'S COMING BACK TO LIFE, I WANT TO BE TRAINED BY HIM.
TOO BAD. HE'S POWERFUL, BUT HE'S NO COMBAT-MASTER.
LOOK AT THE WAY HE'S COSSETED YOU. HE DOESN'T HAVE THE *TOUGHNESS* THAT IS PLAINLY NEEDED...
A-CHOO!!
sniff...
?
AND SO HE RUNS AND RUNS AND RUNS... LITTLE DREAMING OF HIS ONLY SON'S MISERY...

NEXT: MISERY LOVES COMPANY

DBZ : 13 • Son Gohan, the Inconsolable

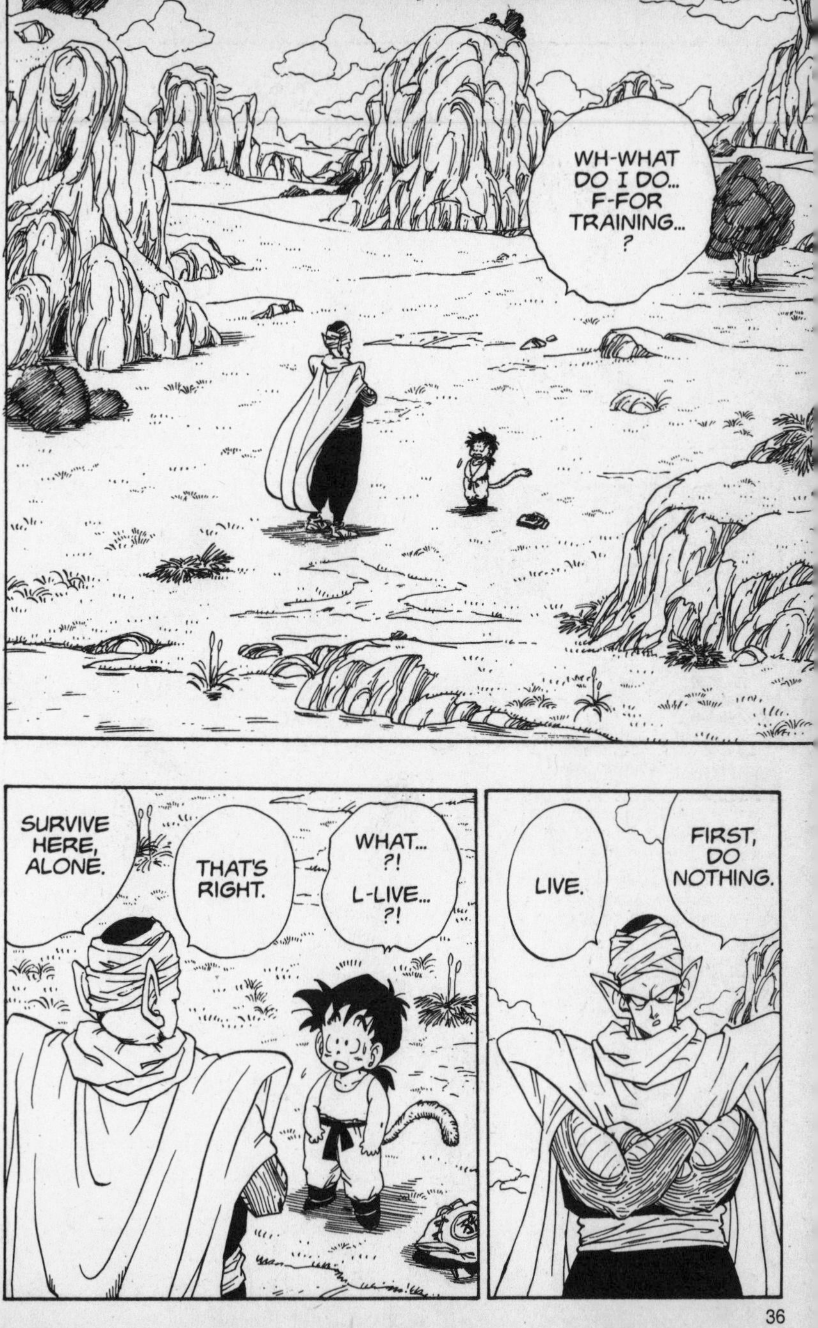
WH-WHAT DO I DO... F-FOR TRAINING... ?
FIRST, DO NOTHING.
LIVE.
WHAT... ?! L-LIVE... ?!
THAT'S RIGHT.
SURVIVE HERE, ALONE.

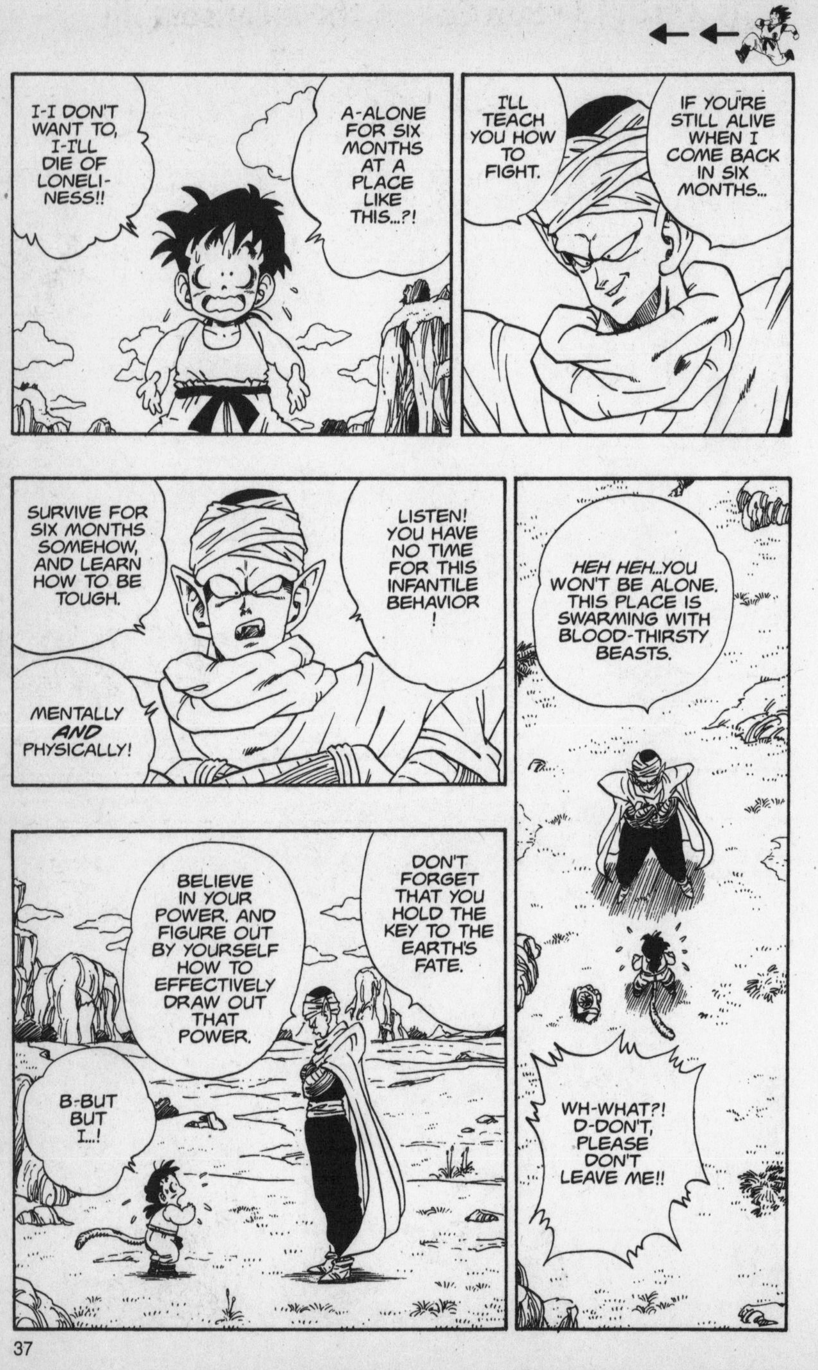
IF YOU'RE STILL ALIVE WHEN I COME BACK IN SIX MONTHS...
I'LL TEACH YOU HOW TO FIGHT.
A-ALONE FOR SIX MONTHS AT A PLACE LIKE THIS...?!
I-I DON'T WANT TO, I-I'LL DIE OF LONELI-NESS!!
HEH HEH...YOU WON'T BE ALONE. THIS PLACE IS SWARMING WITH BLOOD-THIRSTY BEASTS.
WH-WHAT?! D-DON'T, PLEASE DON'T LEAVE ME!!
LISTEN! YOU HAVE NO TIME FOR THIS INFANTILE BEHAVIOR!
SURVIVE FOR SIX MONTHS SOMEHOW, AND LEARN HOW TO BE TOUGH.
MENTALLY *AND* PHYSICALLY!
DON'T FORGET THAT YOU HOLD THE KEY TO THE EARTH'S FATE.
BELIEVE IN YOUR POWER. AND FIGURE OUT BY YOURSELF HOW TO EFFECTIVELY DRAW OUT THAT POWER.
B-BUT BUT I...!

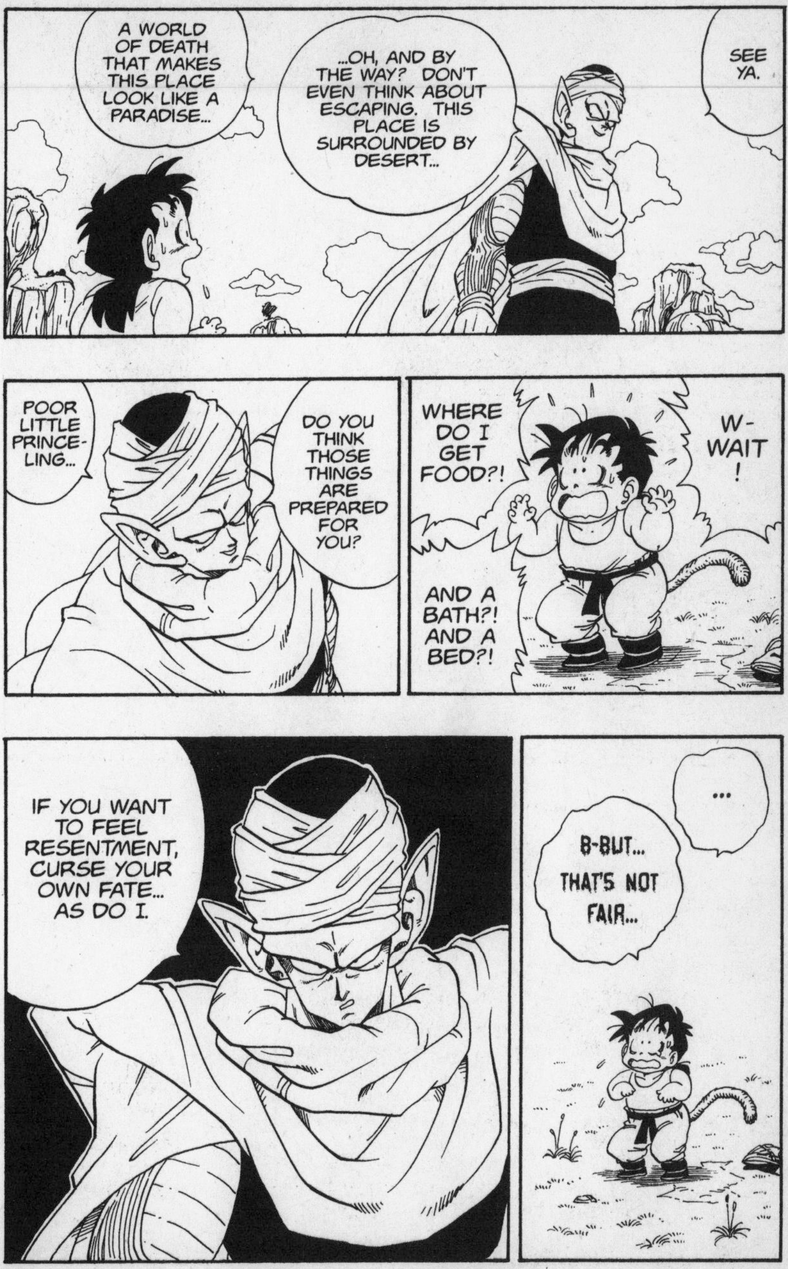
SEE YA.
...OH, AND BY THE WAY? DON'T EVEN THINK ABOUT ESCAPING. THIS PLACE IS SURROUNDED BY DESERT...
A WORLD OF DEATH THAT MAKES THIS PLACE LOOK LIKE A PARADISE...
W-WAIT!
WHERE DO I GET FOOD?!
AND A BATH?! AND A BED?!
DO YOU THINK THOSE THINGS ARE PREPARED FOR YOU?
POOR LITTLE PRINCE-LING...
...
B-BUT... THAT'S NOT FAIR...
IF YOU WANT TO FEEL RESENTMENT, CURSE YOUR OWN FATE... AS DO I.

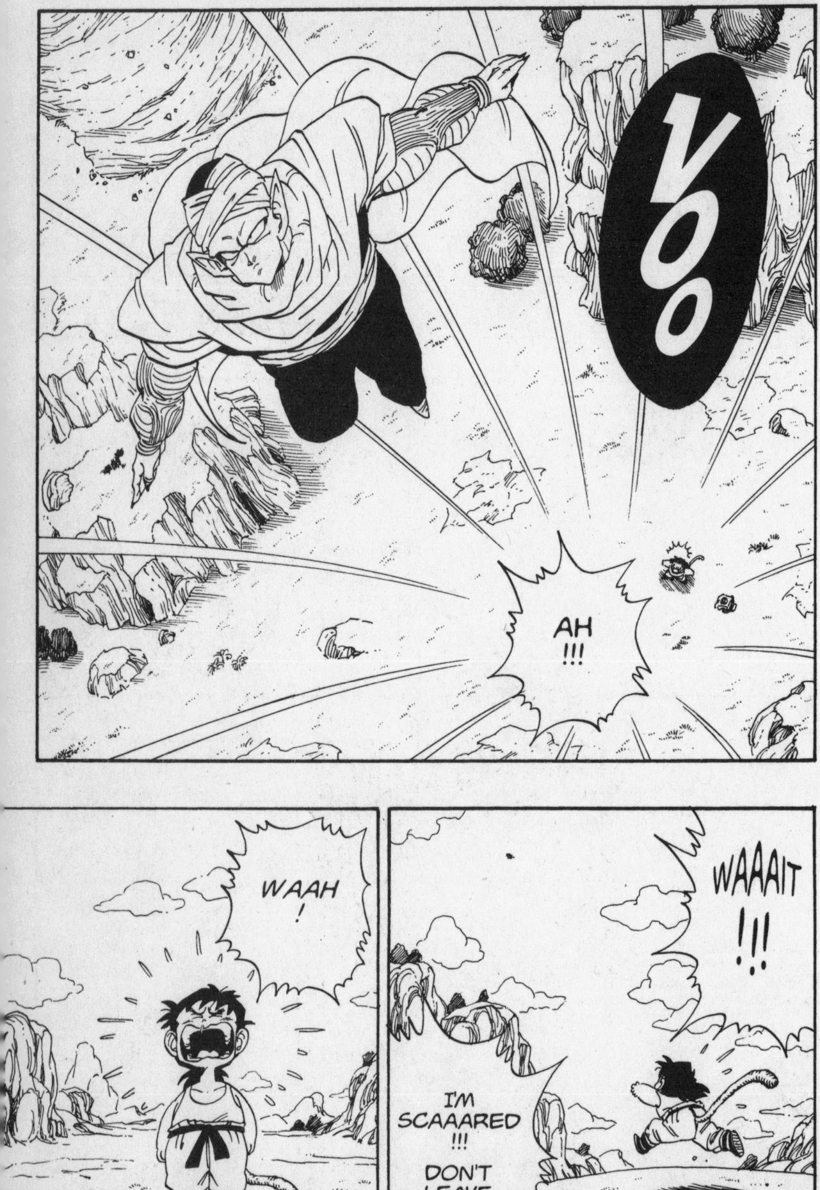
VOO
AH!!!
WAAAIT!!!
I'M SCAAARED!!! DON'T LEAVE MEEE!
WAAH!

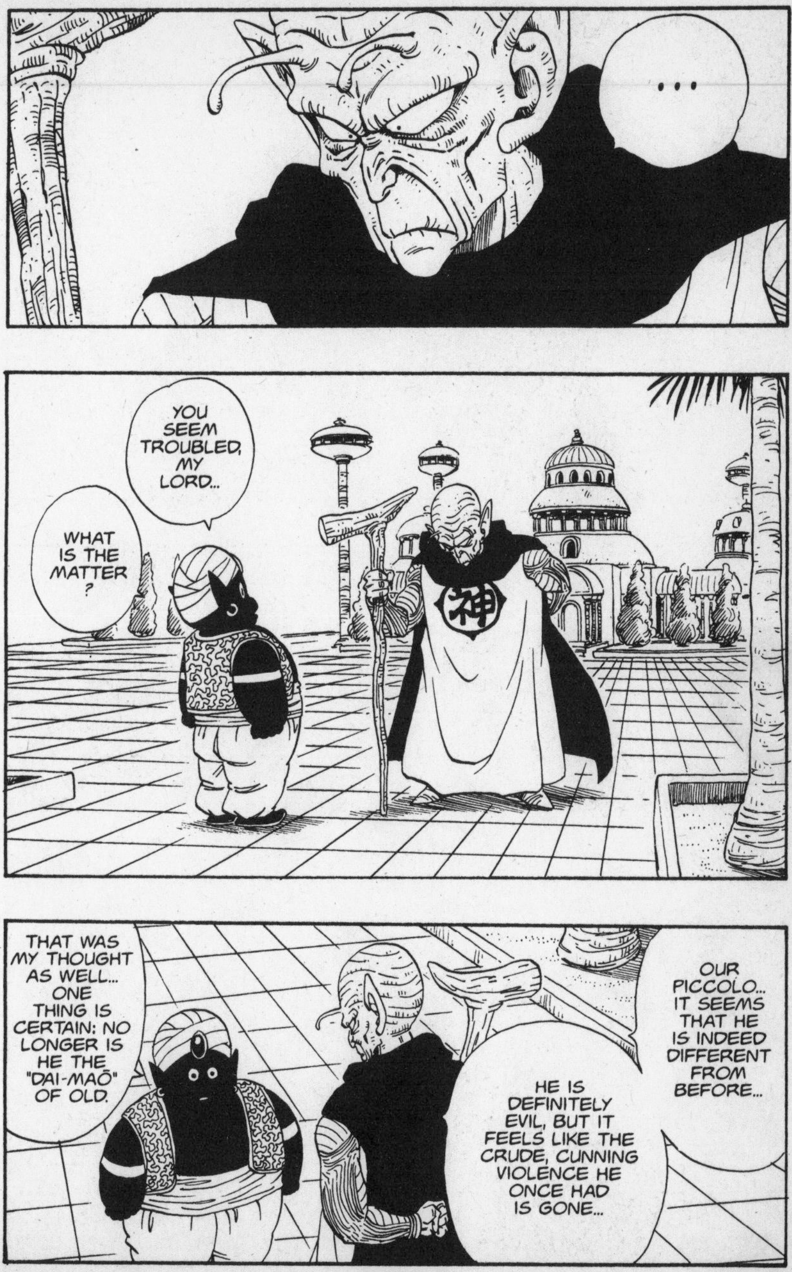
...
YOU SEEM TROUBLED, MY LORD...
WHAT IS THE MATTER ?
OUR PICCOLO... IT SEEMS THAT HE IS INDEED DIFFERENT FROM BEFORE...
HE IS DEFINITELY EVIL, BUT IT FEELS LIKE THE CRUDE, CUNNING VIOLENCE HE ONCE HAD IS GONE...
THAT WAS MY THOUGHT AS WELL... ONE THING IS CERTAIN: NO LONGER IS HE THE "DAI-MAŌ" OF OLD.

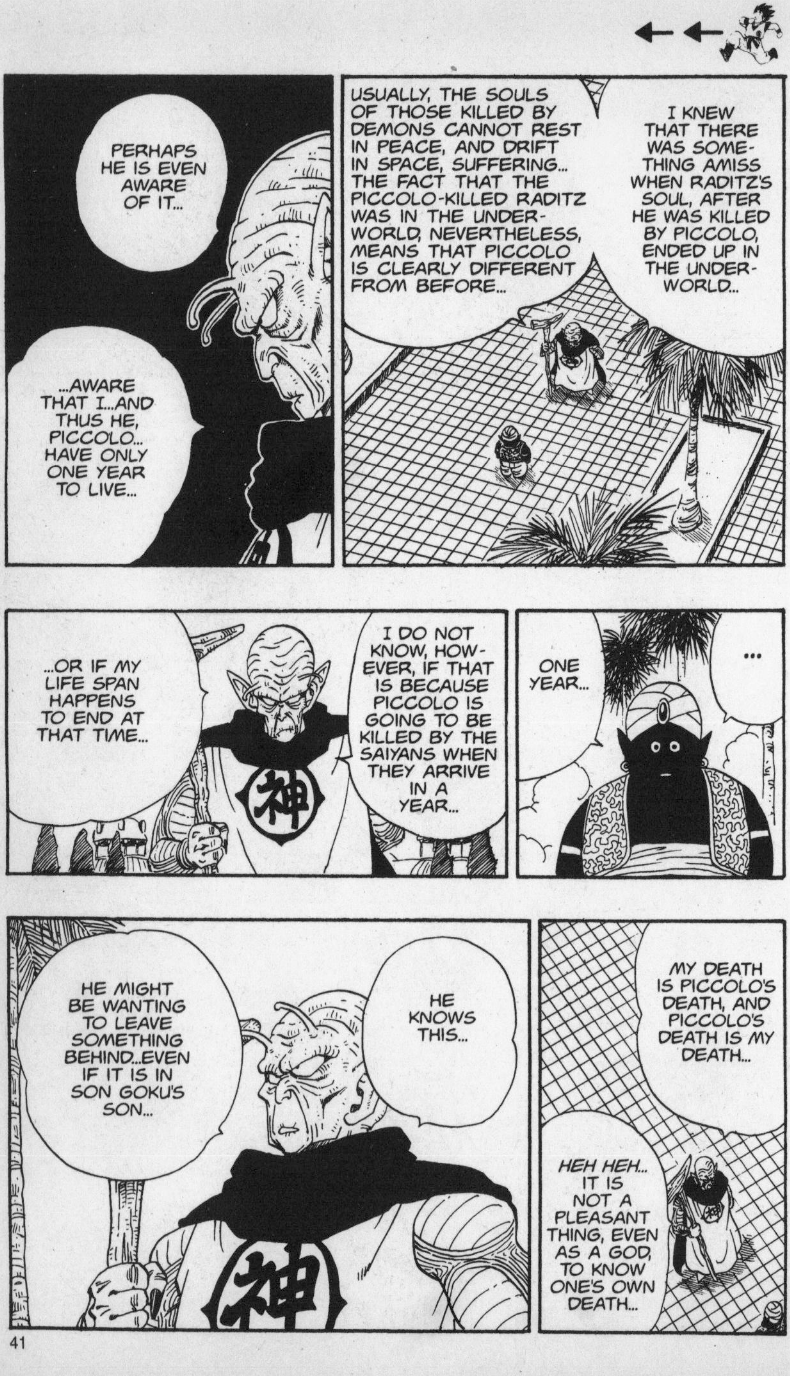
I KNEW THAT THERE WAS SOMETHING AMISS WHEN RADITZ'S SOUL, AFTER HE WAS KILLED BY PICCOLO, ENDED UP IN THE UNDERWORLD...
USUALLY, THE SOULS OF THOSE KILLED BY DEMONS CANNOT REST IN PEACE, AND DRIFT IN SPACE, SUFFERING... THE FACT THAT THE PICCOLO-KILLED RADITZ WAS IN THE UNDERWORLD, NEVERTHELESS, MEANS THAT PICCOLO IS CLEARLY DIFFERENT FROM BEFORE...
PERHAPS HE IS EVEN AWARE OF IT...
...AWARE THAT I...AND THUS HE, PICCOLO... HAVE ONLY ONE YEAR TO LIVE...
...
ONE YEAR...
I DO NOT KNOW, HOWEVER, IF THAT IS BECAUSE PICCOLO IS GOING TO BE KILLED BY THE SAIYANS WHEN THEY ARRIVE IN A YEAR...
...OR IF MY LIFE SPAN HAPPENS TO END AT THAT TIME...
MY DEATH IS PICCOLO'S DEATH, AND PICCOLO'S DEATH IS MY DEATH...
HEH HEH... IT IS NOT A PLEASANT THING, EVEN AS A GOD, TO KNOW ONE'S OWN DEATH...
HE KNOWS THIS...
HE MIGHT BE WANTING TO LEAVE SOMETHING BEHIND...EVEN IF IT IS IN SON GOKU'S SON...

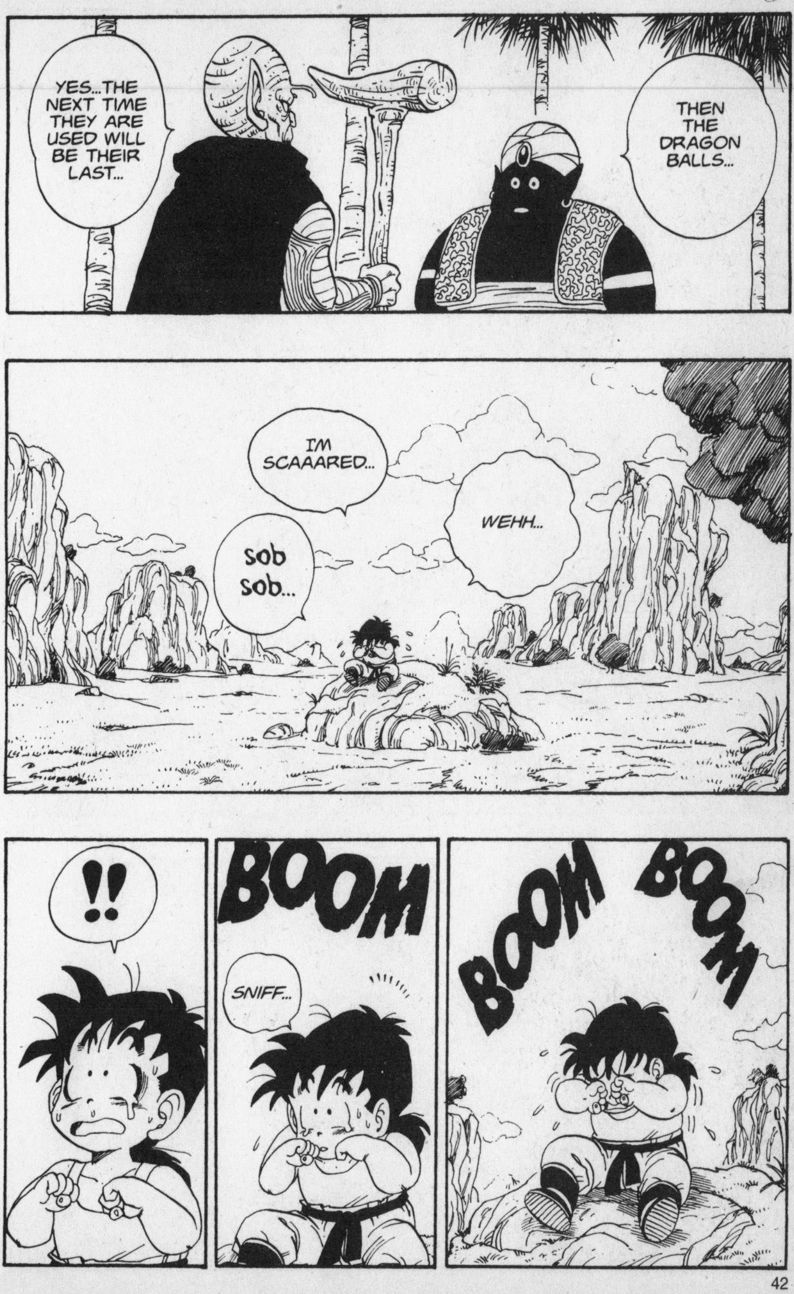
THEN THE DRAGON BALLS...
YES...THE NEXT TIME THEY ARE USED WILL BE THEIR LAST...
WEHH...
I'M SCAAARED...
sob sob...
BOOM BOOM
BOOM
BOOM
SNIFF...
!!

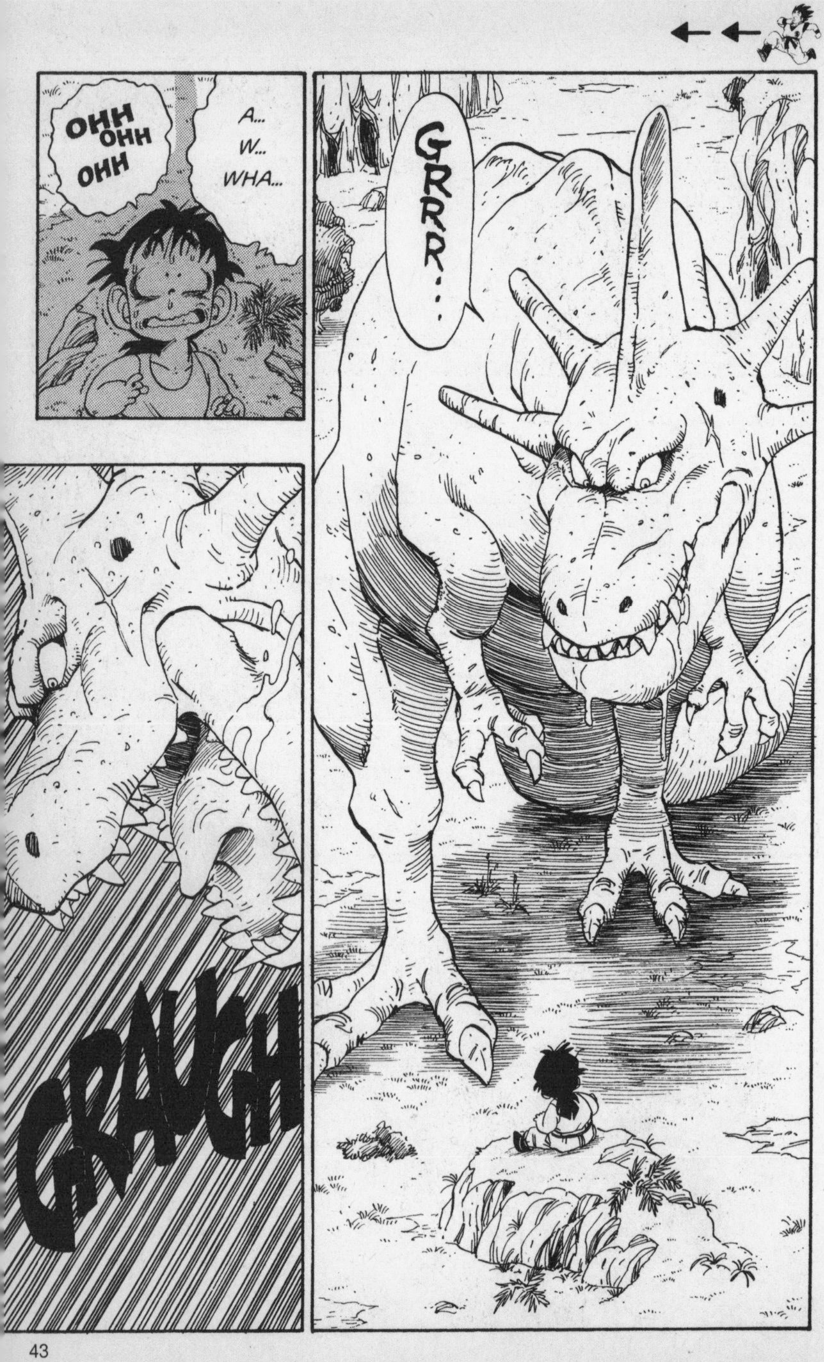
GRRR...
A... W... WHA...
OHH OHH OHH
CRAUGH

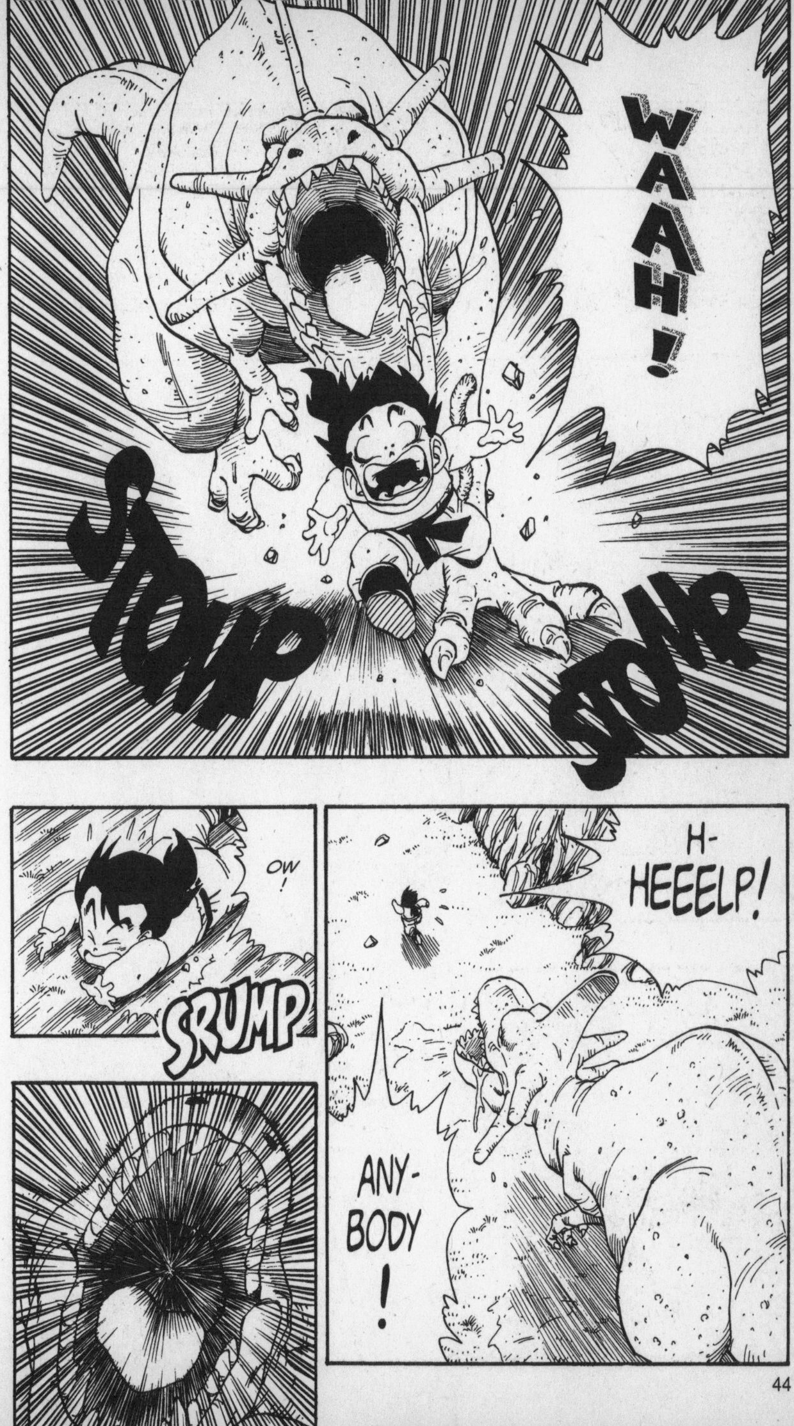
WAAH!
STOMP
STOMP
H-HEEELP!
ANY-BODY!
OW!
SRUMP

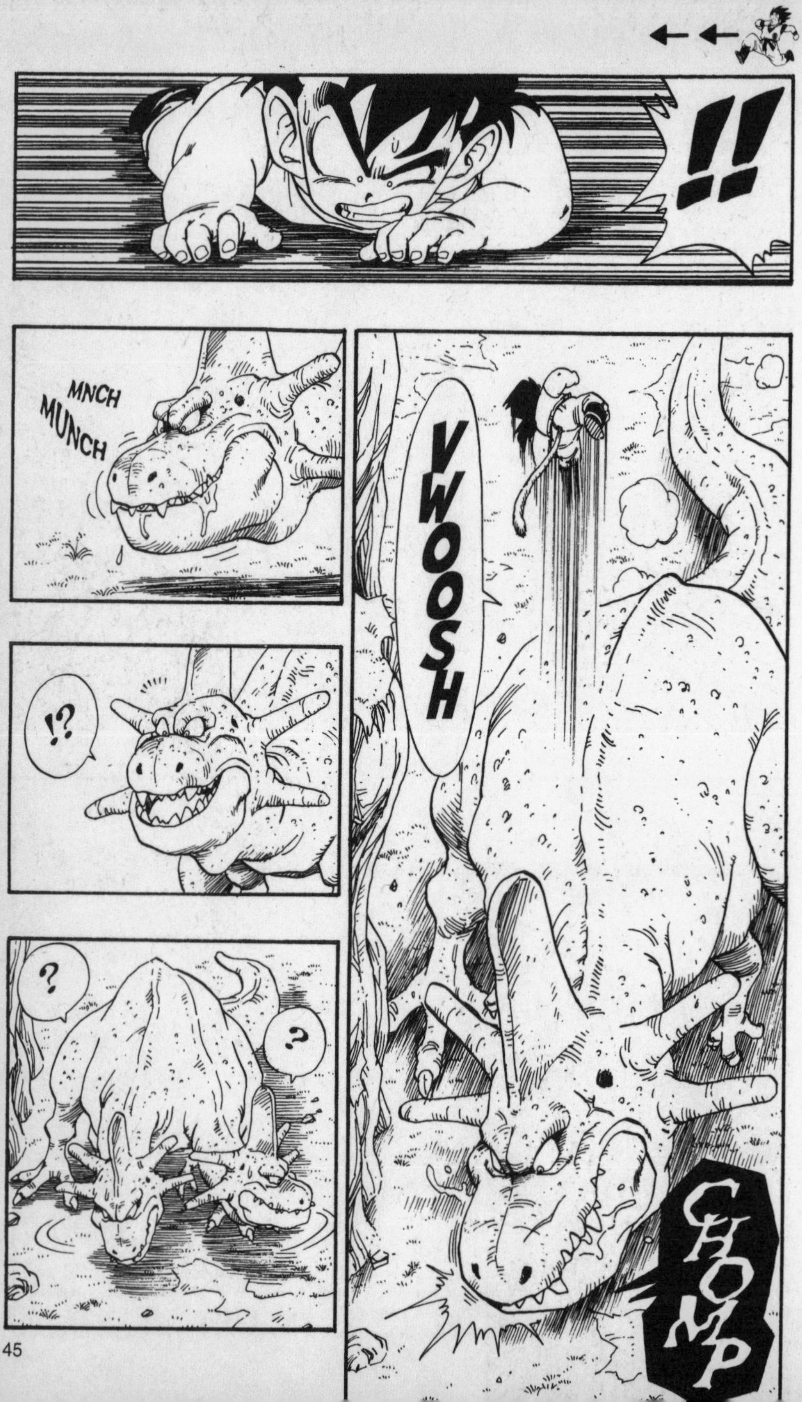
!!
VWOOSH
CHOMP
MNCH
MUNCH
!?
?
?

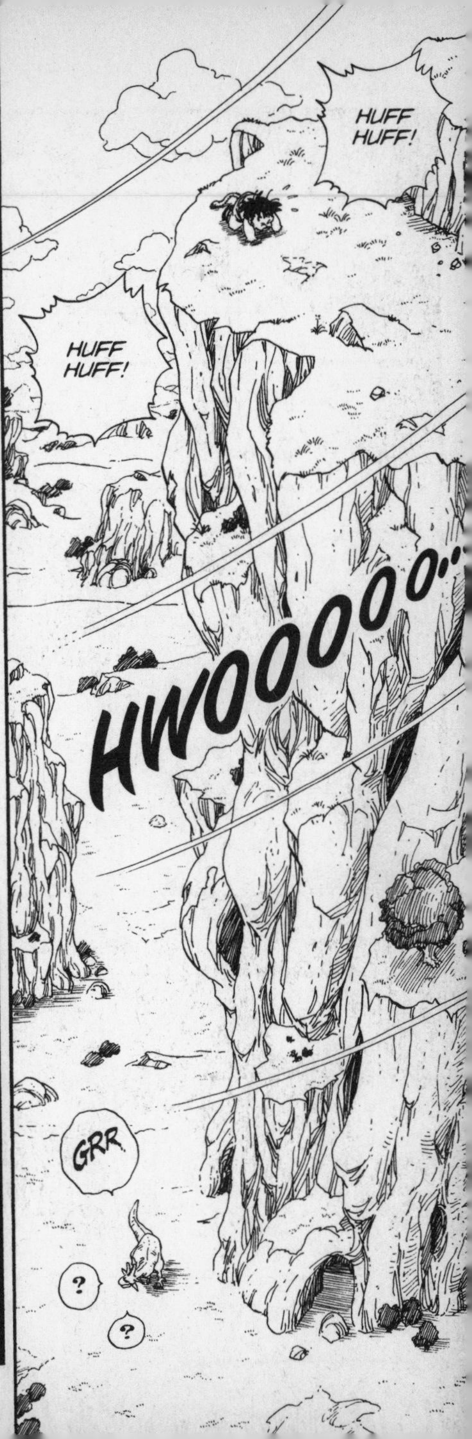
HUFF HUFF!
HUFF HUFF!
HWOOOOOO...
GRR
?
?

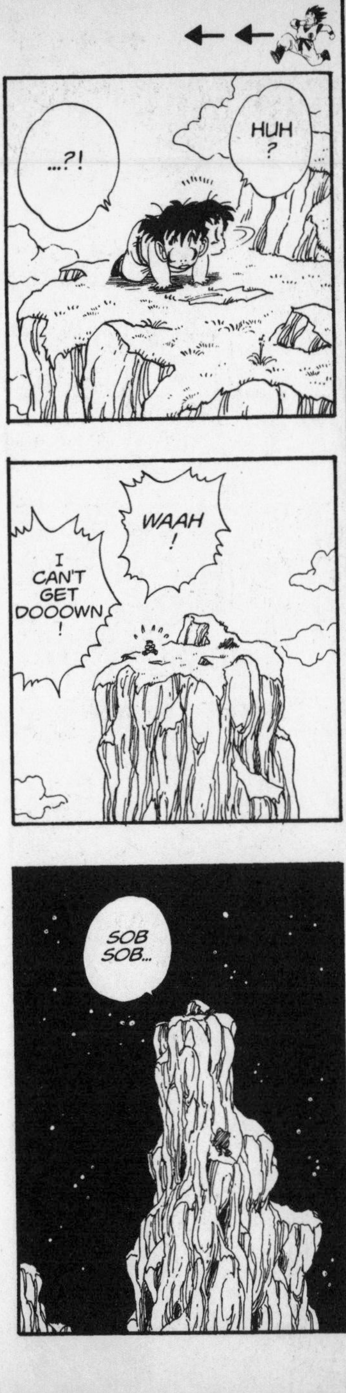
HUH ?
...?!
WAAH !
I CAN'T GET DOOOWN !
SOB SOB...

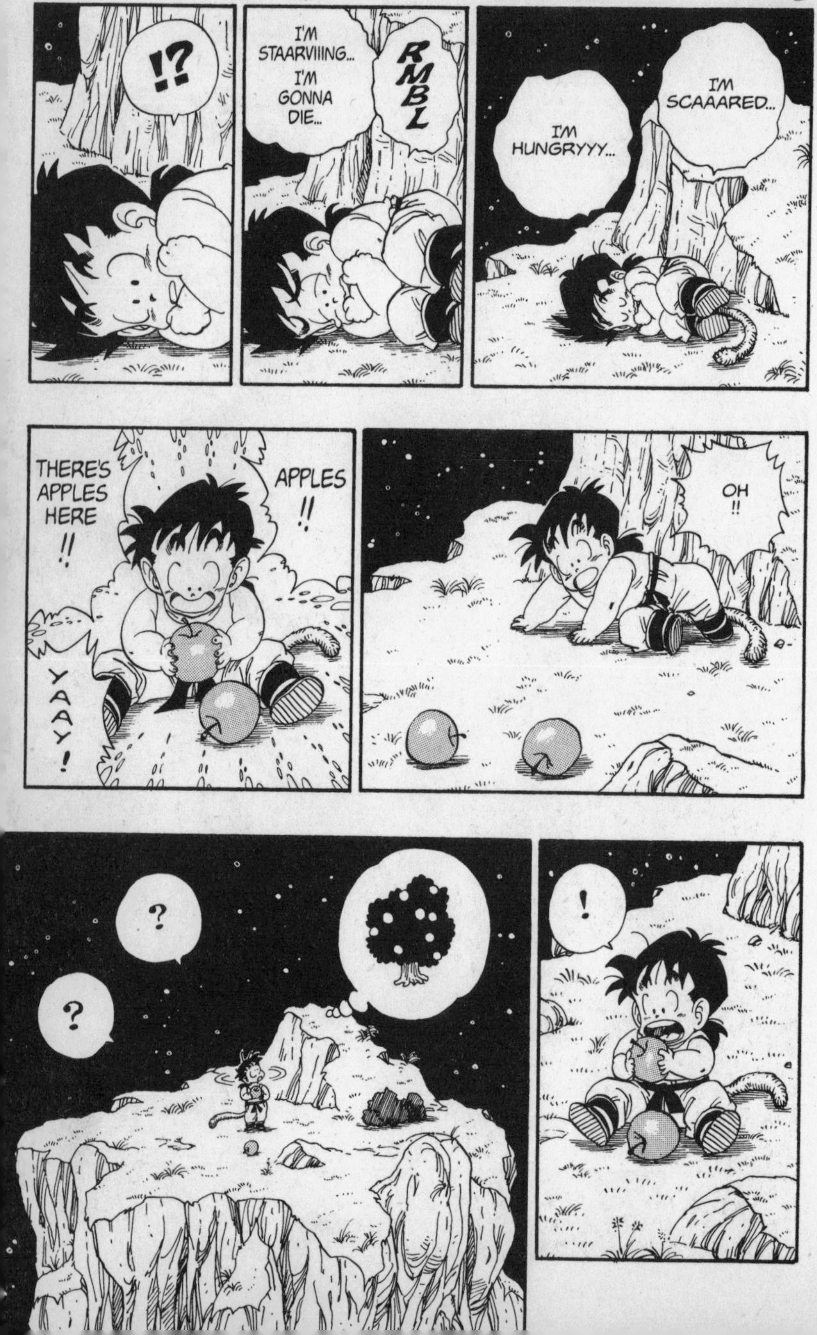
I'M SCAAARED...
I'M HUNGRYYY...
RMBL
I'M STAARVIIING... I'M GONNA DIE...
!?
OH !!
APPLES !!
THERE'S APPLES HERE !!
YAAAY!
!
?
?

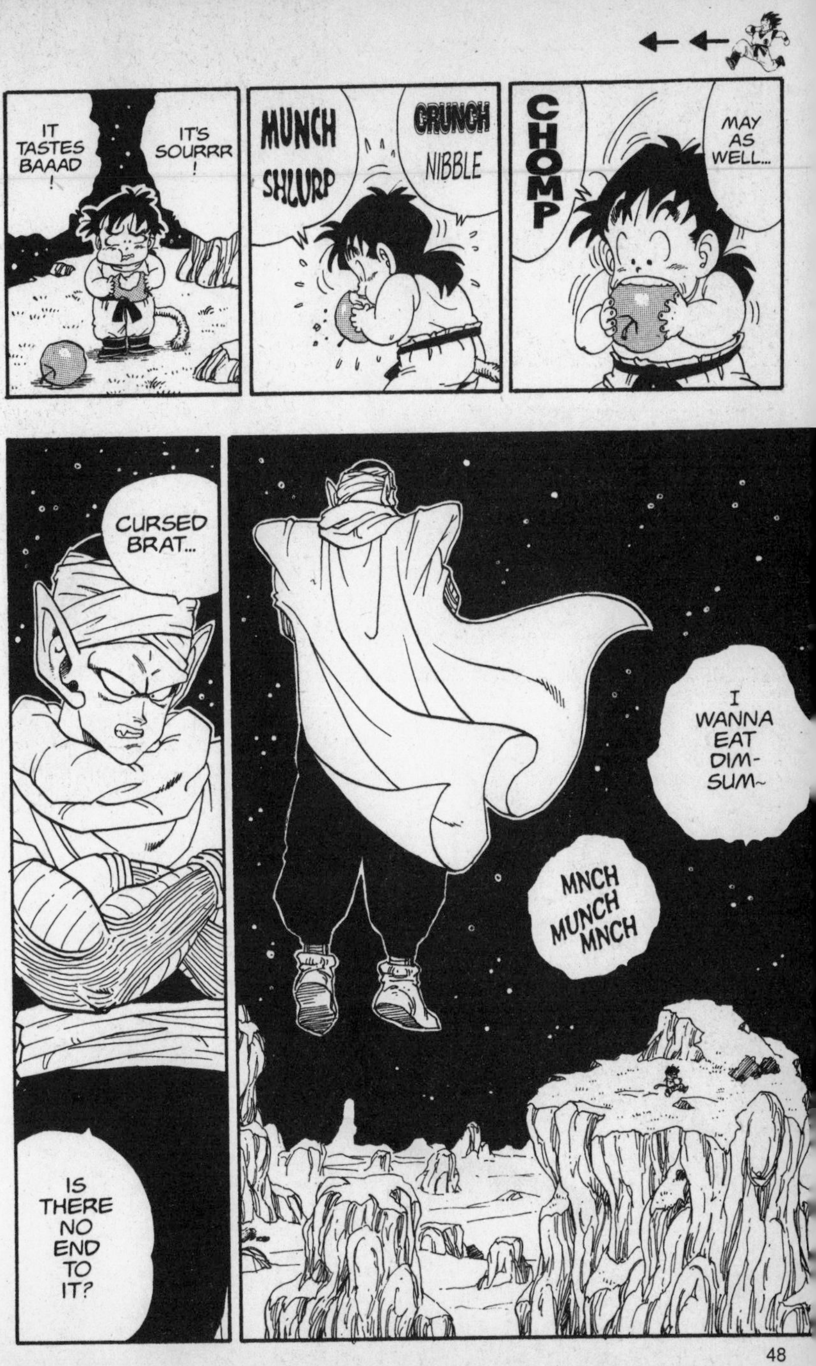
MAY AS WELL...
CHOMP
CRUNCH
NIBBLE
MUNCH
SHLURP
IT'S SOURRR!
IT TASTES BAAAD!
I WANNA EAT DIM-SUM~
MNCH MUNCH MNCH
CURSED BRAT...
IS THERE NO END TO IT?

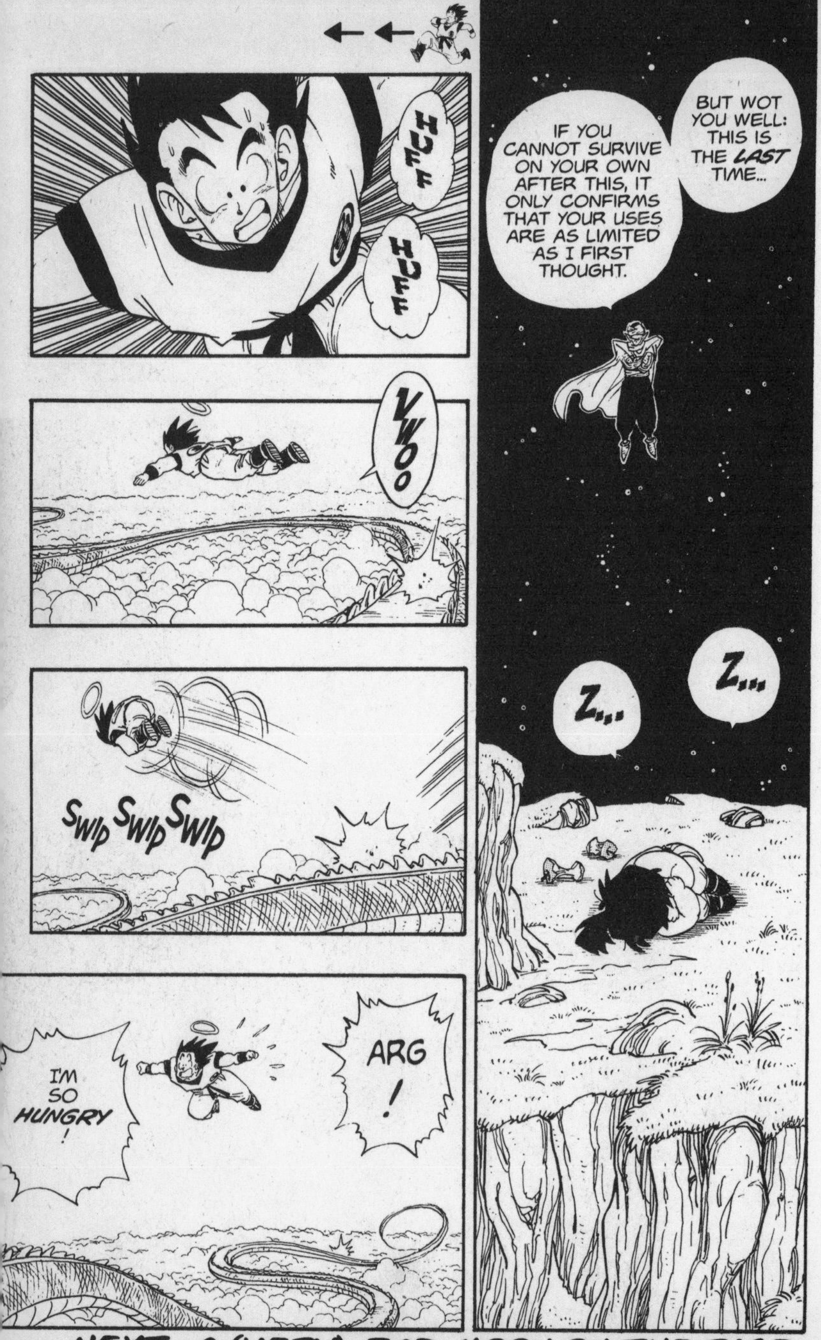
BUT WOT YOU WELL: THIS IS THE *LAST* TIME...
IF YOU CANNOT SURVIVE ON YOUR OWN AFTER THIS, IT ONLY CONFIRMS THAT YOUR USES ARE AS LIMITED AS I FIRST THOUGHT.
Z...
Z...
HUFF
HUFF
VWOOO
SWIP SWIP SWIP
ARG !
I'M SO *HUNGRY* !

NEXT: A (VERY) BAD MOON ON THE RISE

DBZ : 14 • Deeds Done by the Full Moon

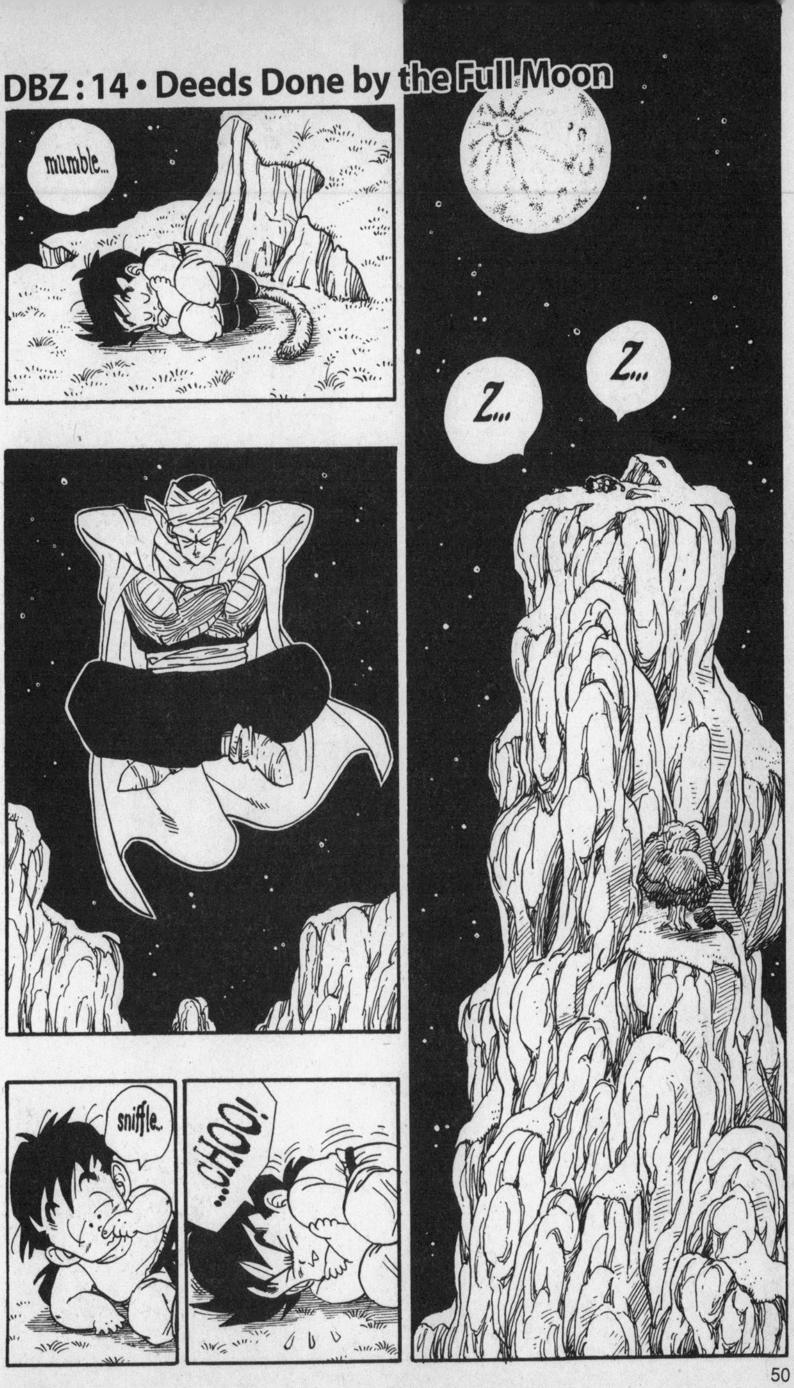
Z...
Z...
mumble...
...CHOO!
sniffle..

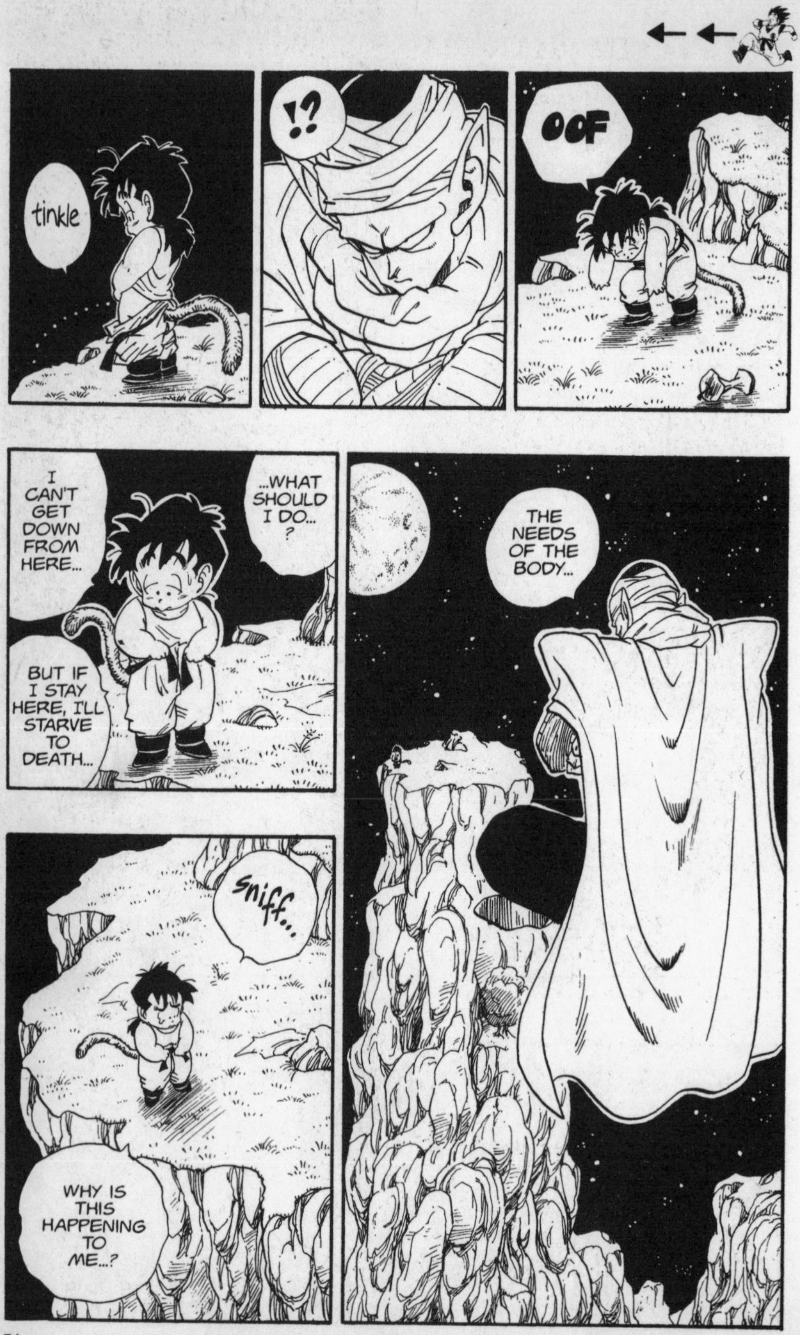
OOF
!?
tinkle
THE NEEDS OF THE BODY...
...WHAT SHOULD I DO...?
I CAN'T GET DOWN FROM HERE...
BUT IF I STAY HERE, I'LL STARVE TO DEATH...
sniff...
WHY IS THIS HAPPENING TO ME...?

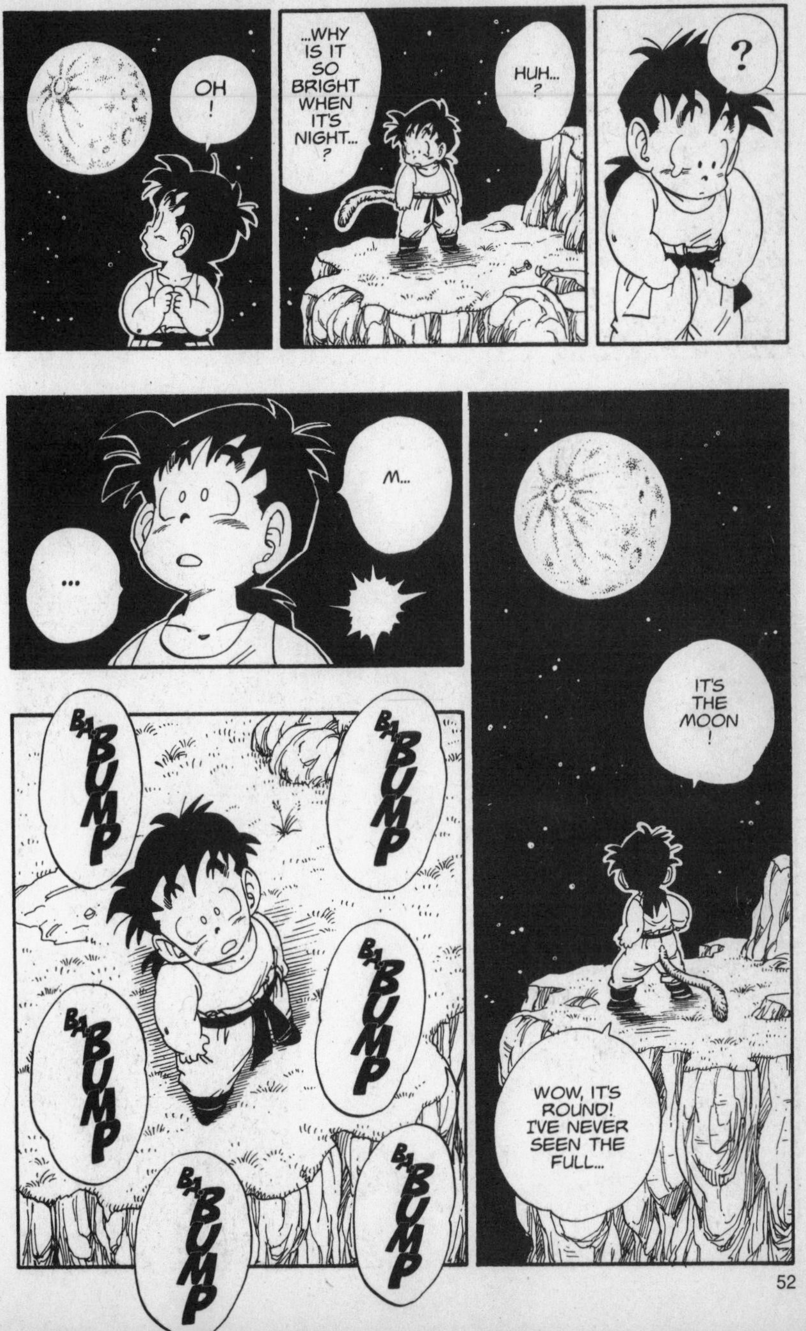
?
HUH...?
...WHY IS IT SO BRIGHT WHEN IT'S NIGHT...?
OH!
IT'S THE MOON!
WOW, IT'S ROUND! I'VE NEVER SEEN THE FULL...
M...
...
BA-BUMP
BA-BUMP
BA-BUMP
BA-BUMP
BA-BUMP
BA-BUMP

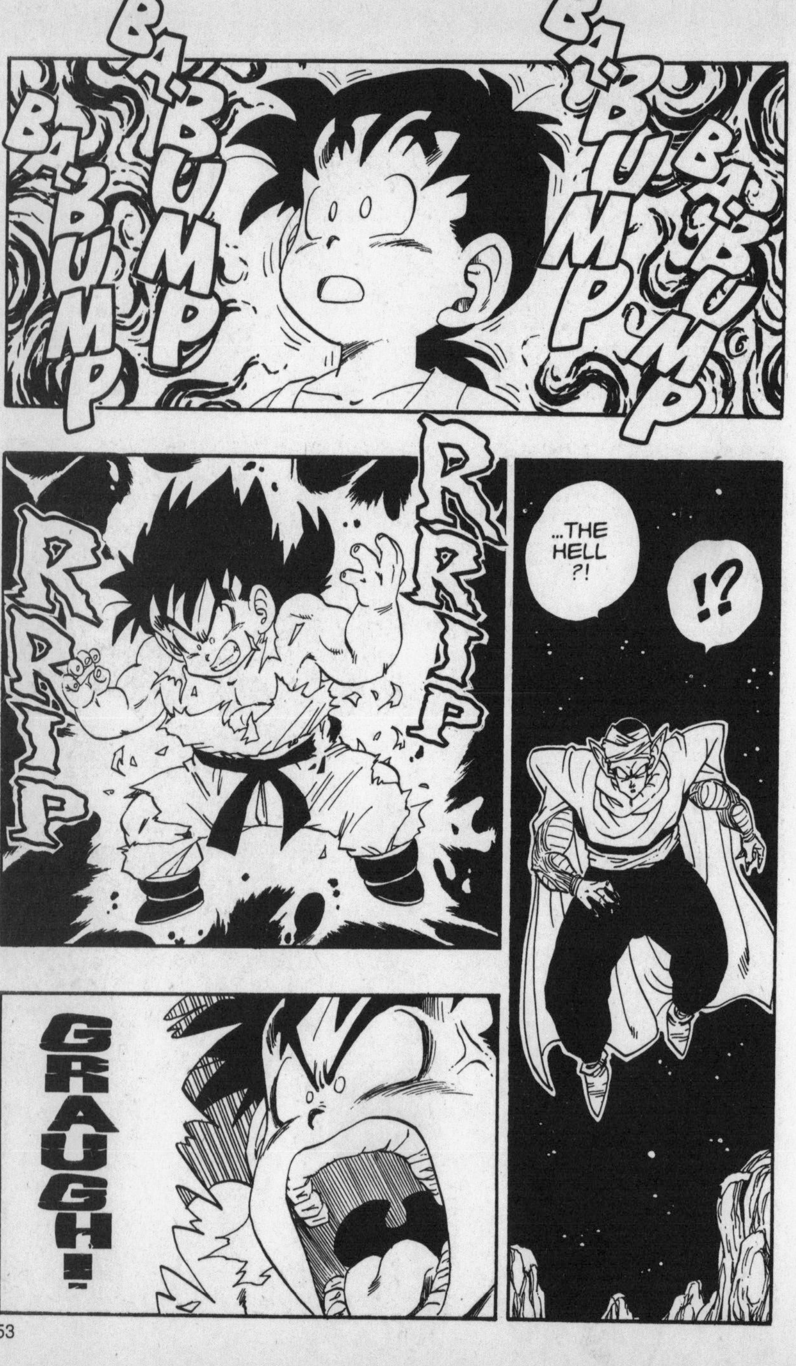
BA-BUMP
BA-BUMP
BA-BUMP
BA-BUMP
!?
...THE HELL ?!
RRIP
RRIP
GRAUGH!!

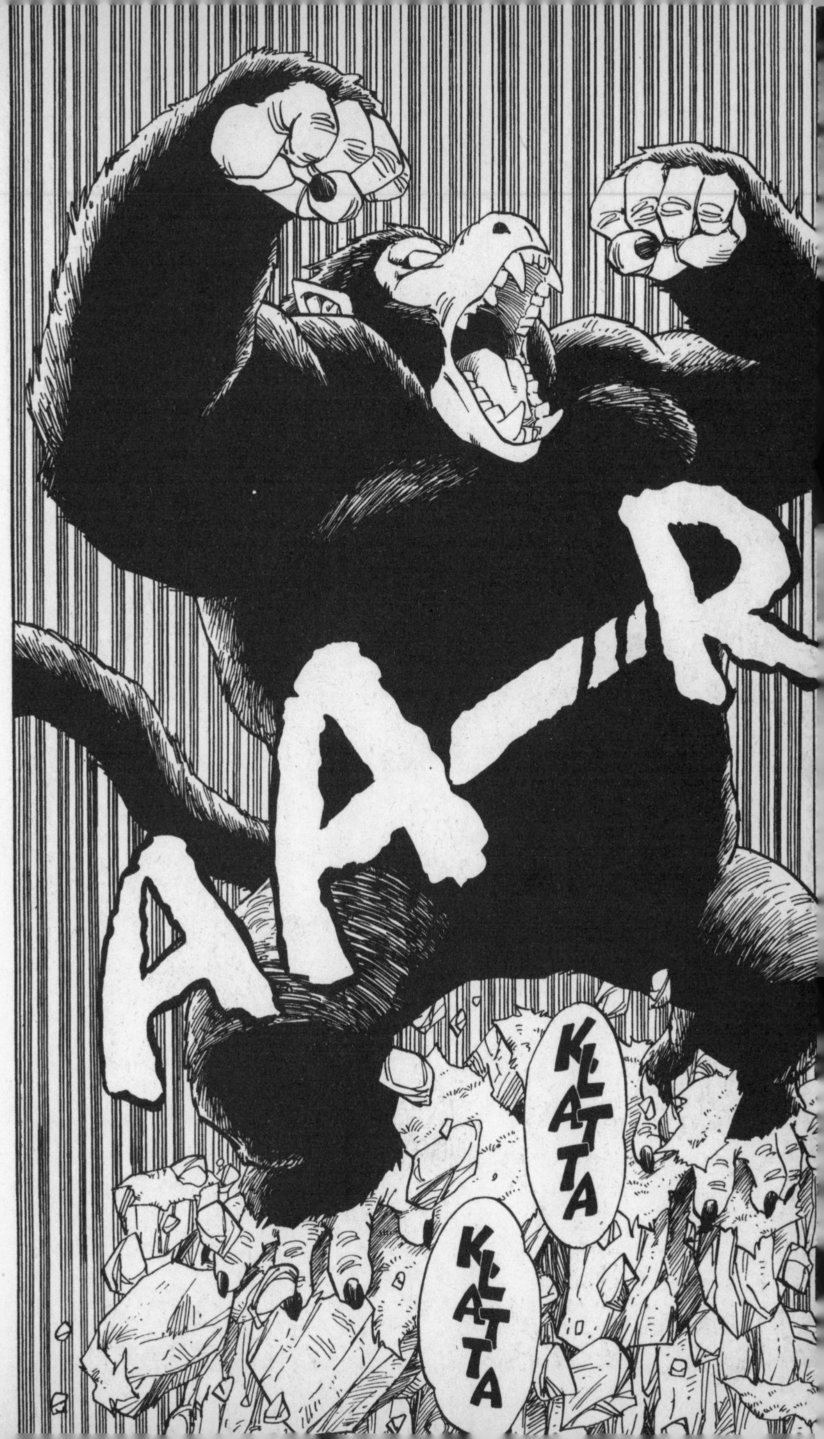
AA–R
KLATTA
KLATTA

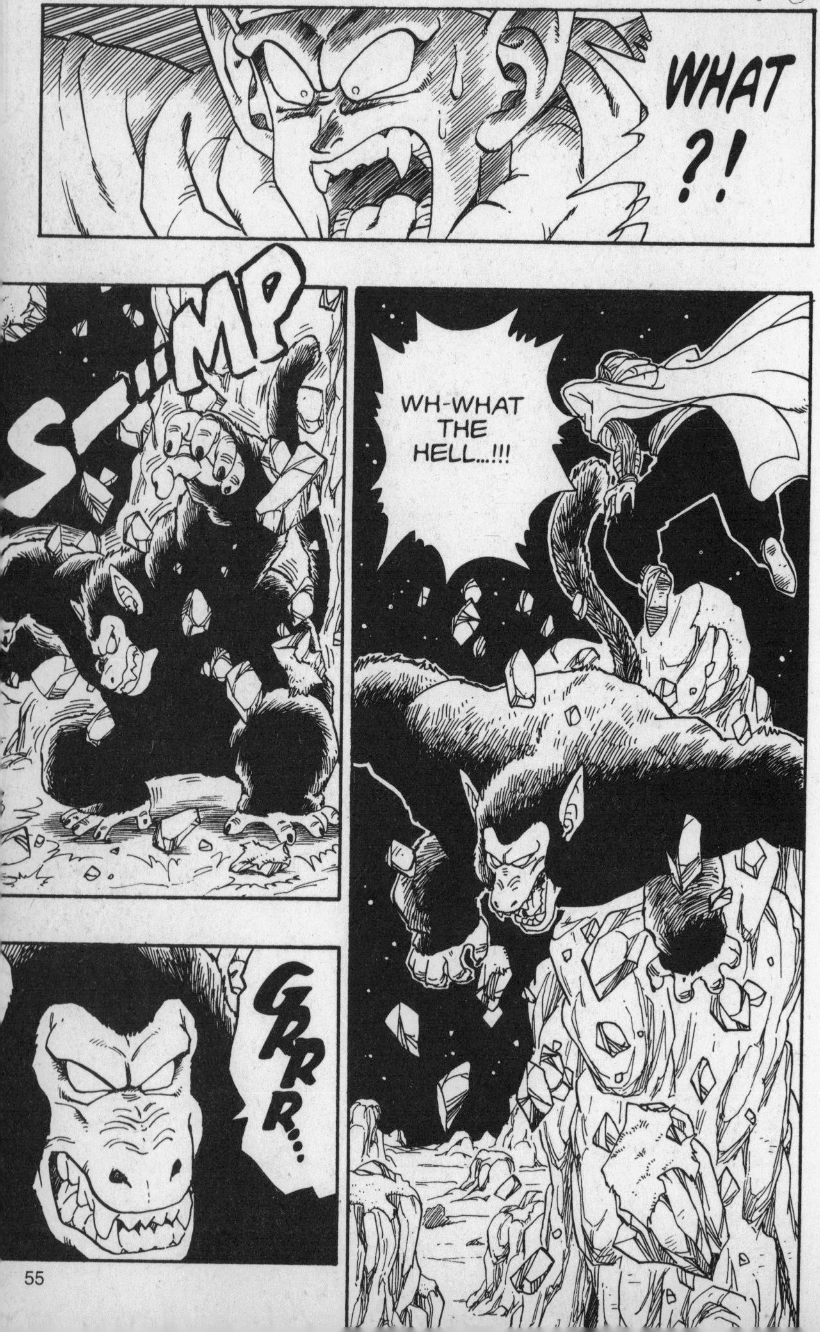
WHAT ?!
WH-WHAT THE HELL...!!!
S...MP
GRRR...

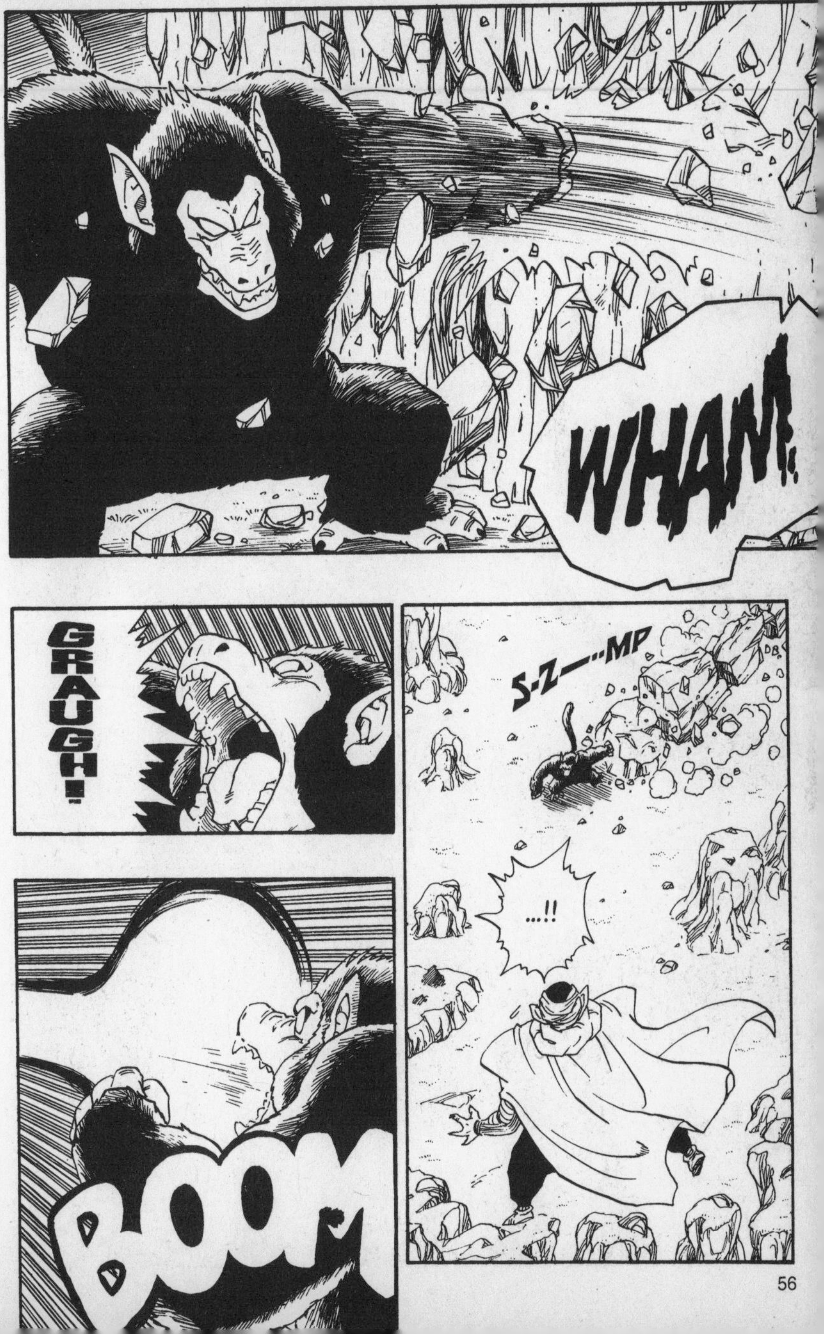
WHAM!!
S-Z---MP
...!!
GRAUGH!!
BOOM

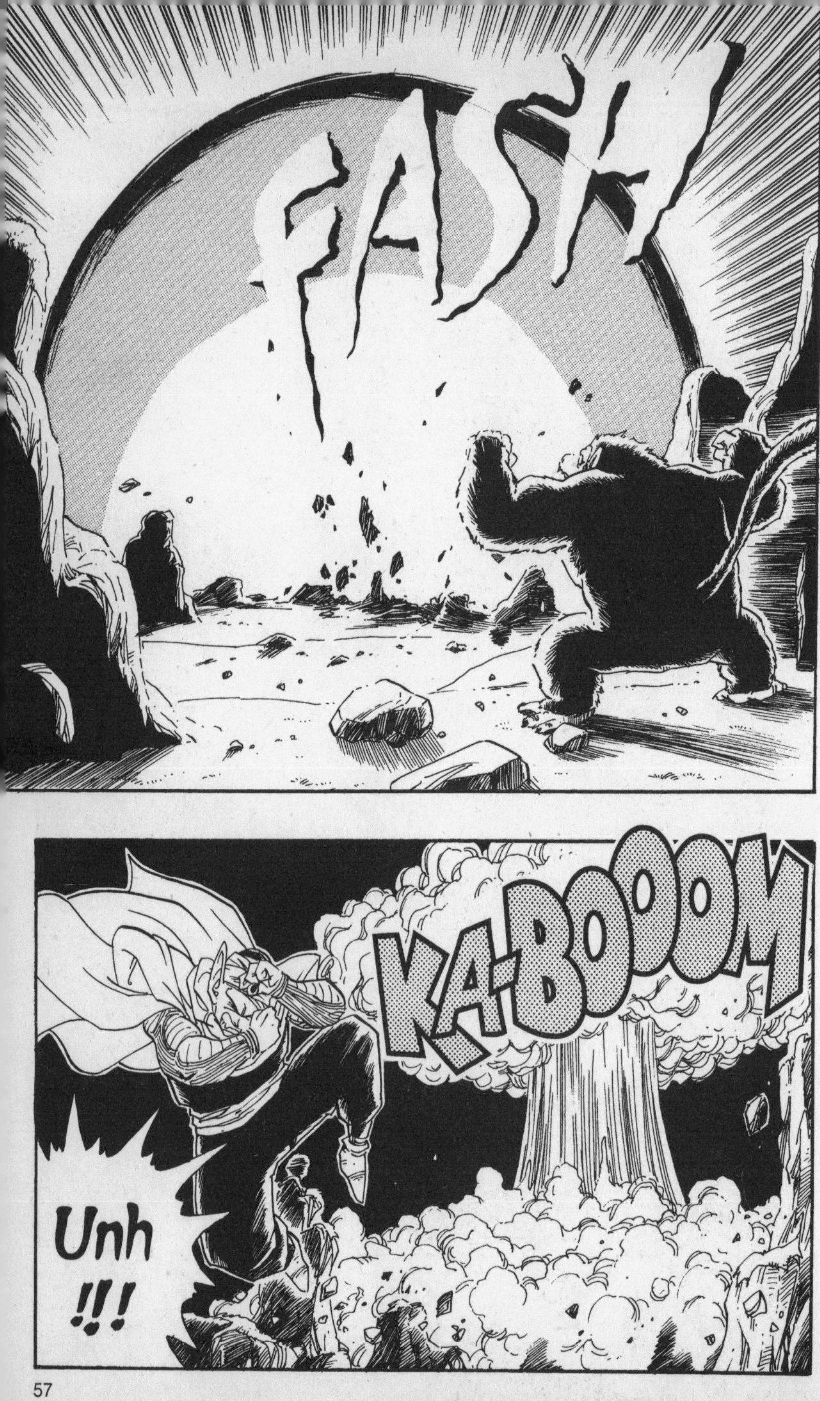
FASH!
KA-BOOOM
Unh !!!

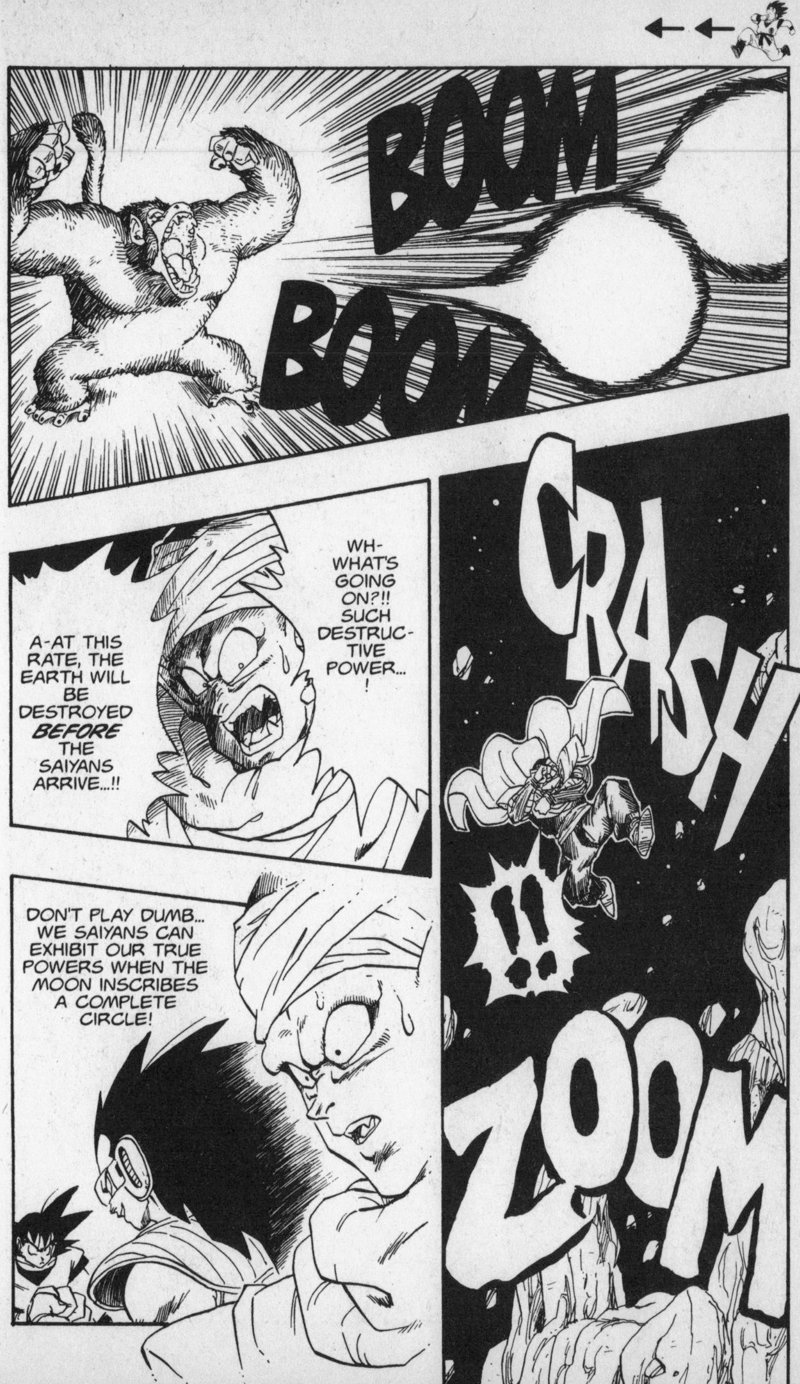

BOOM
BOOM
CRASH
!!
ZOOM
WH- WHAT'S GOING ON?!! SUCH DESTRUCTIVE POWER...!
A-AT THIS RATE, THE EARTH WILL BE DESTROYED *BEFORE* THE SAIYANS ARRIVE...!!
DON'T PLAY DUMB... WE SAIYANS CAN EXHIBIT OUR TRUE POWERS WHEN THE MOON INSCRIBES A COMPLETE CIRCLE!

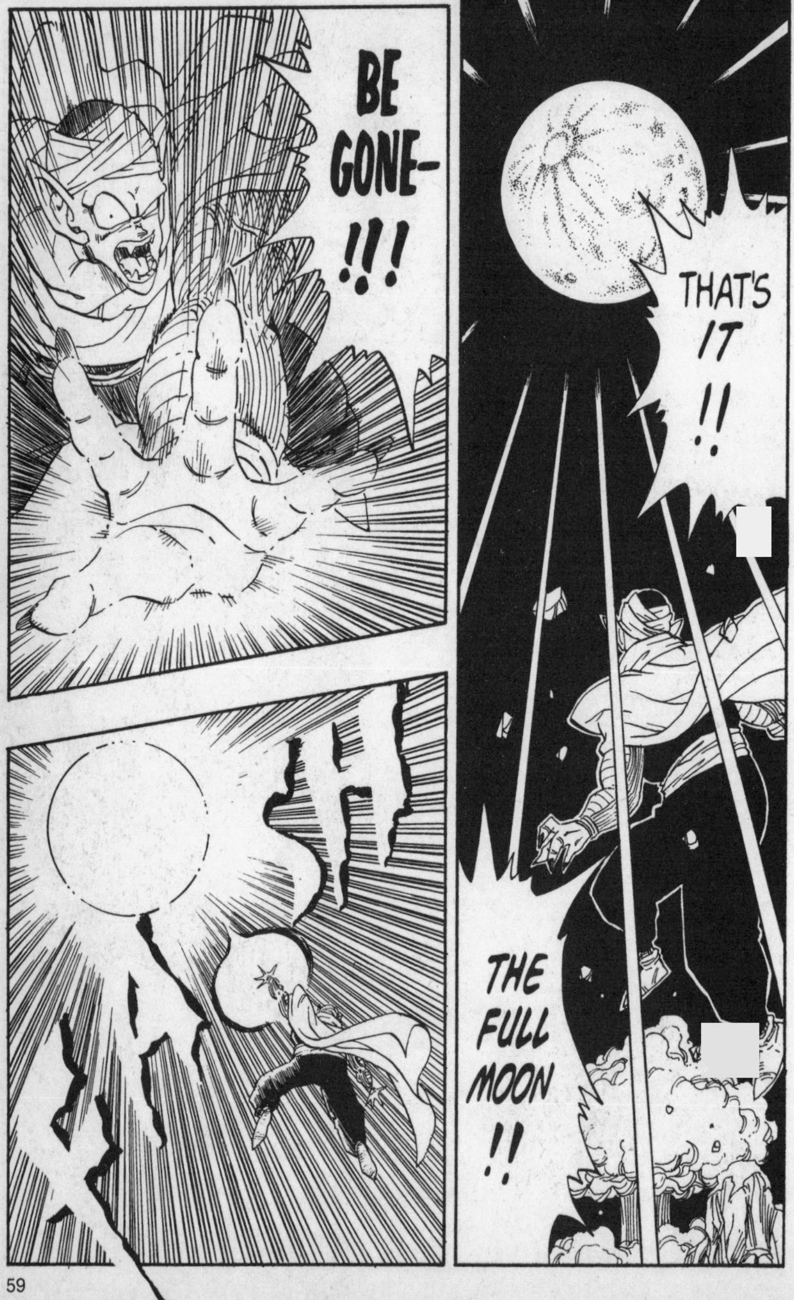
THAT'S IT!!
THE FULL MOON!!
BE GONE-!!!

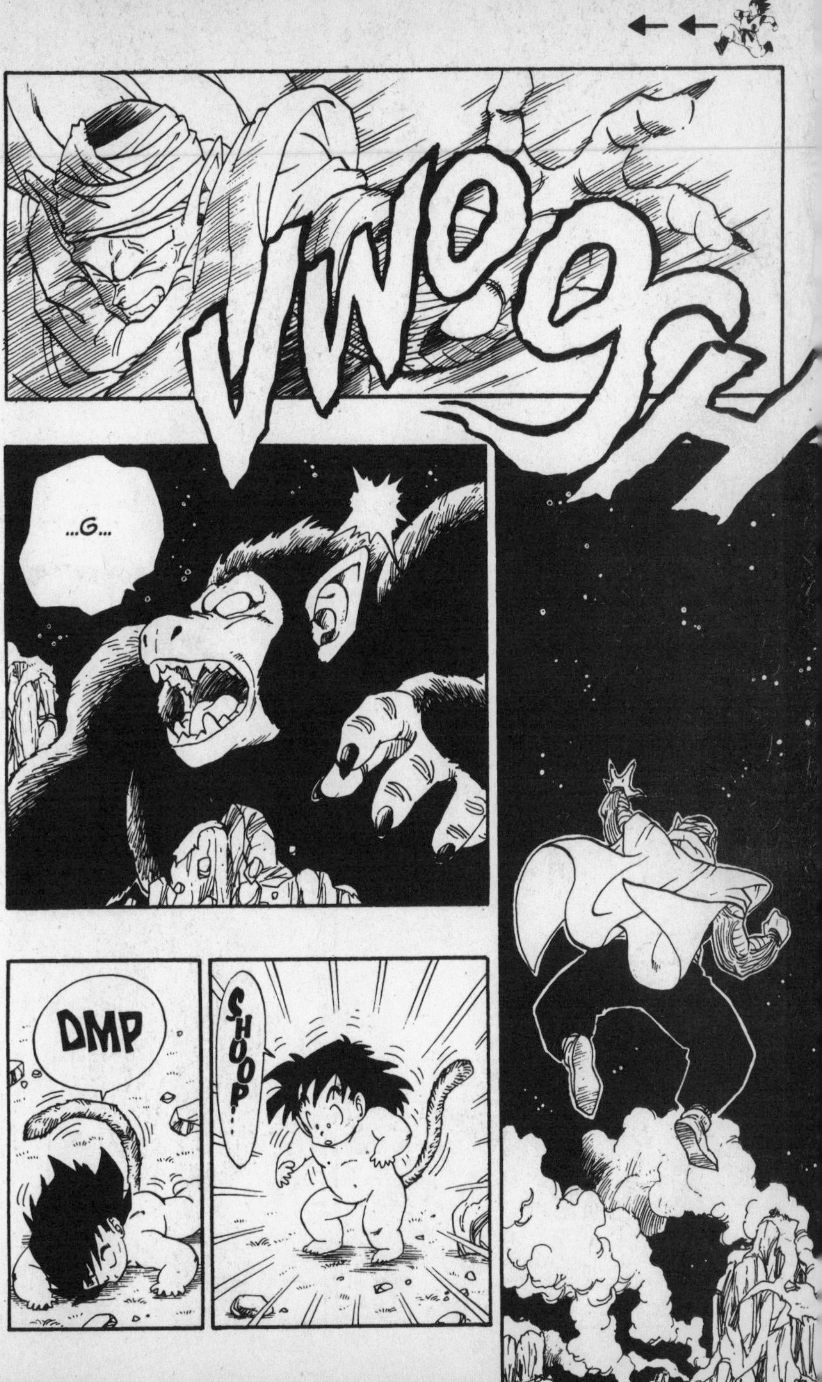
...G...
SHOOP...
DMP

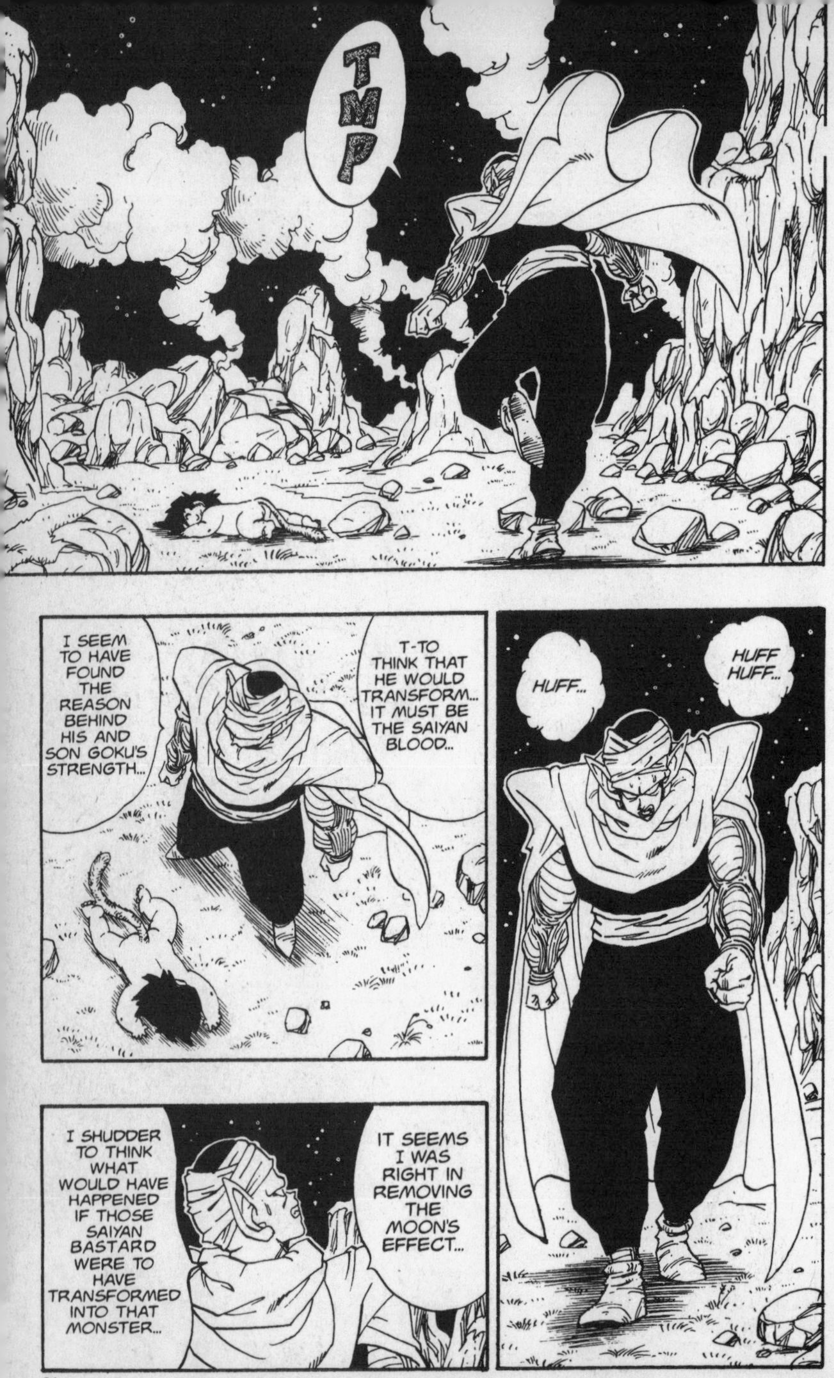
TMP
HUFF HUFF...
HUFF...
T-TO THINK THAT HE WOULD TRANSFORM... IT MUST BE THE SAIYAN BLOOD...
I SEEM TO HAVE FOUND THE REASON BEHIND HIS AND SON GOKU'S STRENGTH...
IT SEEMS I WAS RIGHT IN REMOVING THE MOON'S EFFECT...
I SHUDDER TO THINK WHAT WOULD HAVE HAPPENED IF THOSE SAIYAN BASTARD WERE TO HAVE TRANSFORMED INTO THAT MONSTER...

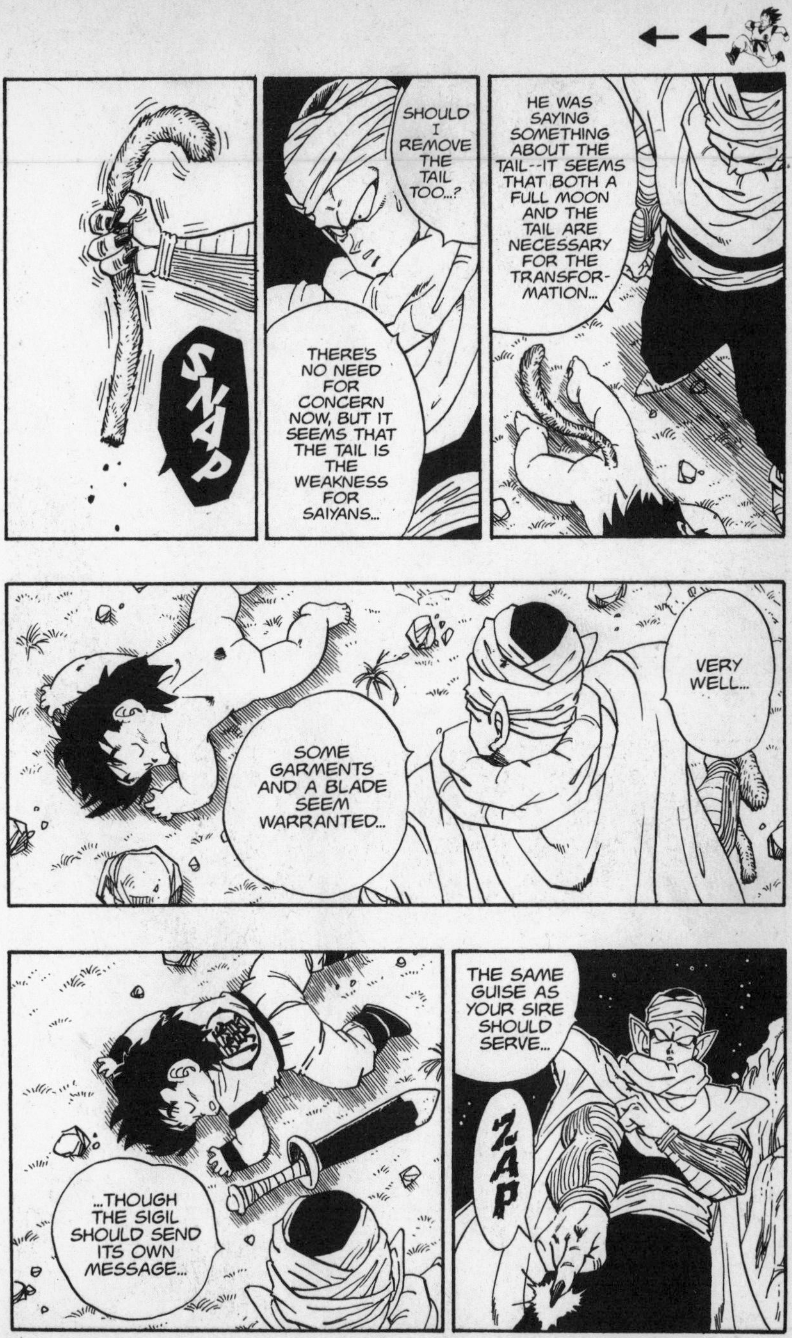
HE WAS SAYING SOMETHING ABOUT THE TAIL--IT SEEMS THAT BOTH A FULL MOON AND THE TAIL ARE NECESSARY FOR THE TRANSFORMATION...
SHOULD I REMOVE THE TAIL TOO...?
THERE'S NO NEED FOR CONCERN NOW, BUT IT SEEMS THAT THE TAIL IS THE WEAKNESS FOR SAIYANS...
SNAP
VERY WELL...
SOME GARMENTS AND A BLADE SEEM WARRANTED...
THE SAME GUISE AS YOUR SIRE SHOULD SERVE...
ZAP
...THOUGH THE SIGIL SHOULD SEND ITS OWN MESSAGE...

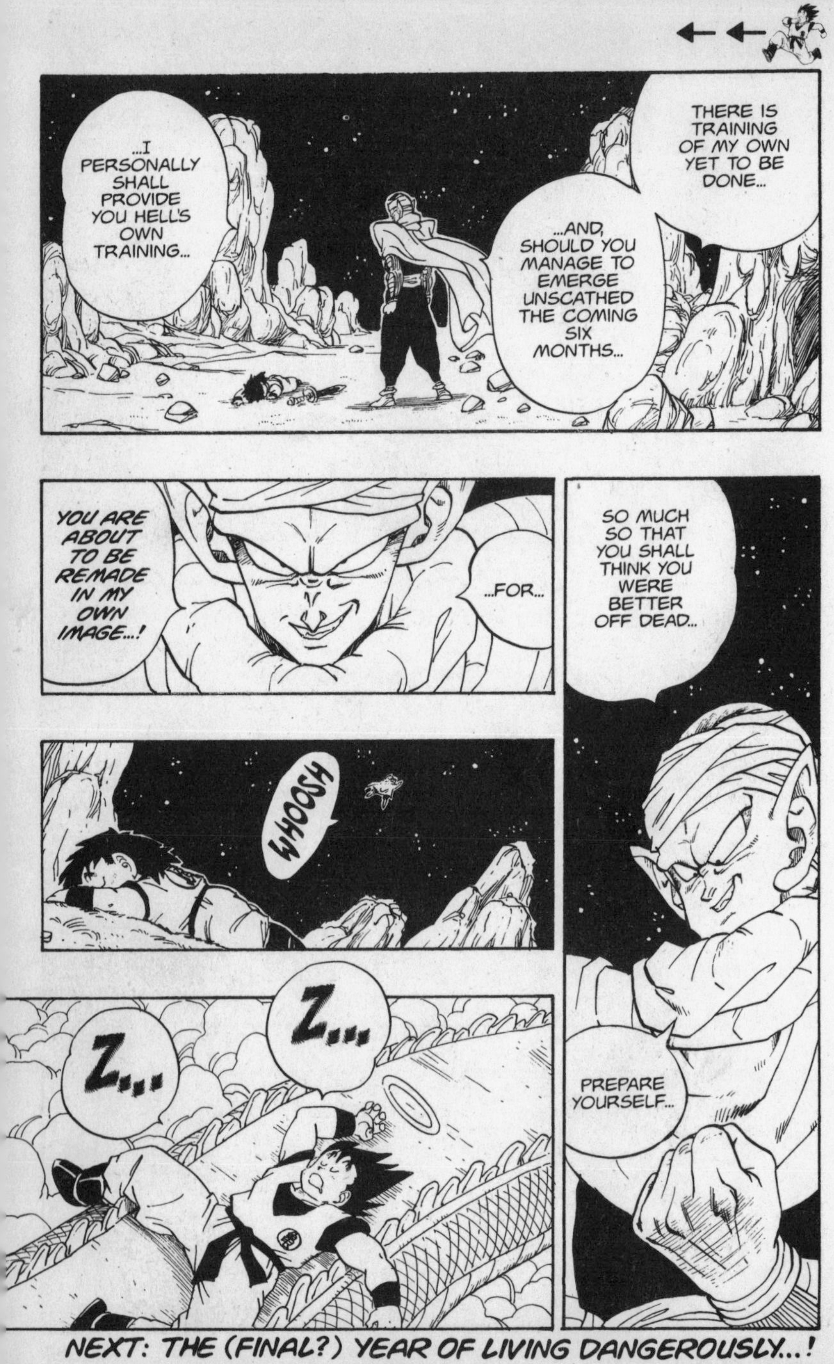
THERE IS TRAINING OF MY OWN YET TO BE DONE...
...AND, SHOULD YOU MANAGE TO EMERGE UNSCATHED THE COMING SIX MONTHS...
...I PERSONALLY SHALL PROVIDE YOU HELL'S OWN TRAINING...
SO MUCH SO THAT YOU SHALL THINK YOU WERE BETTER OFF DEAD...
PREPARE YOURSELF...
...FOR...
YOU ARE ABOUT TO BE REMADE IN MY OWN IMAGE...!
WHOOSH
Z...
Z...

NEXT: THE (FINAL?) YEAR OF LIVING DANGEROUSLY...!

DBZ : 15 • Goku and Gohan's Training Begins!!!

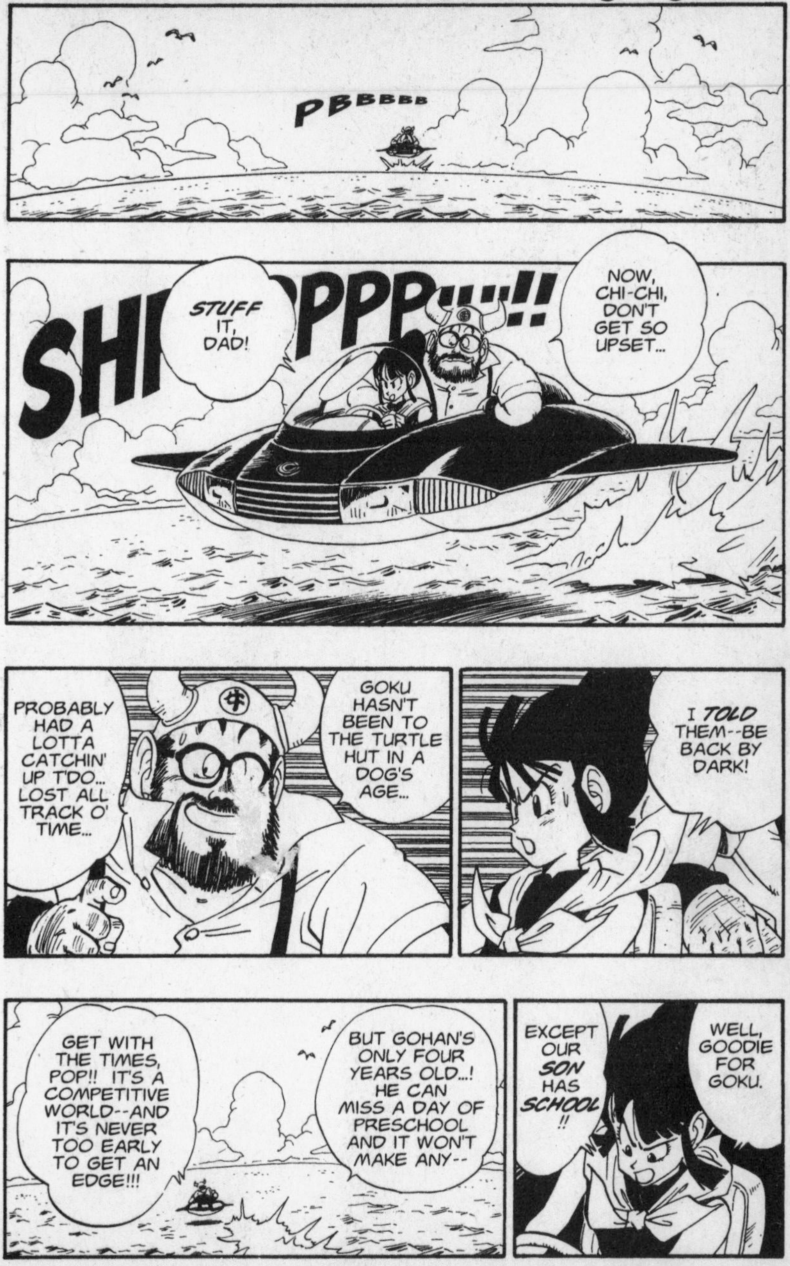

PBBBBB
NOW, CHI-CHI, DON'T GET SO UPSET...
SHI
PPPP!!!!!
STUFF IT, DAD!
I TOLD THEM--BE BACK BY DARK!
GOKU HASN'T BEEN TO THE TURTLE HUT IN A DOG'S AGE...
PROBABLY HAD A LOTTA CATCHIN' UP T'DO... LOST ALL TRACK O' TIME...
WELL, GOODIE FOR GOKU.
EXCEPT OUR SON HAS SCHOOL!!
BUT GOHAN'S ONLY FOUR YEARS OLD...! HE CAN MISS A DAY OF PRESCHOOL AND IT WON'T MAKE ANY--
GET WITH THE TIMES, POP!! IT'S A COMPETITIVE WORLD--AND IT'S NEVER TOO EARLY TO GET AN EDGE!!!

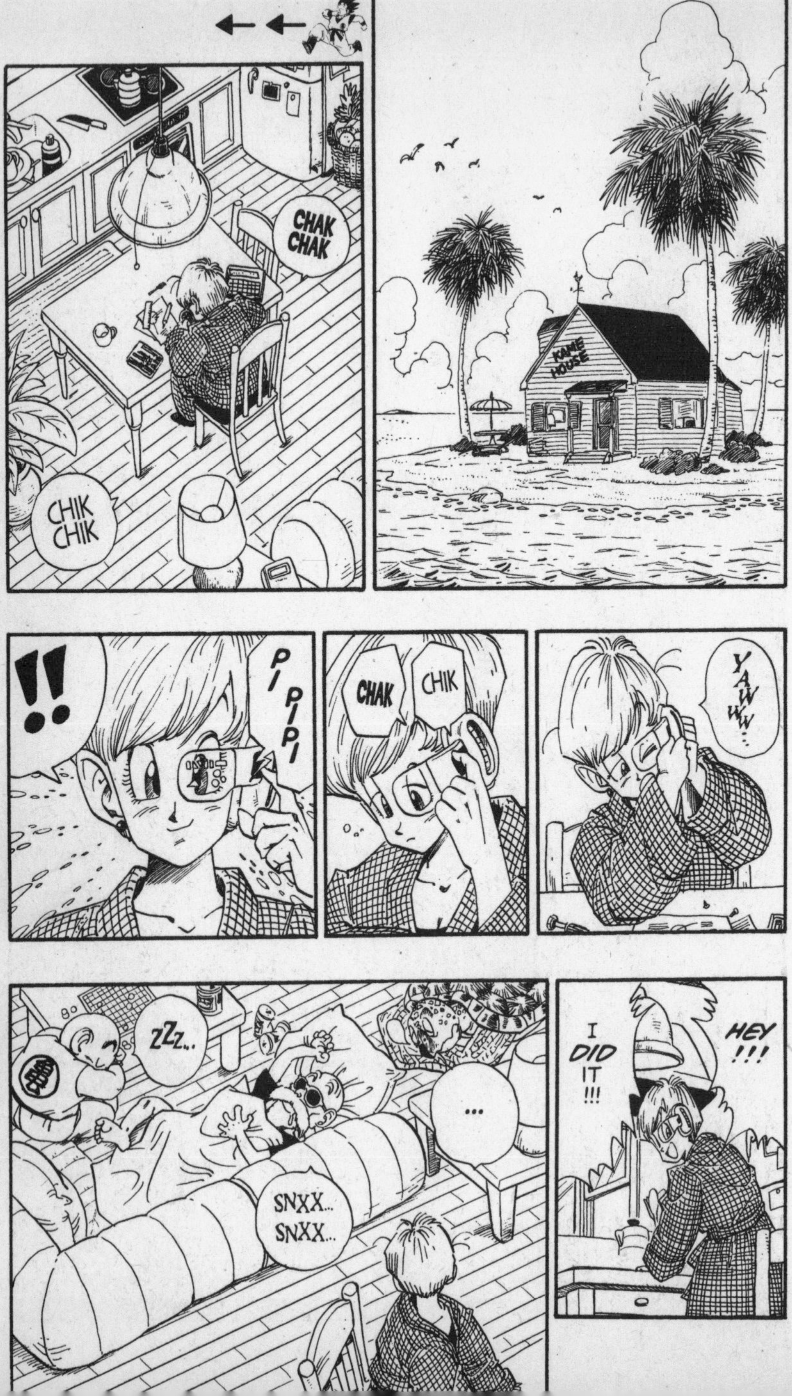
KAME HOUSE
CHAK CHAK
CHIK CHIK
YAWWW...
CHIK
CHAK
PI PIPIPI
!!
HEY!!!
I DID IT!!!
ZZz..
...
SNXX... SNXX...

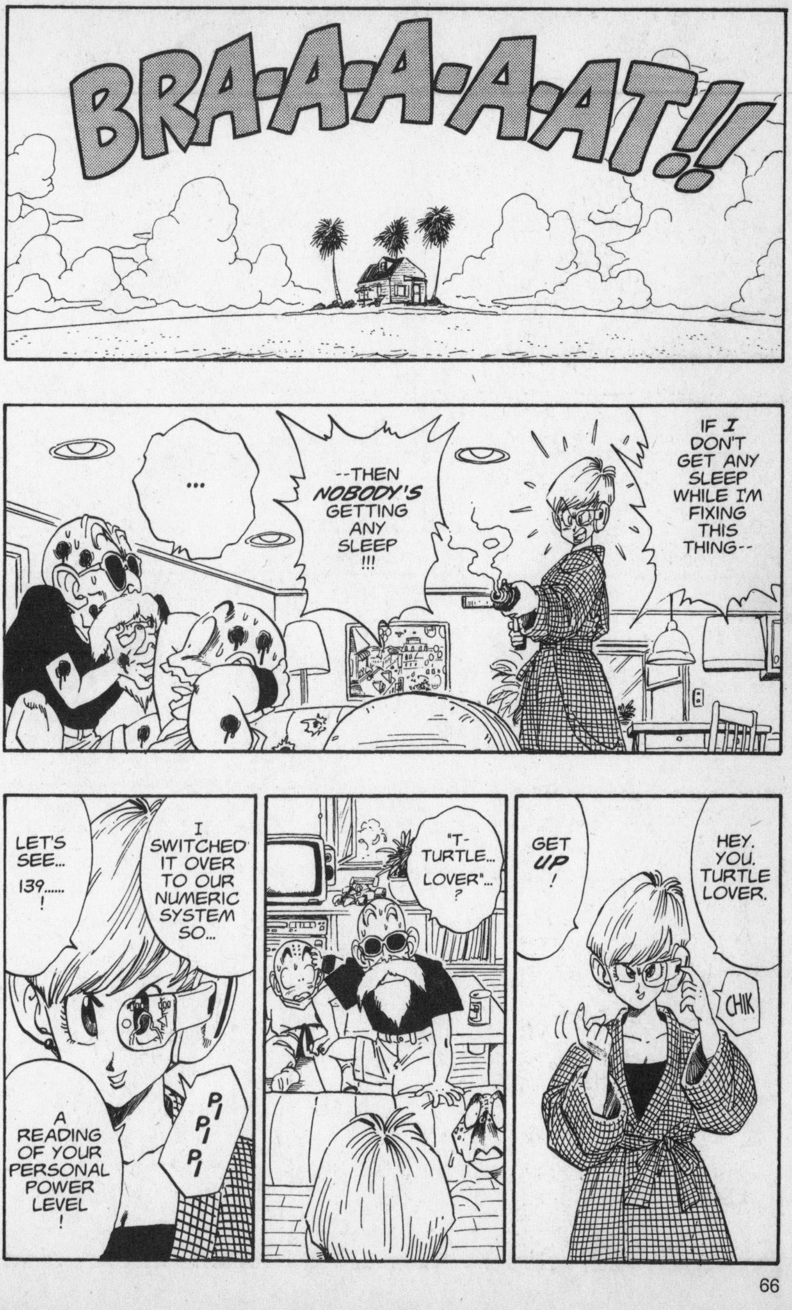
BRA-A-A-A-AT!!
IF I DON'T GET ANY SLEEP WHILE I'M FIXING THIS THING--
--THEN NOBODY'S GETTING ANY SLEEP!!!
...
HEY. YOU. TURTLE LOVER.
CHIK
GET UP!
"T-TURTLE... LOVER"...?
I SWITCHED IT OVER TO OUR NUMERIC SYSTEM SO...
LET'S SEE... 139......!
PI PI PI
A READING OF YOUR PERSONAL POWER LEVEL!

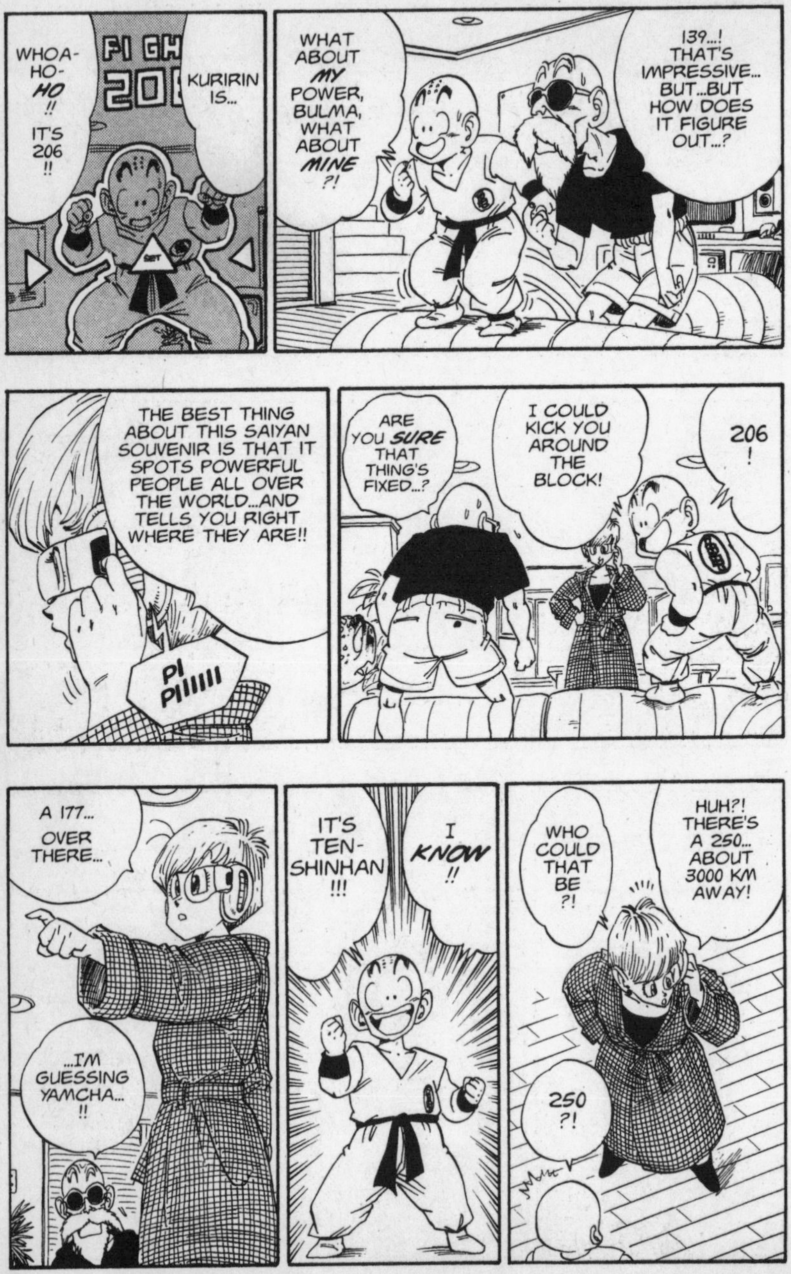
139...! THAT'S IMPRESSIVE... BUT...BUT HOW DOES IT FIGURE OUT...?
WHAT ABOUT MY POWER, BULMA, WHAT ABOUT MINE ?!
KURIRIN IS...
WHOA-HO-HO !! IT'S 206 !!
206 !
I COULD KICK YOU AROUND THE BLOCK!
ARE YOU SURE THAT THING'S FIXED...?
THE BEST THING ABOUT THIS SAIYAN SOUVENIR IS THAT IT SPOTS POWERFUL PEOPLE ALL OVER THE WORLD...AND TELLS YOU RIGHT WHERE THEY ARE!!
PI PI!!!!!
HUH?! THERE'S A 250... ABOUT 3000 KM AWAY!
WHO COULD THAT BE ?!
250 ?!
I KNOW !!
IT'S TEN-SHINHAN !!!
A 177... OVER THERE...
...I'M GUESSING YAMCHA... !!

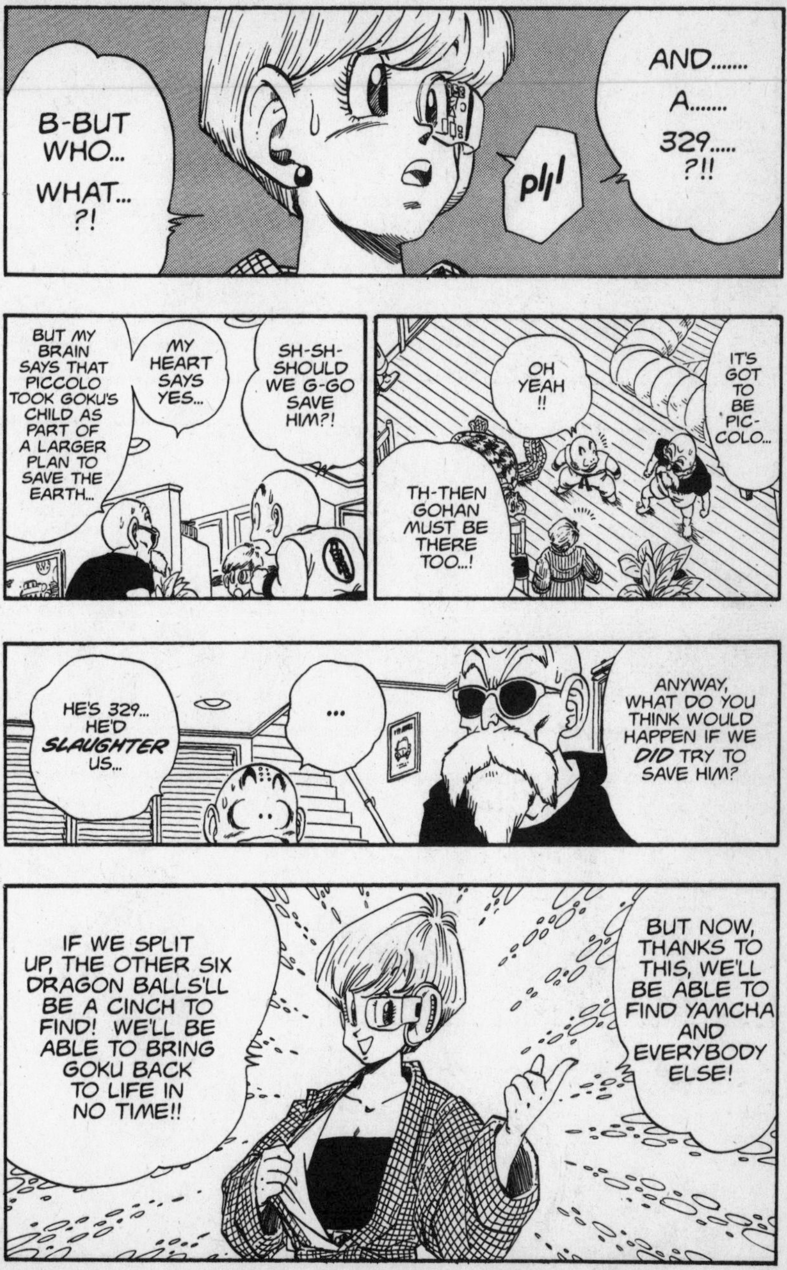
AND....... A....... 329..... ?!!
B-BUT WHO... WHAT... ?!
IT'S GOT TO BE PIC-COLO...
OH YEAH !!
TH-THEN GOHAN MUST BE THERE TOO...!
SH-SH-SHOULD WE G-GO SAVE HIM?!
MY HEART SAYS YES...
BUT MY BRAIN SAYS THAT PICCOLO TOOK GOKU'S CHILD AS PART OF A LARGER PLAN TO SAVE THE EARTH...
ANYWAY, WHAT DO YOU THINK WOULD HAPPEN IF WE *DID* TRY TO SAVE HIM?
...
HE'S 329... HE'D *SLAUGHTER* US...
BUT NOW, THANKS TO THIS, WE'LL BE ABLE TO FIND YAMCHA AND EVERYBODY ELSE!
IF WE SPLIT UP, THE OTHER SIX DRAGON BALLS'LL BE A CINCH TO FIND! WE'LL BE ABLE TO BRING GOKU BACK TO LIFE IN NO TIME!!

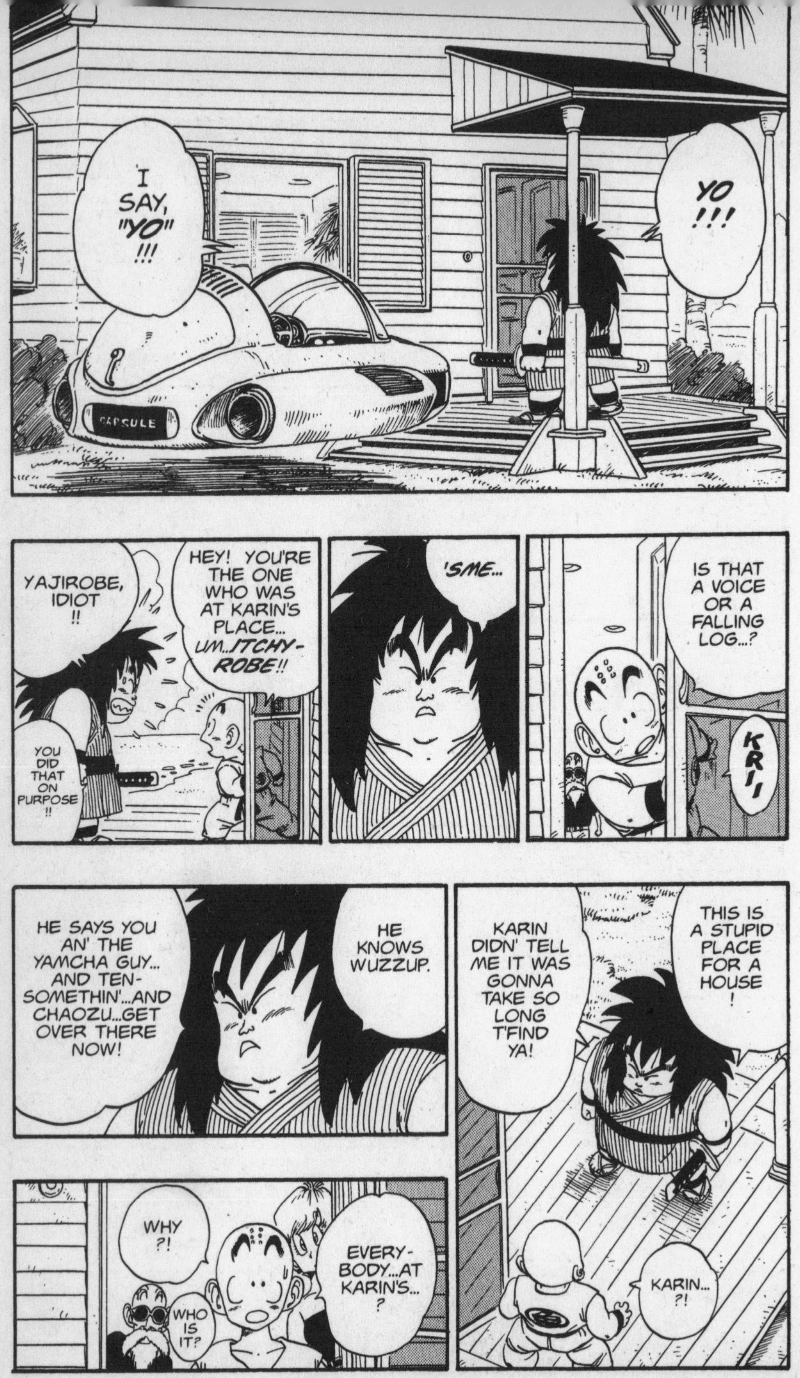
YO !!!
I SAY, "YO" !!!
IS THAT A VOICE OR A FALLING LOG...?
KRI
'SME...
HEY! YOU'RE THE ONE WHO WAS AT KARIN'S PLACE... UM...ITCHY-ROBE!!
YAJIROBE, IDIOT !!
YOU DID THAT ON PURPOSE !!
THIS IS A STUPID PLACE FOR A HOUSE !
KARIN DIDN' TELL ME IT WAS GONNA TAKE SO LONG T'FIND YA!
KARIN... ?!
HE KNOWS WUZZUP.
HE SAYS YOU AN' THE YAMCHA GUY... AND TEN-SOMETHIN'...AND CHAOZU...GET OVER THERE NOW!
EVERY-BODY...AT KARIN'S... ?
WHY ?!
WHO IS IT?

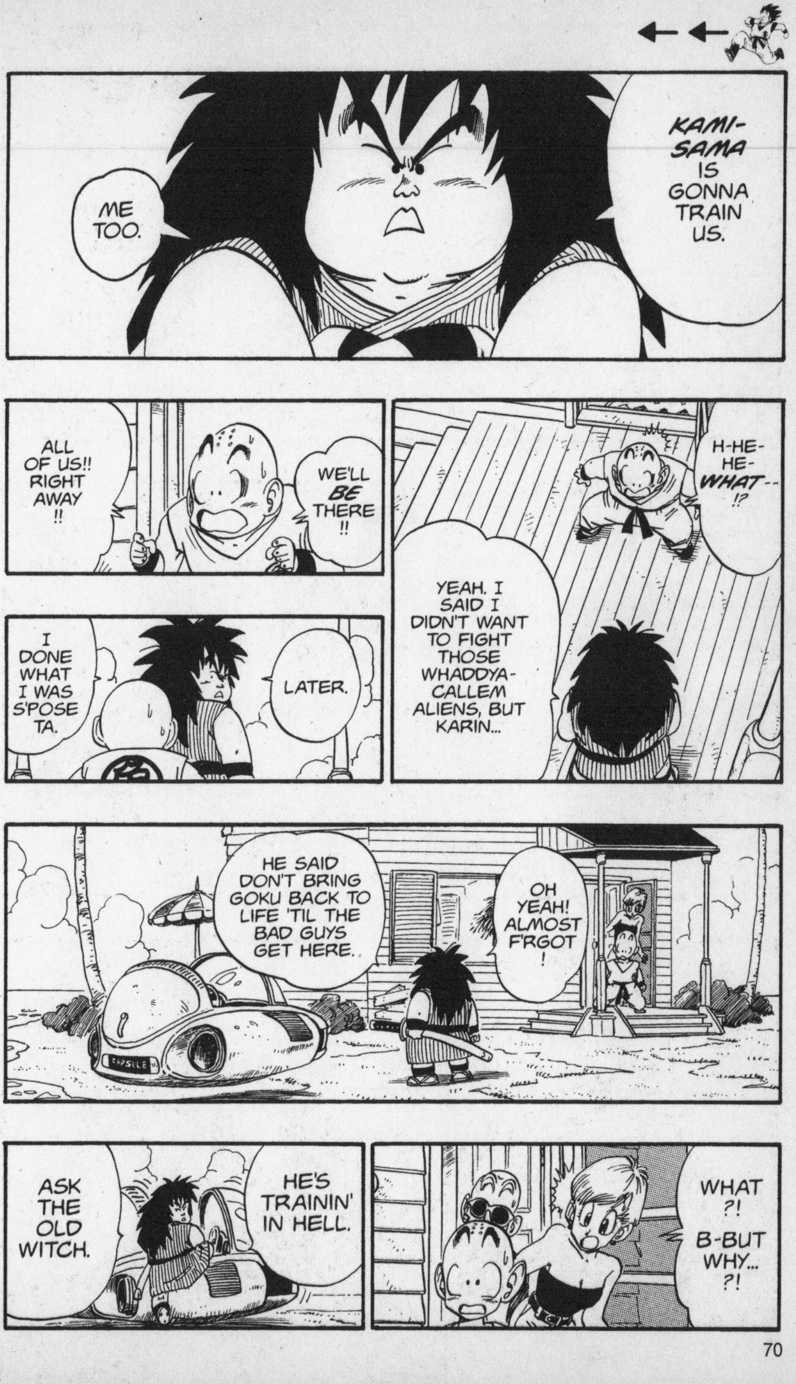
KAMI-SAMA IS GONNA TRAIN US.
ME TOO.
H-HE-HE WHAT--!?
YEAH. I SAID I DIDN'T WANT TO FIGHT THOSE WHADDYA-CALLEM ALIENS, BUT KARIN...
WE'LL BE THERE!!
ALL OF US!! RIGHT AWAY!!
LATER.
I DONE WHAT I WAS S'POSE TA.
OH YEAH! ALMOST F'RGOT!
HE SAID DON'T BRING GOKU BACK TO LIFE 'TIL THE BAD GUYS GET HERE.
WHAT?! B-BUT WHY...?!
HE'S TRAININ' IN HELL.
ASK THE OLD WITCH.

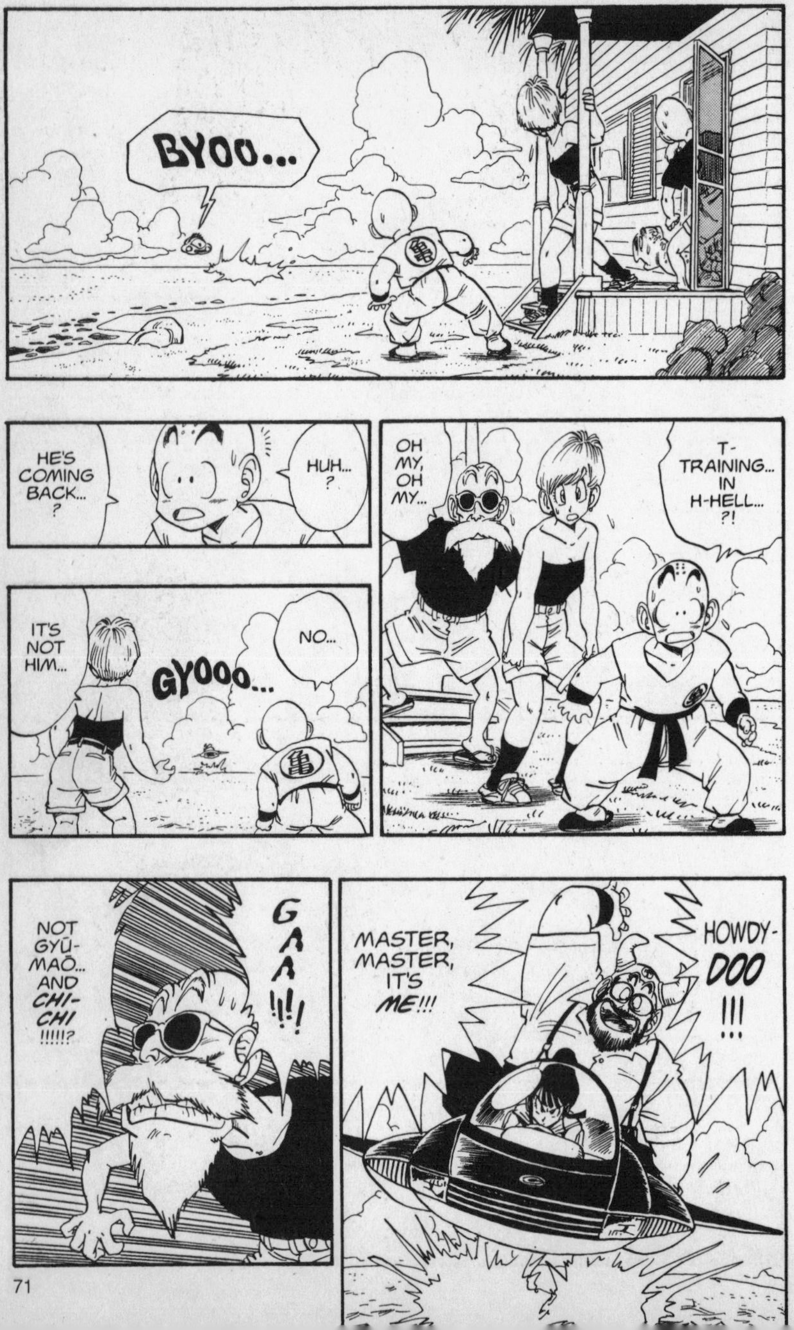
BYOO...
T-TRAINING... IN H-HELL...?!
OH MY, OH MY...
HUH...?
HE'S COMING BACK...?
NO...
GYOOO...
IT'S NOT HIM...
HOWDY-DOO!!!
MASTER, MASTER, IT'S ME!!!
GAAA!!!!
NOT GYŪ-MAŌ... AND CHI-CHI!!!!!?

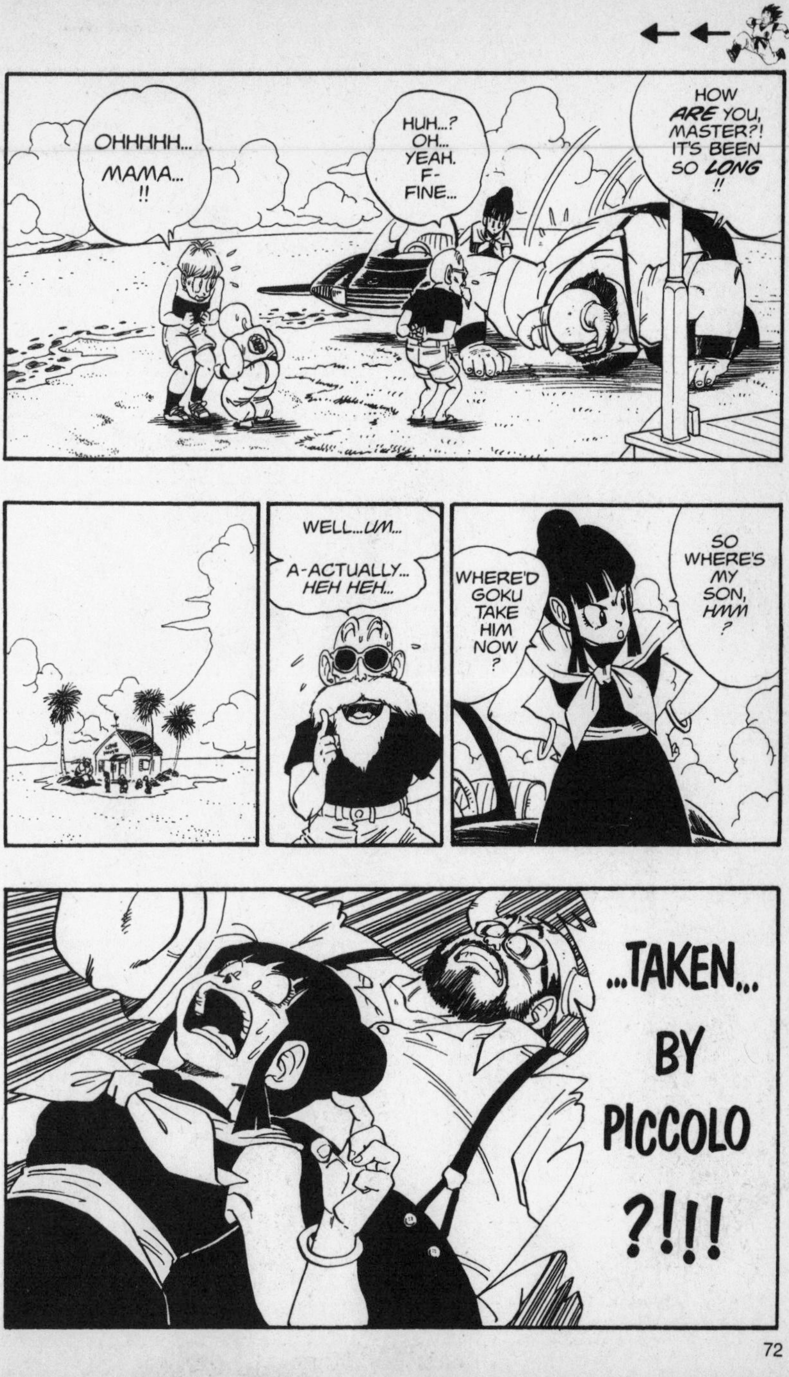
HOW ARE YOU, MASTER?! IT'S BEEN SO LONG!!
HUH...? OH... YEAH. F-FINE...
OHHHHH... MAMA...!!
SO WHERE'S MY SON, HMM?
WHERE'D GOKU TAKE HIM NOW?
WELL...UM...
A-ACTUALLY... HEH HEH...
...TAKEN... BY PICCOLO?!!!

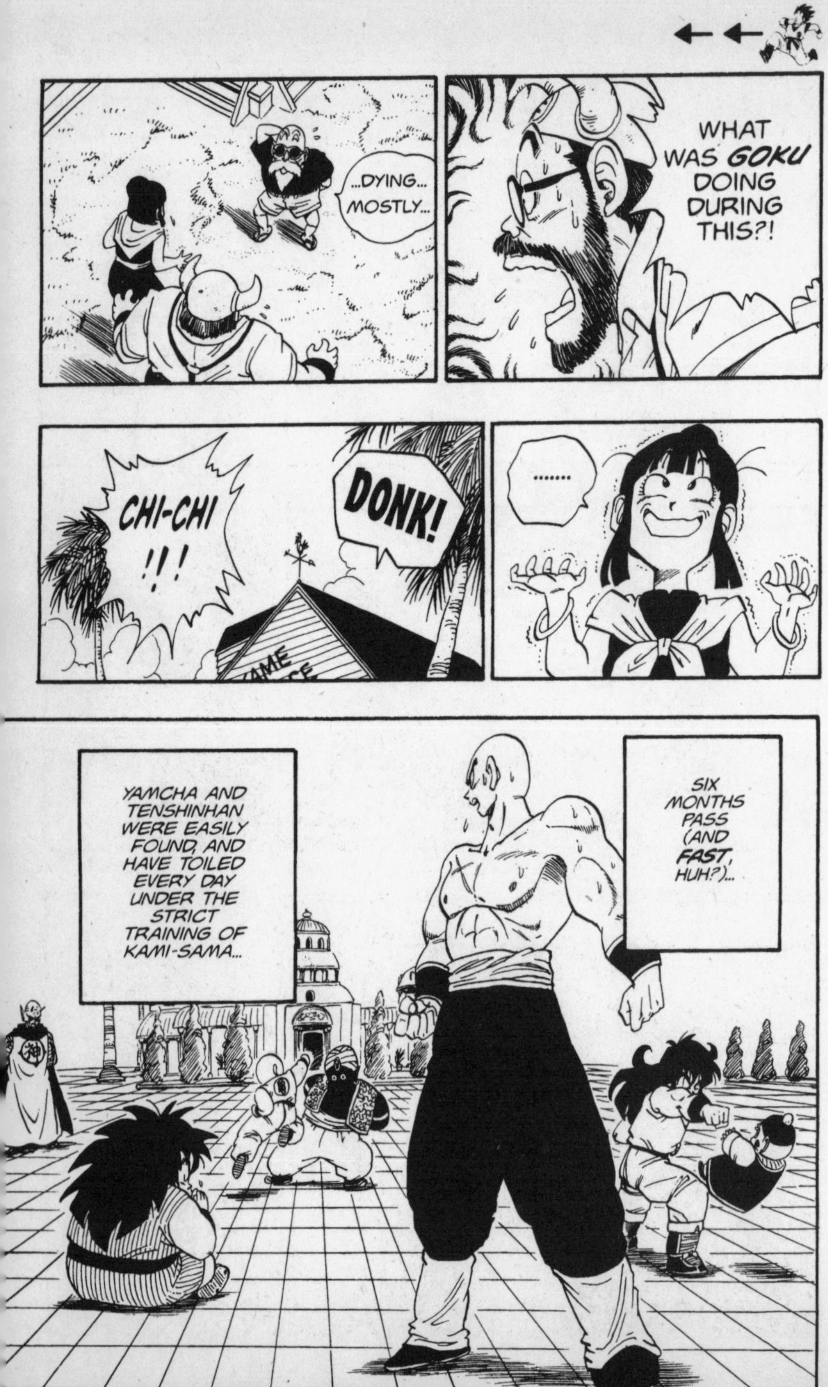
WHAT WAS GOKU DOING DURING THIS?!
...DYING... MOSTLY...
......
DONK!
CHI-CHI !!!
KAME HOUSE
SIX MONTHS PASS (AND FAST, HUH?)...
YAMCHA AND TENSHINHAN WERE EASILY FOUND, AND HAVE TOILED EVERY DAY UNDER THE STRICT TRAINING OF KAMI-SAMA...

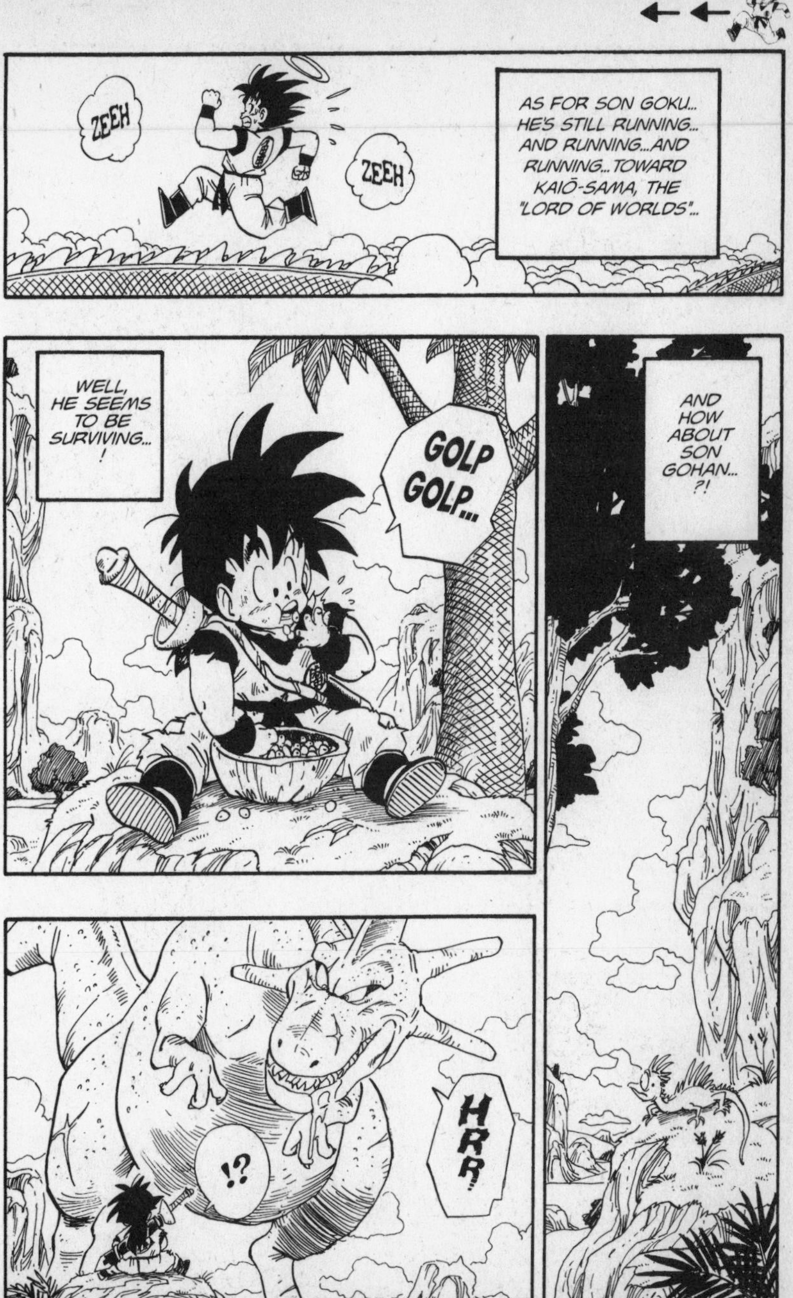

AS FOR SON GOKU... HE'S STILL RUNNING... AND RUNNING...AND RUNNING...TOWARD KAIŌ-SAMA, THE "LORD OF WORLDS"...
ZEEH
ZEEH
AND HOW ABOUT SON GOHAN...?!
WELL, HE SEEMS TO BE SURVIVING...!
GOLP GOLP...
HRR
!?

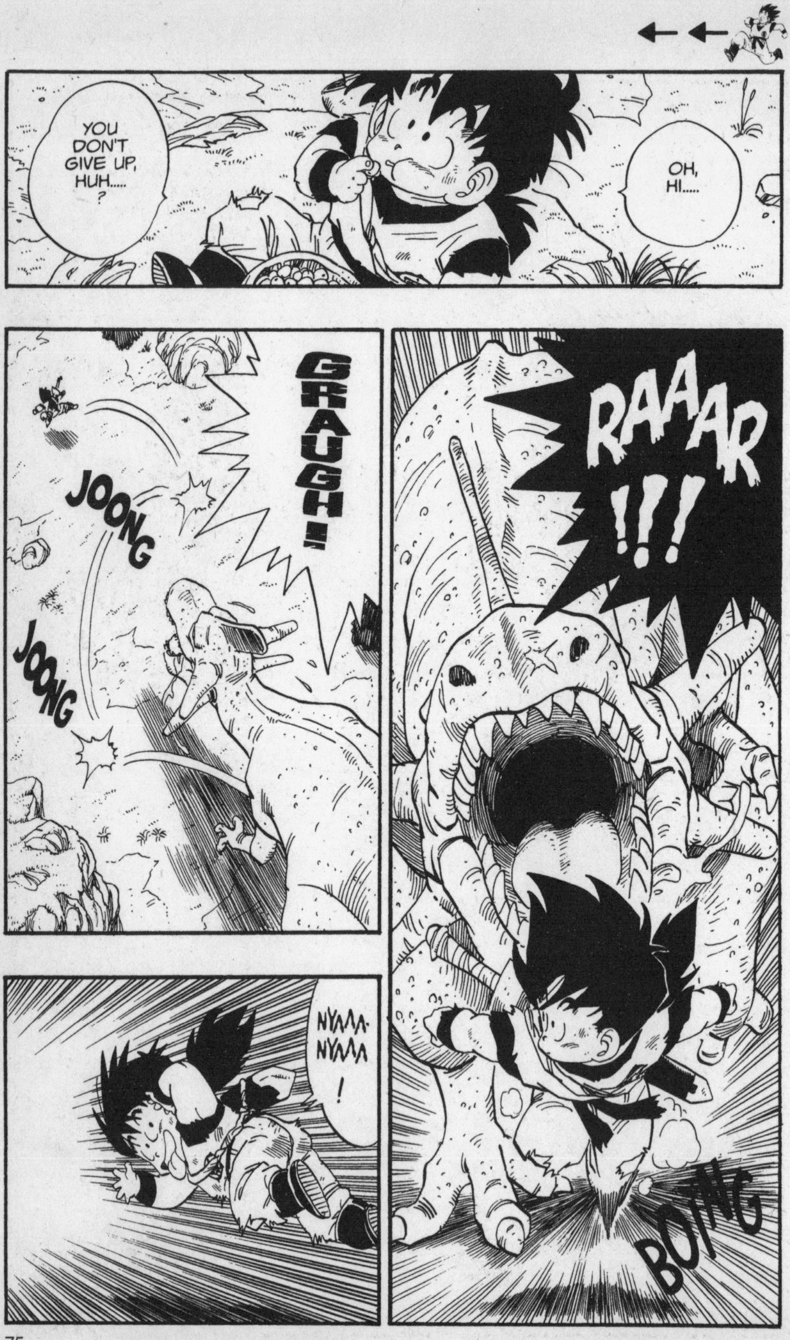
OH, HI.....
YOU DON'T GIVE UP, HUH.....?
RAAAR!!!
BOING
GRAUGH!!
JOONG
JOONG
NYAAA-NYAAA!

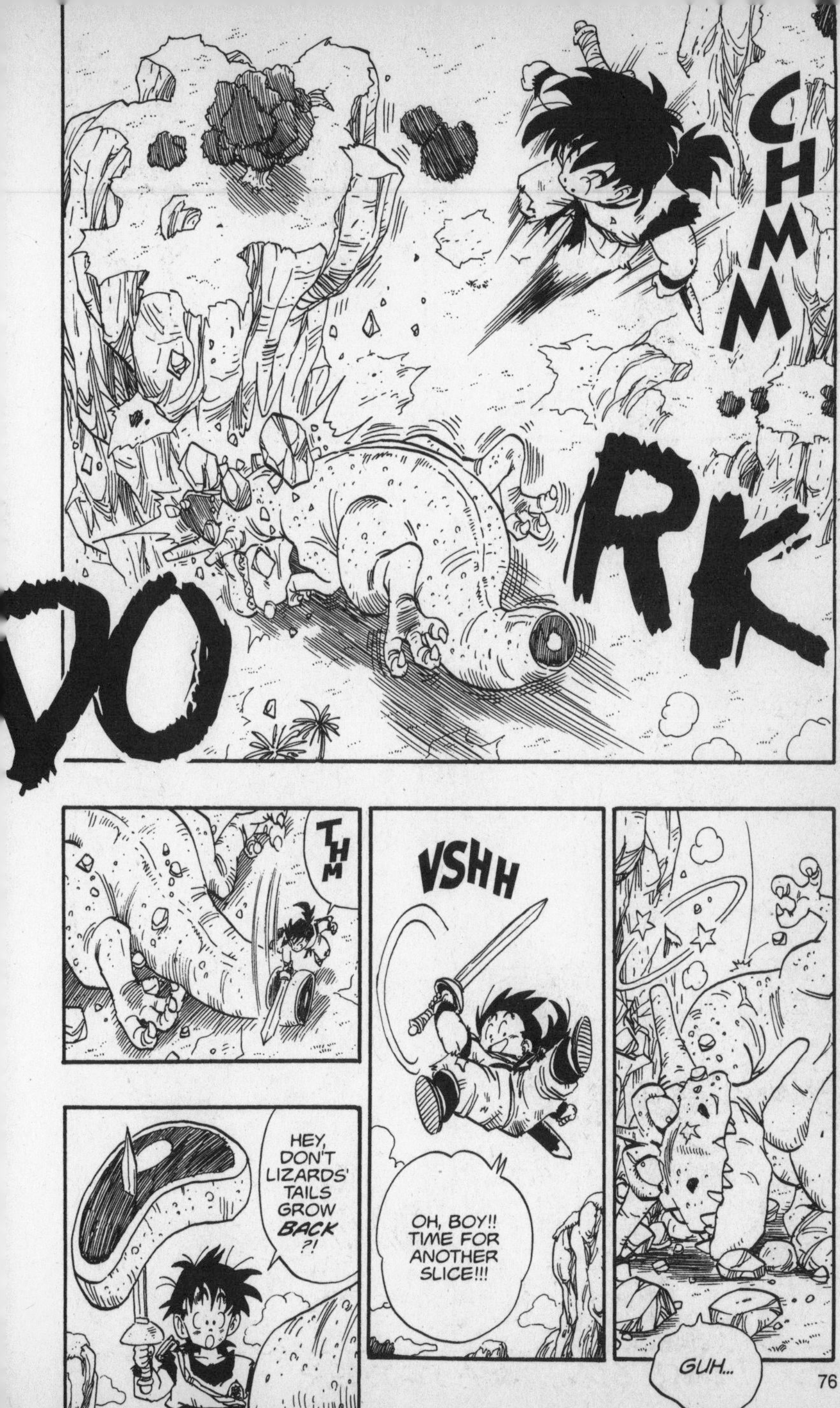
CHMM
DORK
GUH...
VSHH
OH, BOY!! TIME FOR ANOTHER SLICE!!!
THM
HEY, DON'T LIZARDS' TAILS GROW BACK ?!

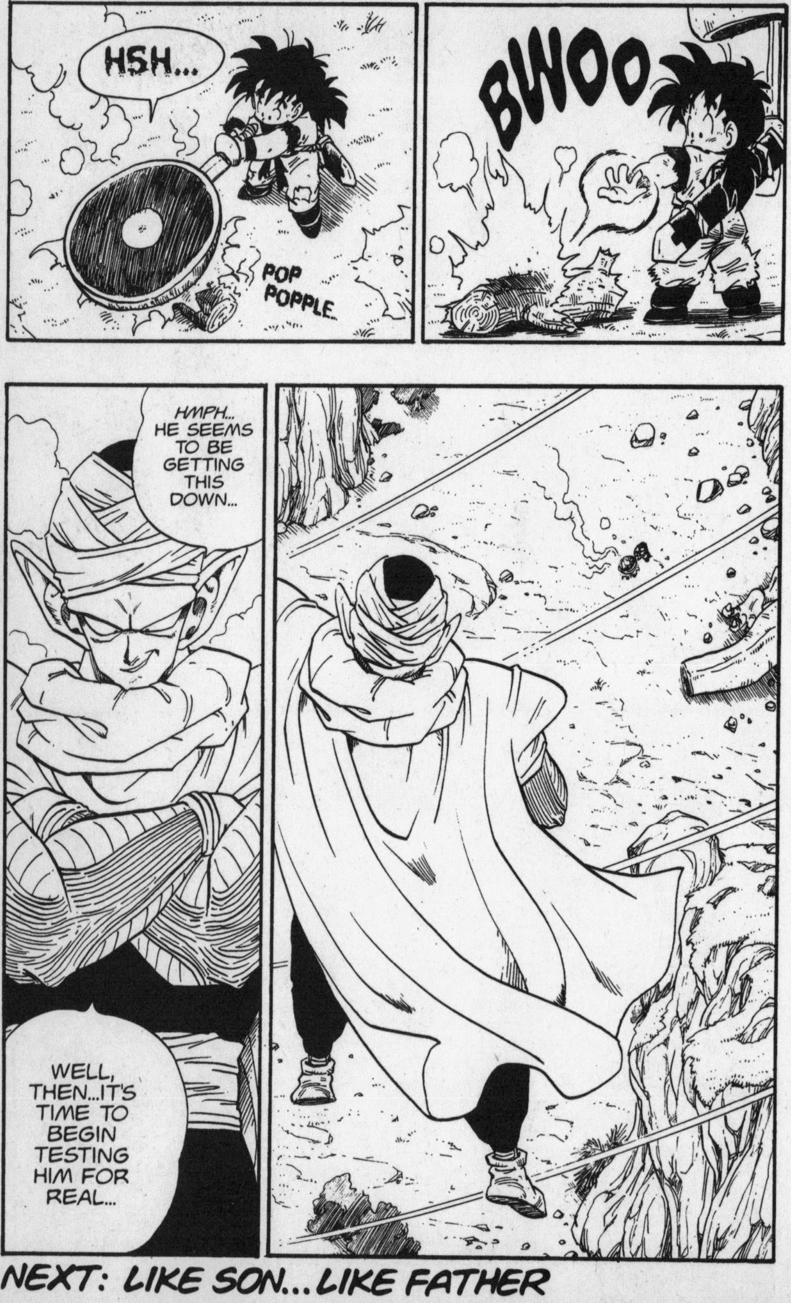
BWOO
HSH...
POP POPPLE
HMPH... HE SEEMS TO BE GETTING THIS DOWN...
WELL, THEN...IT'S TIME TO BEGIN TESTING HIM FOR REAL...

NEXT: LIKE SON... LIKE FATHER

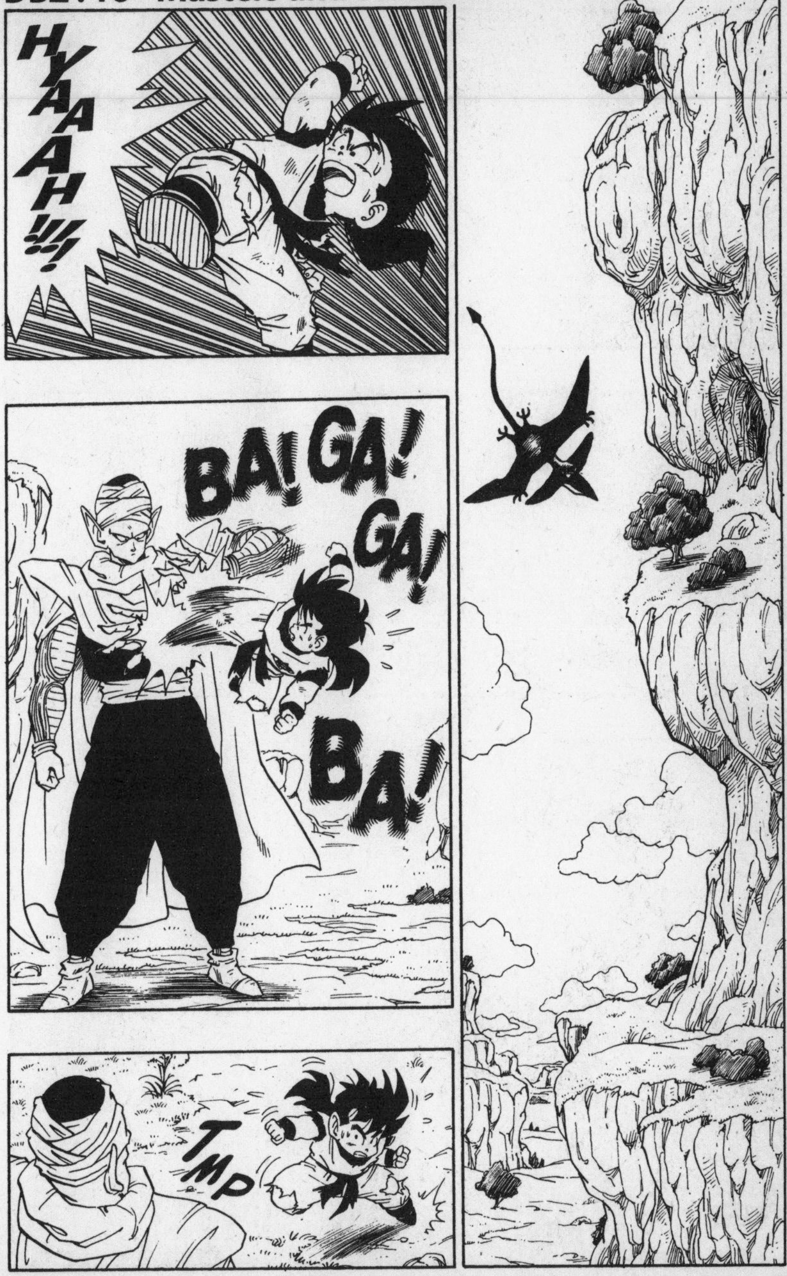
HYAAAH!!!!
BA! GA!
GA!
BA!
TMP

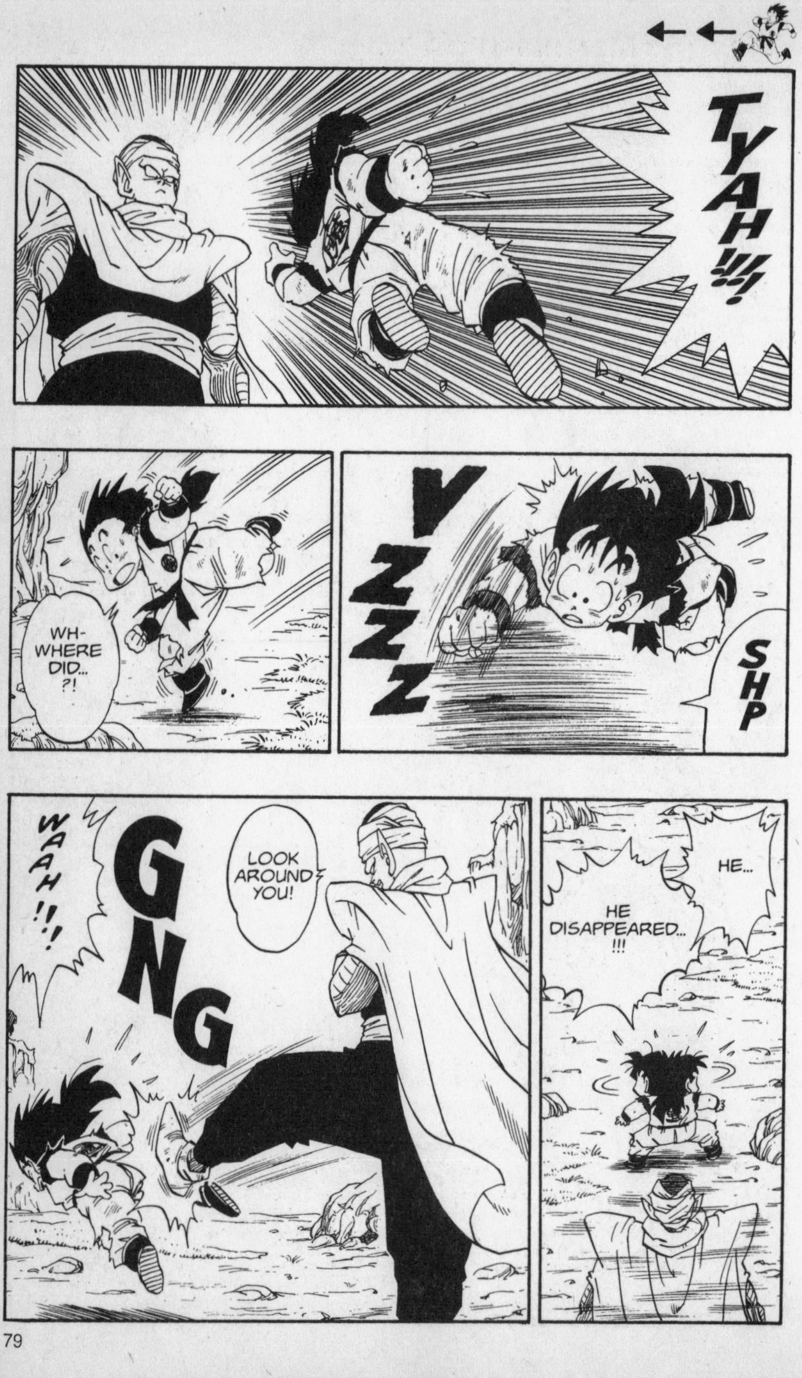
TYAH!!!!
SHP
VZZZ
WH-WHERE DID...?!
HE...
HE DISAPPEARED...!!!
LOOK AROUND YOU!
GNG
WAAH!!!

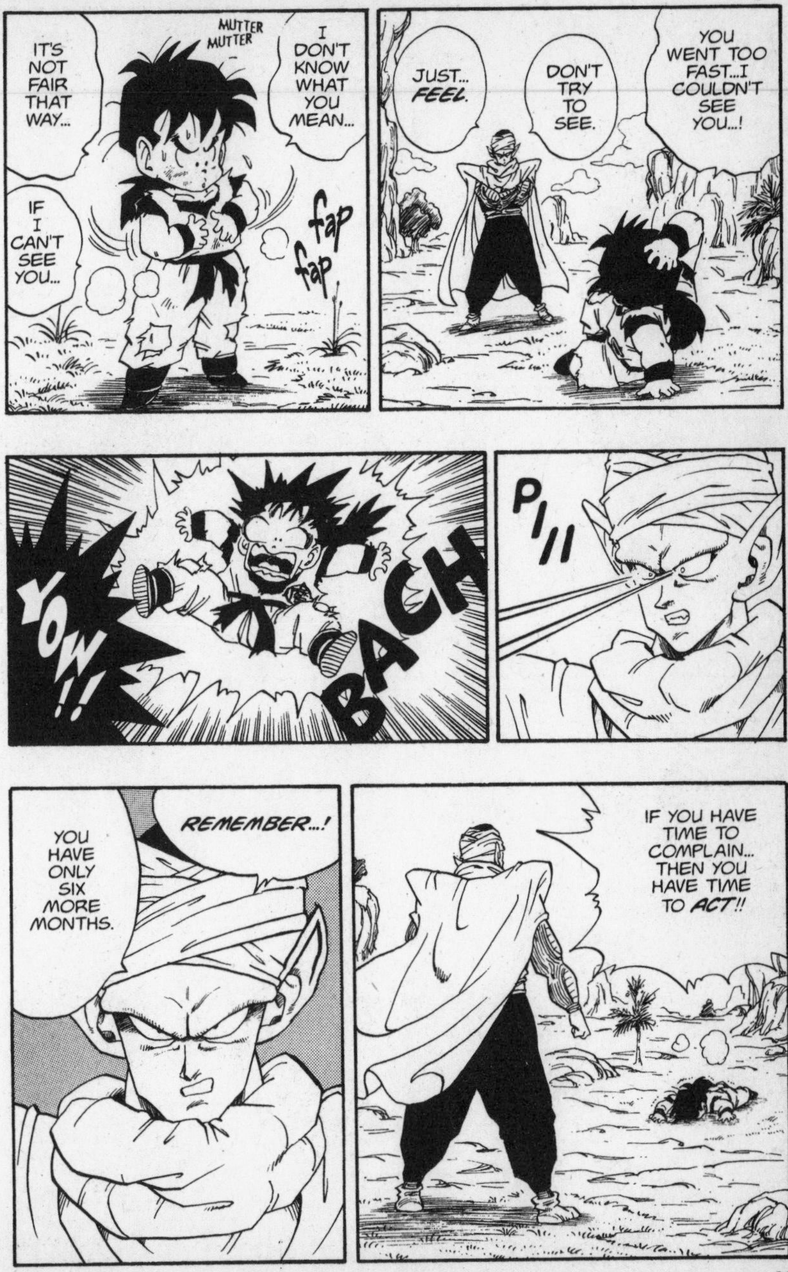
YOU WENT TOO FAST...I COULDN'T SEE YOU...!
DON'T TRY TO SEE.
JUST... *FEEL*.
I DON'T KNOW WHAT YOU MEAN...
MUTTER MUTTER
IT'S NOT FAIR THAT WAY...
IF I CAN'T SEE YOU...
fap fap
PI//
BACH
YOW!!
IF YOU HAVE TIME TO COMPLAIN... THEN YOU HAVE TIME TO *ACT*!!
REMEMBER...!
YOU HAVE ONLY SIX MORE MONTHS.

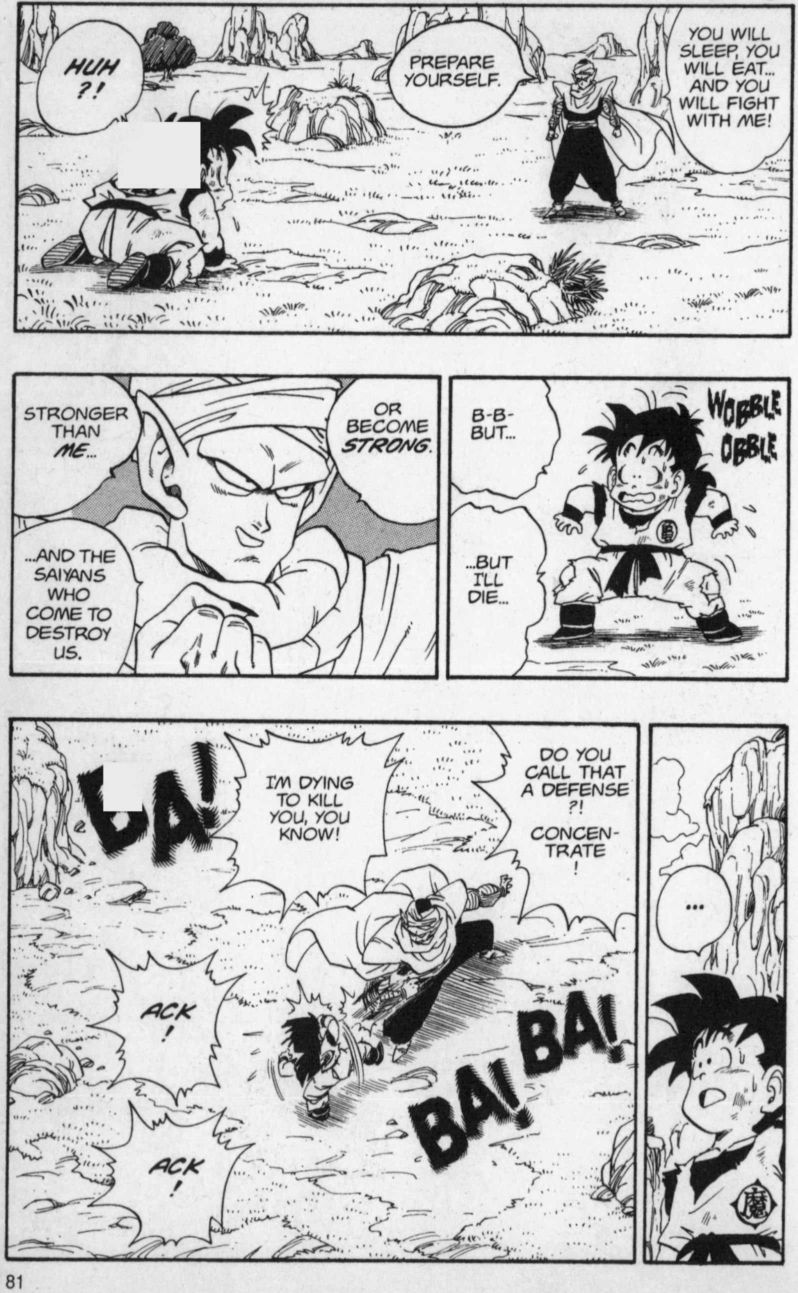
YOU WILL SLEEP, YOU WILL EAT... AND YOU WILL FIGHT WITH ME!
PREPARE YOURSELF.
HUH ?!
WOBBLE OBBLE
B-B-BUT...
...BUT I'LL DIE...
OR BECOME STRONG.
STRONGER THAN ME...
...AND THE SAIYANS WHO COME TO DESTROY US.
...
DO YOU CALL THAT A DEFENSE ?!
CONCENTRATE!
I'M DYING TO KILL YOU, YOU KNOW!
BA!
BA! BA!
BA!
ACK!
ACK!

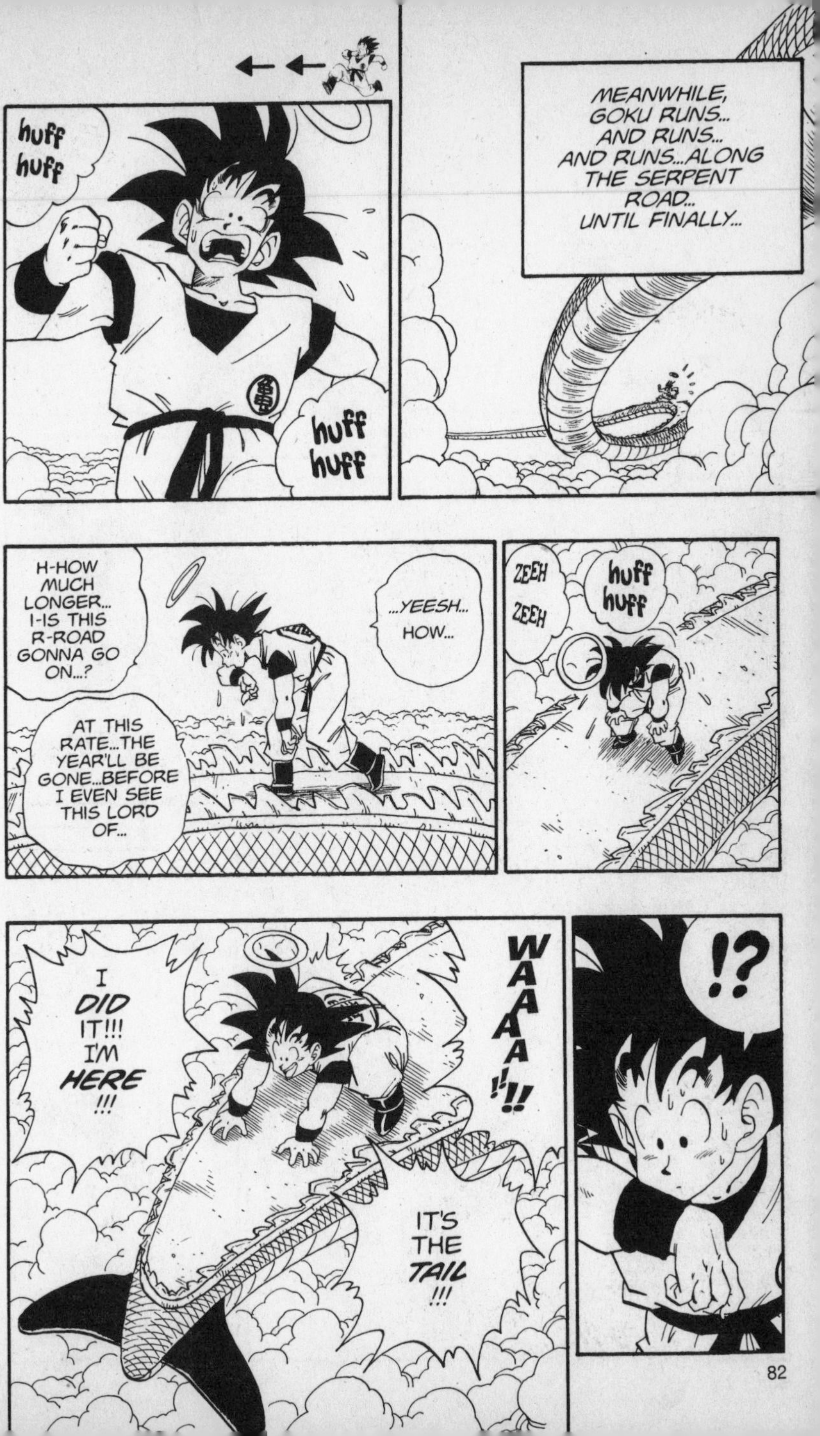
MEANWHILE, GOKU RUNS... AND RUNS... AND RUNS...ALONG THE SERPENT ROAD... UNTIL FINALLY...
huff huff
huff huff
huff huff
ZEEH ZEEH
...YEESH... HOW...
H-HOW MUCH LONGER... I-IS THIS R-ROAD GONNA GO ON...?
AT THIS RATE...THE YEAR'LL BE GONE...BEFORE I EVEN SEE THIS LORD OF...
!?
WAAAA!!!!
I DID IT!!! I'M HERE!!!
IT'S THE TAIL!!!

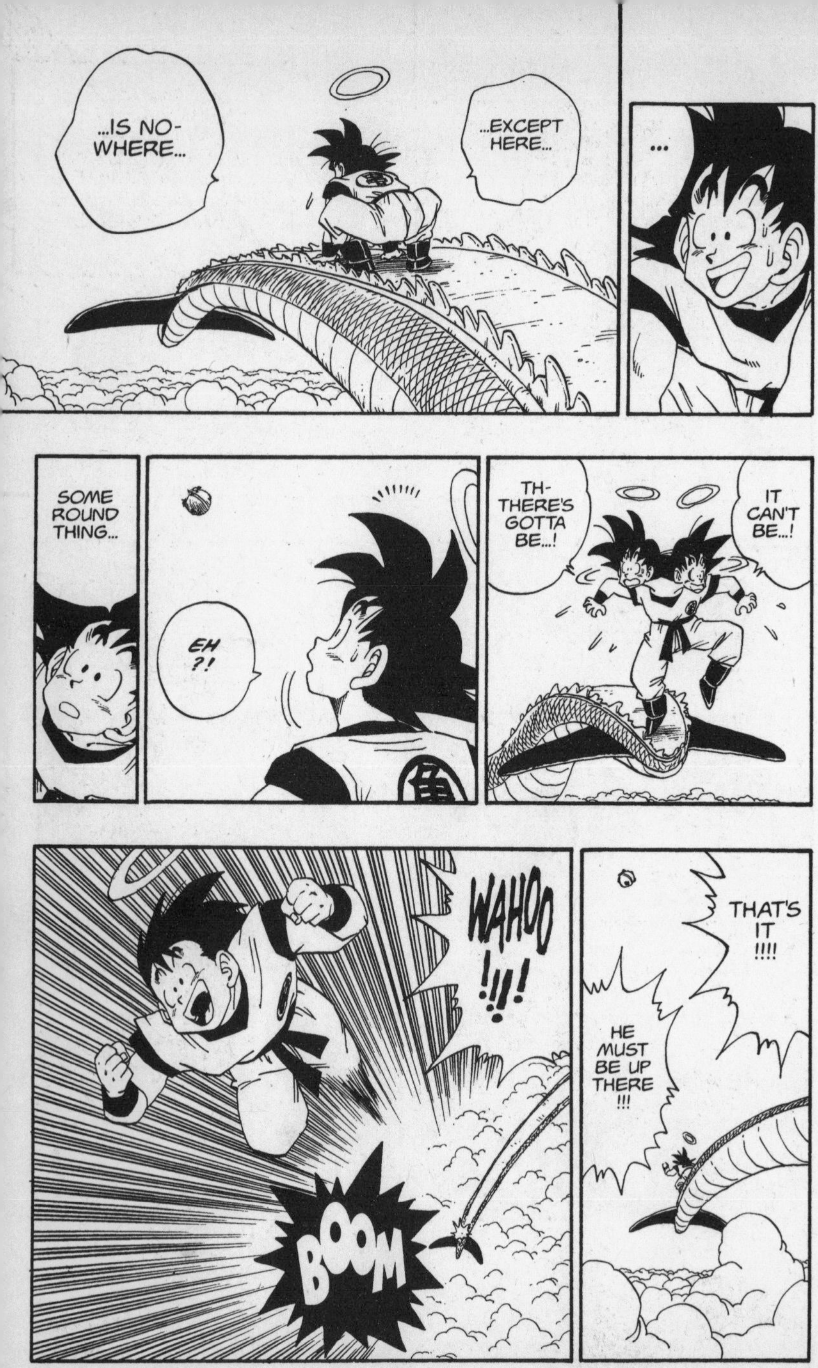
...
...IS NO-WHERE...
...EXCEPT HERE...
IT CAN'T BE...!
TH-THERE'S GOTTA BE...!
EH ?!
SOME ROUND THING...
THAT'S IT !!!!
HE MUST BE UP THERE !!!
WAHOO !!!!
BOOM

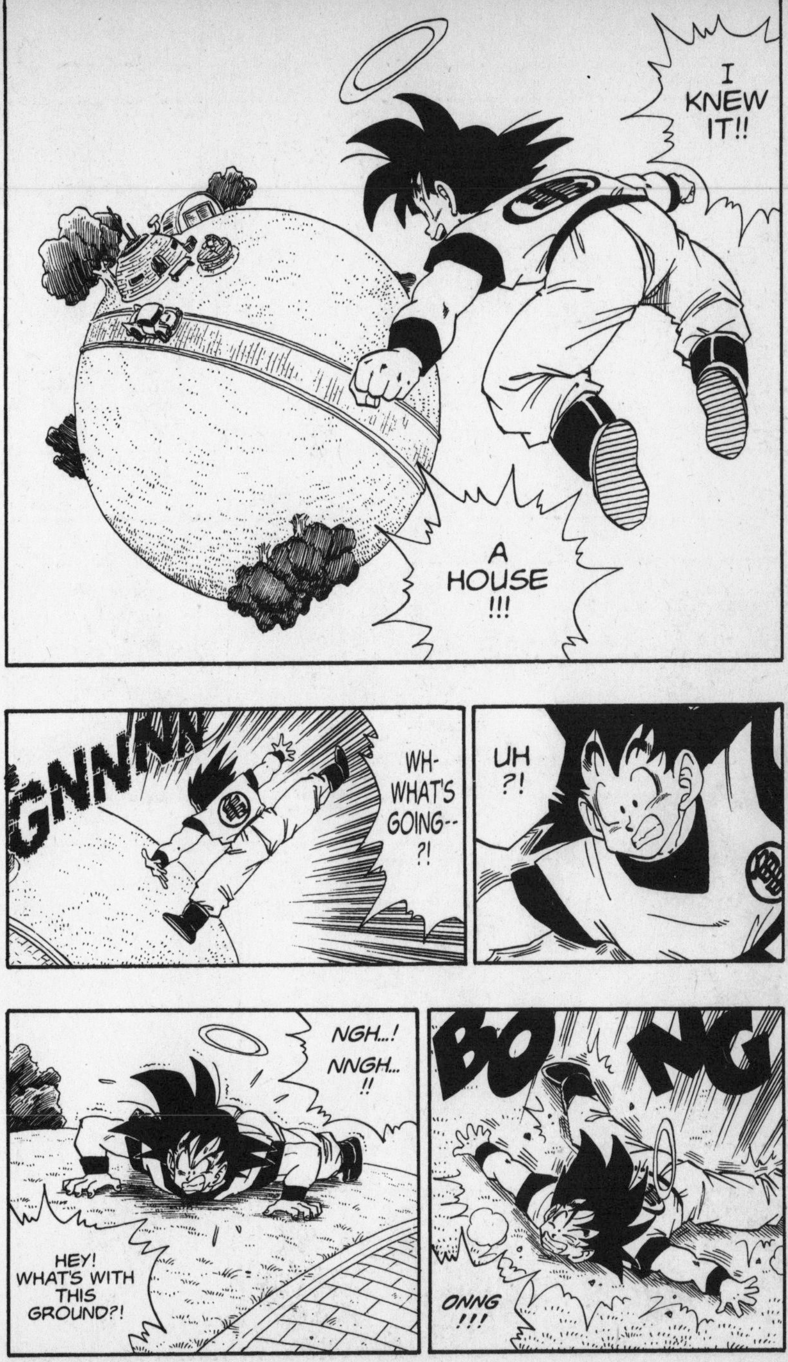
I KNEW IT!!
A HOUSE !!!
UH ?!
GNNNN
WH- WHAT'S GOING-- ?!
BO NG
ONNG !!!
NGH...! NNGH... !!
HEY! WHAT'S WITH THIS GROUND?!

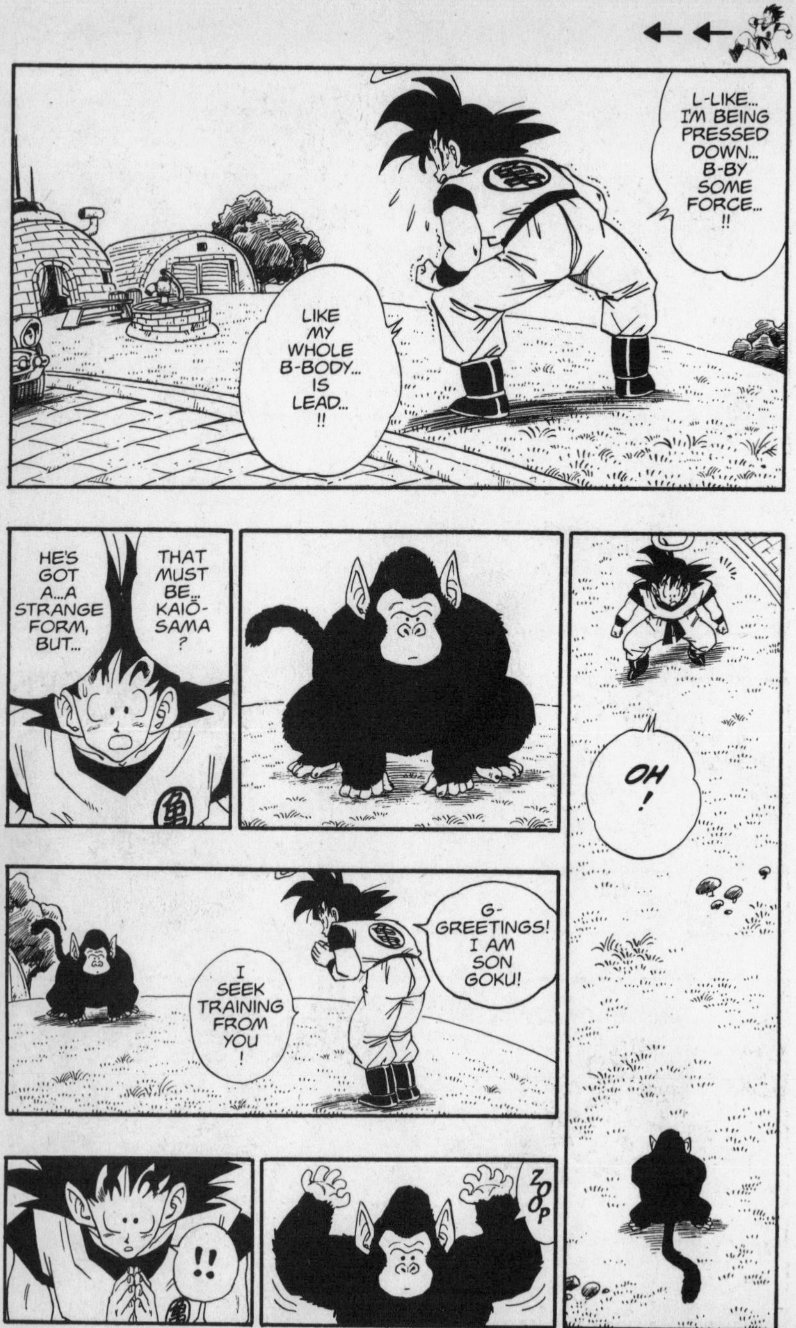
L-LIKE... I'M BEING PRESSED DOWN... B-BY SOME FORCE... !!
LIKE MY WHOLE B-BODY... IS LEAD... !!
OH !
THAT MUST BE... KAIŌ-SAMA ?
HE'S GOT A...A STRANGE FORM, BUT...
G-GREETINGS! I AM SON GOKU!
I SEEK TRAINING FROM YOU !
ZOOP
!!

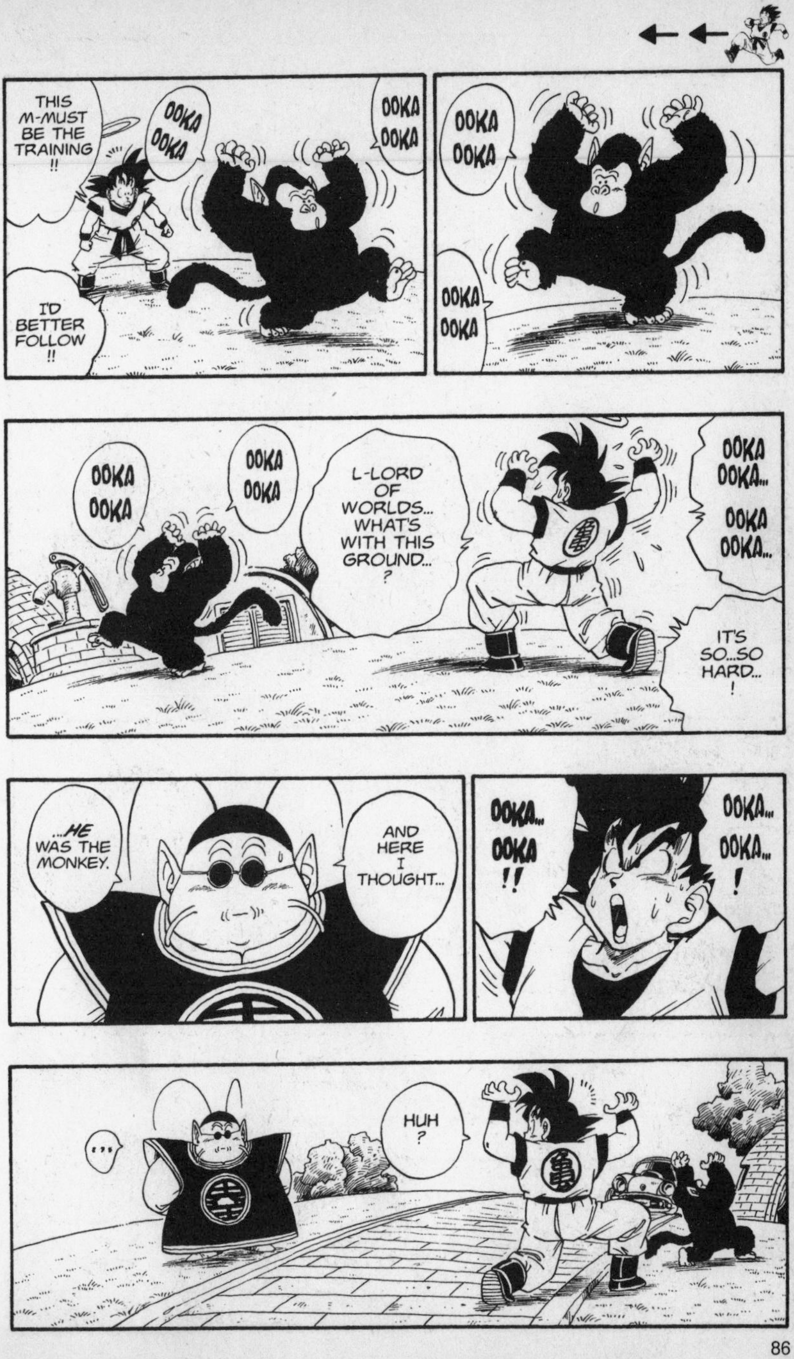
OOKA OOKA
OOKA OOKA
OOKA OOKA
OOKA OOKA
THIS M-MUST BE THE TRAINING !!
I'D BETTER FOLLOW !!
OOKA OOKA... OOKA OOKA...
IT'S SO...SO HARD... !
L-LORD OF WORLDS... WHAT'S WITH THIS GROUND... ?
OOKA OOKA
OOKA OOKA
OOKA... OOKA... !
OOKA... OOKA !!
AND HERE I THOUGHT...
...HE WAS THE MONKEY.
HUH ?
...

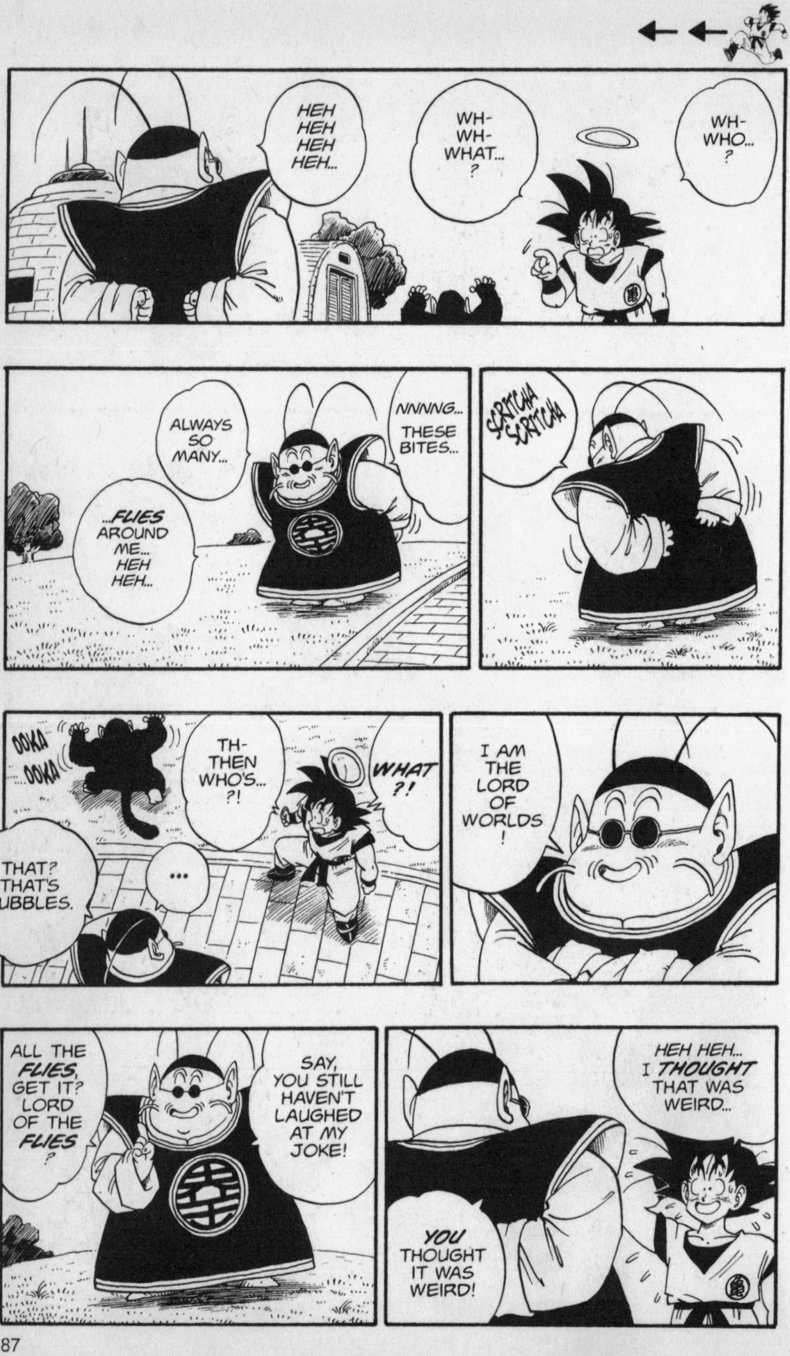
WH- WHO...?
WH- WH- WHAT...?
HEH HEH HEH HEH...
SCRITCHA SCRITCHA
NNNNG... THESE BITES...
ALWAYS SO MANY...
...FLIES AROUND ME... HEH HEH...
I AM THE LORD OF WORLDS!
WHAT?!
TH- THEN WHO'S...?!
OOKA OOKA
...
THAT? THAT'S BUBBLES.
HEH HEH... I THOUGHT THAT WAS WEIRD...
YOU THOUGHT IT WAS WEIRD!
SAY, YOU STILL HAVEN'T LAUGHED AT MY JOKE!
ALL THE FLIES, GET IT? LORD OF THE FLIES?

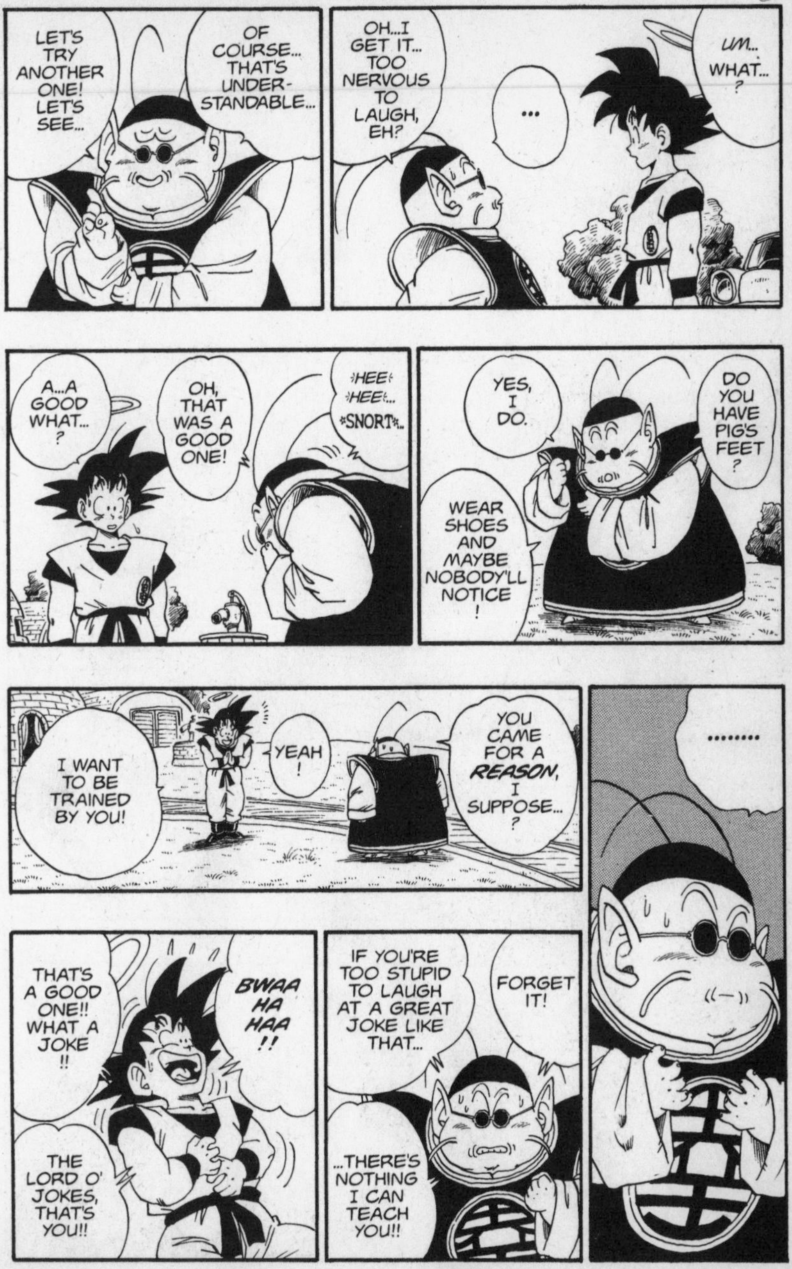
UM... WHAT...?
...
OH...I GET IT... TOO NERVOUS TO LAUGH, EH?
OF COURSE... THAT'S UNDERSTANDABLE...
LET'S TRY ANOTHER ONE! LET'S SEE...
DO YOU HAVE PIG'S FEET?
YES, I DO.
WEAR SHOES AND MAYBE NOBODY'LL NOTICE!
HEE *HEE*... *SNORT*..
OH, THAT WAS A GOOD ONE!
A...A GOOD WHAT...?
....
YOU CAME FOR A *REASON*, I SUPPOSE...?
YEAH!
I WANT TO BE TRAINED BY YOU!
FORGET IT!
IF YOU'RE TOO STUPID TO LAUGH AT A GREAT JOKE LIKE THAT...
...THERE'S NOTHING I CAN TEACH YOU!!
BWAA HA HAA!!
THAT'S A GOOD ONE!! WHAT A JOKE!!
THE LORD O' JOKES, THAT'S YOU!!

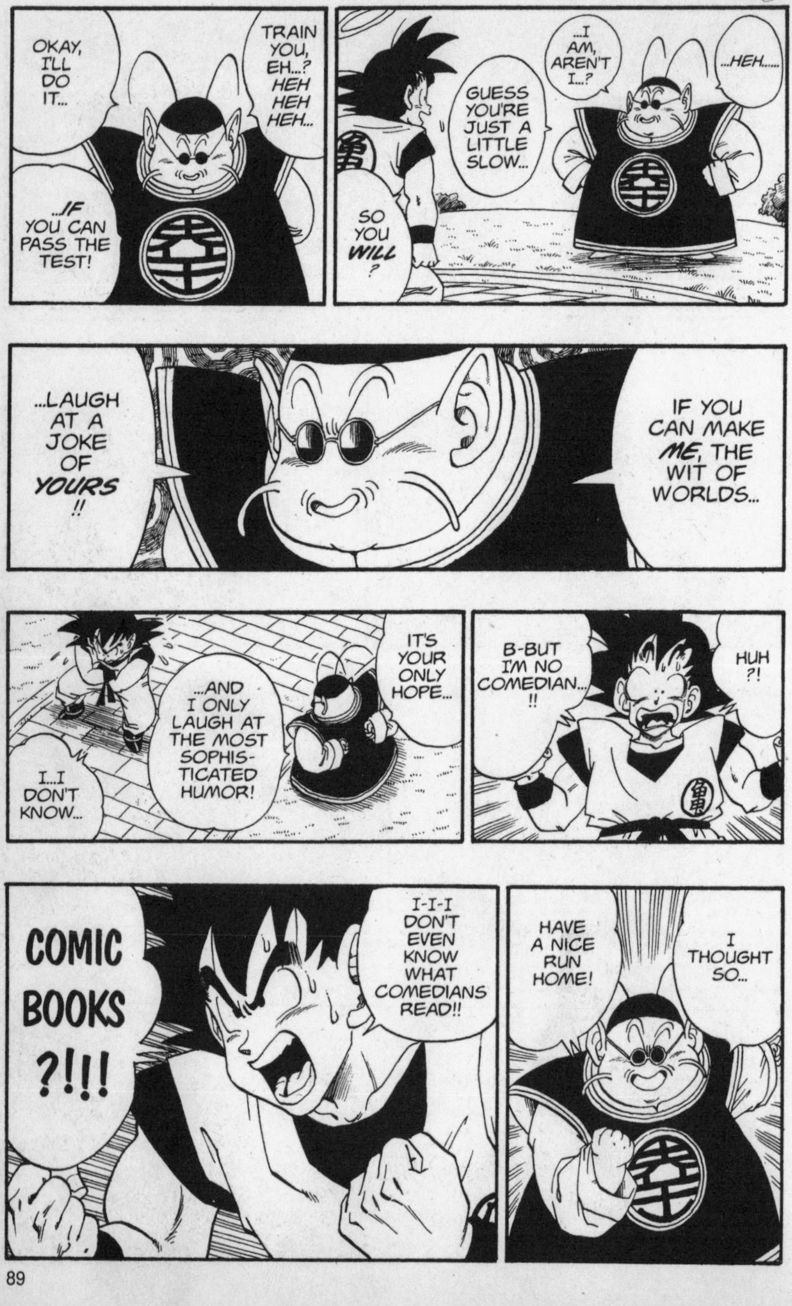
...HEH.....
...I AM, AREN'T I...?
GUESS YOU'RE JUST A LITTLE SLOW...
SO YOU WILL?
TRAIN YOU, EH...? HEH HEH HEH...
OKAY, I'LL DO IT...
...IF YOU CAN PASS THE TEST!
IF YOU CAN MAKE ME, THE WIT OF WORLDS...
...LAUGH AT A JOKE OF YOURS !!
HUH ?!
B-BUT I'M NO COMEDIAN... !!
IT'S YOUR ONLY HOPE...
...AND I ONLY LAUGH AT THE MOST SOPHISTICATED HUMOR!
I...I DON'T KNOW...
I THOUGHT SO...
HAVE A NICE RUN HOME!
I-I-I DON'T EVEN KNOW WHAT COMEDIANS READ!!
COMIC BOOKS ?!!!

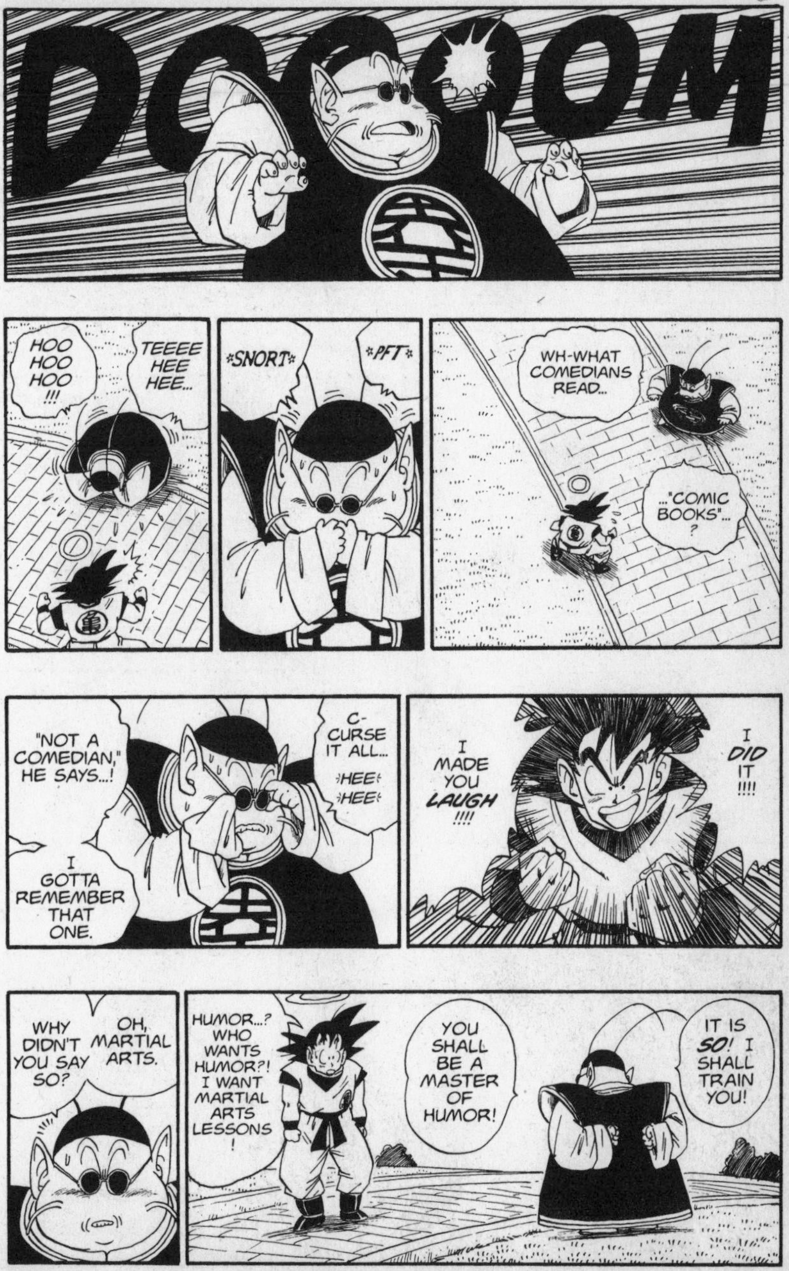
DOOOOM
WH-WHAT COMEDIANS READ...
..."COMIC BOOKS"...?
PFT
SNORT
TEEEE HEE HEE...
HOO HOO HOO !!!
I DID IT !!!!
I MADE YOU LAUGH !!!!
C-CURSE IT ALL... HEE HEE
"NOT A COMEDIAN," HE SAYS...!
I GOTTA REMEMBER THAT ONE.
IT IS SO! I SHALL TRAIN YOU!
YOU SHALL BE A MASTER OF HUMOR!
HUMOR...? WHO WANTS HUMOR?! I WANT MARTIAL ARTS LESSONS!
OH, MARTIAL ARTS.
WHY DIDN'T YOU SAY SO?

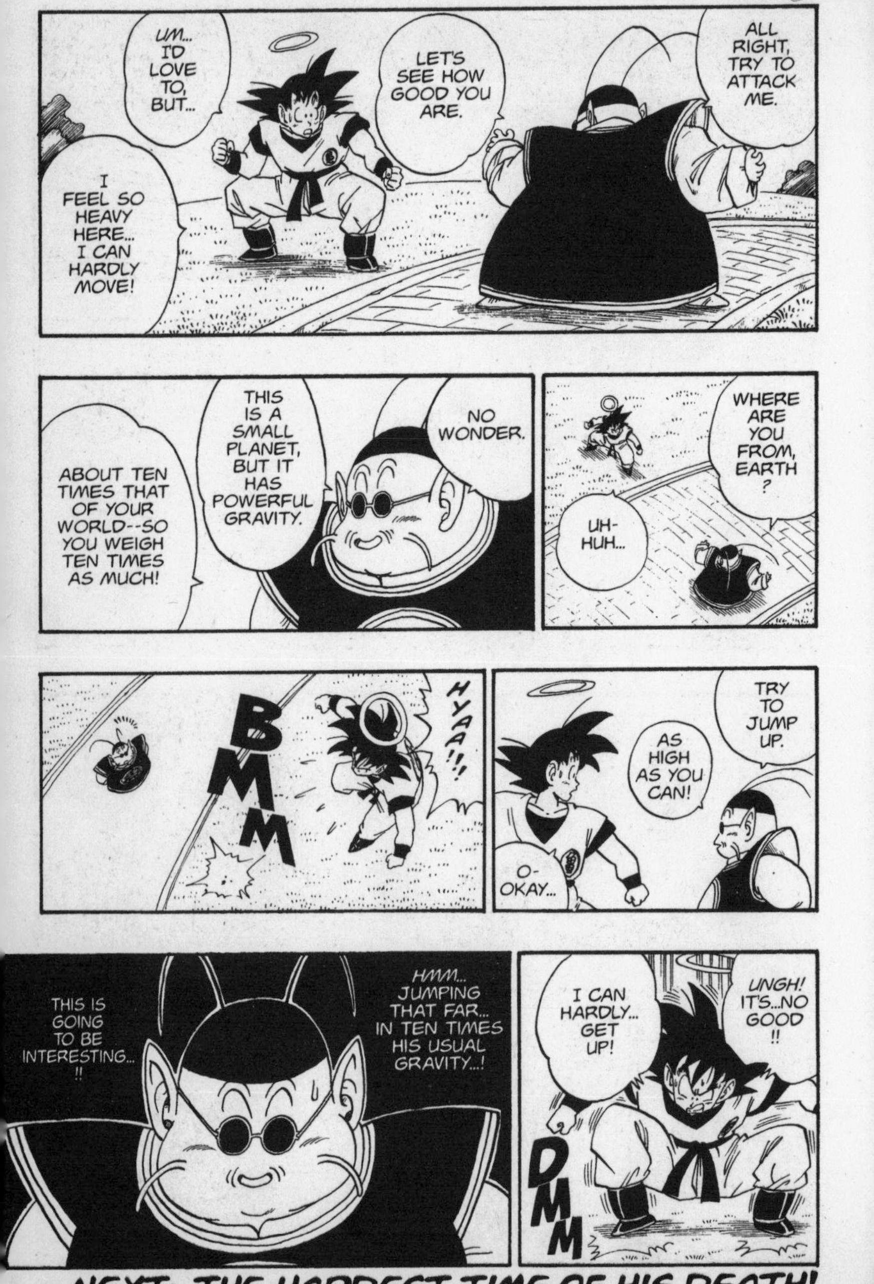
ALL RIGHT, TRY TO ATTACK ME.
LET'S SEE HOW GOOD YOU ARE.
UM... I'D LOVE TO, BUT...
I FEEL SO HEAVY HERE... I CAN HARDLY MOVE!
WHERE ARE YOU FROM, EARTH?
UH-HUH...
NO WONDER.
THIS IS A SMALL PLANET, BUT IT HAS POWERFUL GRAVITY.
ABOUT TEN TIMES THAT OF YOUR WORLD--SO YOU WEIGH TEN TIMES AS MUCH!
TRY TO JUMP UP.
AS HIGH AS YOU CAN!
O-OKAY...
HYAA!!!
BMM
UNGH! IT'S...NO GOOD!!
I CAN HARDLY... GET UP!
DMM
HMM... JUMPING THAT FAR... IN TEN TIMES HIS USUAL GRAVITY...!
THIS IS GOING TO BE INTERESTING...!!

NEXT: THE HARDEST TIME OF HIS DEATH!

DBZ : 17 • The Hardest Time of His Death

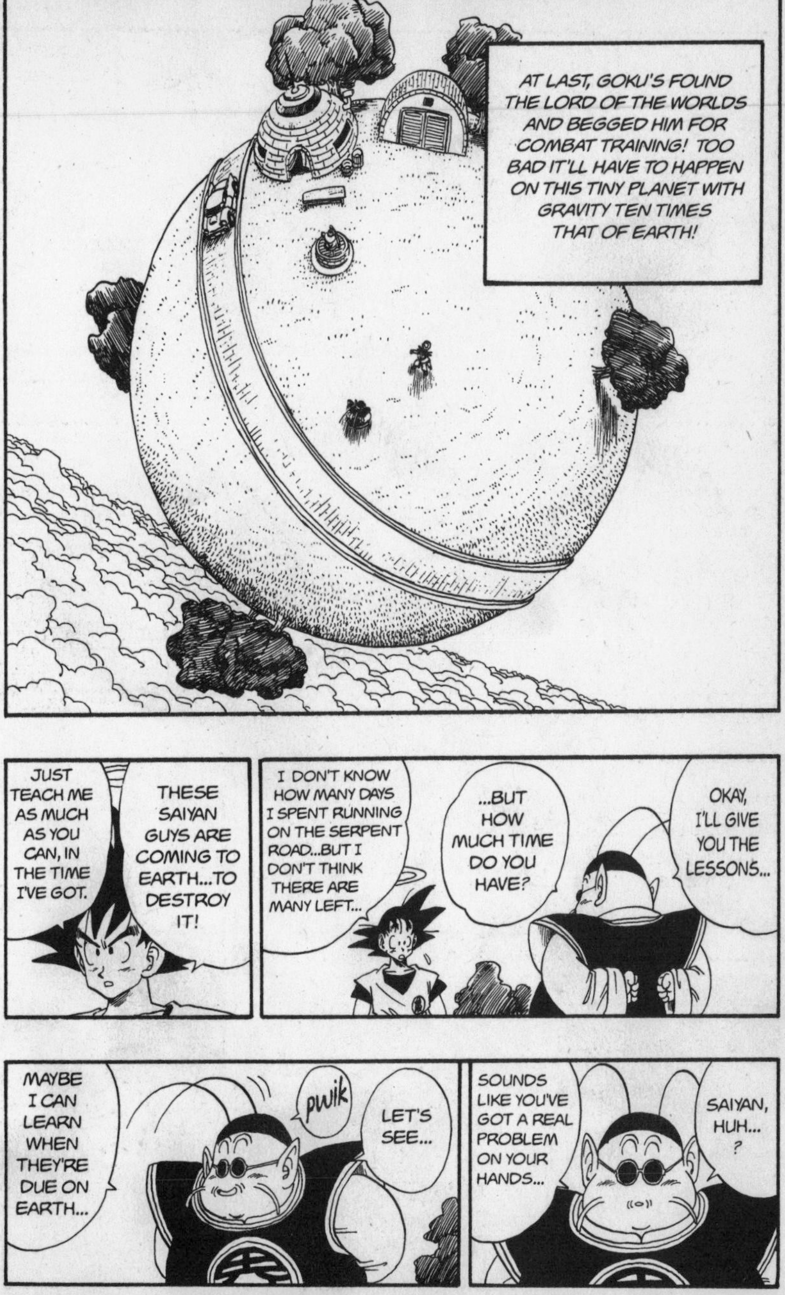
AT LAST, GOKU'S FOUND THE LORD OF THE WORLDS AND BEGGED HIM FOR COMBAT TRAINING! TOO BAD IT'LL HAVE TO HAPPEN ON THIS TINY PLANET WITH GRAVITY TEN TIMES THAT OF EARTH!
OKAY, I'LL GIVE YOU THE LESSONS...
...BUT HOW MUCH TIME DO YOU HAVE?
I DON'T KNOW HOW MANY DAYS I SPENT RUNNING ON THE SERPENT ROAD...BUT I DON'T THINK THERE ARE MANY LEFT...
THESE SAIYAN GUYS ARE COMING TO EARTH...TO DESTROY IT!
JUST TEACH ME AS MUCH AS YOU CAN, IN THE TIME I'VE GOT.
SAIYAN, HUH...?
SOUNDS LIKE YOU'VE GOT A REAL PROBLEM ON YOUR HANDS...
LET'S SEE...
pwik
MAYBE I CAN LEARN WHEN THEY'RE DUE ON EARTH...

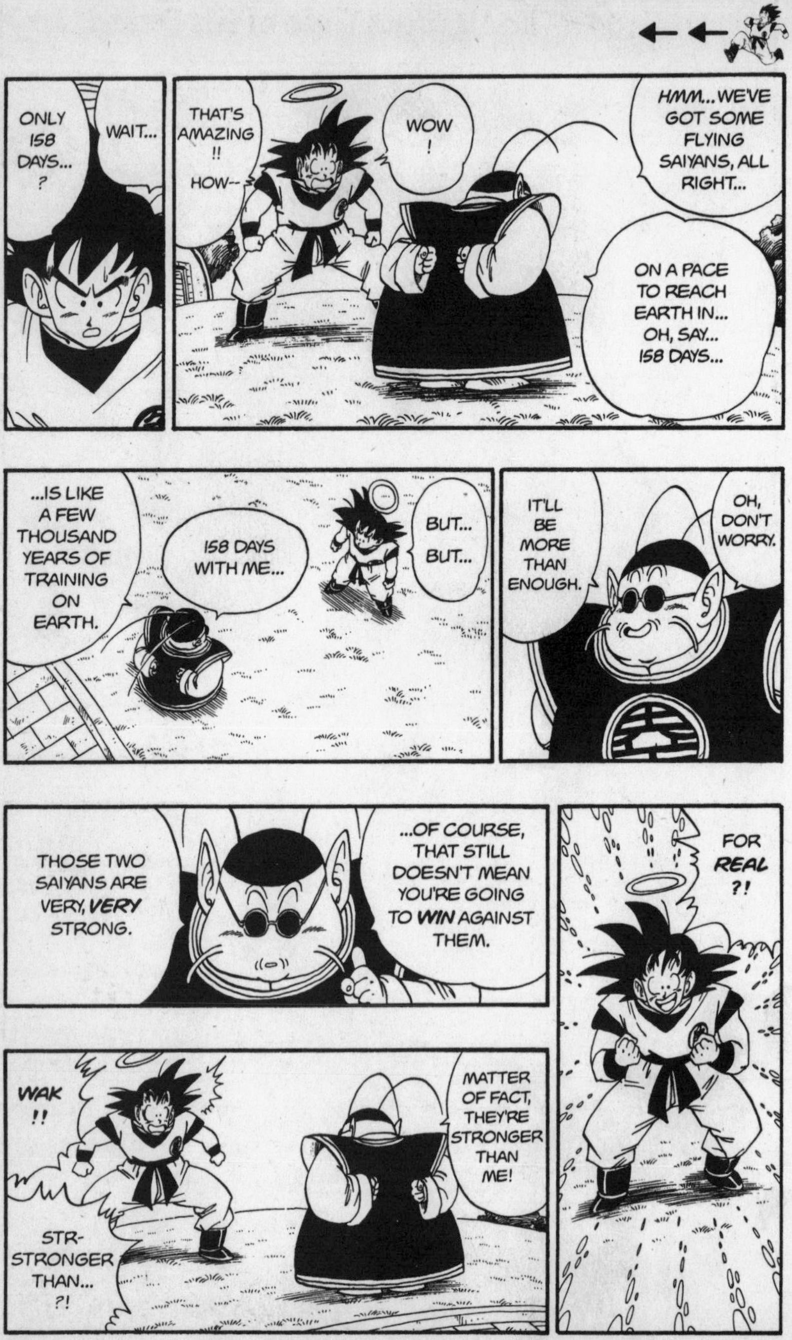
HMM...WE'VE GOT SOME FLYING SAIYANS, ALL RIGHT...
ON A PACE TO REACH EARTH IN... OH, SAY... 158 DAYS...
WOW !
THAT'S AMAZING !! HOW--
WAIT...
ONLY 158 DAYS... ?
OH, DON'T WORRY.
IT'LL BE MORE THAN ENOUGH.
BUT... BUT...
158 DAYS WITH ME...
...IS LIKE A FEW THOUSAND YEARS OF TRAINING ON EARTH.
FOR REAL ?!
...OF COURSE, THAT STILL DOESN'T MEAN YOU'RE GOING TO WIN AGAINST THEM.
THOSE TWO SAIYANS ARE VERY, VERY STRONG.
MATTER OF FACT, THEY'RE STRONGER THAN ME!
WAK !!
STR-STRONGER THAN... ?!

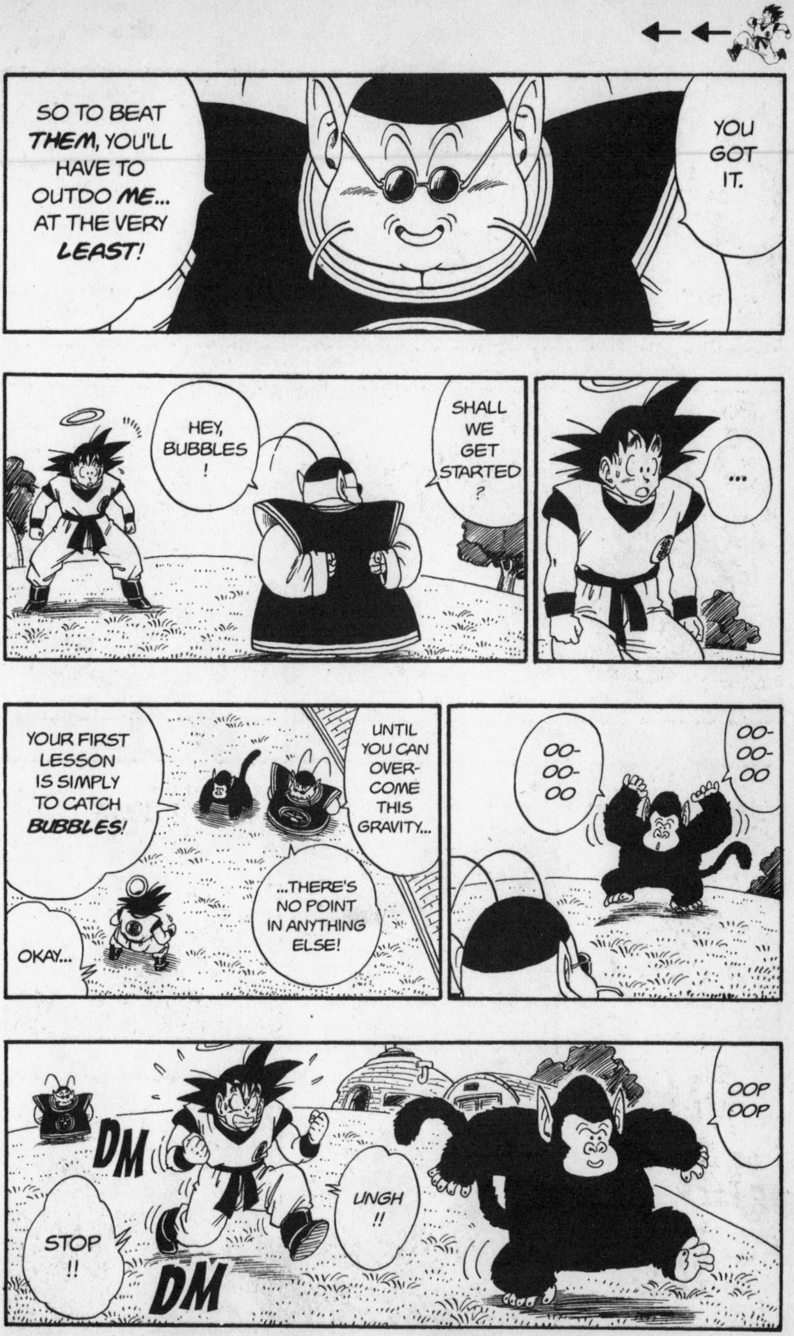
YOU GOT IT.
SO TO BEAT THEM, YOU'LL HAVE TO OUTDO ME... AT THE VERY LEAST!
...
SHALL WE GET STARTED ?
HEY, BUBBLES !
OO-OO-OO
OO-OO-OO
UNTIL YOU CAN OVER-COME THIS GRAVITY...
...THERE'S NO POINT IN ANYTHING ELSE!
YOUR FIRST LESSON IS SIMPLY TO CATCH BUBBLES!
OKAY...
OOP OOP
UNGH !!
DM
STOP !!
DM

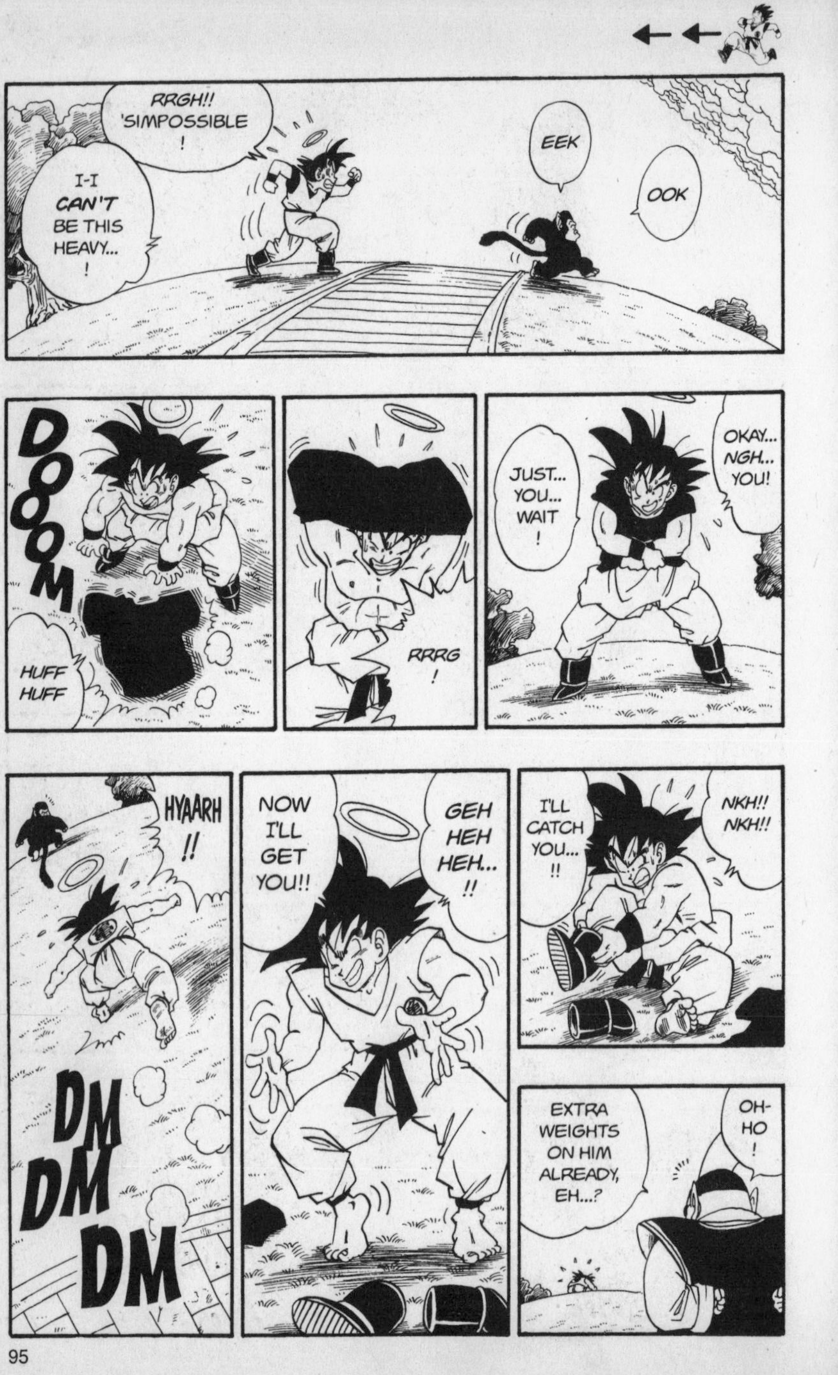
OOK
EEK
RRGH!! 'SIMPOSSIBLE !
I-I CAN'T BE THIS HEAVY... !
OKAY... NGH... YOU!
JUST... YOU... WAIT !
RRRG !
DOOOM
HUFF HUFF
NKH!! NKH!!
I'LL CATCH YOU... !!
OH-HO !
EXTRA WEIGHTS ON HIM ALREADY, EH...?
GEH HEH HEH... !!
NOW I'LL GET YOU!!
HYAARH !!
DM DM DM DM DM

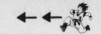

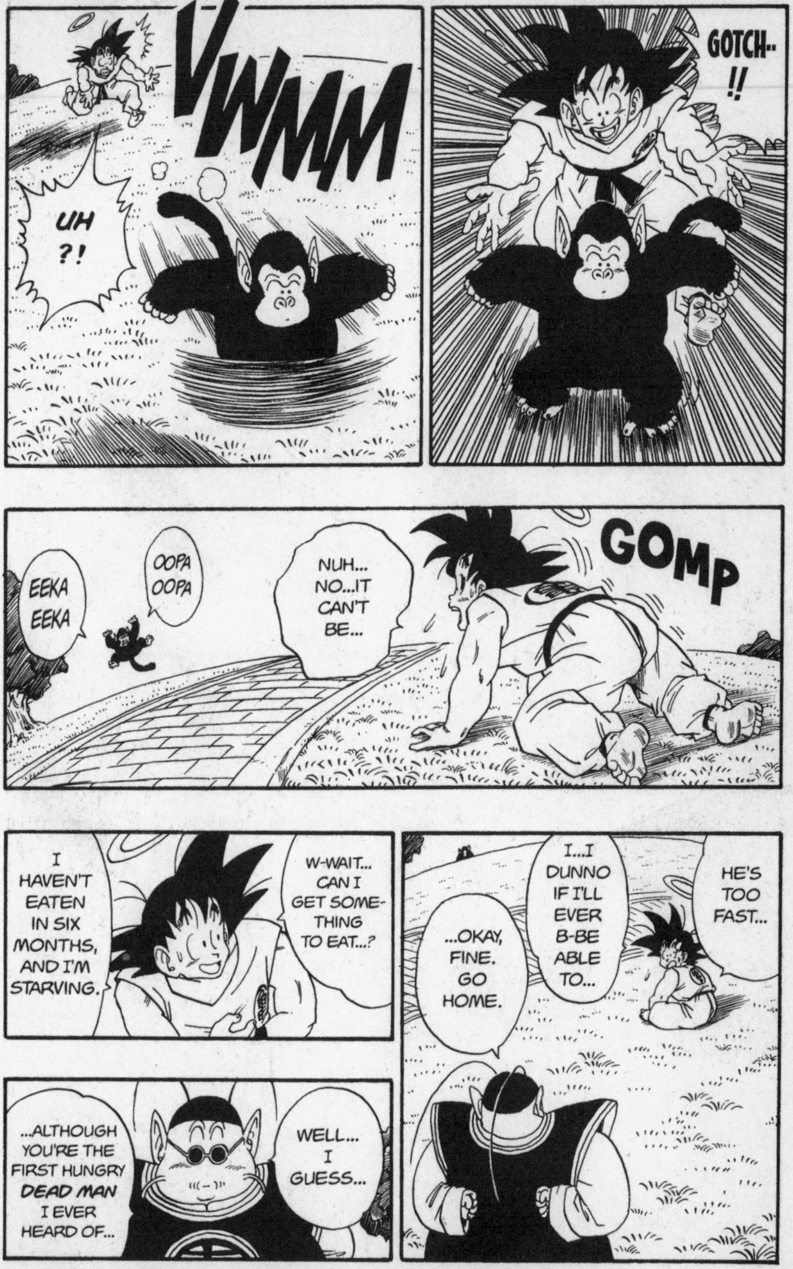
GOTCH-- !!
VWMM
UH ?!
GOMP
NUH... NO...IT CAN'T BE...
OOPA OOPA
EEKA EEKA
HE'S TOO FAST...
I...I DUNNO IF I'LL EVER B-BE ABLE TO...
...OKAY, FINE. GO HOME.
W-WAIT... CAN I GET SOME-THING TO EAT...?
I HAVEN'T EATEN IN SIX MONTHS, AND I'M STARVING.
WELL... I GUESS...
...ALTHOUGH YOU'RE THE FIRST HUNGRY DEAD MAN I EVER HEARD OF...

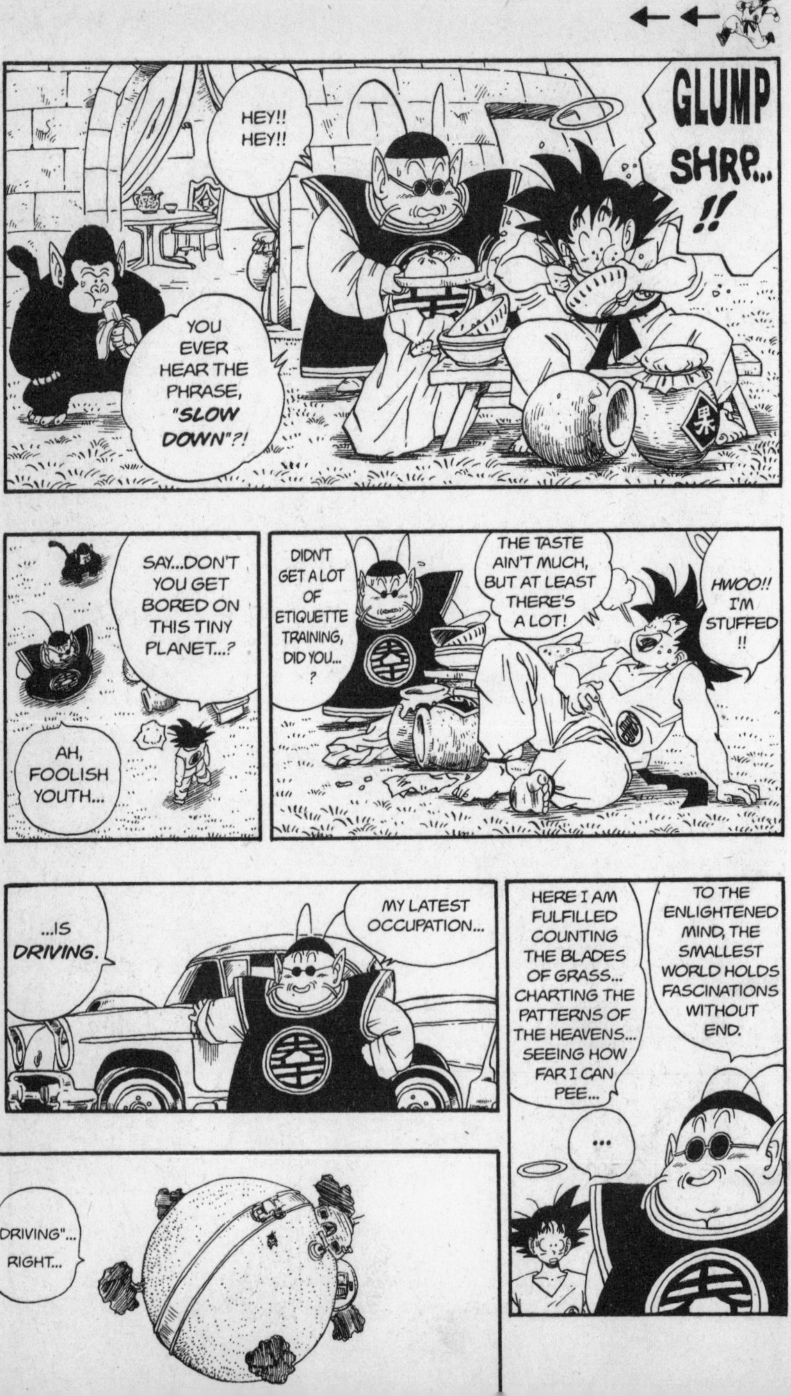
GLUMP SHRP... !!
HEY!! HEY!!
YOU EVER HEAR THE PHRASE, "SLOW DOWN"?!
HWOO!! I'M STUFFED !!
THE TASTE AIN'T MUCH, BUT AT LEAST THERE'S A LOT!
DIDN'T GET A LOT OF ETIQUETTE TRAINING, DID YOU... ?
SAY...DON'T YOU GET BORED ON THIS TINY PLANET...?
AH, FOOLISH YOUTH...
TO THE ENLIGHTENED MIND, THE SMALLEST WORLD HOLDS FASCINATIONS WITHOUT END.
HERE I AM FULFILLED COUNTING THE BLADES OF GRASS... CHARTING THE PATTERNS OF THE HEAVENS... SEEING HOW FAR I CAN PEE...
...
MY LATEST OCCUPATION...
...IS DRIVING.
"DRIVING"... RIGHT...

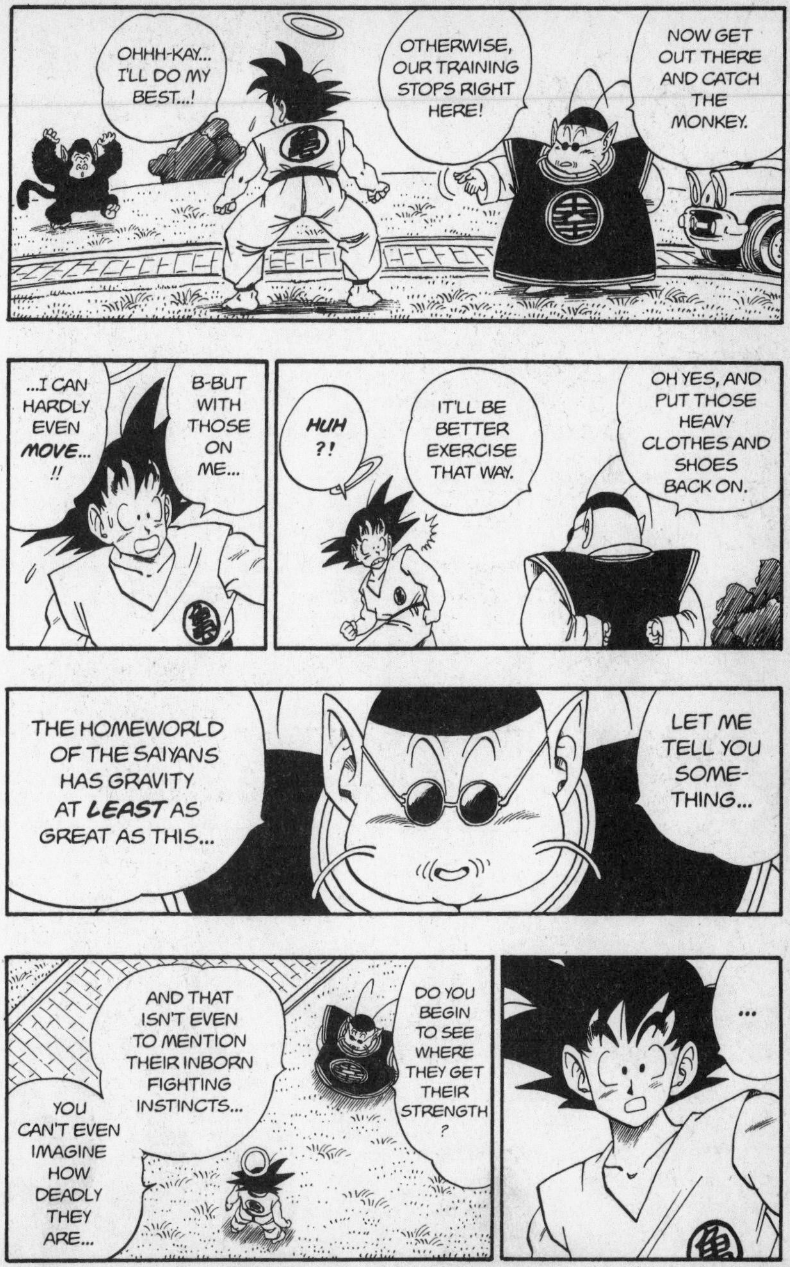

NOW GET OUT THERE AND CATCH THE MONKEY.
OTHERWISE, OUR TRAINING STOPS RIGHT HERE!
OHHH-KAY... I'LL DO MY BEST...!
OH YES, AND PUT THOSE HEAVY CLOTHES AND SHOES BACK ON.
IT'LL BE BETTER EXERCISE THAT WAY.
HUH ?!
B-BUT WITH THOSE ON ME...
...I CAN HARDLY EVEN MOVE... !!
LET ME TELL YOU SOME-THING...
THE HOMEWORLD OF THE SAIYANS HAS GRAVITY AT LEAST AS GREAT AS THIS...
...
DO YOU BEGIN TO SEE WHERE THEY GET THEIR STRENGTH ?
AND THAT ISN'T EVEN TO MENTION THEIR INBORN FIGHTING INSTINCTS...
YOU CAN'T EVEN IMAGINE HOW DEADLY THEY ARE...

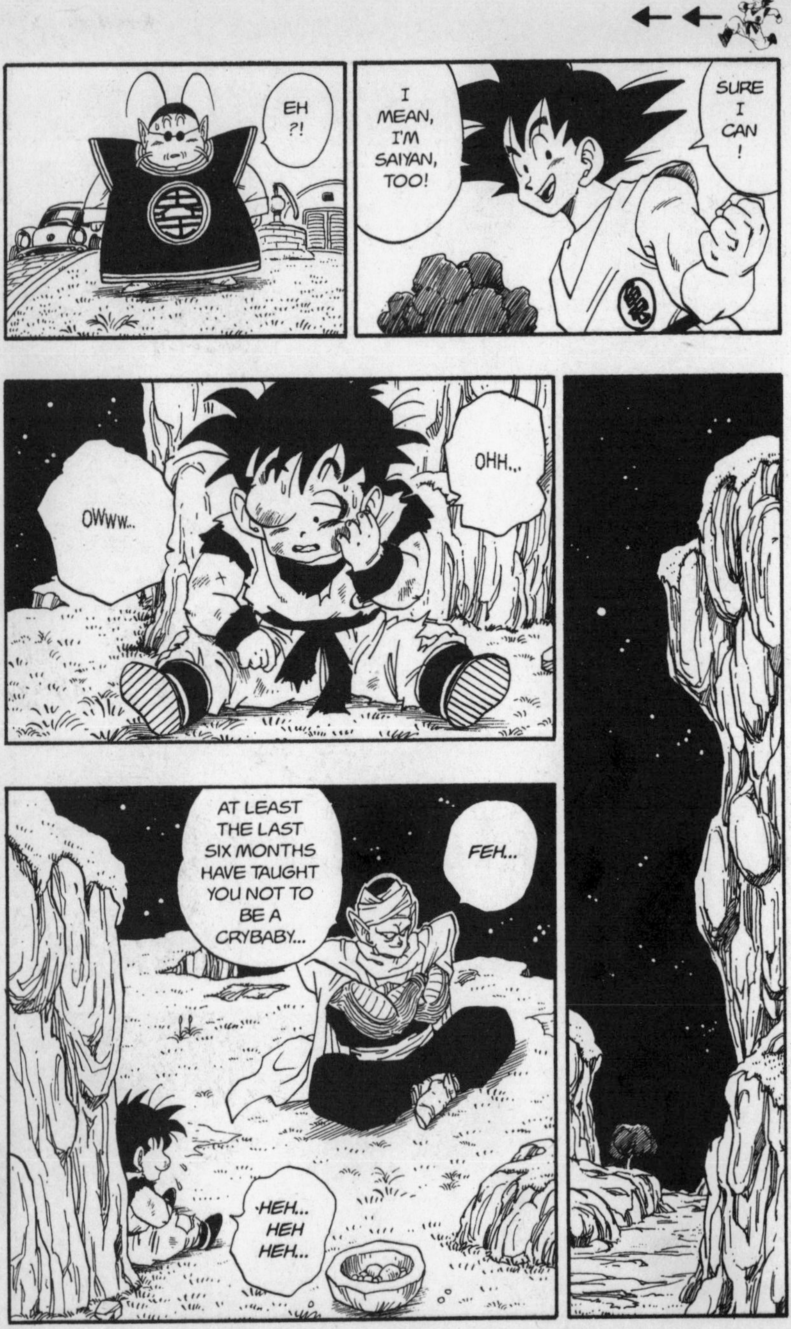
SURE I CAN!
I MEAN, I'M SAIYAN, TOO!
EH ?!
OHH...
OWWW...
FEH...
AT LEAST THE LAST SIX MONTHS HAVE TAUGHT YOU NOT TO BE A CRYBABY...
HEH... HEH HEH...

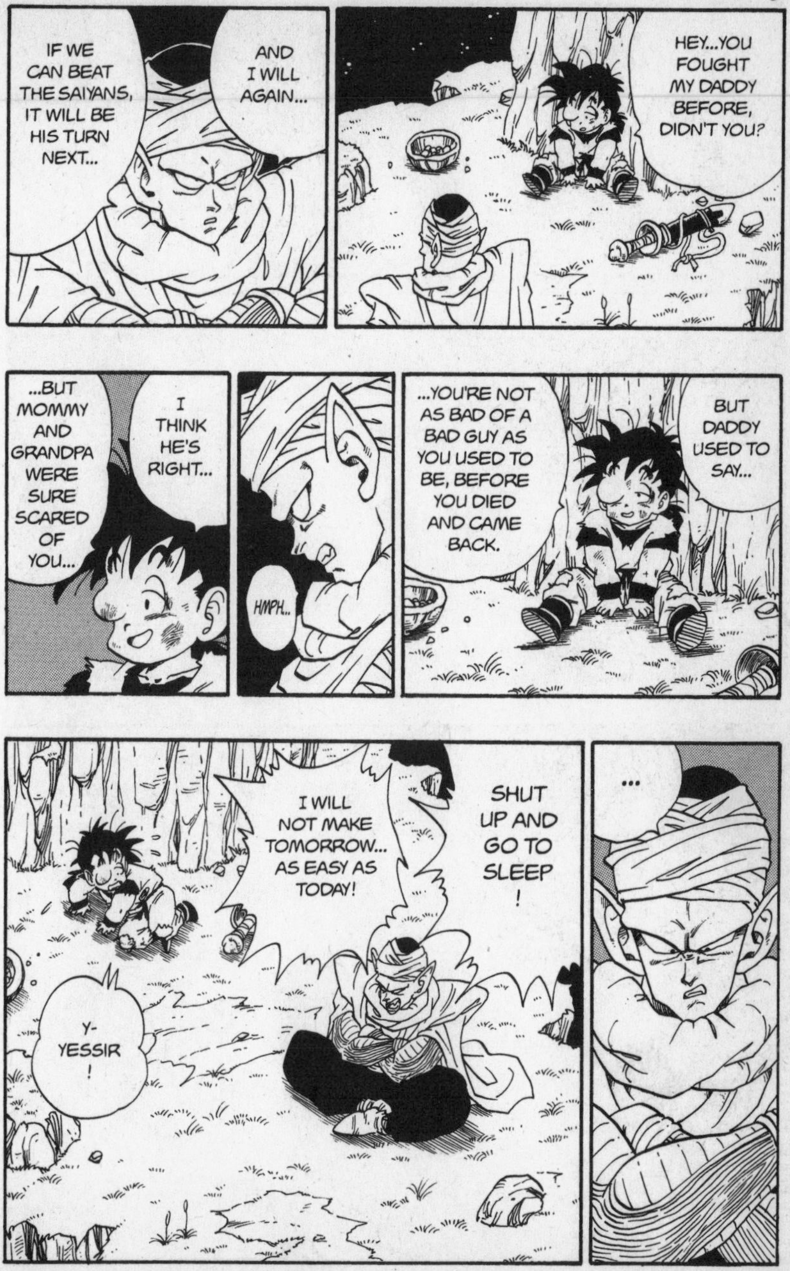
HEY...YOU FOUGHT MY DADDY BEFORE, DIDN'T YOU?
AND I WILL AGAIN...
IF WE CAN BEAT THE SAIYANS, IT WILL BE HIS TURN NEXT...
BUT DADDY USED TO SAY...
...YOU'RE NOT AS BAD OF A BAD GUY AS YOU USED TO BE, BEFORE YOU DIED AND CAME BACK.
HMPH...
I THINK HE'S RIGHT...
...BUT MOMMY AND GRANDPA WERE SURE SCARED OF YOU...
...
SHUT UP AND GO TO SLEEP!
I WILL NOT MAKE TOMORROW... AS EASY AS TODAY!
Y-YESSIR!

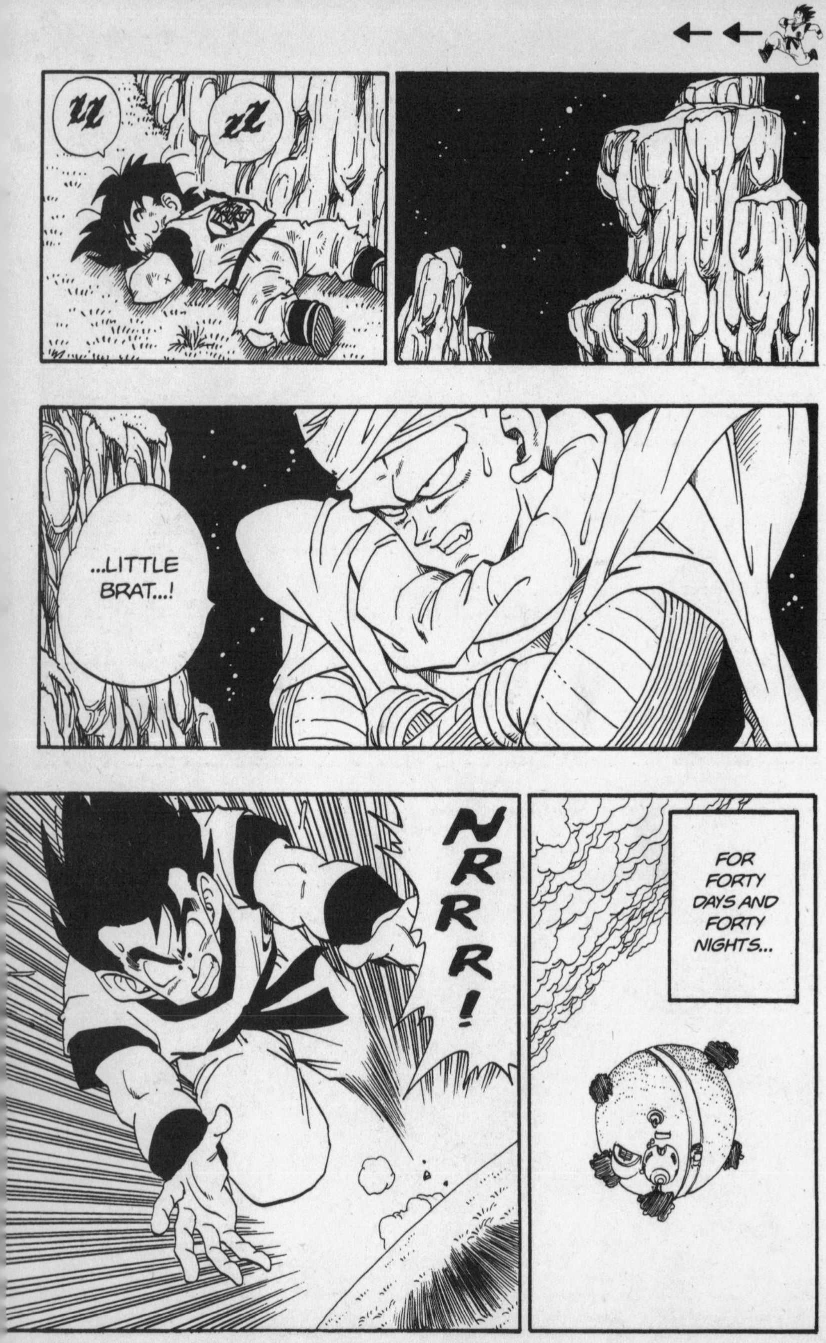
zz
zz
...LITTLE BRAT...!
FOR FORTY DAYS AND FORTY NIGHTS...
NRRR!

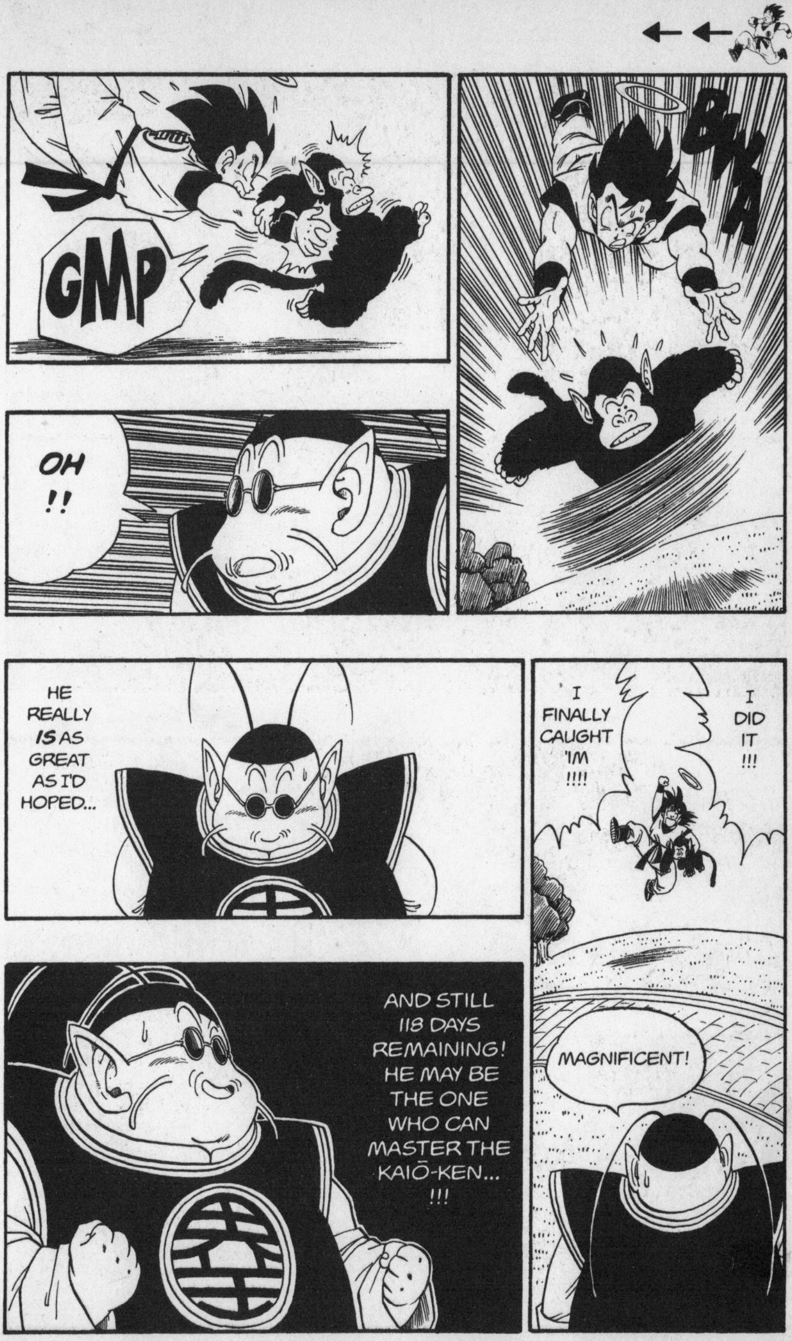
BWA
GMP
OH !!
I DID IT !!!
I FINALLY CAUGHT 'IM !!!!
MAGNIFICENT!
HE REALLY *IS* AS GREAT AS I'D HOPED...
AND STILL 118 DAYS REMAINING! HE MAY BE THE ONE WHO CAN MASTER THE KAIŌ-KEN... !!!

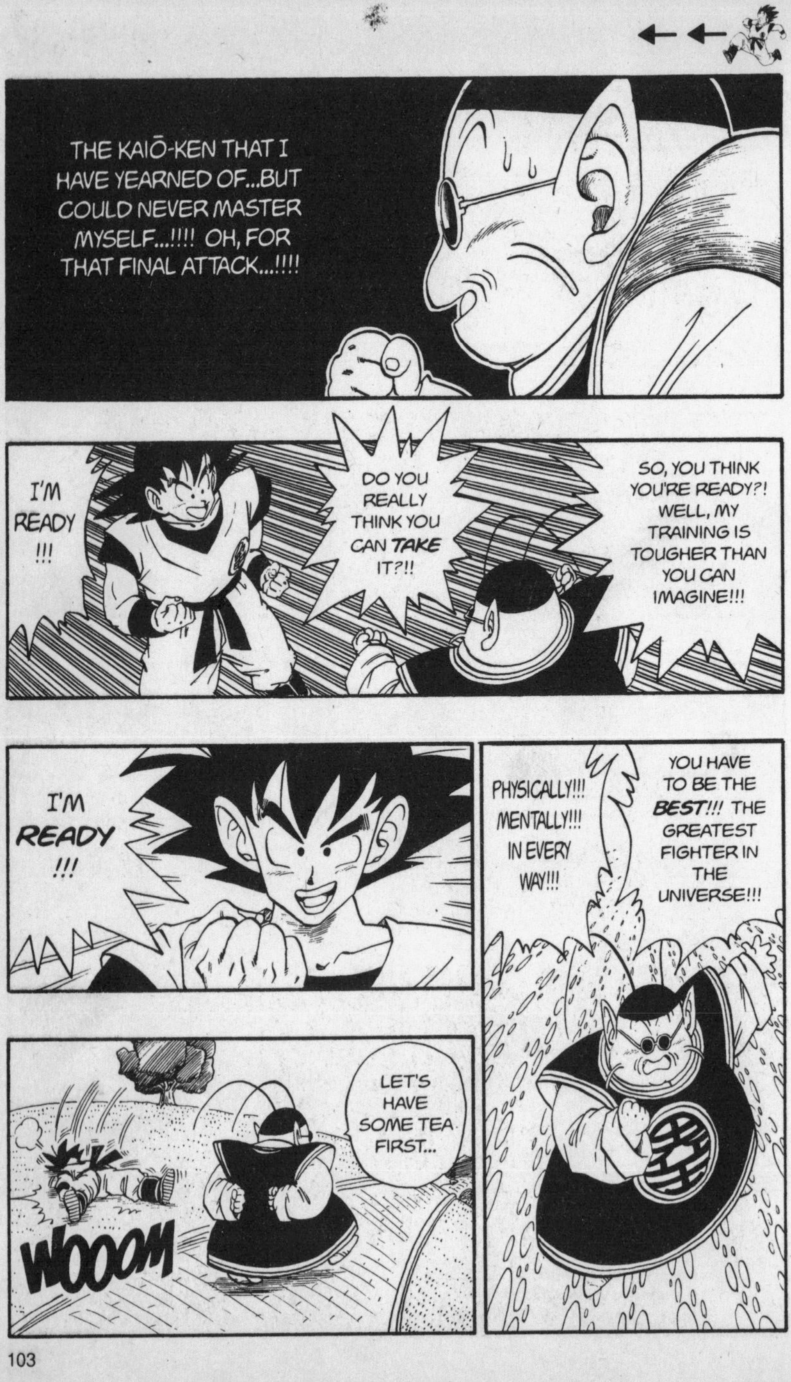
THE KAIŌ-KEN THAT I HAVE YEARNED OF...BUT COULD NEVER MASTER MYSELF...!!!! OH, FOR THAT FINAL ATTACK...!!!!
SO, YOU THINK YOU'RE READY?! WELL, MY TRAINING IS TOUGHER THAN YOU CAN IMAGINE!!!
DO YOU REALLY THINK YOU CAN *TAKE* IT?!!
I'M READY !!!
YOU HAVE TO BE THE *BEST*!!! THE GREATEST FIGHTER IN THE UNIVERSE!!!
PHYSICALLY!!! MENTALLY!!! IN EVERY WAY!!!
I'M *READY* !!!
LET'S HAVE SOME TEA FIRST...
WOOOM

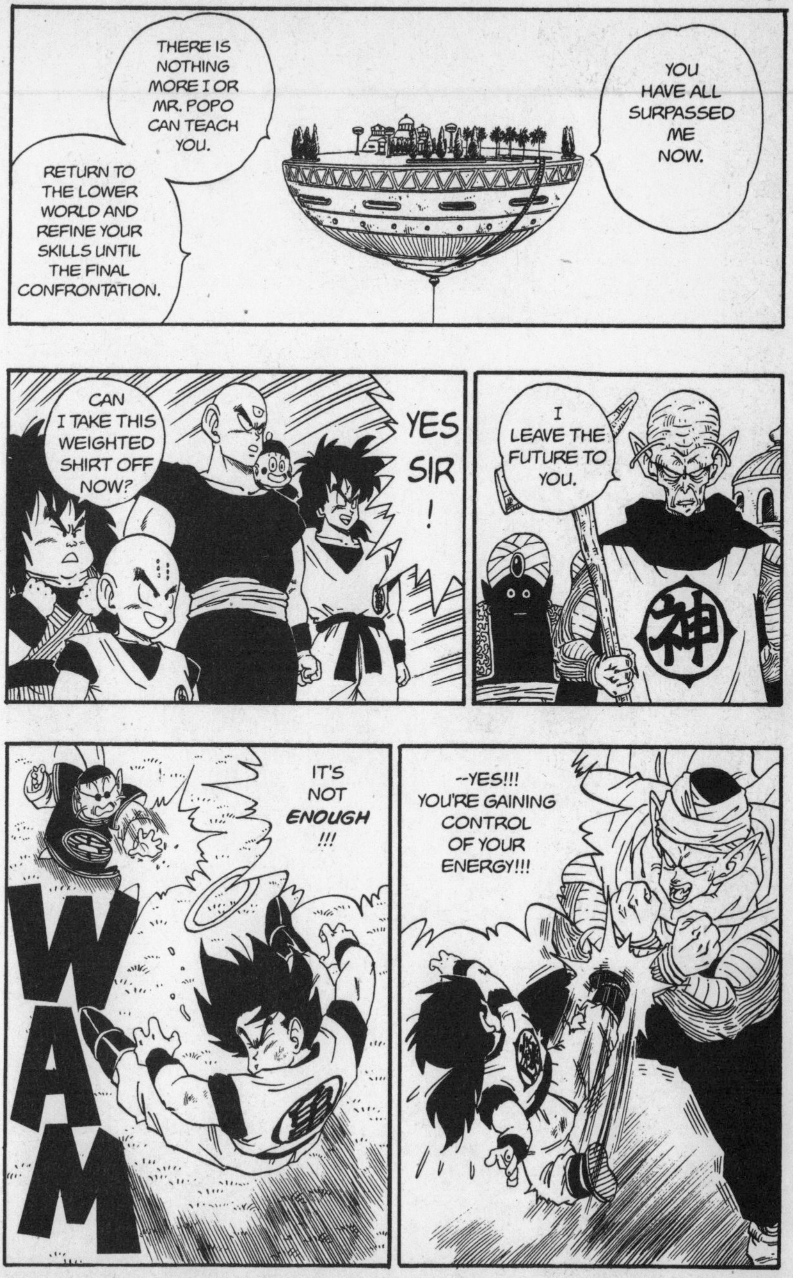
YOU HAVE ALL SURPASSED ME NOW.
THERE IS NOTHING MORE I OR MR. POPO CAN TEACH YOU.
RETURN TO THE LOWER WORLD AND REFINE YOUR SKILLS UNTIL THE FINAL CONFRONTATION.
I LEAVE THE FUTURE TO YOU.
YES SIR!
CAN I TAKE THIS WEIGHTED SHIRT OFF NOW?
--YES!!! YOU'RE GAINING CONTROL OF YOUR ENERGY!!!
IT'S NOT ENOUGH!!!
WAM

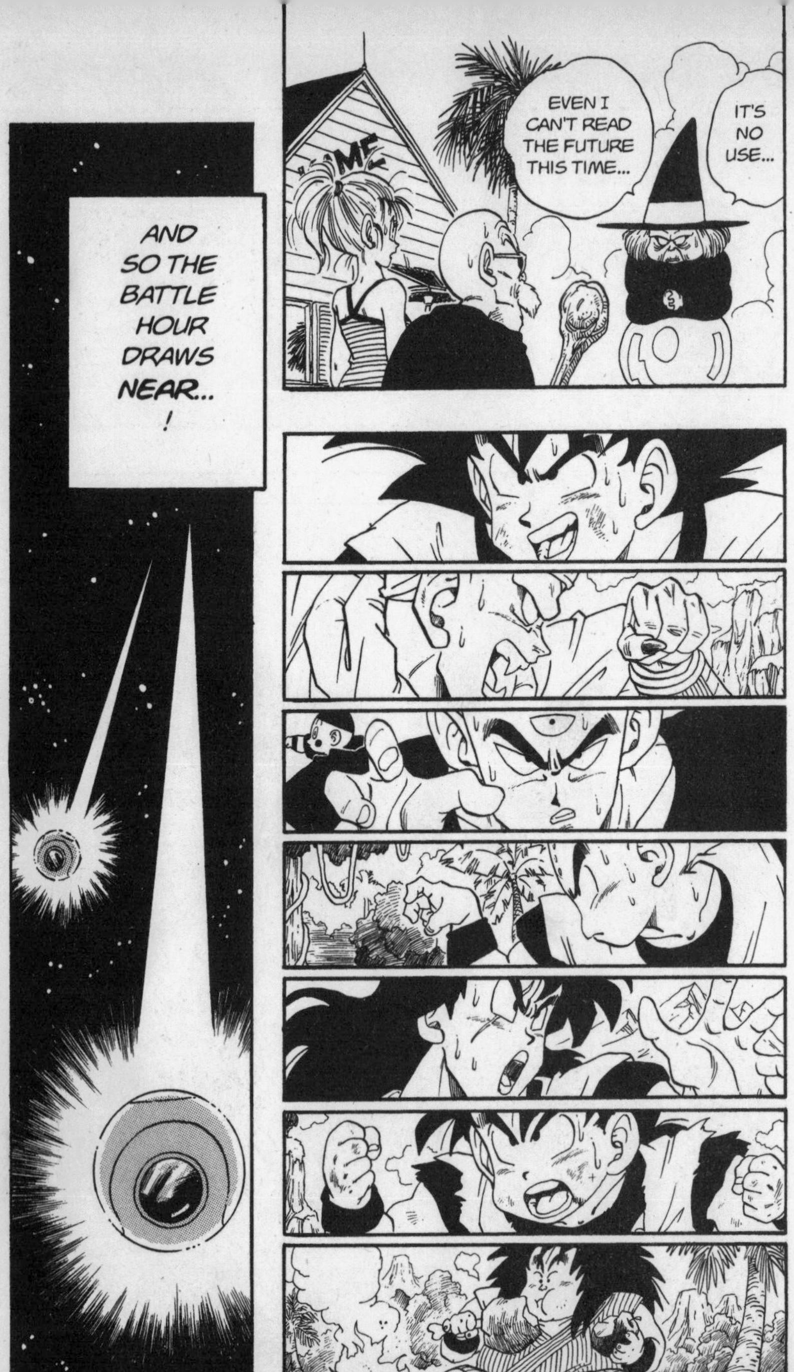
IT'S NO USE...
EVEN I CAN'T READ THE FUTURE THIS TIME...
ME
AND SO THE BATTLE HOUR DRAWS NEAR...!

NEXT: THE LAST DAY!

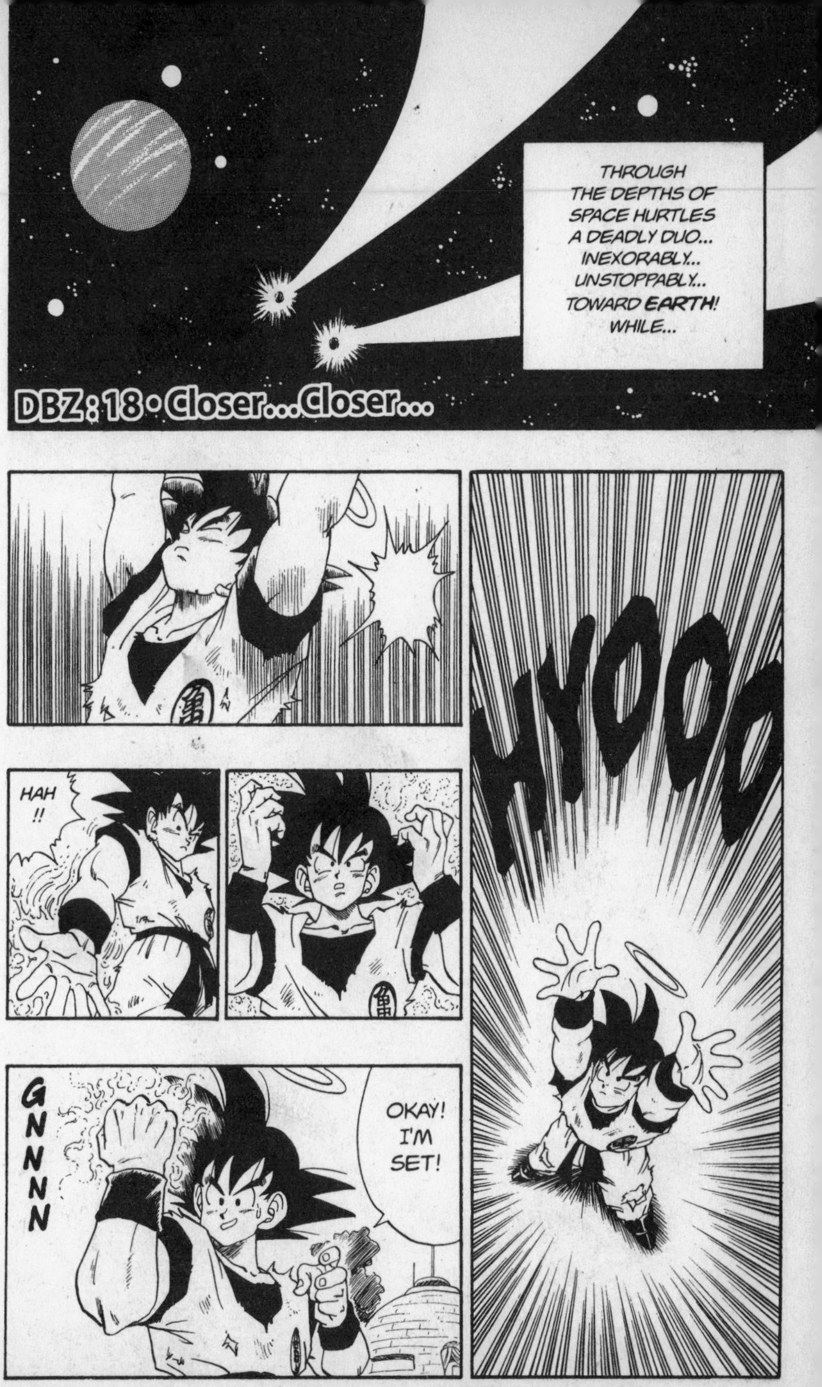
THROUGH THE DEPTHS OF SPACE HURTLES A DEADLY DUO... INEXORABLY... UNSTOPPABLY... TOWARD EARTH! WHILE...
DBZ : 18 • Closer...Closer...
HYOOO
HAH !!
OKAY! I'M SET!
GNNNN

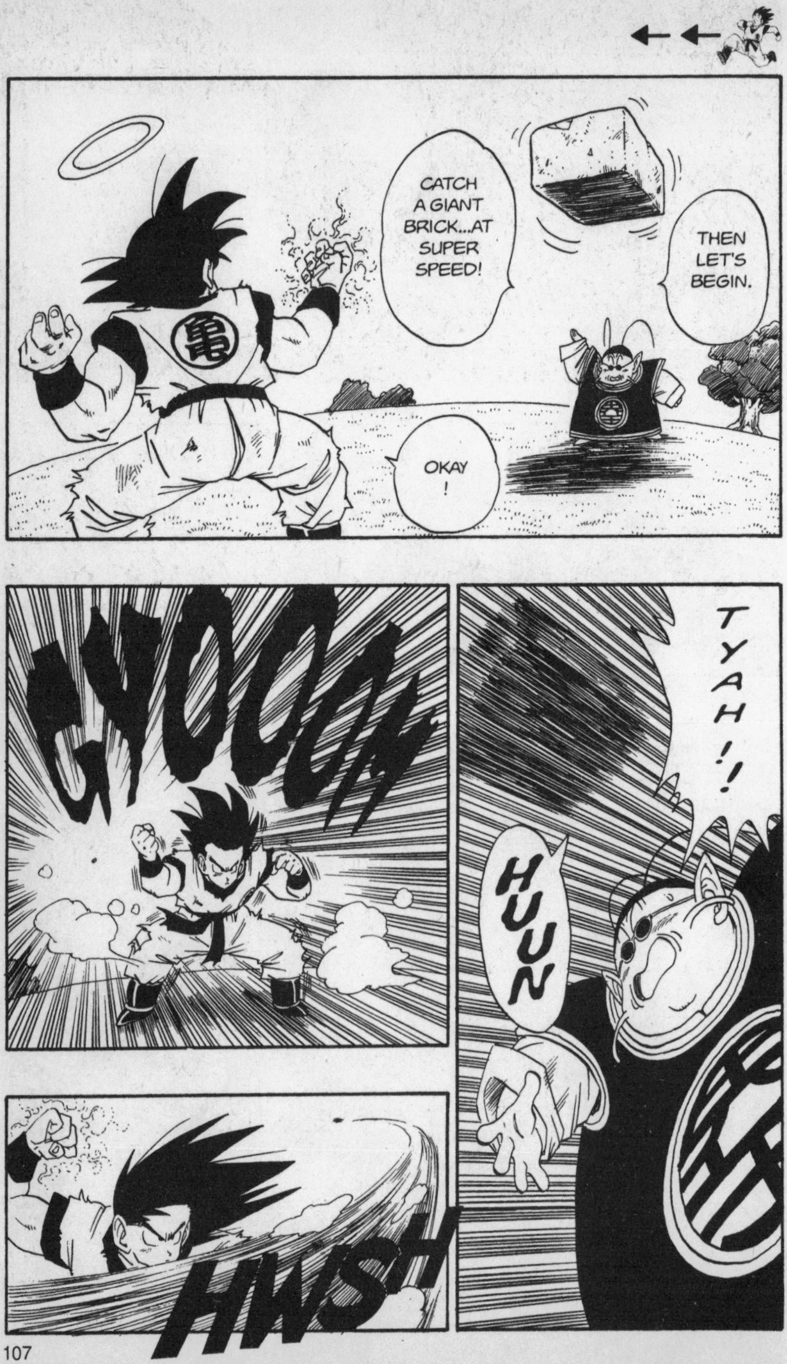
THEN LET'S BEGIN.
CATCH A GIANT BRICK...AT SUPER SPEED!
OKAY!
TYAH!!
HUUN
GYOOM
HWSH

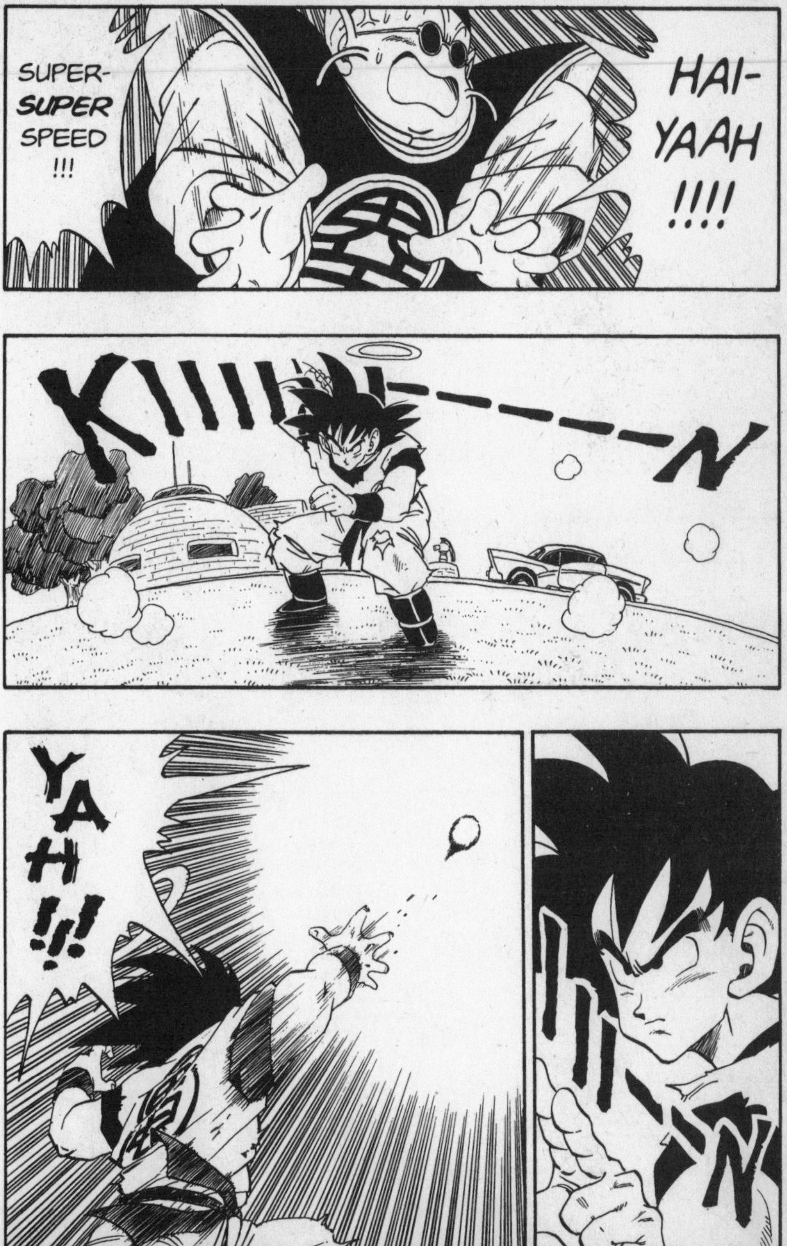
HAI-YAAH!!!!
SUPER-SUPER SPEED!!!
KIIIII------N
YAH!!!

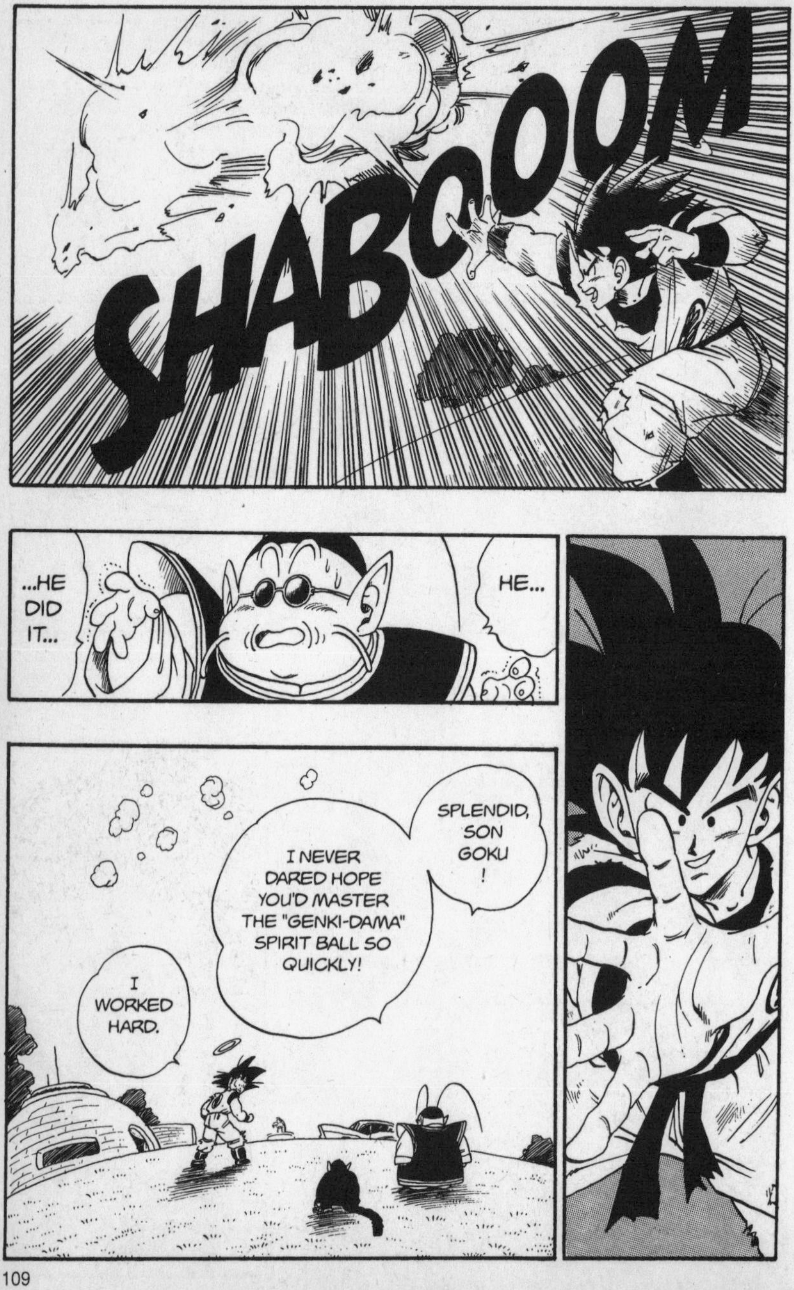
SHABOOOM
HE...
...HE DID IT...
SPLENDID, SON GOKU!
I NEVER DARED HOPE YOU'D MASTER THE "GENKI-DAMA" SPIRIT BALL SO QUICKLY!
I WORKED HARD.

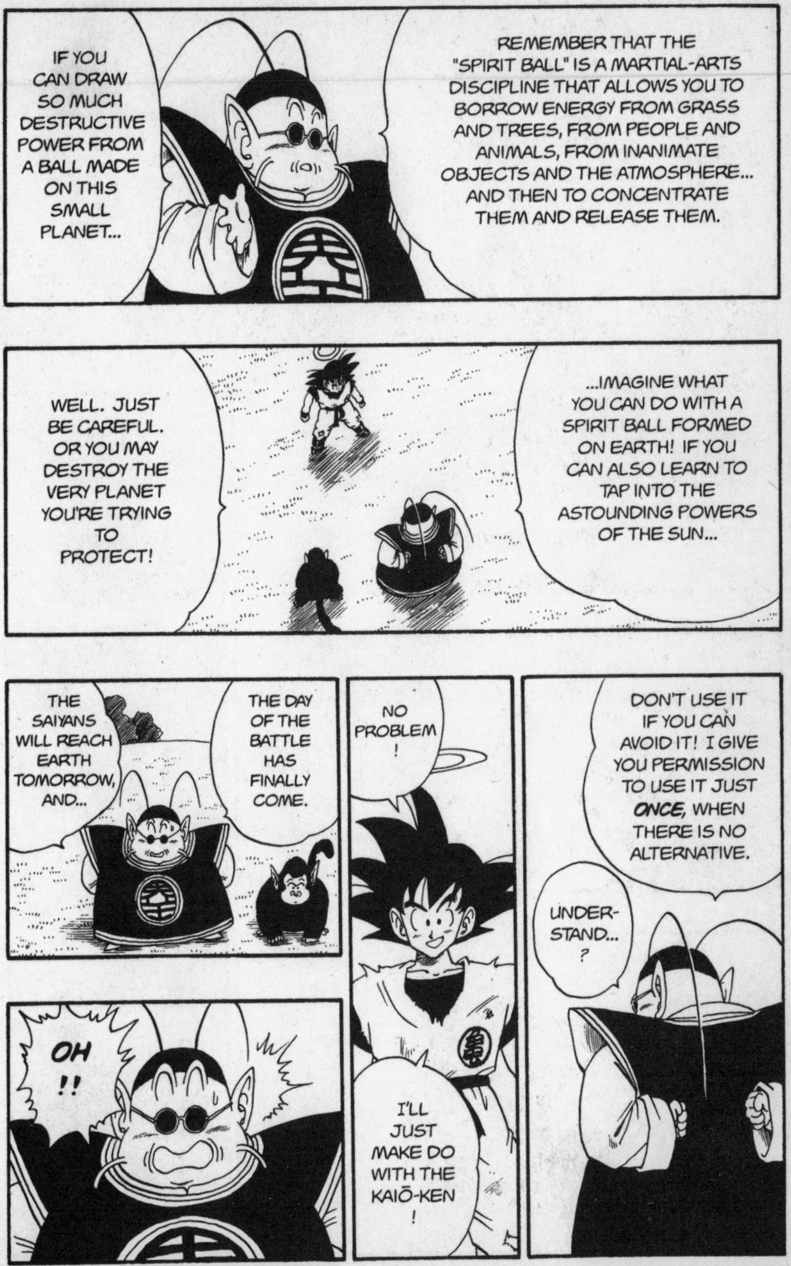
REMEMBER THAT THE "SPIRIT BALL" IS A MARTIAL-ARTS DISCIPLINE THAT ALLOWS YOU TO BORROW ENERGY FROM GRASS AND TREES, FROM PEOPLE AND ANIMALS, FROM INANIMATE OBJECTS AND THE ATMOSPHERE... AND THEN TO CONCENTRATE THEM AND RELEASE THEM.
IF YOU CAN DRAW SO MUCH DESTRUCTIVE POWER FROM A BALL MADE ON THIS SMALL PLANET...
...IMAGINE WHAT YOU CAN DO WITH A SPIRIT BALL FORMED ON EARTH! IF YOU CAN ALSO LEARN TO TAP INTO THE ASTOUNDING POWERS OF THE SUN...
WELL. JUST BE CAREFUL. OR YOU MAY DESTROY THE VERY PLANET YOU'RE TRYING TO PROTECT!
DON'T USE IT IF YOU CAN AVOID IT! I GIVE YOU PERMISSION TO USE IT JUST *ONCE*, WHEN THERE IS NO ALTERNATIVE.
UNDER-STAND...?
NO PROBLEM!
I'LL JUST MAKE DO WITH THE KAIŌ-KEN!
THE DAY OF THE BATTLE HAS FINALLY COME.
THE SAIYANS WILL REACH EARTH TOMORROW, AND...
OH!!

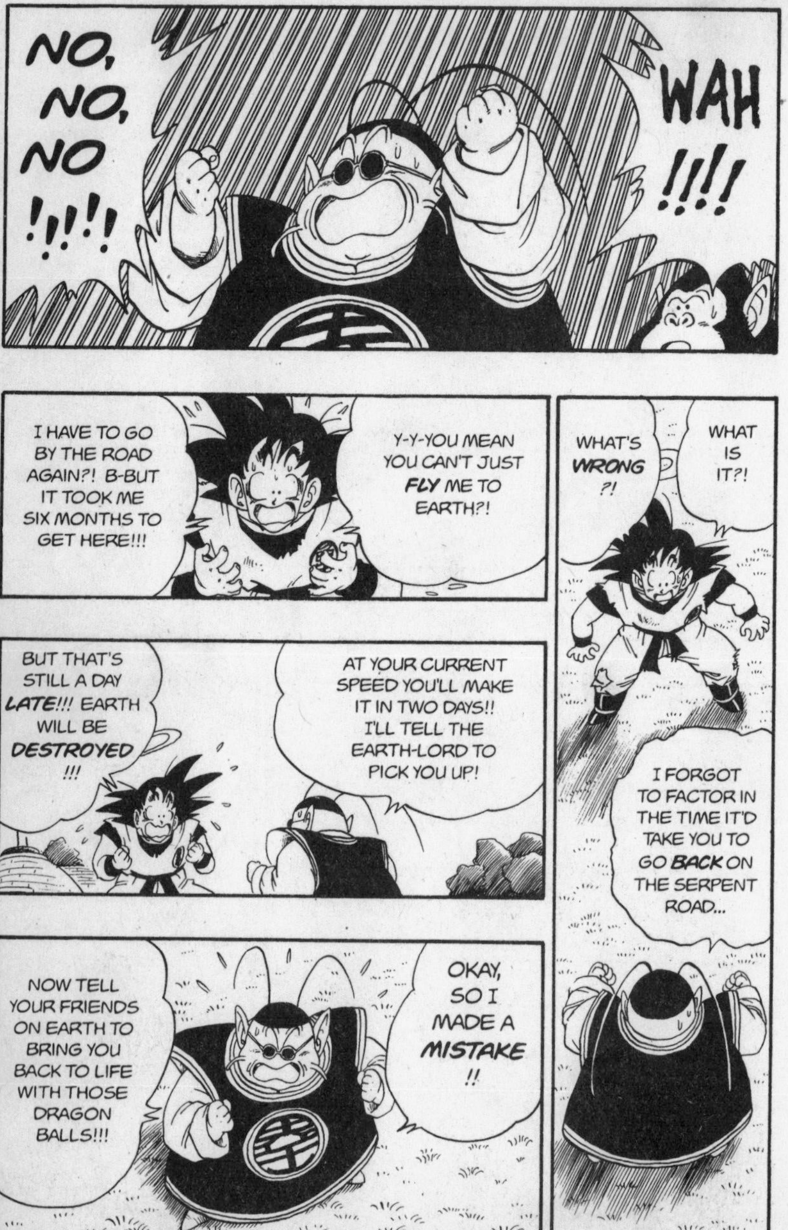
WAH !!!!
NO, NO, NO !!!!!
WHAT IS IT?!
WHAT'S WRONG ?!
I FORGOT TO FACTOR IN THE TIME IT'D TAKE YOU TO GO BACK ON THE SERPENT ROAD...
Y-Y-YOU MEAN YOU CAN'T JUST FLY ME TO EARTH?!
I HAVE TO GO BY THE ROAD AGAIN?! B-BUT IT TOOK ME SIX MONTHS TO GET HERE!!!
AT YOUR CURRENT SPEED YOU'LL MAKE IT IN TWO DAYS!! I'LL TELL THE EARTH-LORD TO PICK YOU UP!
BUT THAT'S STILL A DAY LATE!!! EARTH WILL BE DESTROYED !!!
OKAY, SO I MADE A MISTAKE !!
NOW TELL YOUR FRIENDS ON EARTH TO BRING YOU BACK TO LIFE WITH THOSE DRAGON BALLS!!!

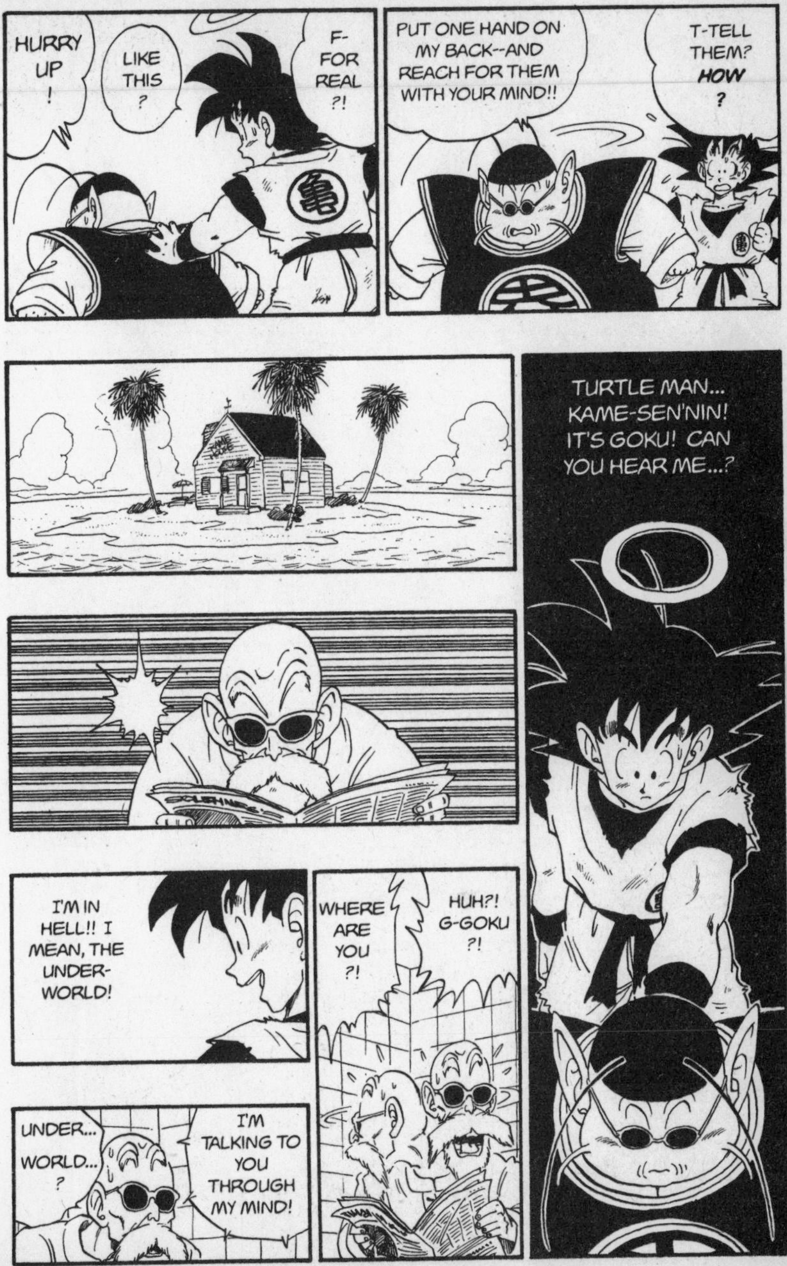
T-TELL THEM? HOW?
PUT ONE HAND ON MY BACK--AND REACH FOR THEM WITH YOUR MIND!!
F-FOR REAL?!
LIKE THIS?
HURRY UP!
TURTLE MAN... KAME-SEN'NIN! IT'S GOKU! CAN YOU HEAR ME...?
HUH?! G-GOKU?!
WHERE ARE YOU?!
I'M IN HELL!! I MEAN, THE UNDER-WORLD!
I'M TALKING TO YOU THROUGH MY MIND!
UNDER... WORLD...?

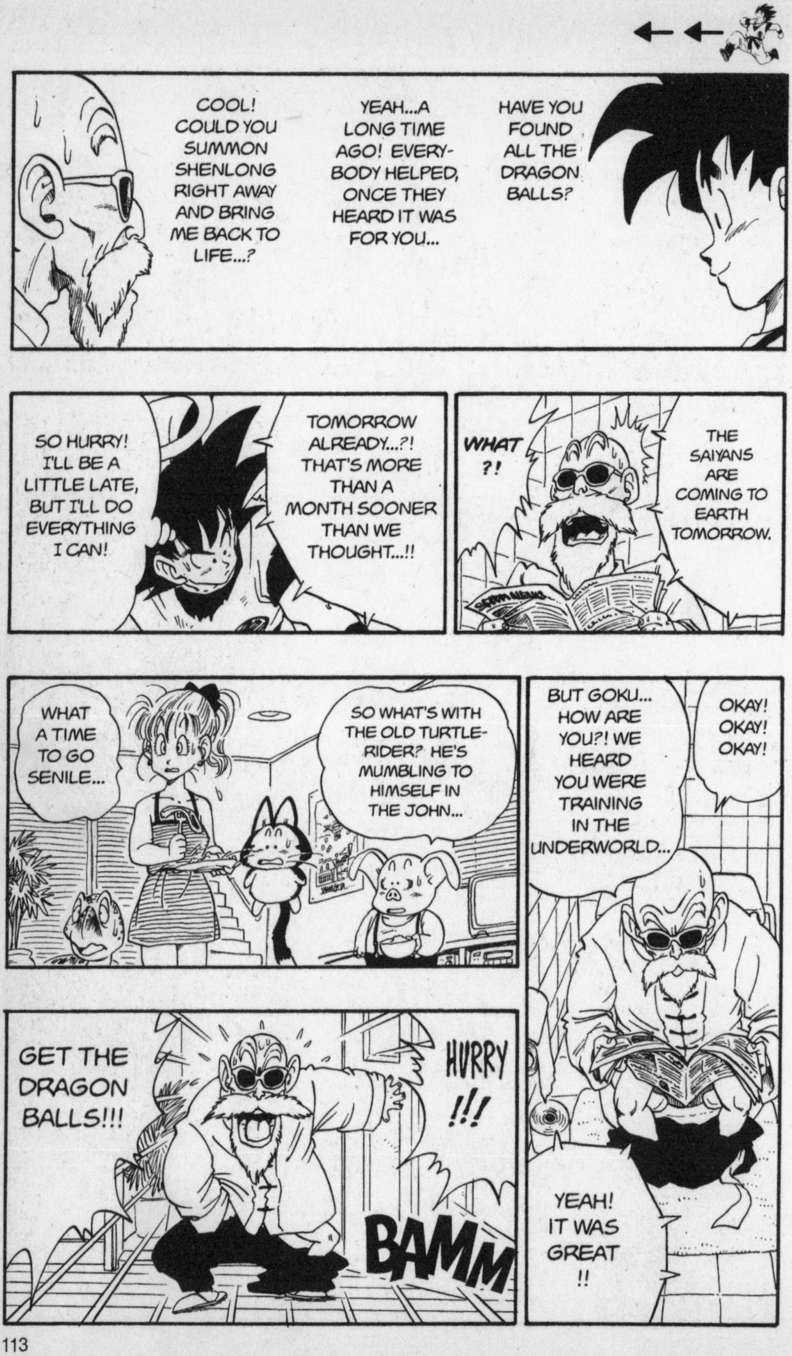
HAVE YOU FOUND ALL THE DRAGON BALLS?
YEAH...A LONG TIME AGO! EVERYBODY HELPED, ONCE THEY HEARD IT WAS FOR YOU...
COOL! COULD YOU SUMMON SHENLONG RIGHT AWAY AND BRING ME BACK TO LIFE...?
THE SAIYANS ARE COMING TO EARTH TOMORROW.
WHAT ?!
TOMORROW ALREADY...?! THAT'S MORE THAN A MONTH SOONER THAN WE THOUGHT...!!
SO HURRY! I'LL BE A LITTLE LATE, BUT I'LL DO EVERYTHING I CAN!
OKAY! OKAY! OKAY!
BUT GOKU... HOW ARE YOU?! WE HEARD YOU WERE TRAINING IN THE UNDERWORLD...
YEAH! IT WAS GREAT !!
SO WHAT'S WITH THE OLD TURTLE-RIDER? HE'S MUMBLING TO HIMSELF IN THE JOHN...
WHAT A TIME TO GO SENILE...
HURRY !!!
GET THE DRAGON BALLS!!!
BAMM

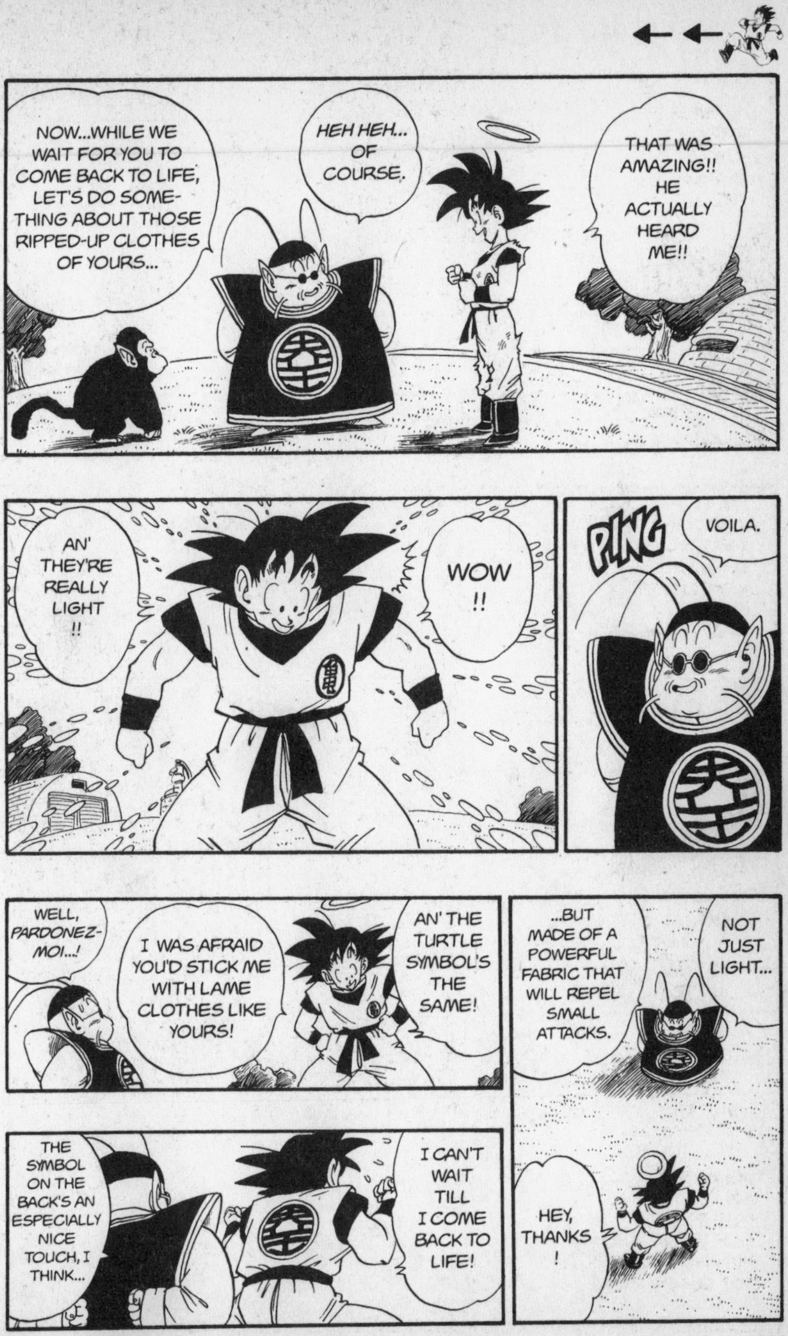
THAT WAS AMAZING!! HE ACTUALLY HEARD ME!!
HEH HEH... OF COURSE.
NOW...WHILE WE WAIT FOR YOU TO COME BACK TO LIFE, LET'S DO SOME-THING ABOUT THOSE RIPPED-UP CLOTHES OF YOURS...
PING
VOILA.
WOW !!
AN' THEY'RE REALLY LIGHT !!
NOT JUST LIGHT...
...BUT MADE OF A POWERFUL FABRIC THAT WILL REPEL SMALL ATTACKS.
HEY, THANKS !
AN' THE TURTLE SYMBOL'S THE SAME!
I WAS AFRAID YOU'D STICK ME WITH LAME CLOTHES LIKE YOURS!
WELL, PARDONEZ-MOI...!
I CAN'T WAIT TILL I COME BACK TO LIFE!
THE SYMBOL ON THE BACK'S AN ESPECIALLY NICE TOUCH, I THINK...

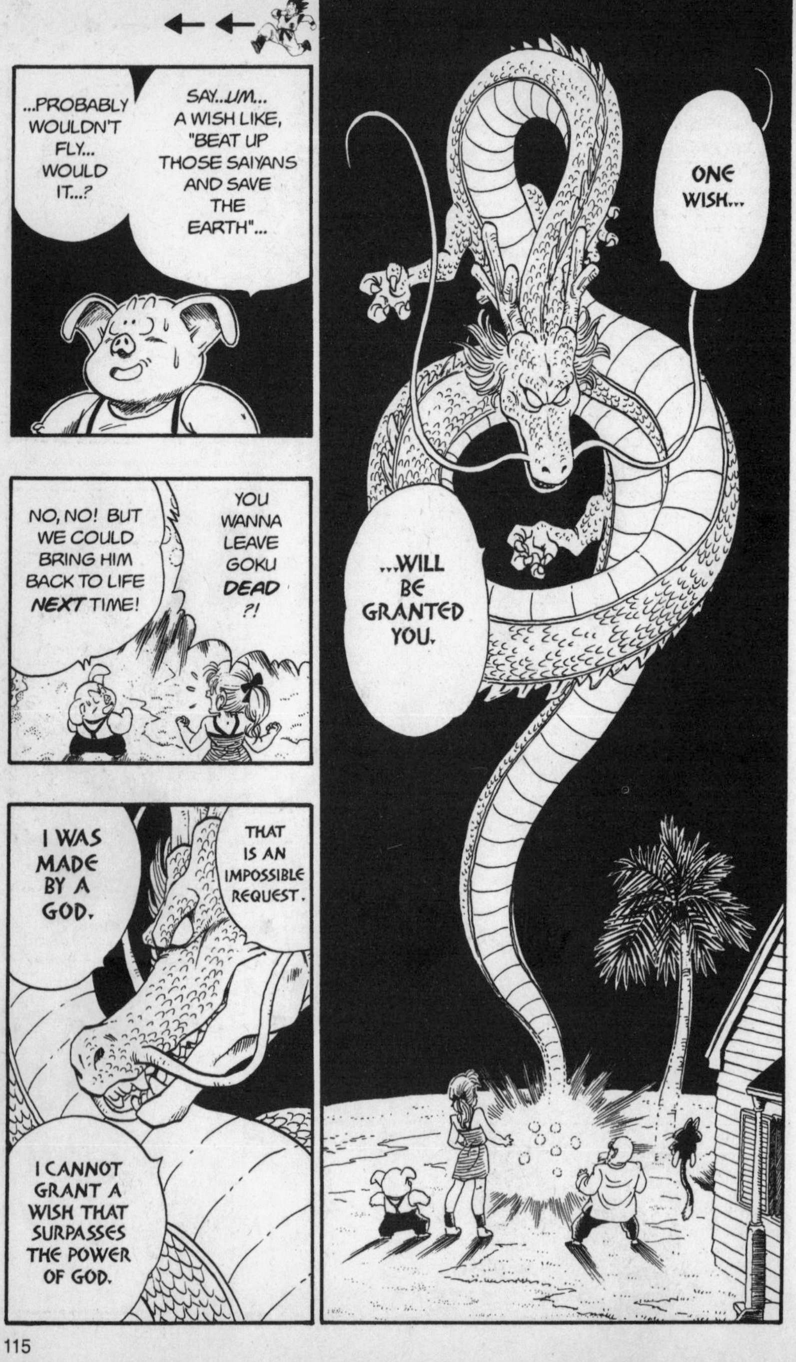
ONE WISH...
...WILL BE GRANTED YOU.
SAY...UM... A WISH LIKE, "BEAT UP THOSE SAIYANS AND SAVE THE EARTH"...
...PROBABLY WOULDN'T FLY... WOULD IT...?
YOU WANNA LEAVE GOKU *DEAD* ?!
NO, NO! BUT WE COULD BRING HIM BACK TO LIFE *NEXT* TIME!
THAT IS AN IMPOSSIBLE REQUEST.
I WAS MADE BY A GOD.
I CANNOT GRANT A WISH THAT SURPASSES THE POWER OF GOD.

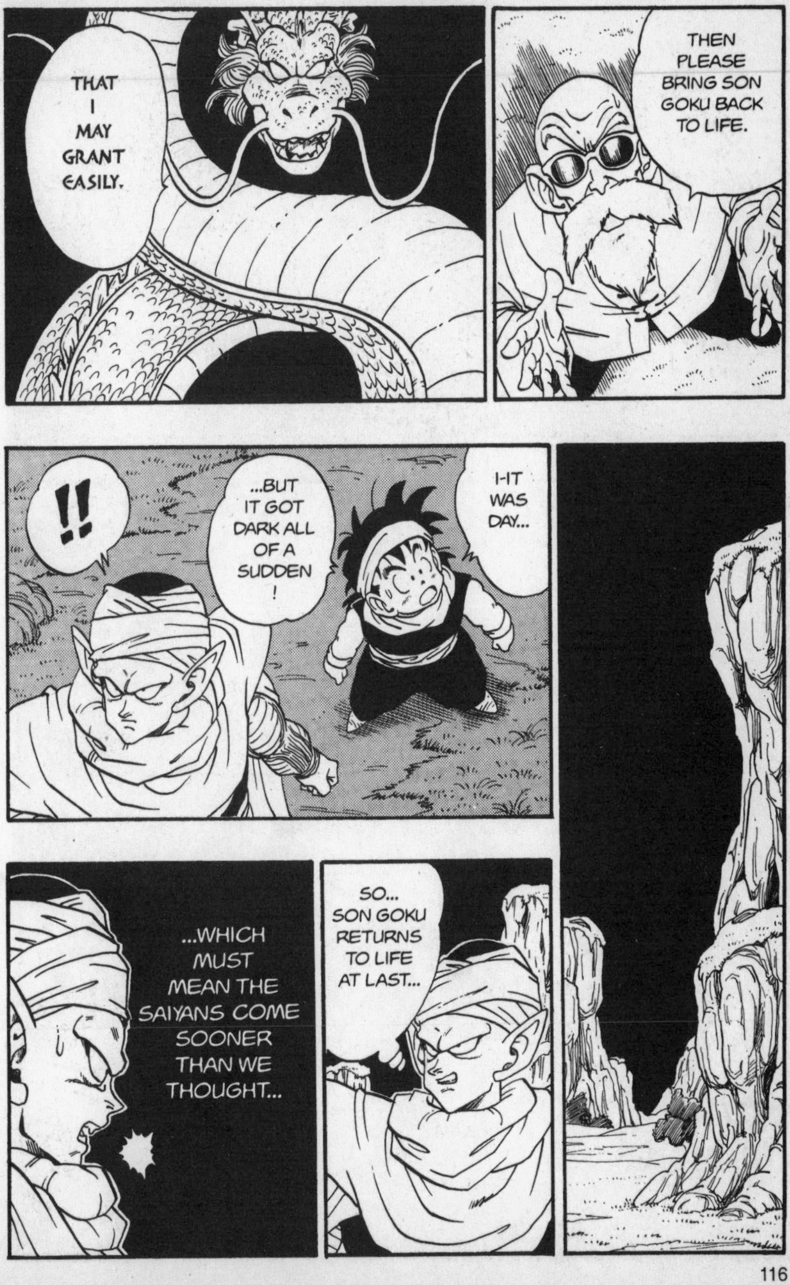
THEN PLEASE BRING SON GOKU BACK TO LIFE.
THAT I MAY GRANT EASILY.
I-IT WAS DAY...
...BUT IT GOT DARK ALL OF A SUDDEN!
!!
SO... SON GOKU RETURNS TO LIFE AT LAST...
...WHICH MUST MEAN THE SAIYANS COME SOONER THAN WE THOUGHT...

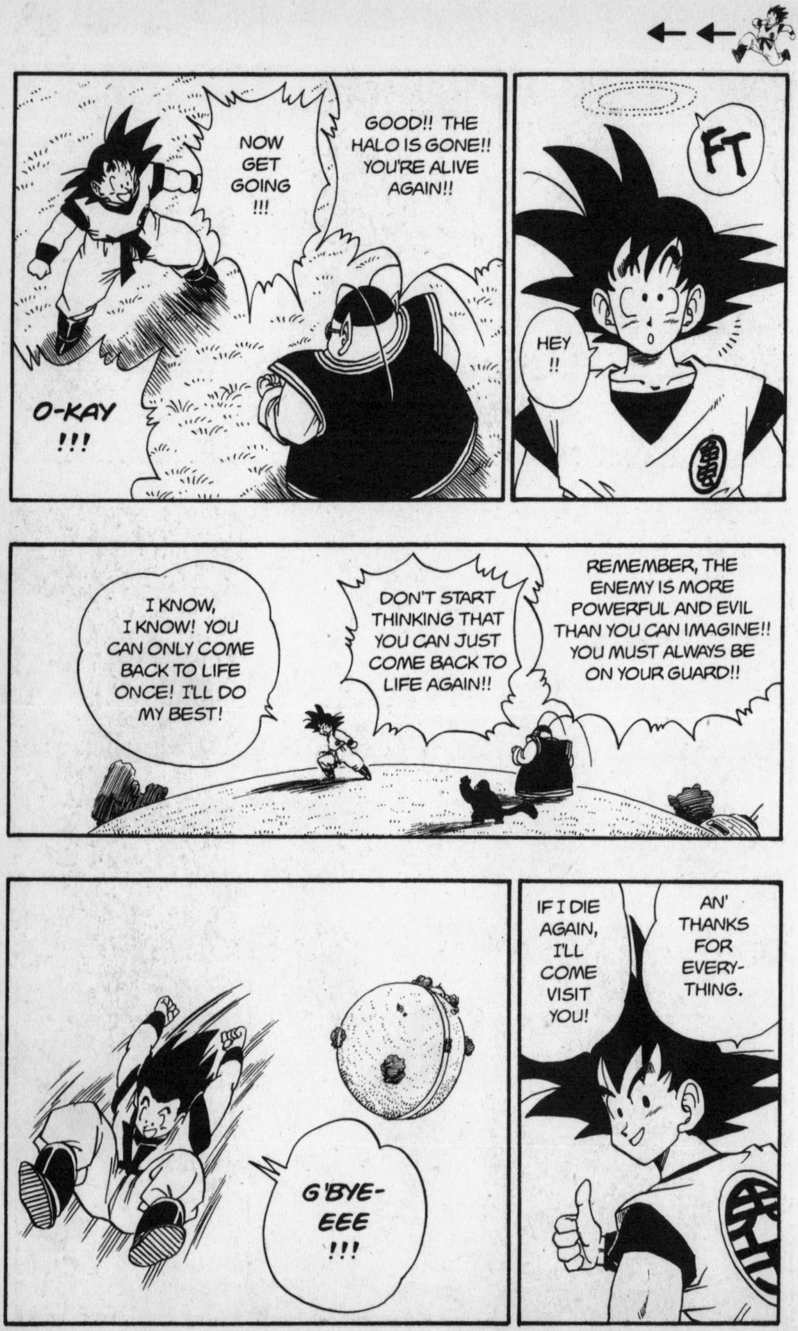
FT
HEY !!
GOOD!! THE HALO IS GONE!! YOU'RE ALIVE AGAIN!!
NOW GET GOING !!!
O-KAY !!!
REMEMBER, THE ENEMY IS MORE POWERFUL AND EVIL THAN YOU CAN IMAGINE!! YOU MUST ALWAYS BE ON YOUR GUARD!!
DON'T START THINKING THAT YOU CAN JUST COME BACK TO LIFE AGAIN!!
I KNOW, I KNOW! YOU CAN ONLY COME BACK TO LIFE ONCE! I'LL DO MY BEST!
AN' THANKS FOR EVERY-THING.
IF I DIE AGAIN, I'LL COME VISIT YOU!
G'BYE-EEE !!!

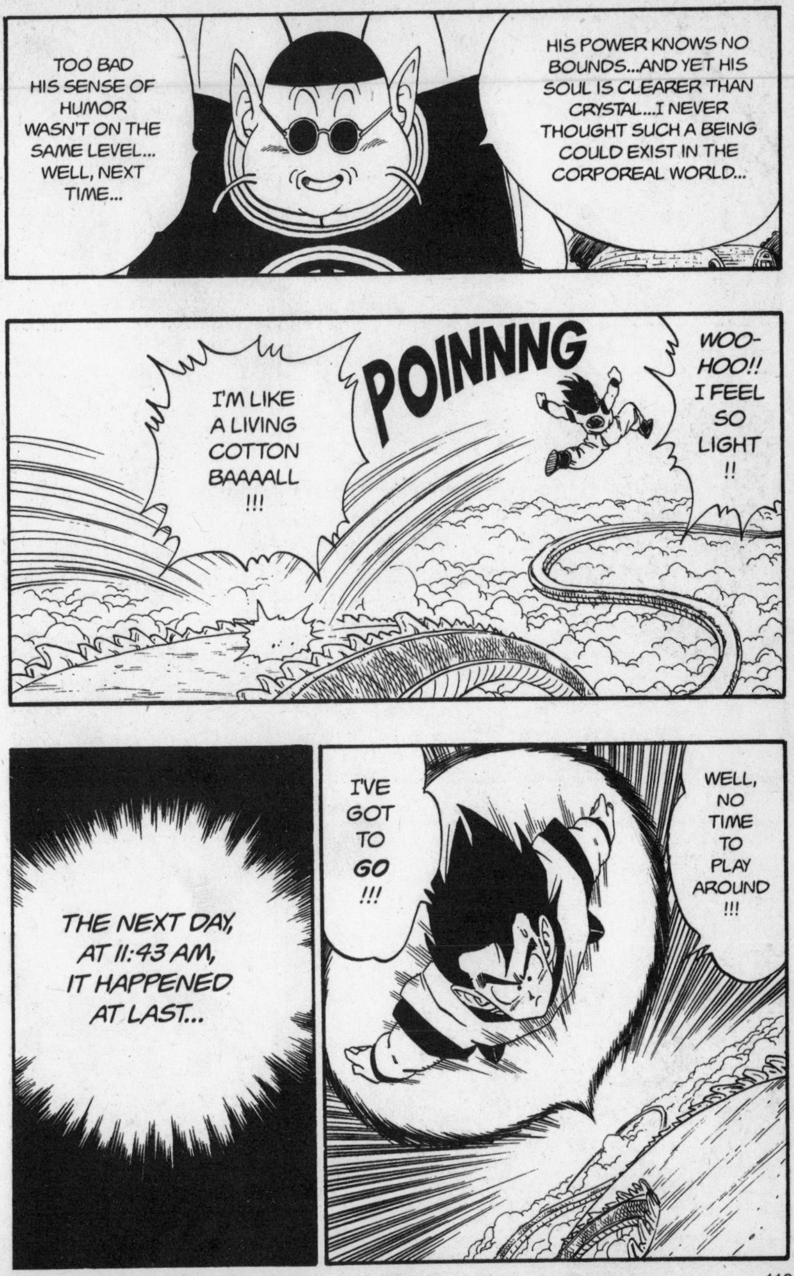
HIS POWER KNOWS NO BOUNDS...AND YET HIS SOUL IS CLEARER THAN CRYSTAL...I NEVER THOUGHT SUCH A BEING COULD EXIST IN THE CORPOREAL WORLD...
TOO BAD HIS SENSE OF HUMOR WASN'T ON THE SAME LEVEL... WELL, NEXT TIME...
WOO-HOO!! I FEEL SO LIGHT!!
POINNNG
I'M LIKE A LIVING COTTON BAAAALL!!!
WELL, NO TIME TO PLAY AROUND!!!
I'VE GOT TO GO!!!
THE NEXT DAY, AT 11:43 AM, IT HAPPENED AT LAST...

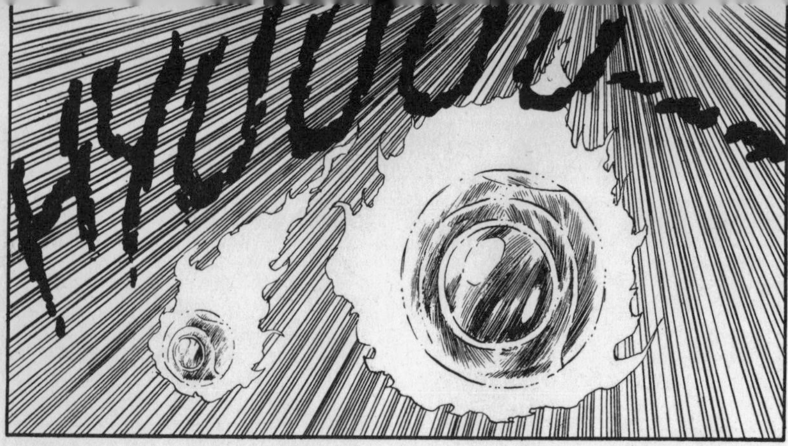

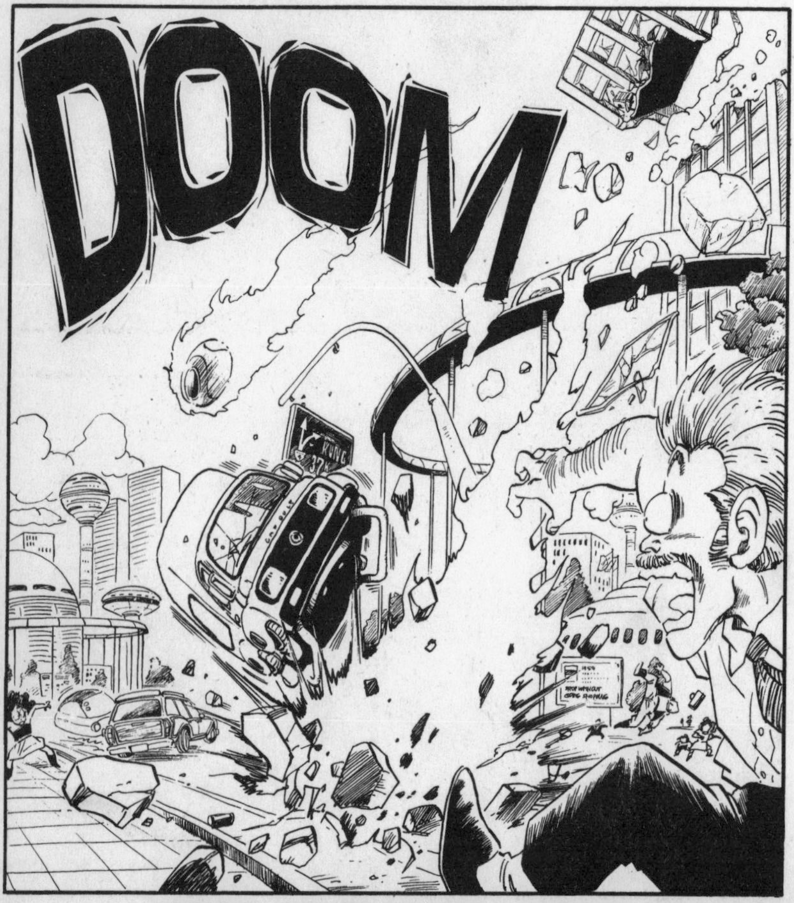
DOOM

NEXT: COME THE SAIYANS...

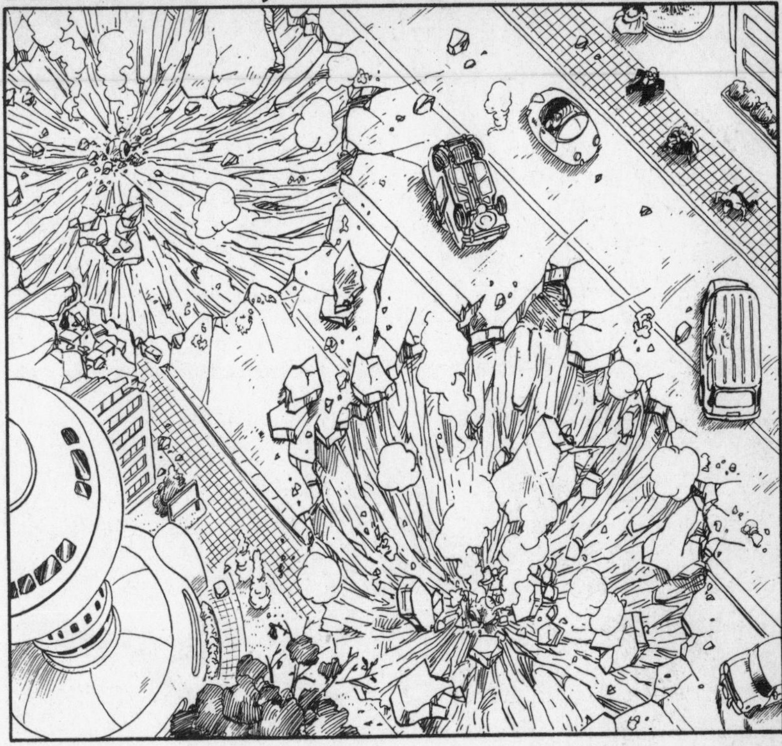

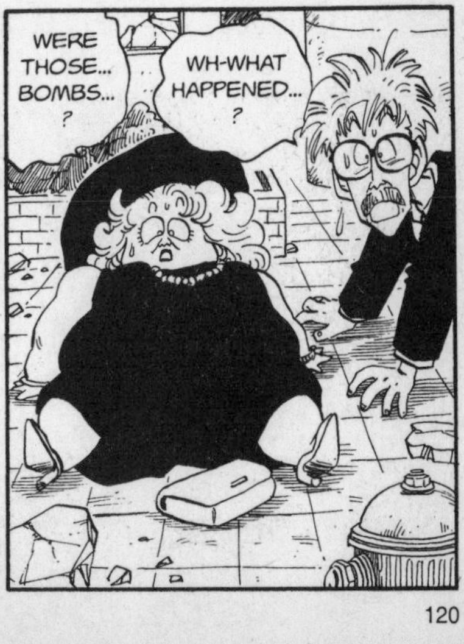
WH-WHAT HAPPENED...?
WERE THOSE... BOMBS...?

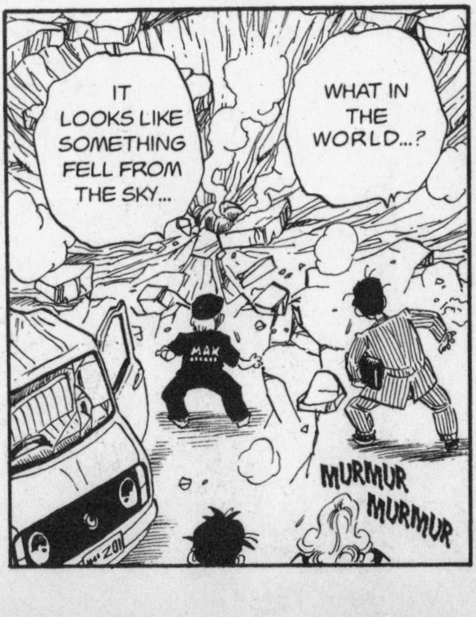
WHAT IN THE WORLD...?
IT LOOKS LIKE SOMETHING FELL FROM THE SKY...
MURMUR MURMUR

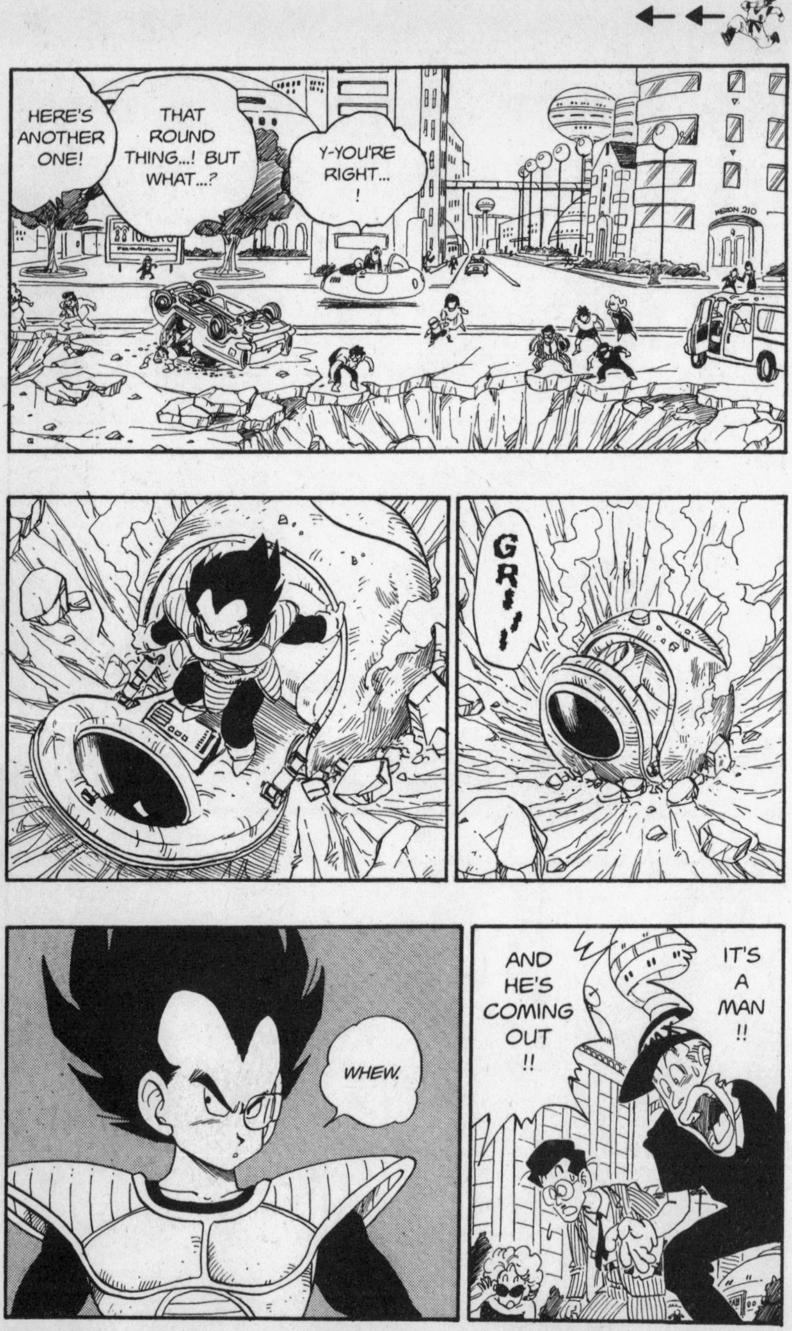
Y-YOU'RE RIGHT... !
THAT ROUND THING...! BUT WHAT...?
HERE'S ANOTHER ONE!
GR!!
IT'S A MAN !!
AND HE'S COMING OUT !!
WHEW.

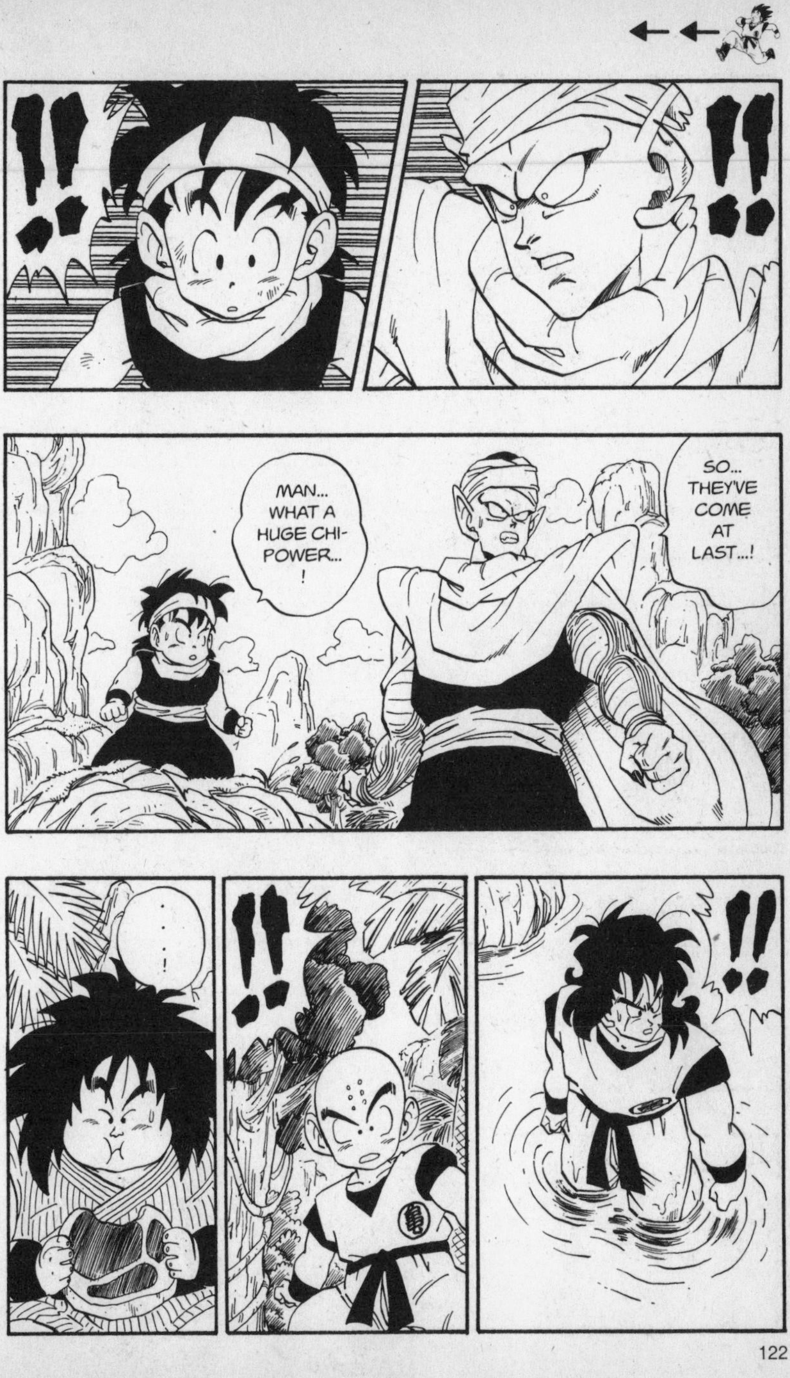
!!
!!
SO... THEY'VE COME AT LAST...!
MAN... WHAT A HUGE CHI-POWER...!
!!
!!
. . . !

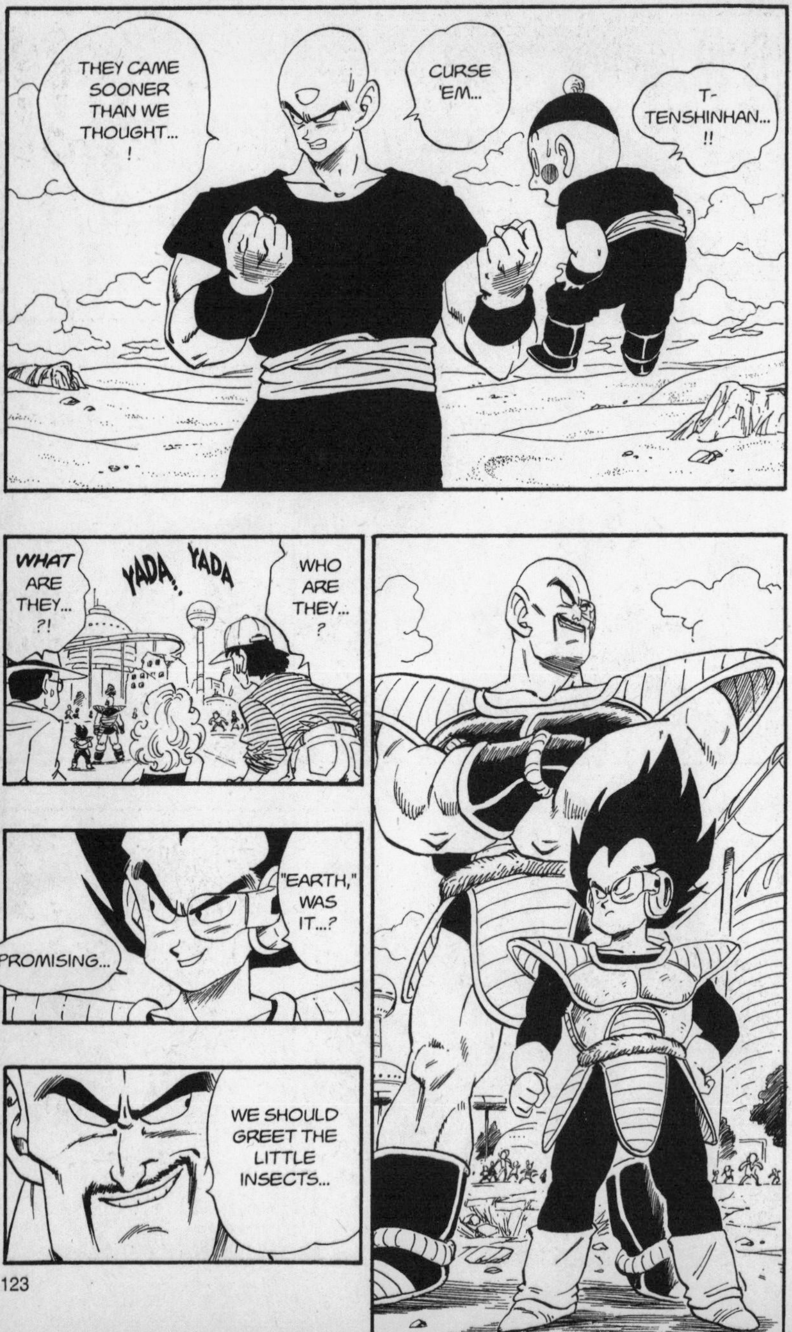
T-TENSHINHAN...!!
CURSE 'EM...
THEY CAME SOONER THAN WE THOUGHT...!
WHO ARE THEY...?
YADA YADA
WHAT ARE THEY...?!
"EARTH," WAS IT...?
PROMISING...
WE SHOULD GREET THE LITTLE INSECTS...

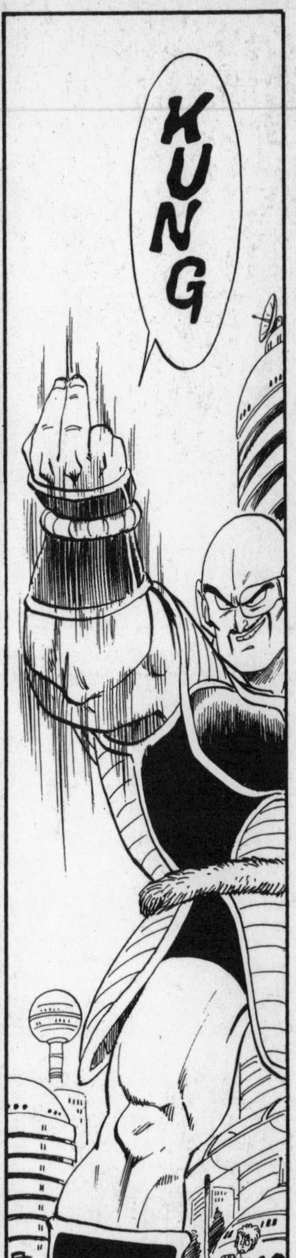
KUNG

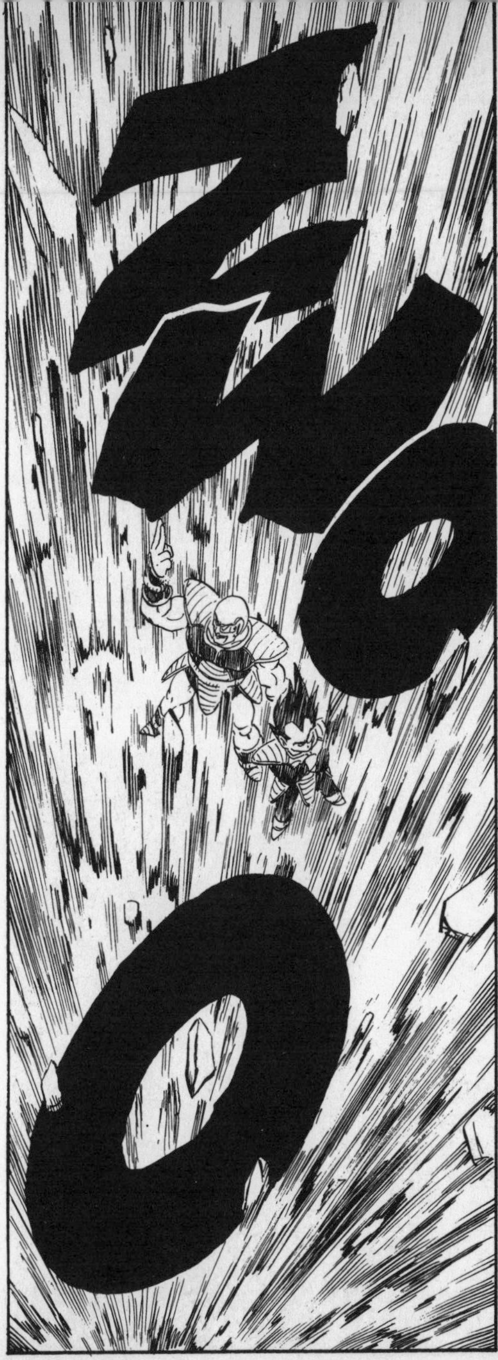

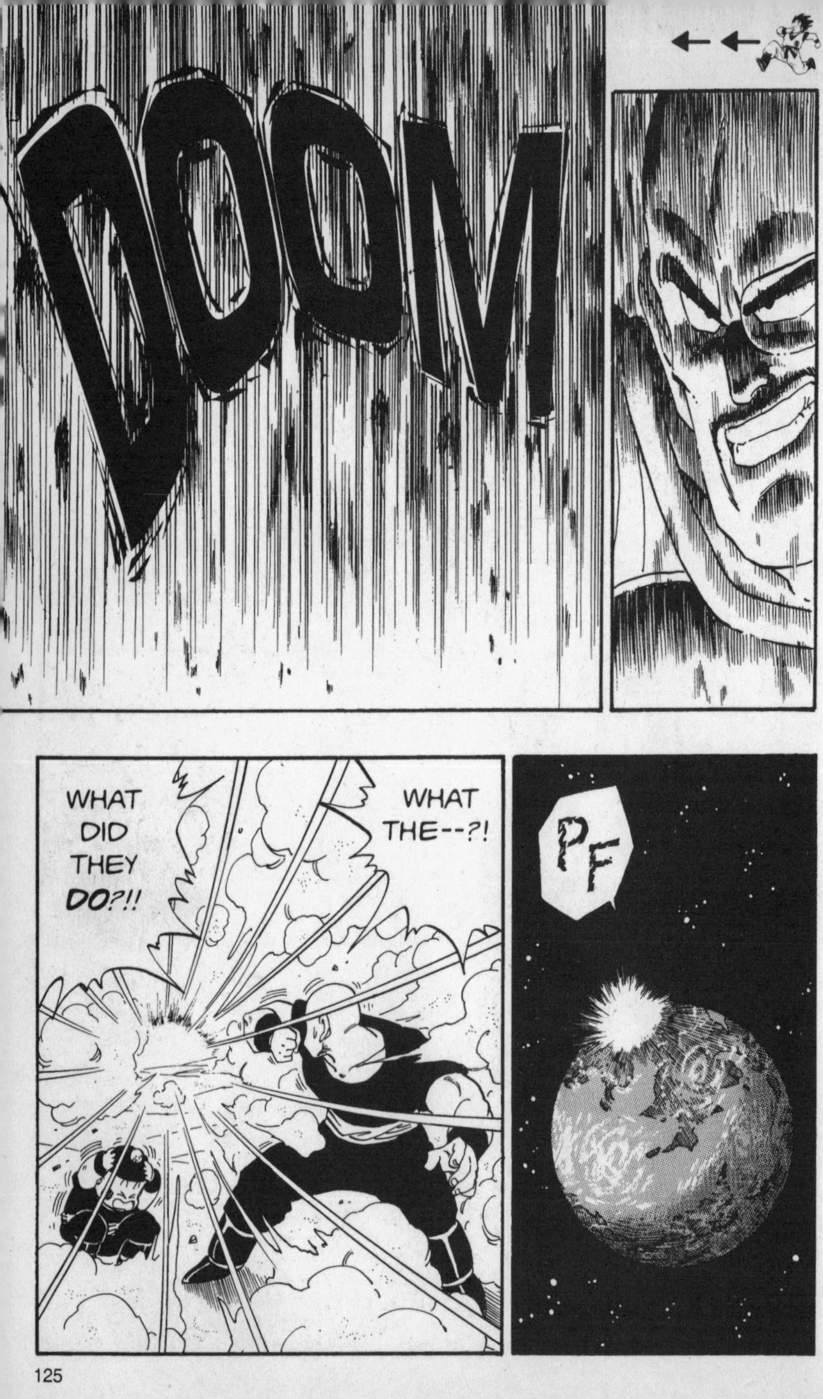
DOOM
PF
WHAT THE--?!
WHAT DID THEY *DO*?!!

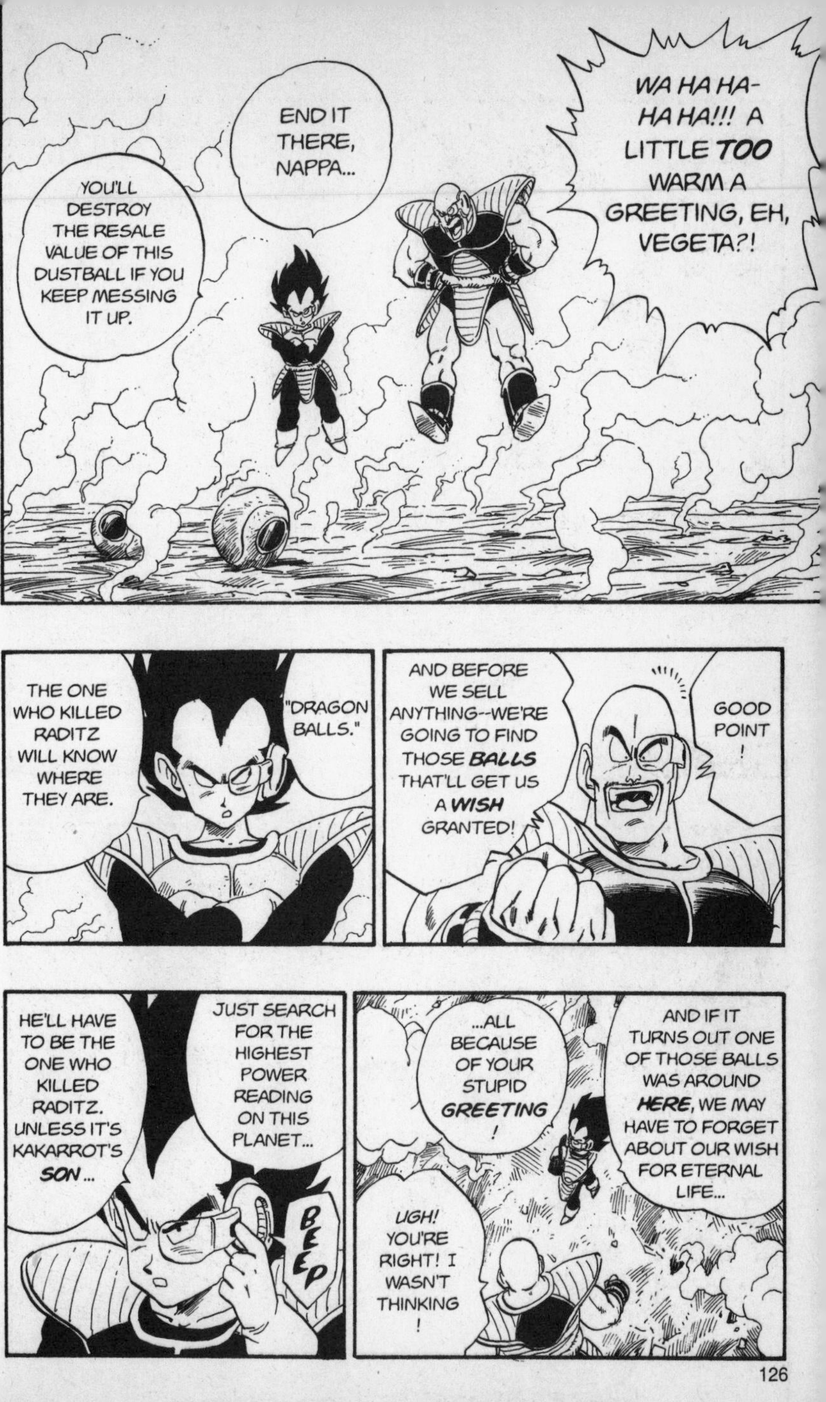
WA HA HA-HA HA!!! A LITTLE TOO WARM A GREETING, EH, VEGETA?!
END IT THERE, NAPPA...
YOU'LL DESTROY THE RESALE VALUE OF THIS DUSTBALL IF YOU KEEP MESSING IT UP.
AND BEFORE WE SELL ANYTHING--WE'RE GOING TO FIND THOSE BALLS THAT'LL GET US A WISH GRANTED!
GOOD POINT!
"DRAGON BALLS."
THE ONE WHO KILLED RADITZ WILL KNOW WHERE THEY ARE.
AND IF IT TURNS OUT ONE OF THOSE BALLS WAS AROUND HERE, WE MAY HAVE TO FORGET ABOUT OUR WISH FOR ETERNAL LIFE...
...ALL BECAUSE OF YOUR STUPID GREETING!
UGH! YOU'RE RIGHT! I WASN'T THINKING!
JUST SEARCH FOR THE HIGHEST POWER READING ON THIS PLANET...
HE'LL HAVE TO BE THE ONE WHO KILLED RADITZ. UNLESS IT'S KAKARROT'S SON...
BEEP

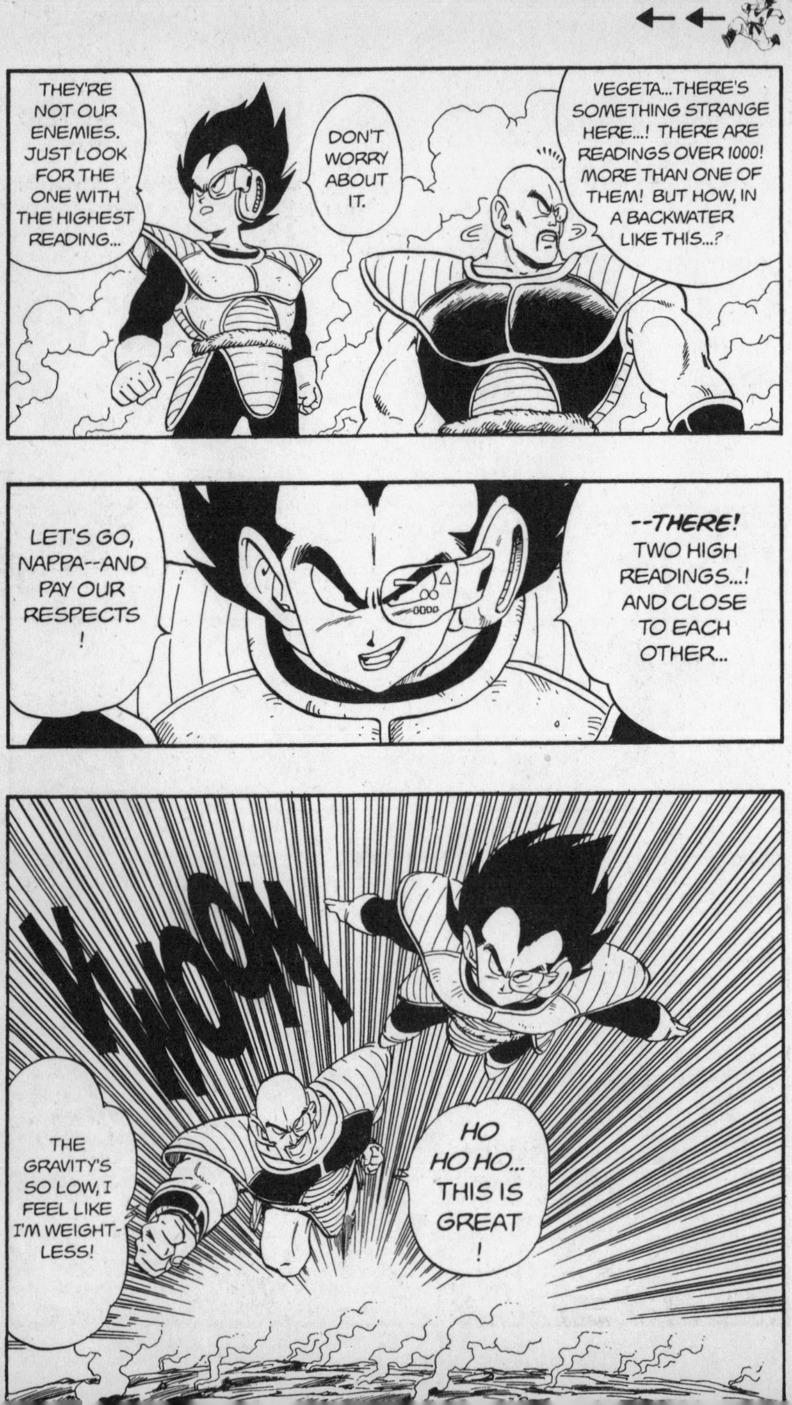
VEGETA...THERE'S SOMETHING STRANGE HERE...! THERE ARE READINGS OVER 1000! MORE THAN ONE OF THEM! BUT HOW, IN A BACKWATER LIKE THIS...?
DON'T WORRY ABOUT IT.
THEY'RE NOT OUR ENEMIES. JUST LOOK FOR THE ONE WITH THE HIGHEST READING...
--THERE! TWO HIGH READINGS...! AND CLOSE TO EACH OTHER...
LET'S GO, NAPPA--AND PAY OUR RESPECTS!
WHOOSH
HO HO HO... THIS IS GREAT!
THE GRAVITY'S SO LOW, I FEEL LIKE I'M WEIGHT-LESS!

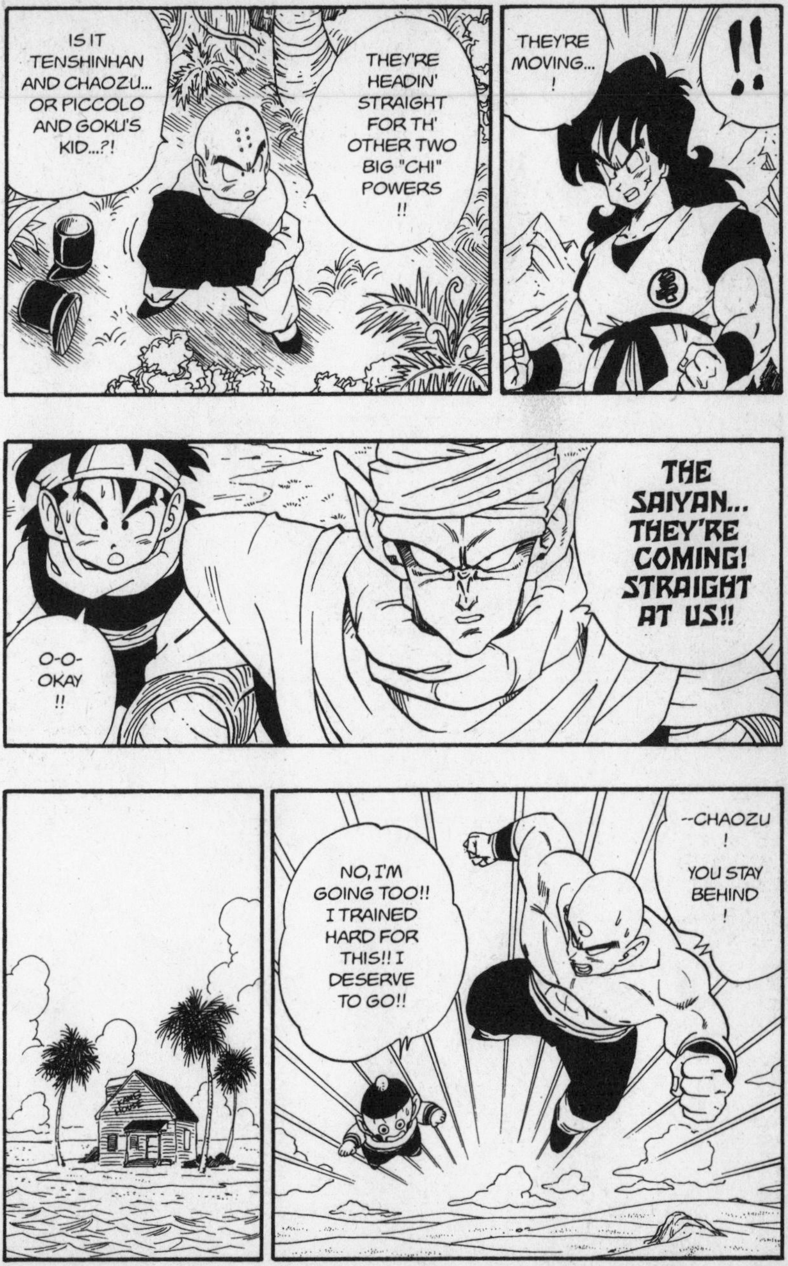
!!
THEY'RE MOVING... !
THEY'RE HEADIN' STRAIGHT FOR TH' OTHER TWO BIG "CHI" POWERS !!
IS IT TENSHINHAN AND CHAOZU... OR PICCOLO AND GOKU'S KID...?!
THE SAIYAN... THEY'RE COMING! STRAIGHT AT US!!
O-O-OKAY !!
--CHAOZU ! YOU STAY BEHIND !
NO, I'M GOING TOO!! I TRAINED HARD FOR THIS!! I DESERVE TO GO!!

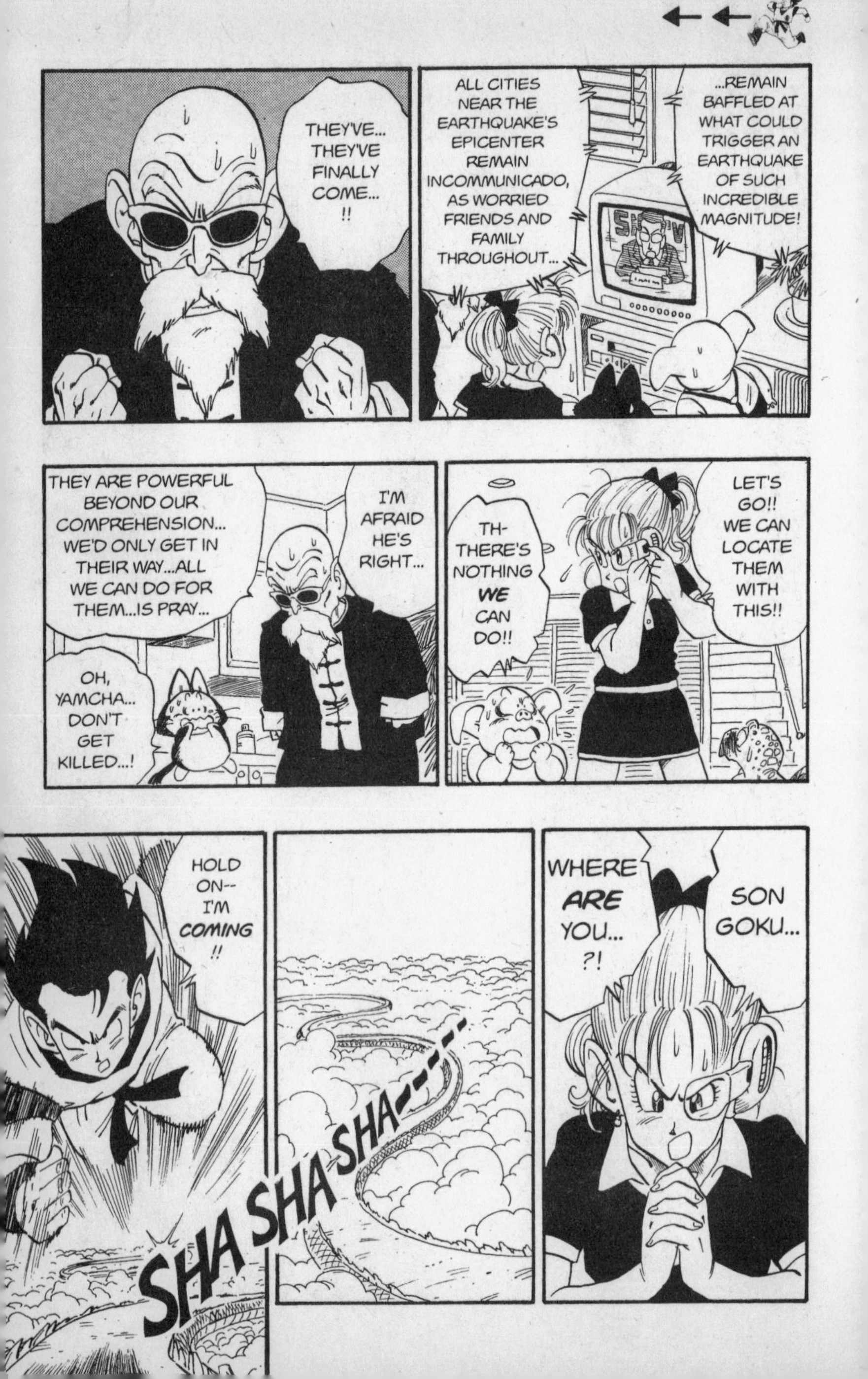
ALL CITIES NEAR THE EARTHQUAKE'S EPICENTER REMAIN INCOMMUNICADO, AS WORRIED FRIENDS AND FAMILY THROUGHOUT...
...REMAIN BAFFLED AT WHAT COULD TRIGGER AN EARTHQUAKE OF SUCH INCREDIBLE MAGNITUDE!
THEY'VE... THEY'VE FINALLY COME... !!
LET'S GO!! WE CAN LOCATE THEM WITH THIS!!
TH- THERE'S NOTHING *WE* CAN DO!!
I'M AFRAID HE'S RIGHT...
THEY ARE POWERFUL BEYOND OUR COMPREHENSION... WE'D ONLY GET IN THEIR WAY...ALL WE CAN DO FOR THEM...IS PRAY...
OH, YAMCHA... DON'T GET KILLED...!
SON GOKU...
WHERE *ARE* YOU... ?!
HOLD ON-- I'M *COMING* !!
SHA SHA SHA---

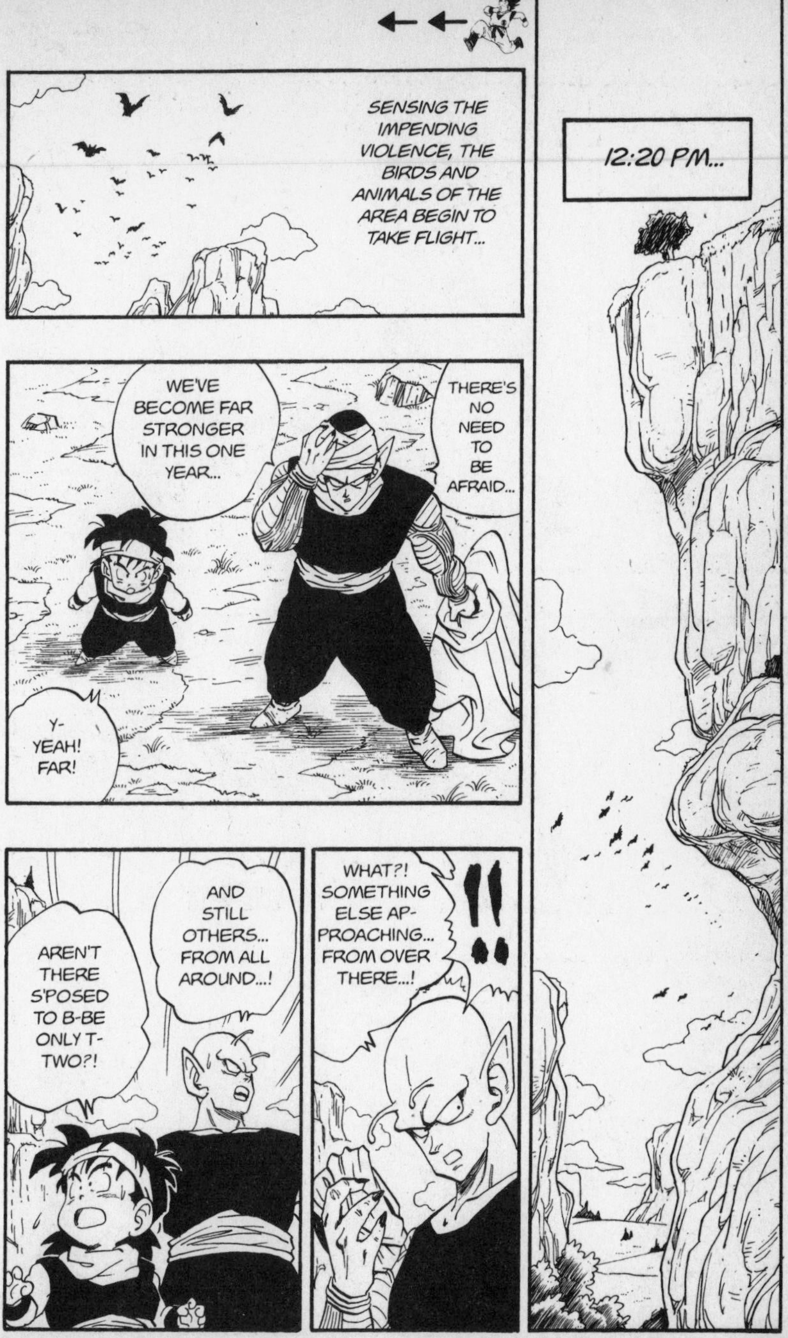

12:20 PM...
SENSING THE IMPENDING VIOLENCE, THE BIRDS AND ANIMALS OF THE AREA BEGIN TO TAKE FLIGHT...
THERE'S NO NEED TO BE AFRAID...
WE'VE BECOME FAR STRONGER IN THIS ONE YEAR...
Y-YEAH! FAR!
!!
WHAT?! SOMETHING ELSE AP-PROACHING... FROM OVER THERE...!
AND STILL OTHERS... FROM ALL AROUND...!
AREN'T THERE S'POSED TO B-BE ONLY T-TWO?!

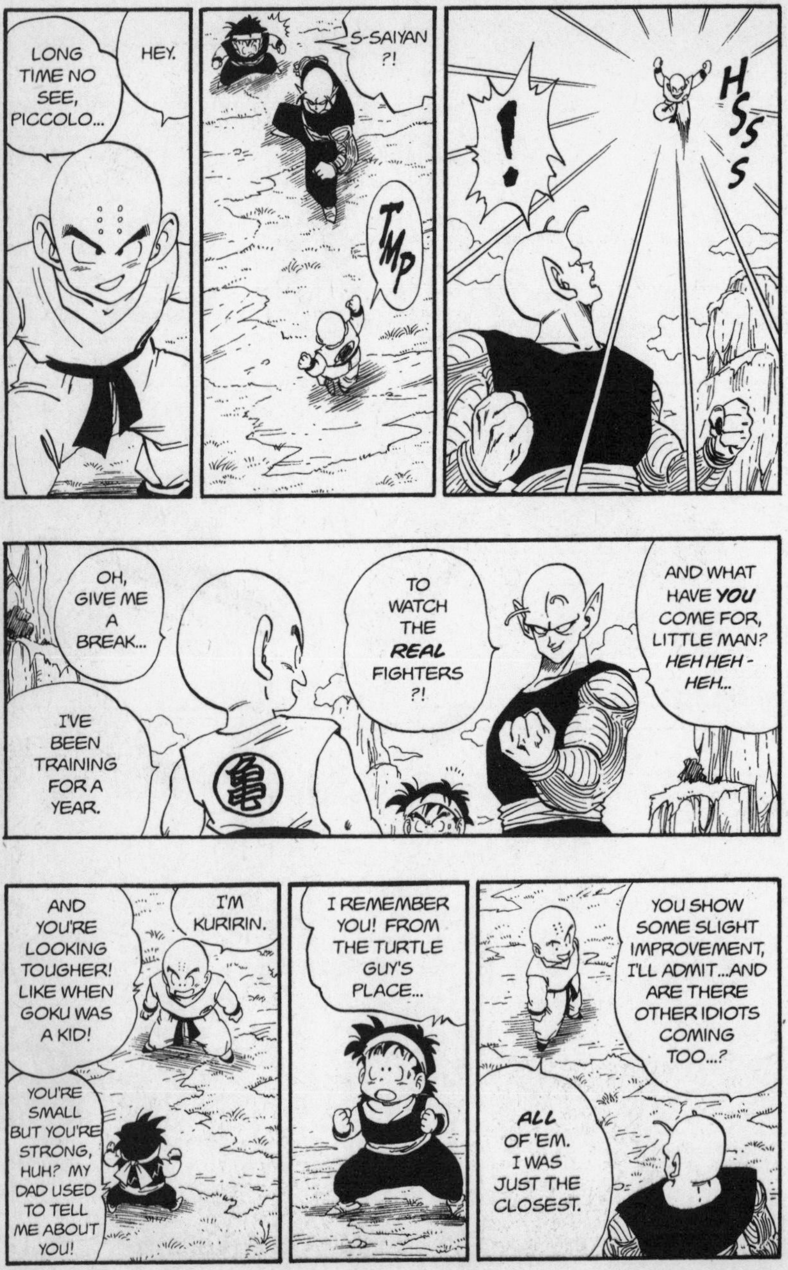
!
HSSS
S-SAIYAN ?!
TMP
HEY.
LONG TIME NO SEE, PICCOLO...
AND WHAT HAVE YOU COME FOR, LITTLE MAN? HEH HEH-HEH...
TO WATCH THE REAL FIGHTERS ?!
OH, GIVE ME A BREAK...
I'VE BEEN TRAINING FOR A YEAR.
YOU SHOW SOME SLIGHT IMPROVEMENT, I'LL ADMIT...AND ARE THERE OTHER IDIOTS COMING TOO...?
ALL OF 'EM. I WAS JUST THE CLOSEST.
I REMEMBER YOU! FROM THE TURTLE GUY'S PLACE...
I'M KURIRIN.
AND YOU'RE LOOKING TOUGHER! LIKE WHEN GOKU WAS A KID!
YOU'RE SMALL BUT YOU'RE STRONG, HUH? MY DAD USED TO TELL ME ABOUT YOU!

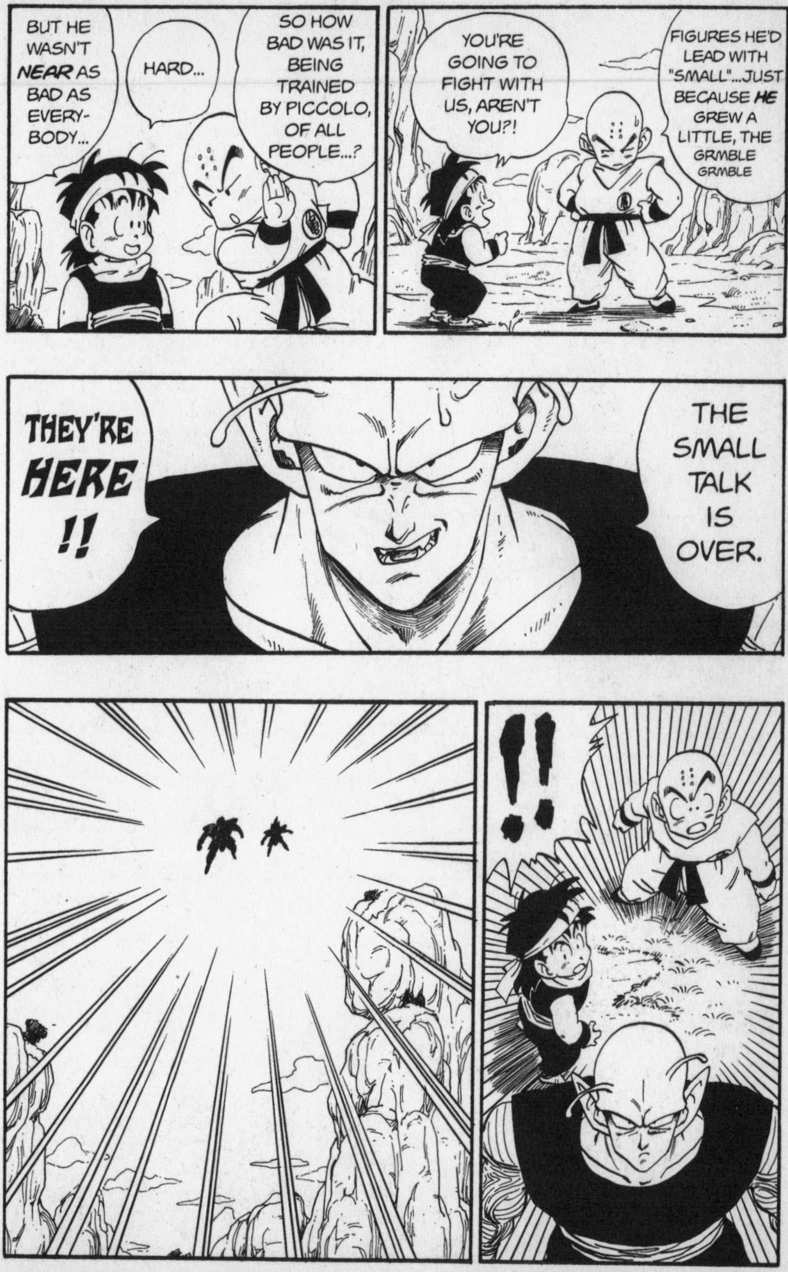

FIGURES HE'D LEAD WITH "SMALL"...JUST BECAUSE HE GREW A LITTLE, THE GRMBLE GRMBLE
YOU'RE GOING TO FIGHT WITH US, AREN'T YOU?!
SO HOW BAD WAS IT, BEING TRAINED BY PICCOLO, OF ALL PEOPLE...?
HARD...
BUT HE WASN'T NEAR AS BAD AS EVERY-BODY...
THE SMALL TALK IS OVER.
THEY'RE HERE!!
!!

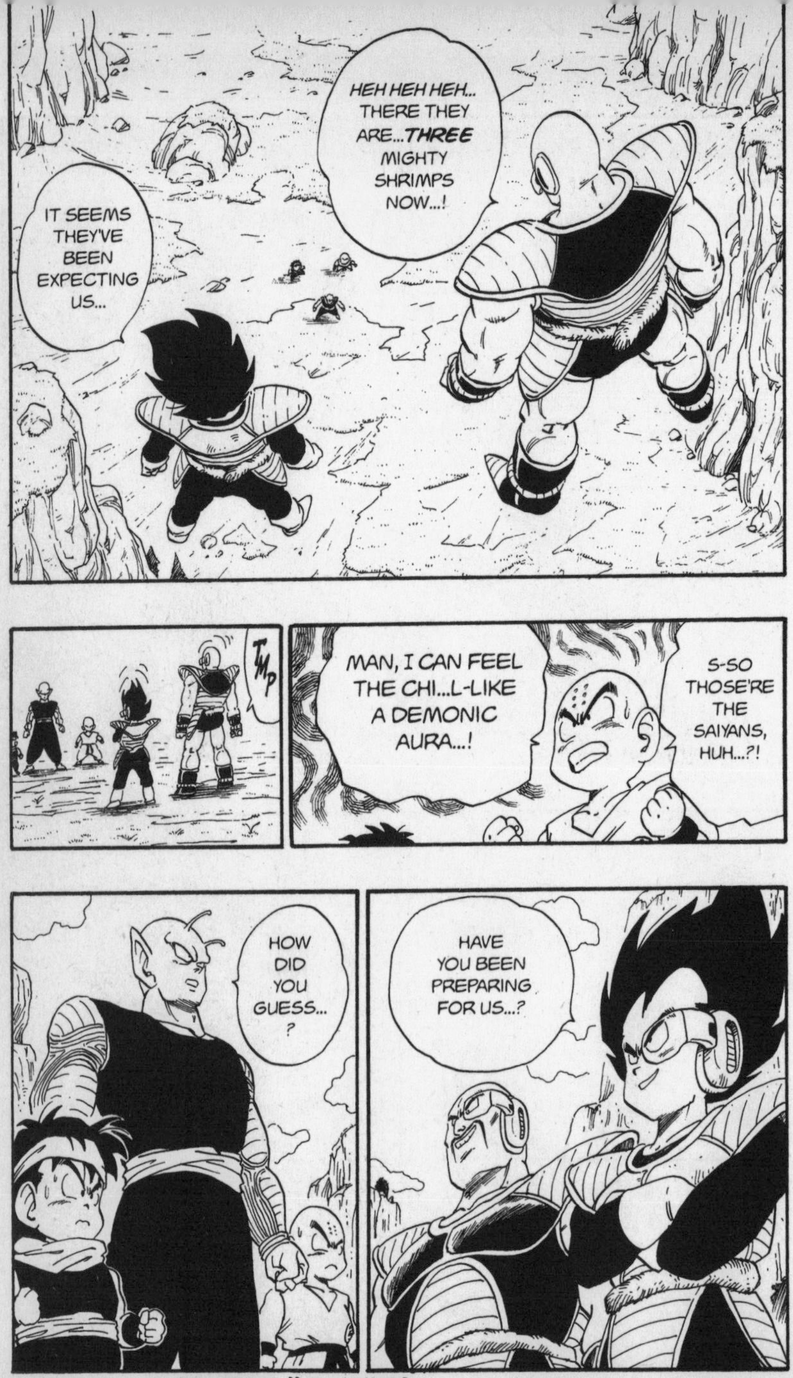
HEH HEH HEH... THERE THEY ARE...**THREE** MIGHTY SHRIMPS NOW...!
IT SEEMS THEY'VE BEEN EXPECTING US...
S-SO THOSE'RE THE SAIYANS, HUH...?!
MAN, I CAN FEEL THE CHI...L-LIKE A DEMONIC AURA...!
TMP
HAVE YOU BEEN PREPARING FOR US...?
HOW DID YOU GUESS...?

NEXT: THE BIG "CHI"S!

DBZ:20 • Let the Games Begin!

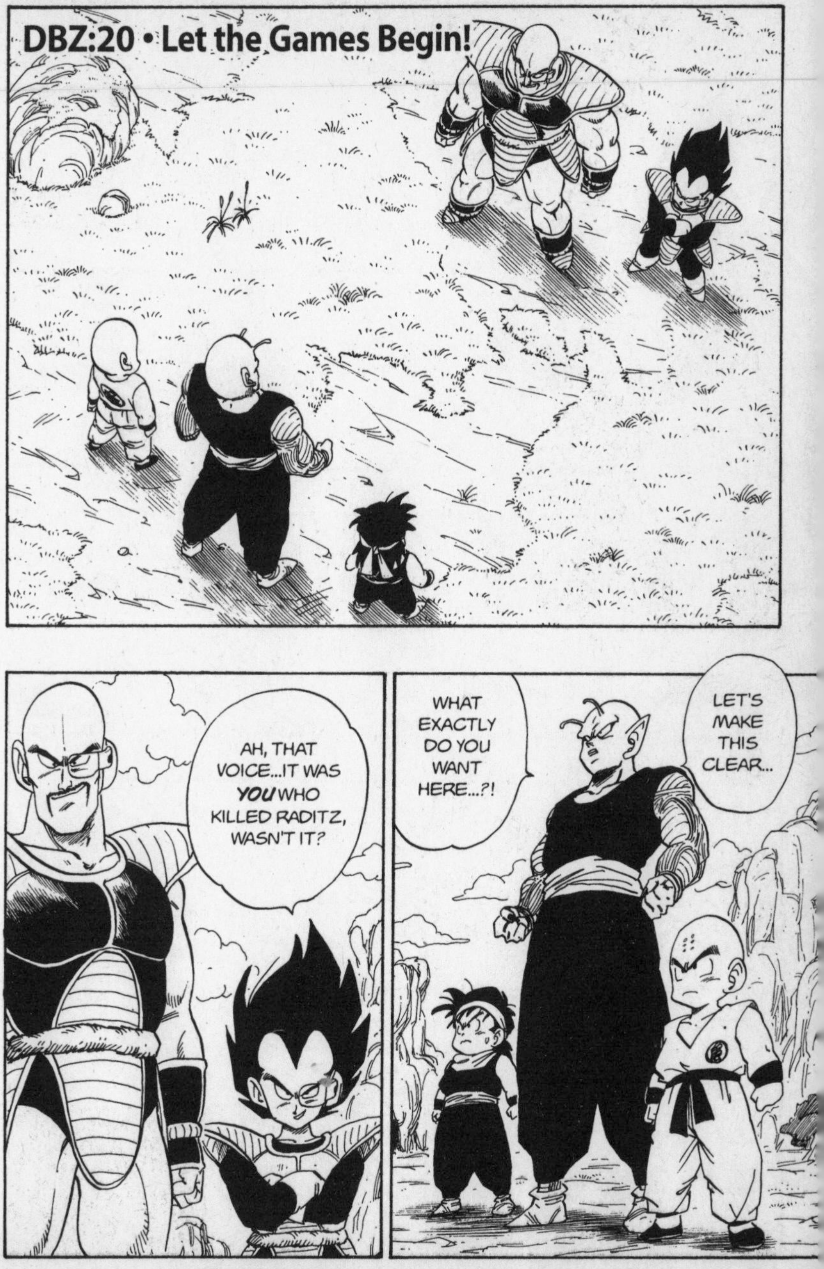
LET'S MAKE THIS CLEAR...
WHAT EXACTLY DO YOU WANT HERE...?!
AH, THAT VOICE...IT WAS ***YOU*** WHO KILLED RADITZ, WASN'T IT?

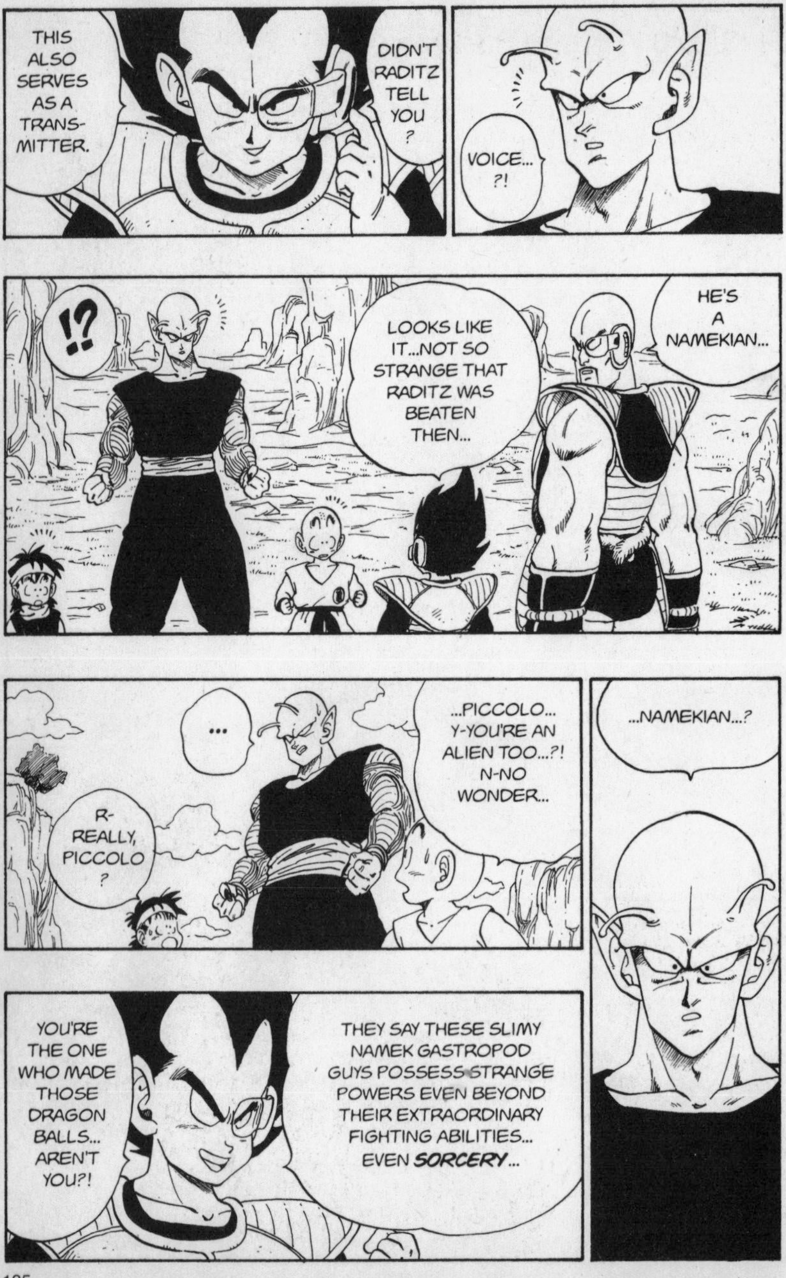
VOICE... ?!
DIDN'T RADITZ TELL YOU ?
THIS ALSO SERVES AS A TRANS-MITTER.
HE'S A NAMEKIAN...
LOOKS LIKE IT...NOT SO STRANGE THAT RADITZ WAS BEATEN THEN...
!?
...NAMEKIAN...?
...PICCOLO... Y-YOU'RE AN ALIEN TOO...?! N-NO WONDER...
...
R-REALLY, PICCOLO ?
THEY SAY THESE SLIMY NAMEK GASTROPOD GUYS POSSESS STRANGE POWERS EVEN BEYOND THEIR EXTRAORDINARY FIGHTING ABILITIES... EVEN SORCERY...
YOU'RE THE ONE WHO MADE THOSE DRAGON BALLS... AREN'T YOU?!

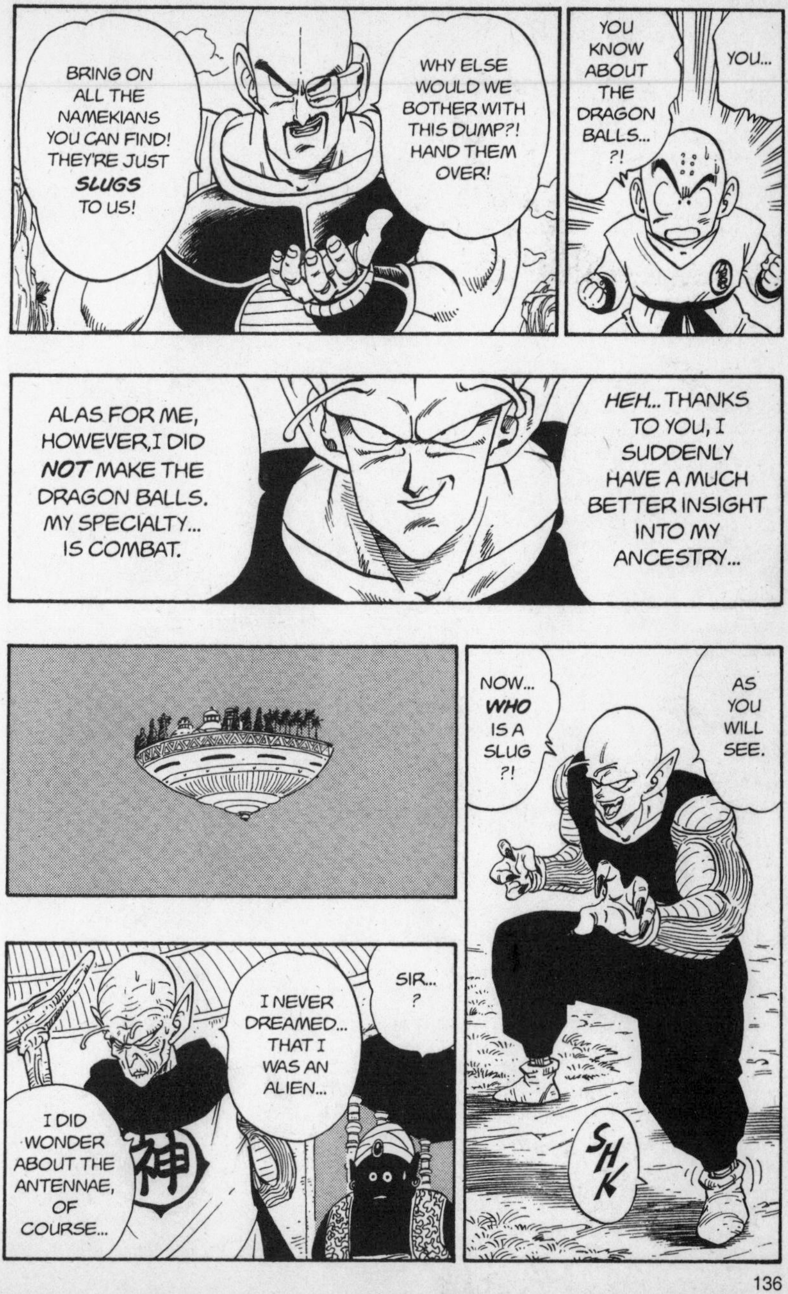
YOU...
YOU KNOW ABOUT THE DRAGON BALLS...?!
WHY ELSE WOULD WE BOTHER WITH THIS DUMP?! HAND THEM OVER!
BRING ON ALL THE NAMEKIANS YOU CAN FIND! THEY'RE JUST **SLUGS** TO US!
HEH... THANKS TO YOU, I SUDDENLY HAVE A MUCH BETTER INSIGHT INTO MY ANCESTRY...
ALAS FOR ME, HOWEVER, I DID ***NOT*** MAKE THE DRAGON BALLS. MY SPECIALTY... IS COMBAT.
AS YOU WILL SEE.
NOW... ***WHO*** IS A SLUG ?!
SHK
SIR... ?
I NEVER DREAMED... THAT I WAS AN ALIEN...
I DID WONDER ABOUT THE ANTENNAE, OF COURSE...

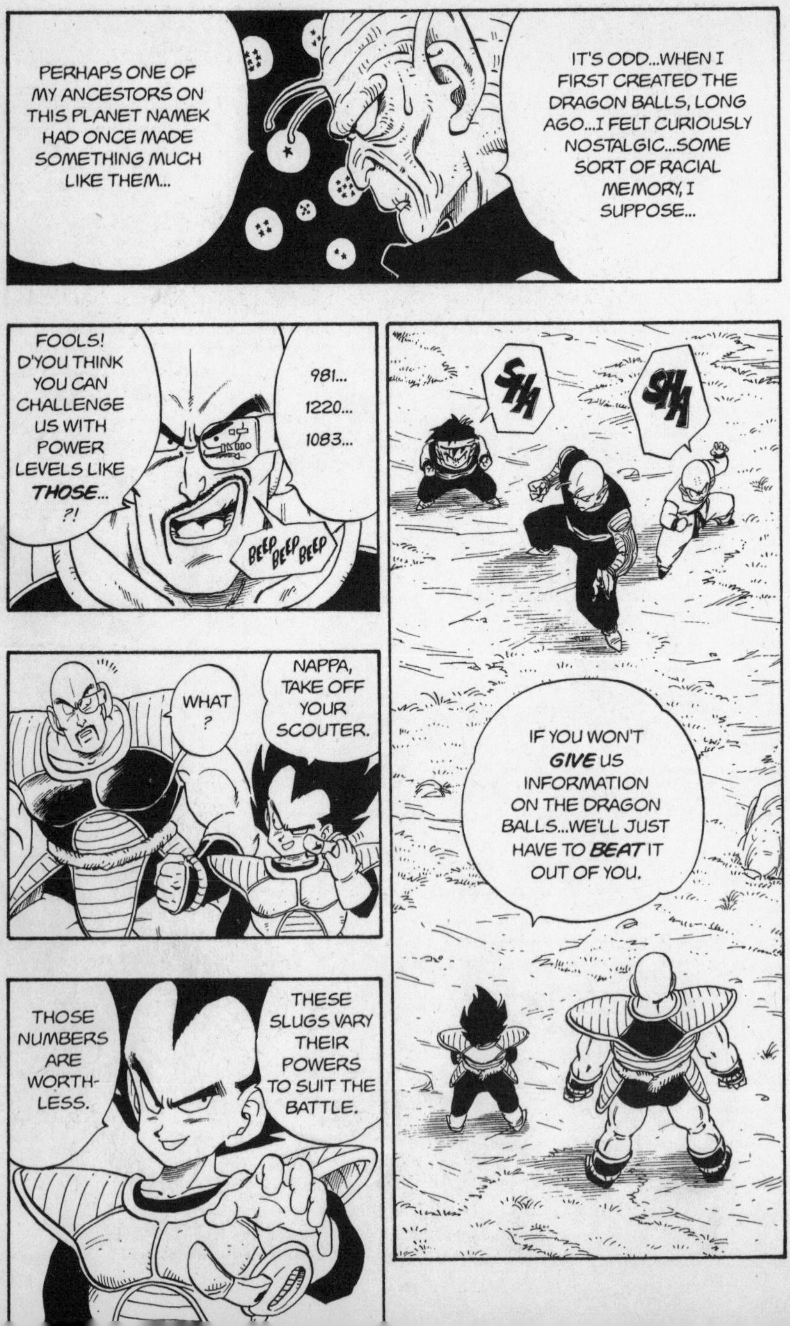
IT'S ODD...WHEN I FIRST CREATED THE DRAGON BALLS, LONG AGO...I FELT CURIOUSLY NOSTALGIC...SOME SORT OF RACIAL MEMORY, I SUPPOSE...
PERHAPS ONE OF MY ANCESTORS ON THIS PLANET NAMEK HAD ONCE MADE SOMETHING MUCH LIKE THEM...
SHA
SHA
IF YOU WON'T GIVE US INFORMATION ON THE DRAGON BALLS...WE'LL JUST HAVE TO BEAT IT OUT OF YOU.
981... 1220... 1083...
FOOLS! D'YOU THINK YOU CAN CHALLENGE US WITH POWER LEVELS LIKE THOSE... ?!
BEEP BEEP BEEP
NAPPA, TAKE OFF YOUR SCOUTER.
WHAT ?
THESE SLUGS VARY THEIR POWERS TO SUIT THE BATTLE.
THOSE NUMBERS ARE WORTH-LESS.

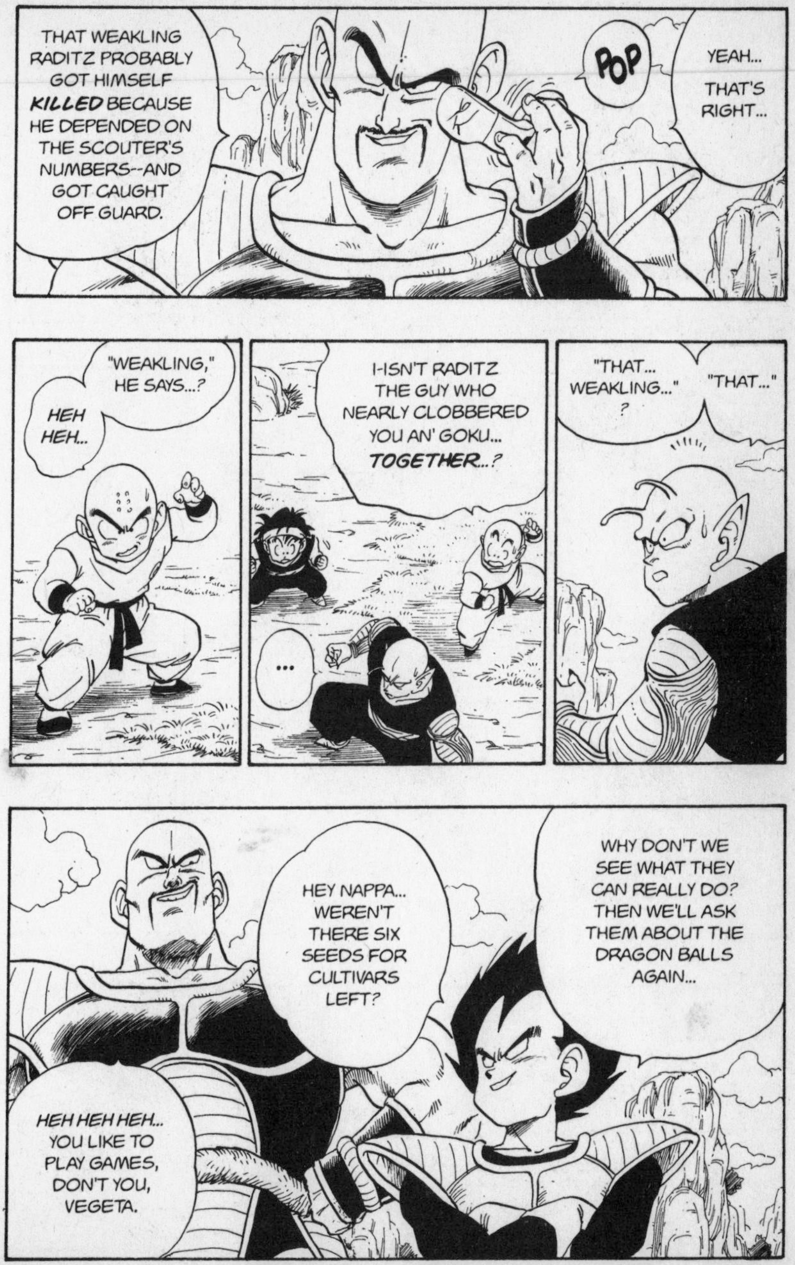
YEAH... THAT'S RIGHT...
POP
THAT WEAKLING RADITZ PROBABLY GOT HIMSELF KILLED BECAUSE HE DEPENDED ON THE SCOUTER'S NUMBERS--AND GOT CAUGHT OFF GUARD.
"THAT..."
"THAT... WEAKLING..." ?
I-ISN'T RADITZ THE GUY WHO NEARLY CLOBBERED YOU AN' GOKU... TOGETHER...?
...
"WEAKLING," HE SAYS...?
HEH HEH...
WHY DON'T WE SEE WHAT THEY CAN REALLY DO? THEN WE'LL ASK THEM ABOUT THE DRAGON BALLS AGAIN...
HEY NAPPA... WEREN'T THERE SIX SEEDS FOR CULTIVARS LEFT?
HEH HEH HEH... YOU LIKE TO PLAY GAMES, DON'T YOU, VEGETA.

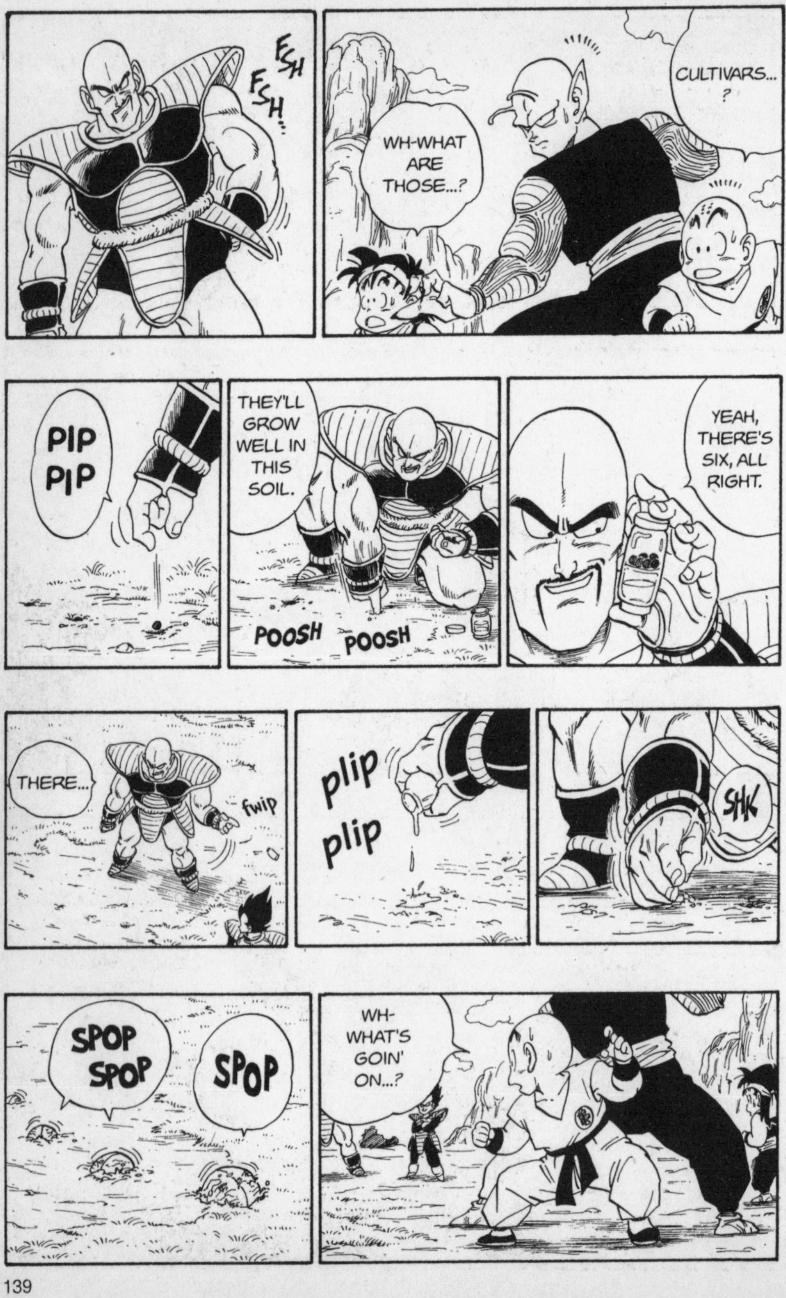
CULTIVARS...?
WH-WHAT ARE THOSE...?
FSH FSH
YEAH, THERE'S SIX, ALL RIGHT.
THEY'LL GROW WELL IN THIS SOIL.
POOSH POOSH
PIP PIP
SHK
plip plip
THERE...
fwip
WH- WHAT'S GOIN' ON...?
SPOP
SPOP SPOP

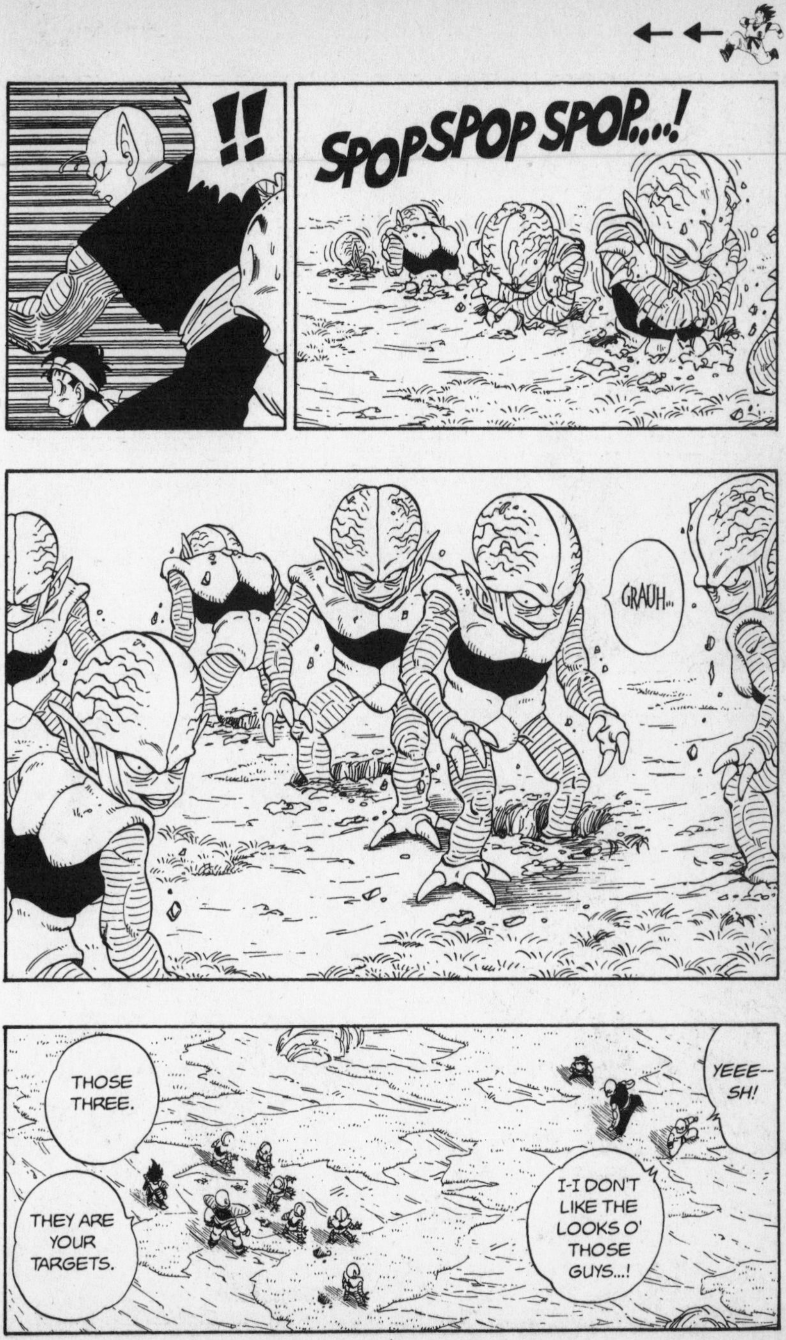
SPOP SPOP SPOP...!
!!
GRAUH...
YEEE--SH!
I-I DON'T LIKE THE LOOKS O' THOSE GUYS...!
THOSE THREE.
THEY ARE YOUR TARGETS.

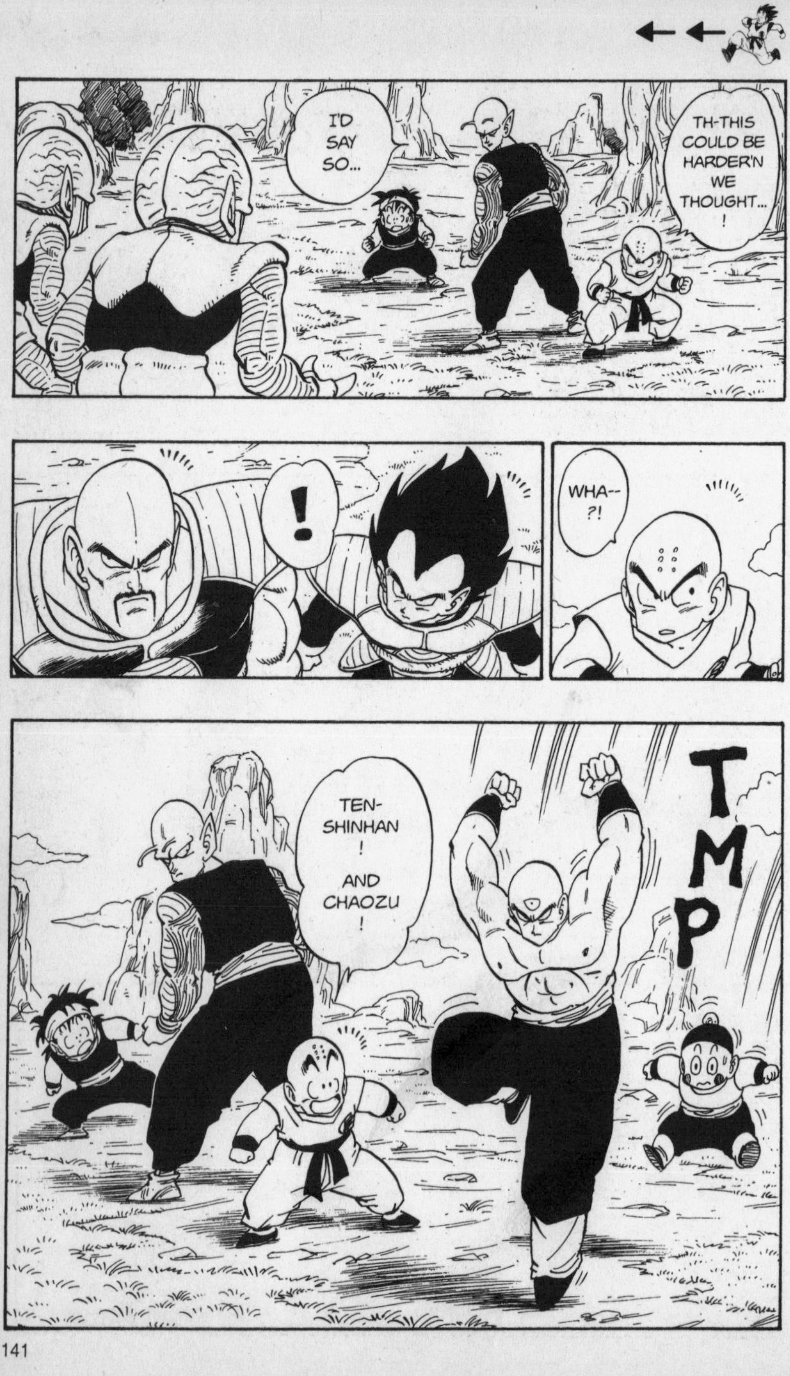
TH-THIS COULD BE HARDER'N WE THOUGHT...!
I'D SAY SO...
WHA--?!
!
TMP
TEN-SHINHAN! AND CHAOZU!

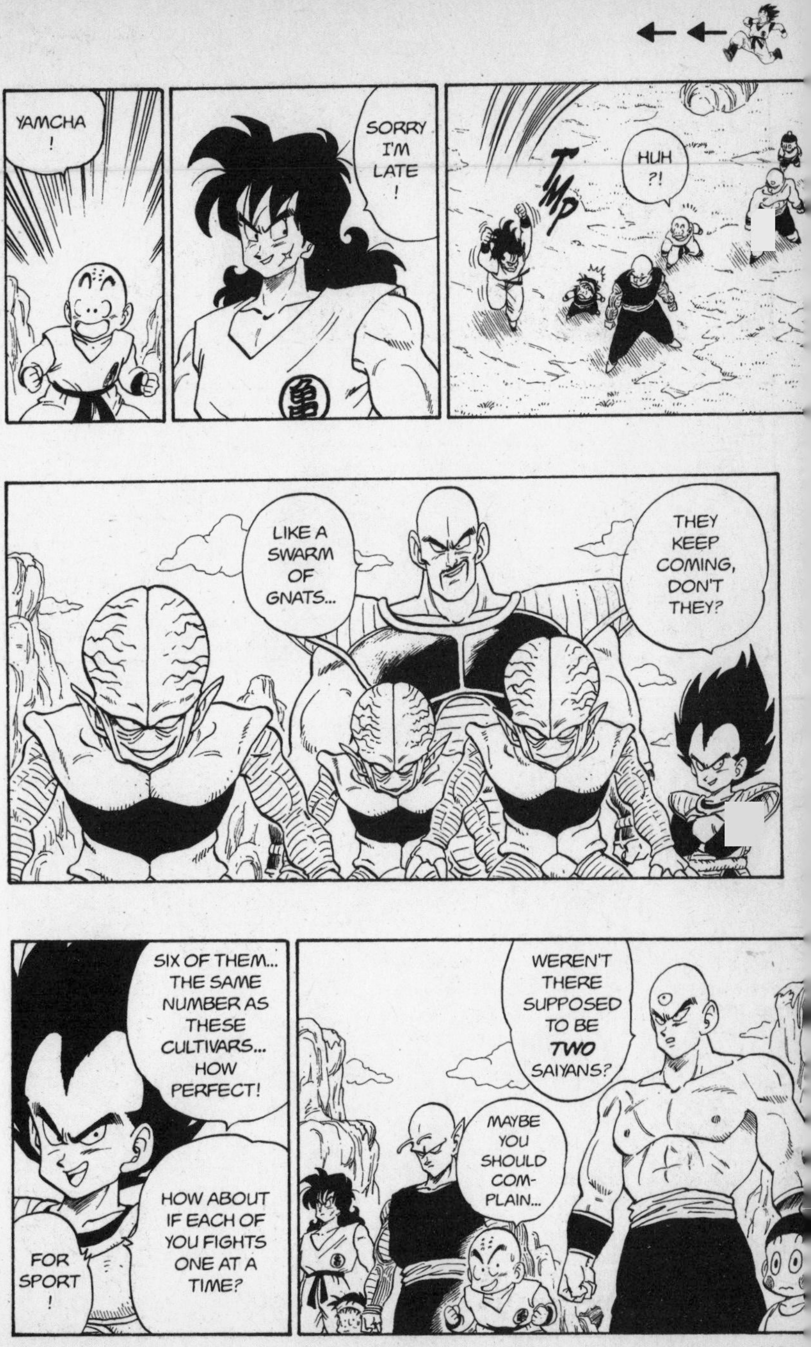
TMP
HUH ?!
SORRY I'M LATE !
YAMCHA !
THEY KEEP COMING, DON'T THEY?
LIKE A SWARM OF GNATS...
WEREN'T THERE SUPPOSED TO BE **TWO** SAIYANS?
MAYBE YOU SHOULD COM-PLAIN...
SIX OF THEM... THE SAME NUMBER AS THESE CULTIVARS... HOW PERFECT!
HOW ABOUT IF EACH OF YOU FIGHTS ONE AT A TIME?
FOR SPORT !

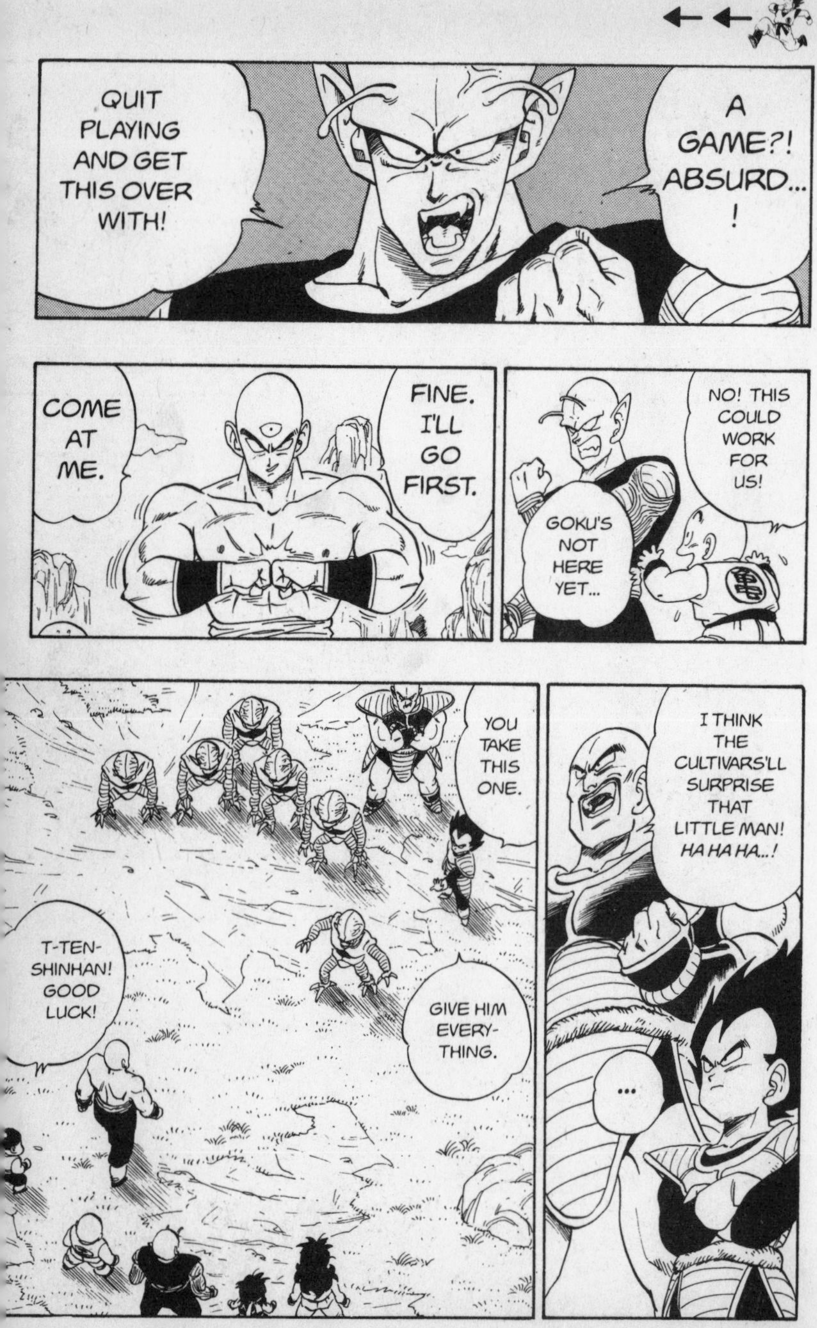

A GAME?! ABSURD... !
QUIT PLAYING AND GET THIS OVER WITH!
NO! THIS COULD WORK FOR US!
GOKU'S NOT HERE YET...
FINE. I'LL GO FIRST.
COME AT ME.
I THINK THE CULTIVARS'LL SURPRISE THAT LITTLE MAN! *HA HA HA...!*
...
YOU TAKE THIS ONE.
GIVE HIM EVERY-THING.
T-TEN-SHINHAN! GOOD LUCK!

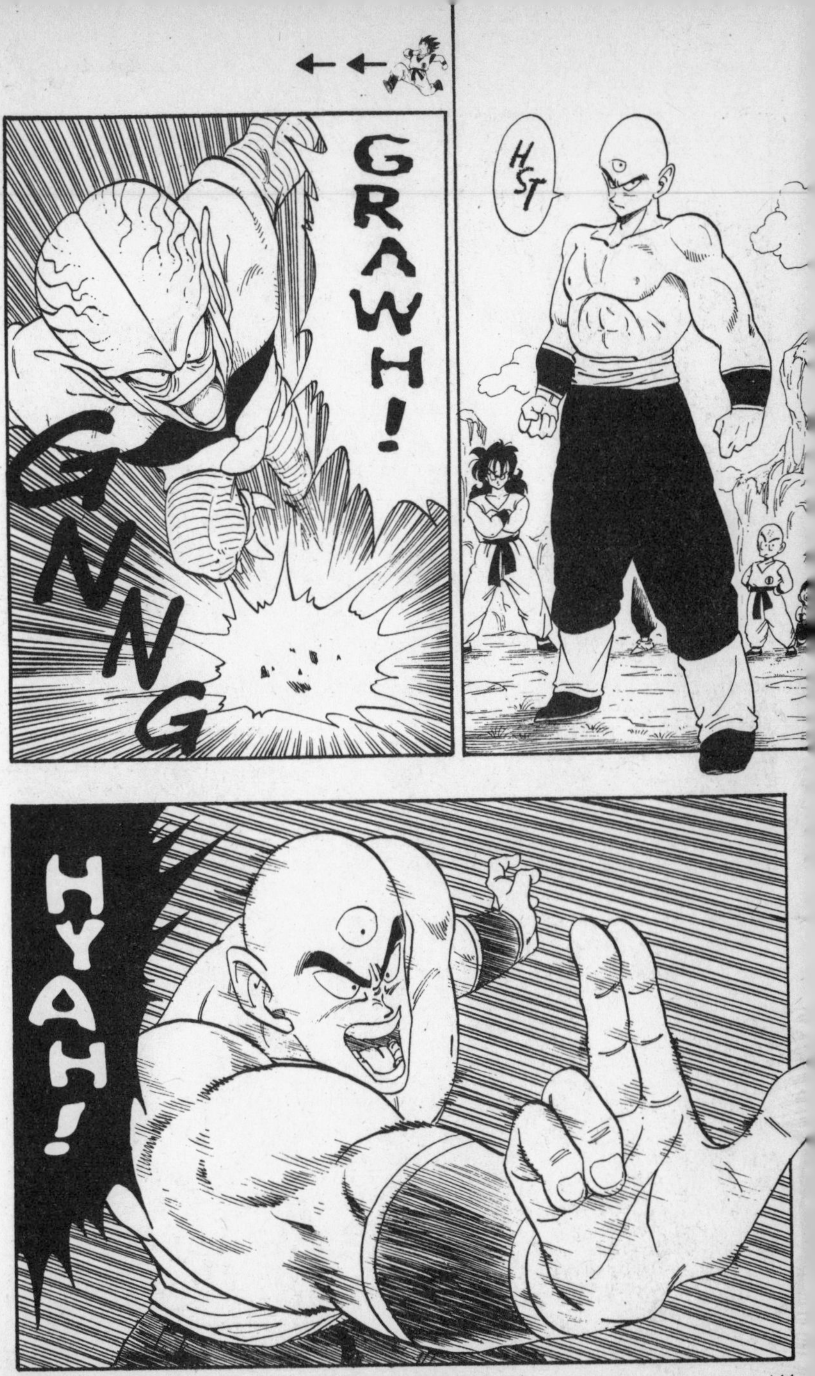
HST
GRAWH!
GNNNG
HYAH!

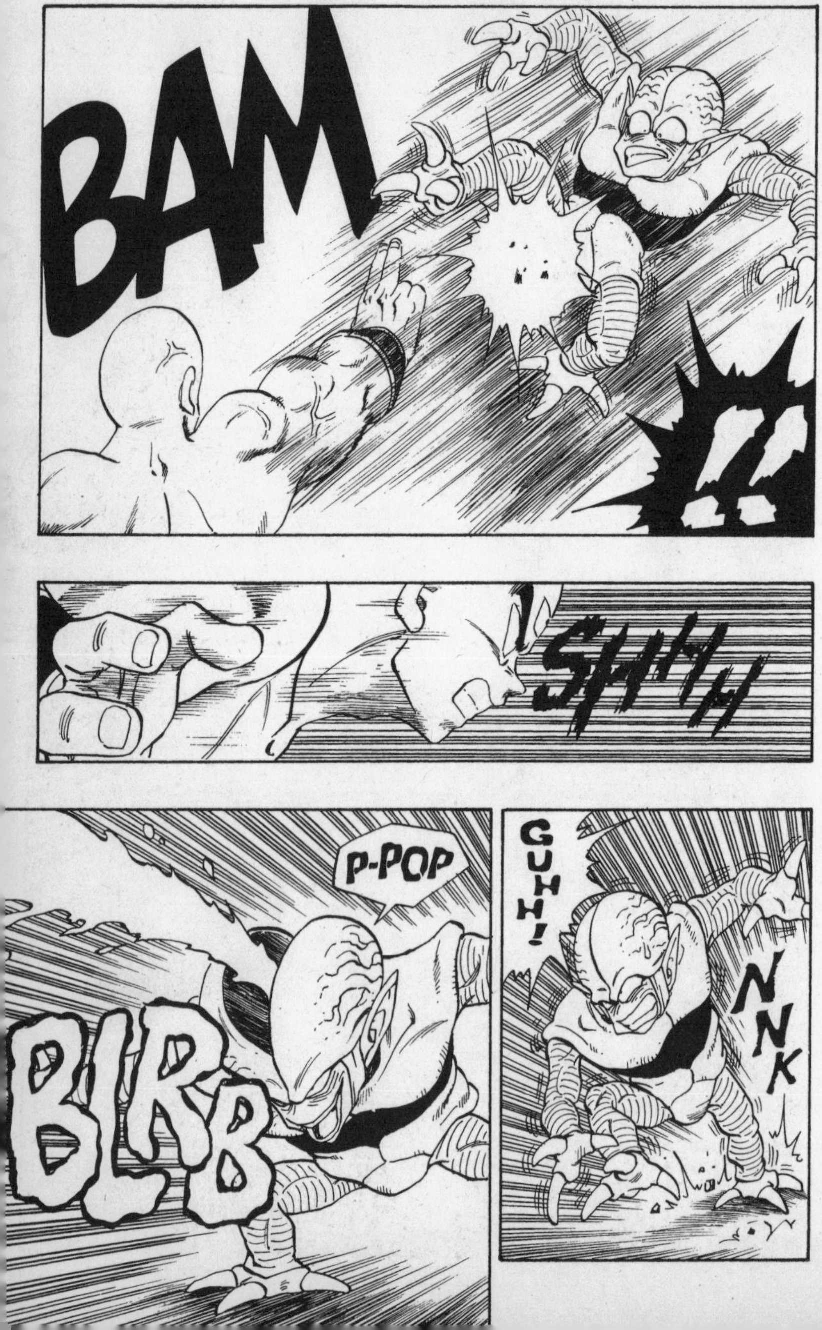
BAM
!!
SHHHH
GUHH!
NNK
P-POP
BLRB

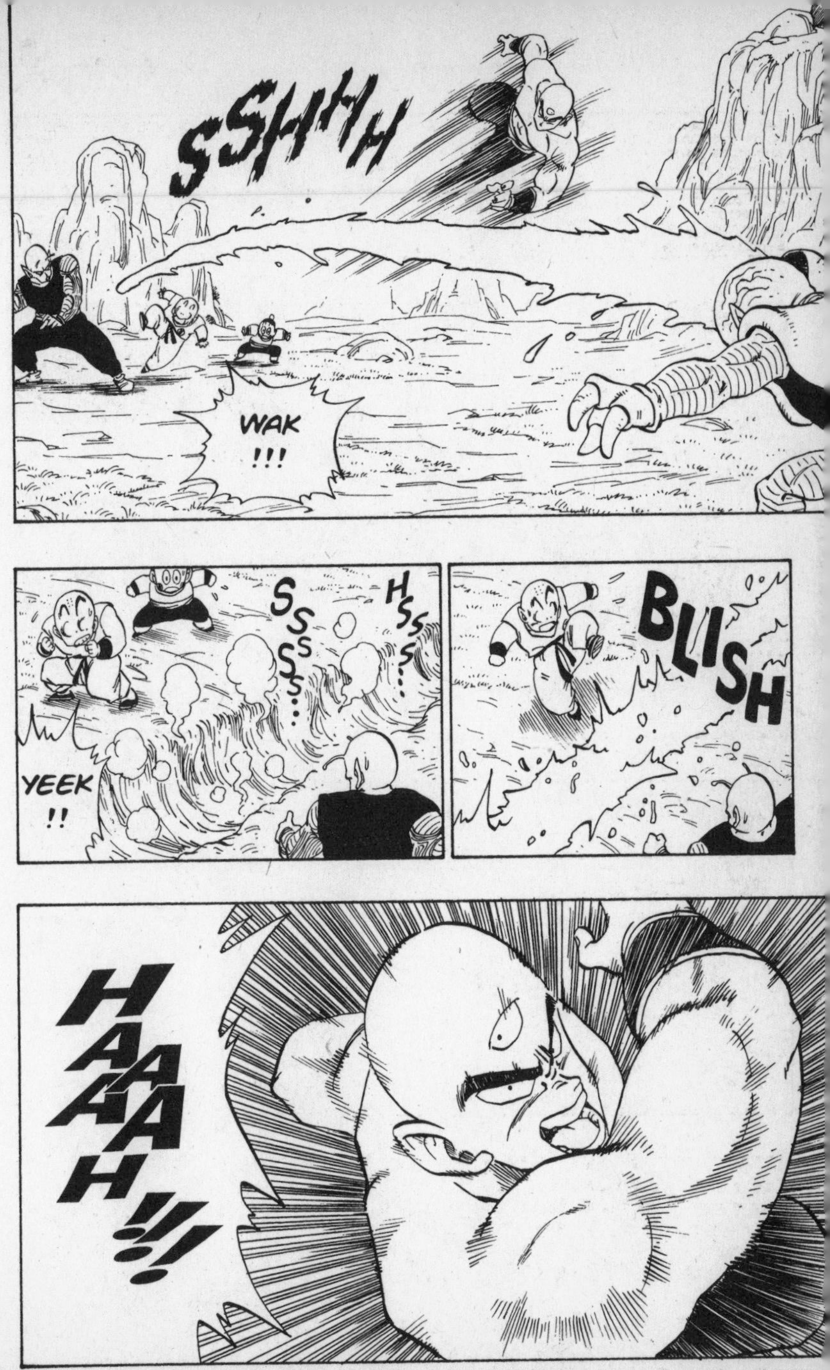
SSHHH
WAK !!!
BLISH
SSSSS...
HSSS...
YEEK !!
HAAAAH!!!

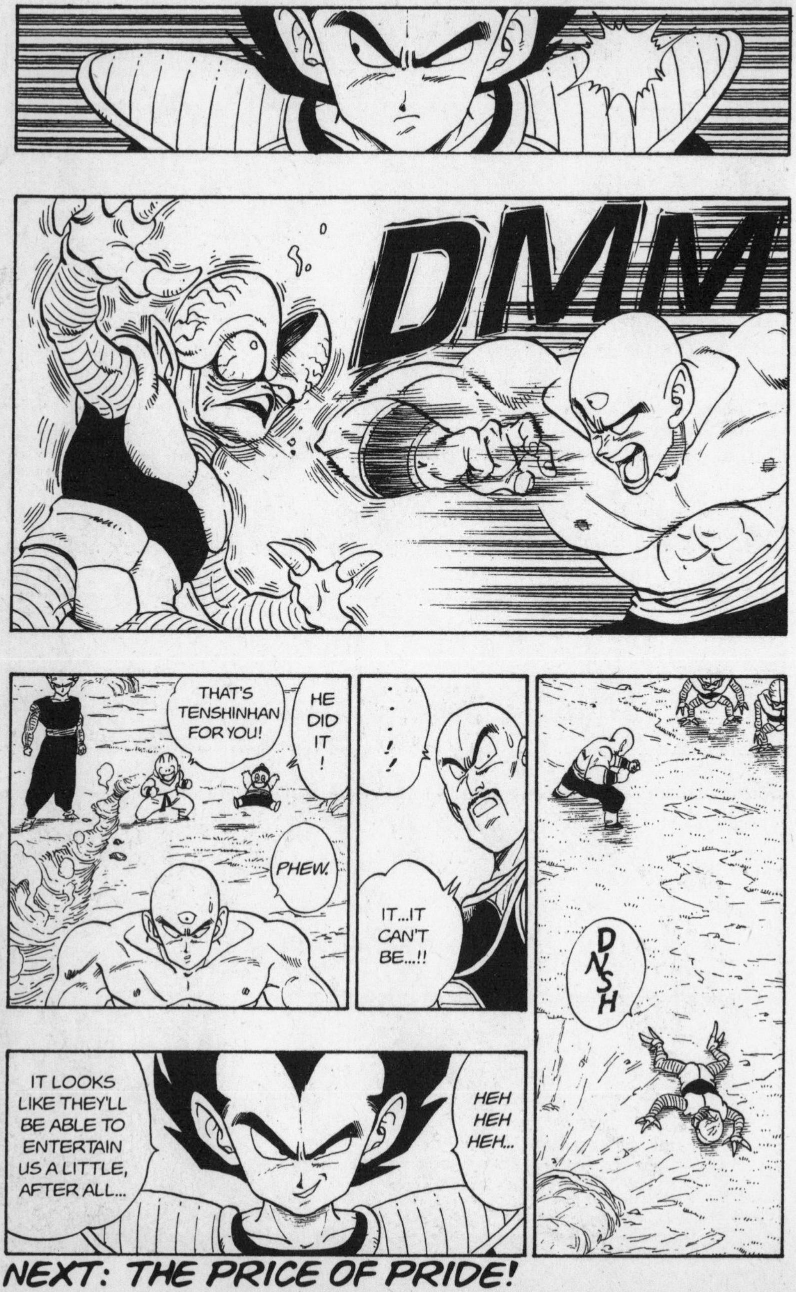
DMM
DNSH
. . . ! !
IT...IT CAN'T BE...!!
HE DID IT!
THAT'S TENSHINHAN FOR YOU!
PHEW.
HEH HEH HEH...
IT LOOKS LIKE THEY'LL BE ABLE TO ENTERTAIN US A LITTLE, AFTER ALL...

NEXT: THE PRICE OF PRIDE!

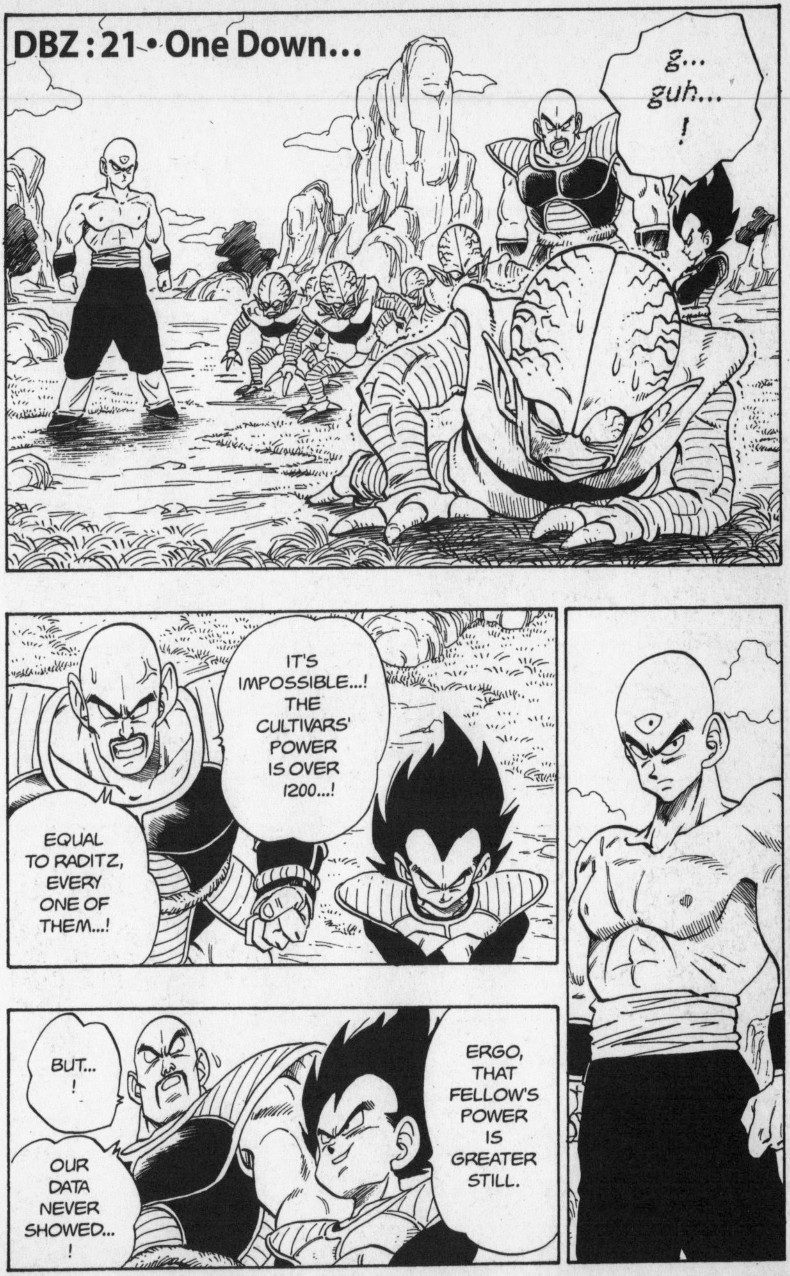
DBZ : 21 • One Down...
g... guh... !
IT'S IMPOSSIBLE...! THE CULTIVARS' POWER IS OVER 1200...!
EQUAL TO RADITZ, EVERY ONE OF THEM...!
ERGO, THAT FELLOW'S POWER IS GREATER STILL.
BUT... !
OUR DATA NEVER SHOWED... !

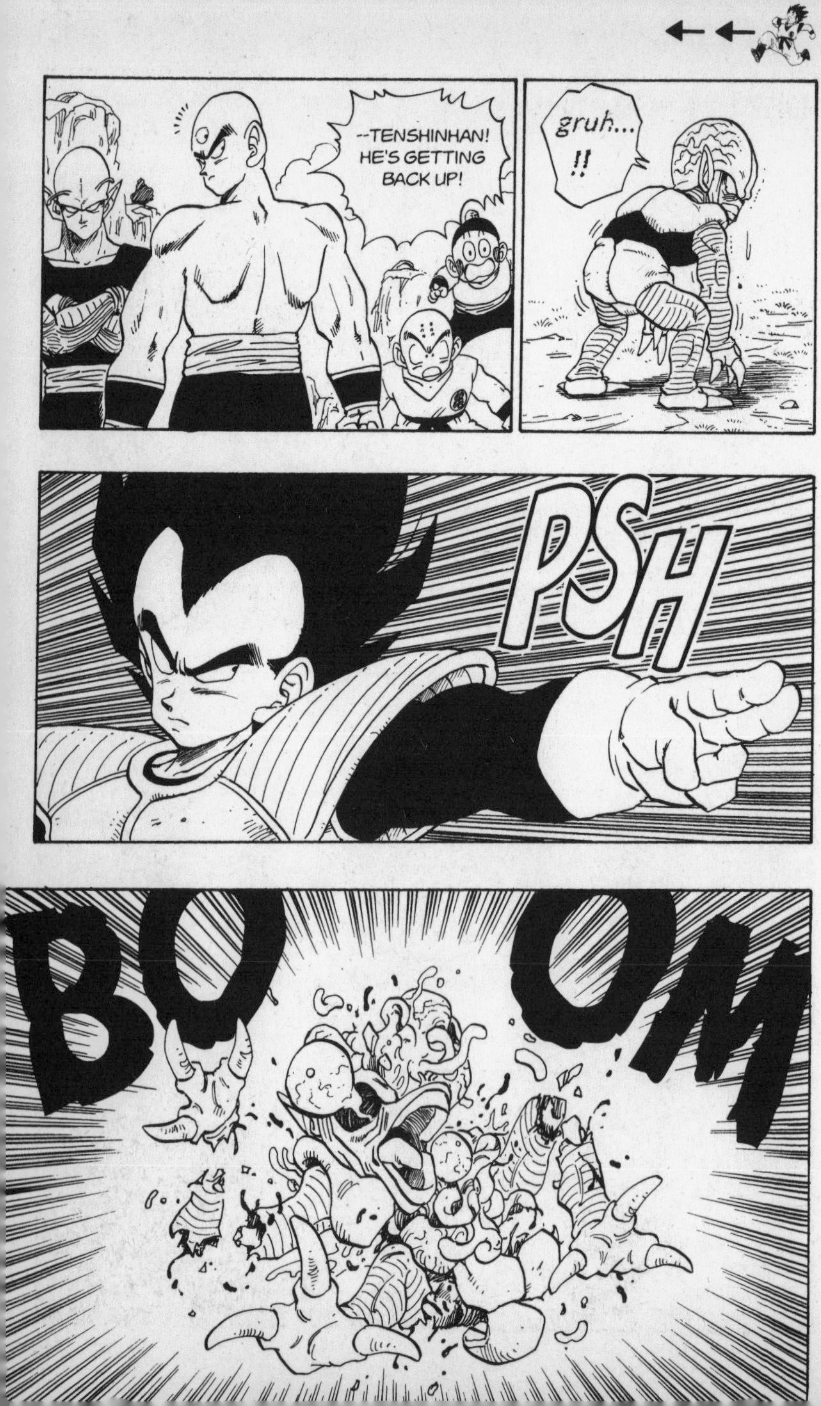
gruh... !!
--TENSHINHAN! HE'S GETTING BACK UP!
PSH
BOOM

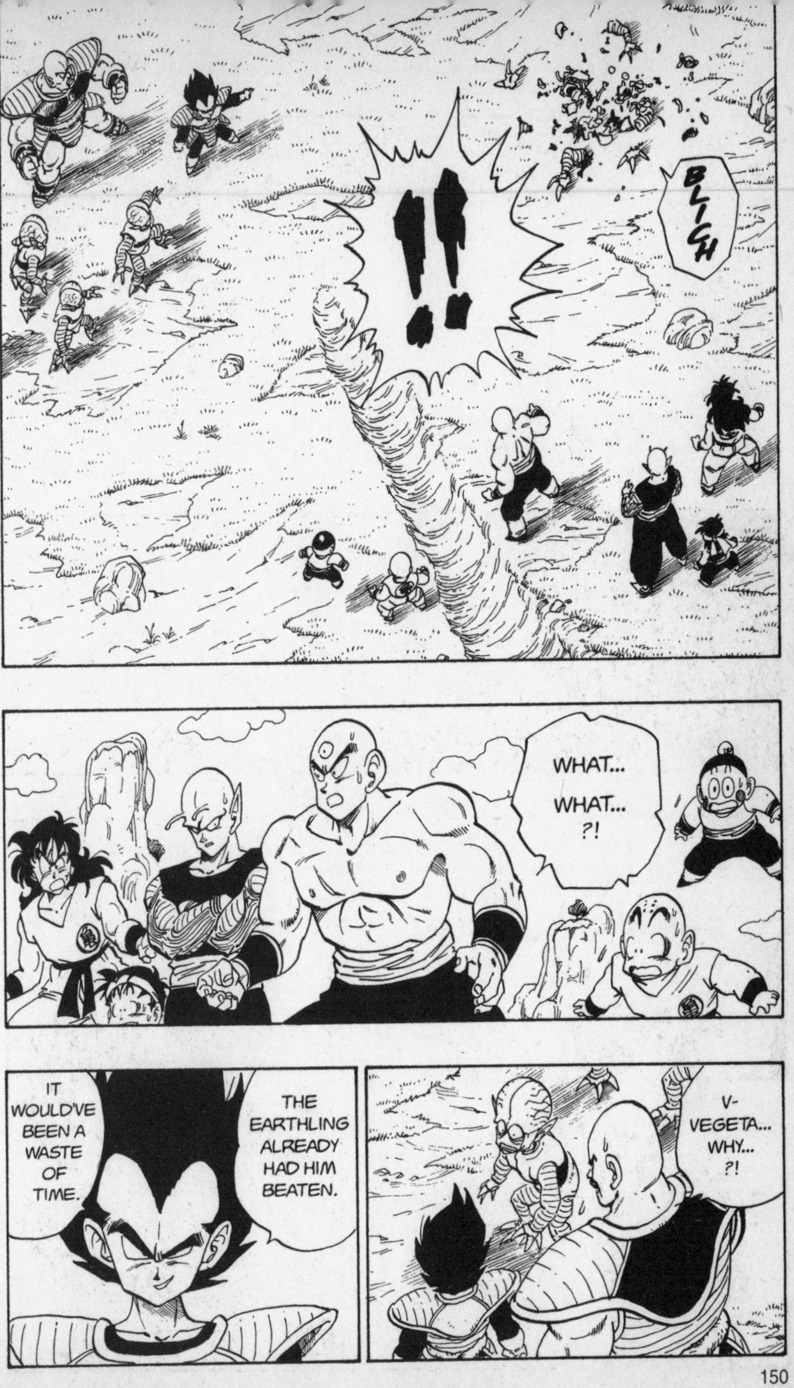
BLICH
!!
WHAT... WHAT... ?!
V-VEGETA... WHY... ?!
THE EARTHLING ALREADY HAD HIM BEATEN.
IT WOULD'VE BEEN A WASTE OF TIME.

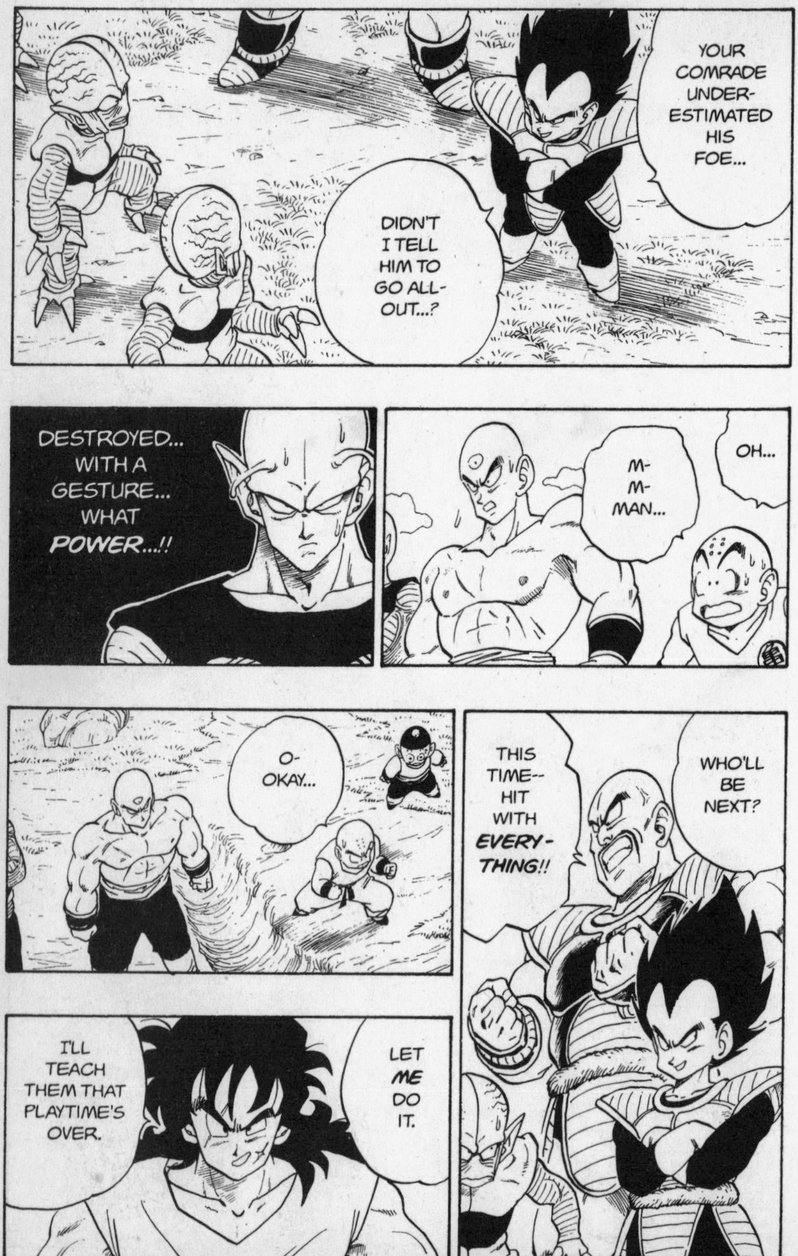
YOUR COMRADE UNDER-ESTIMATED HIS FOE...
DIDN'T I TELL HIM TO GO ALL-OUT...?
OH...
M-M-MAN...
DESTROYED... WITH A GESTURE... WHAT POWER...!!
WHO'LL BE NEXT?
THIS TIME--HIT WITH EVERY-THING!!
O-OKAY...
LET ME DO IT.
I'LL TEACH THEM THAT PLAYTIME'S OVER.

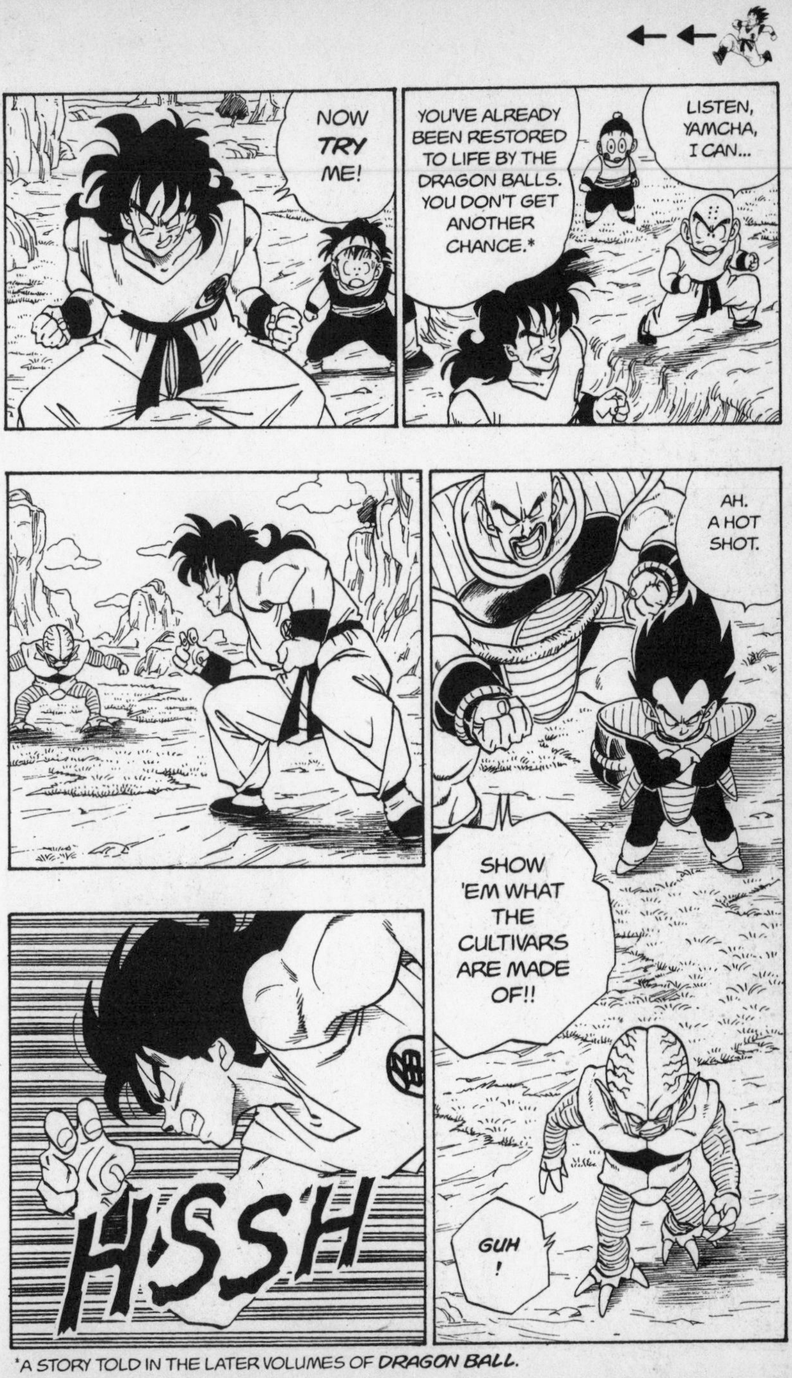
LISTEN, YAMCHA, I CAN...
YOU'VE ALREADY BEEN RESTORED TO LIFE BY THE DRAGON BALLS. YOU DON'T GET ANOTHER CHANCE.*
NOW TRY ME!
AH. A HOT SHOT.
SHOW 'EM WHAT THE CULTIVARS ARE MADE OF!!
GUH!
HSSH

*A STORY TOLD IN THE LATER VOLUMES OF ***DRAGON BALL***.

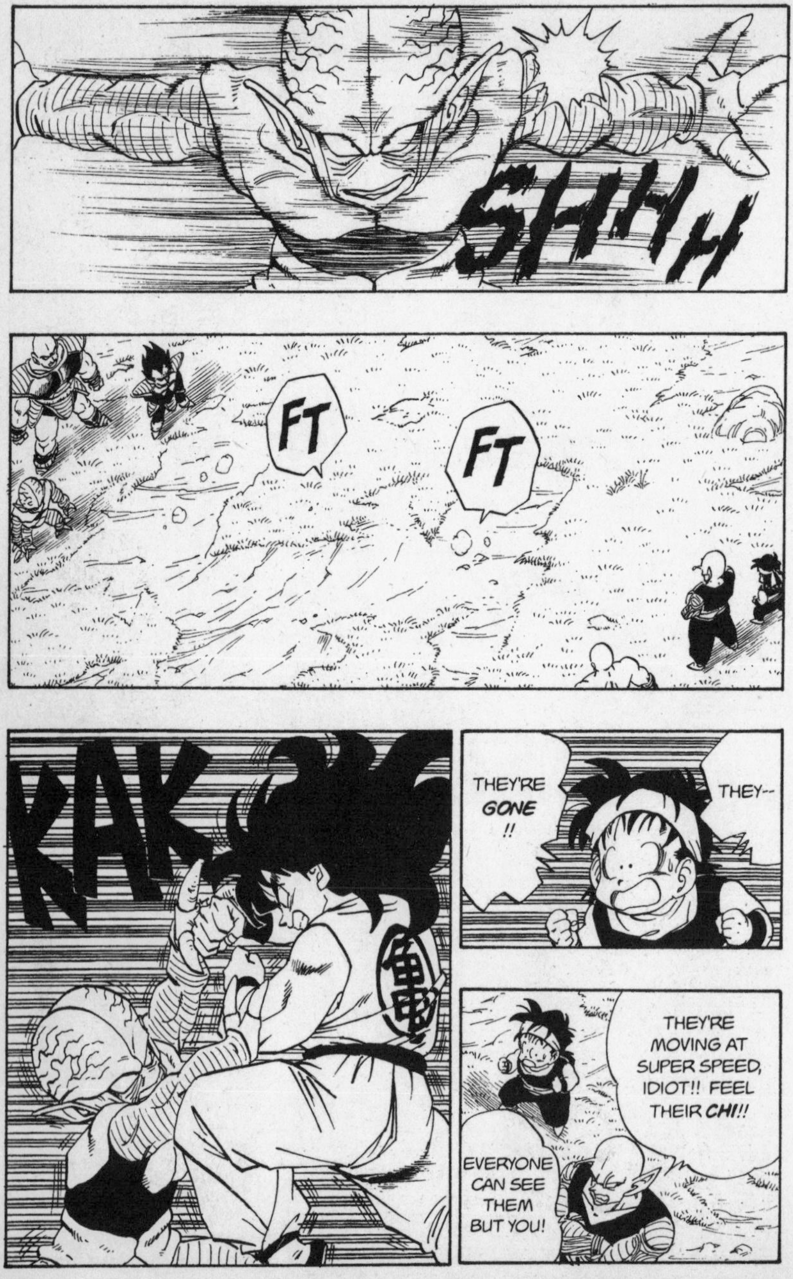
SHHH
FT
FT
THEY--
THEY'RE GONE!!
THEY'RE MOVING AT SUPER SPEED, IDIOT!! FEEL THEIR CHI!!
EVERYONE CAN SEE THEM BUT YOU!
KAK

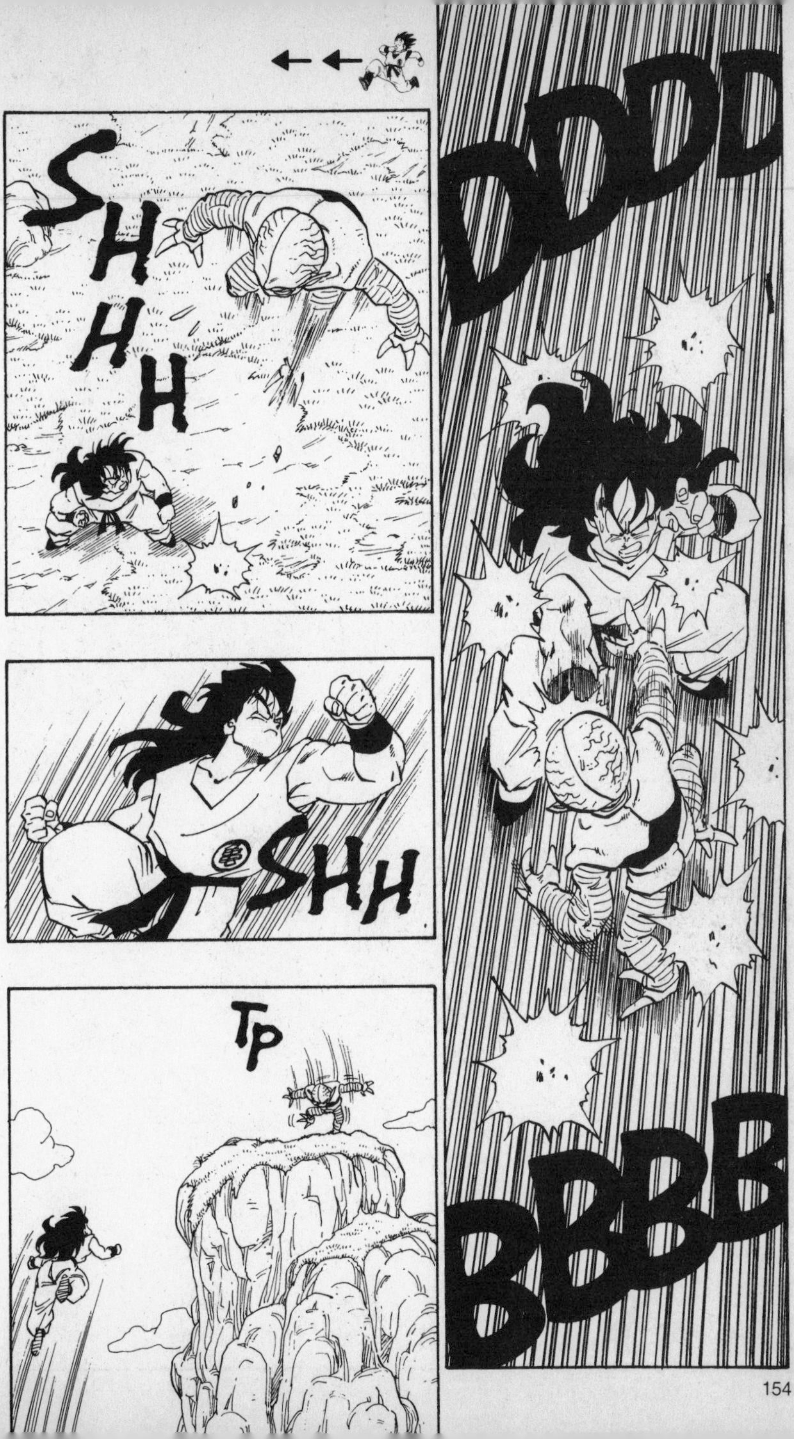
DDDDD
BBBBB
SHHH
SHH
TP

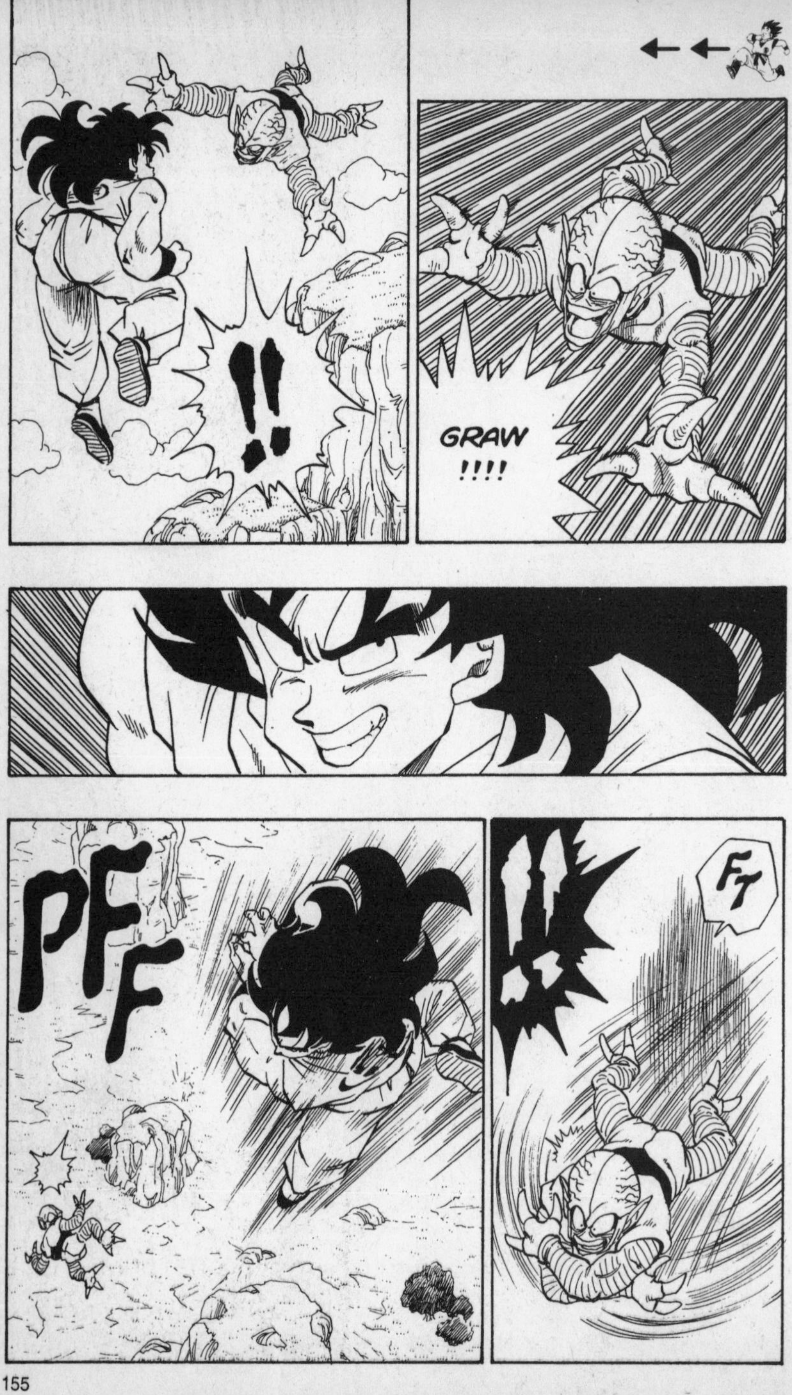
GRAW !!!!
!!
!!
FT
PFF

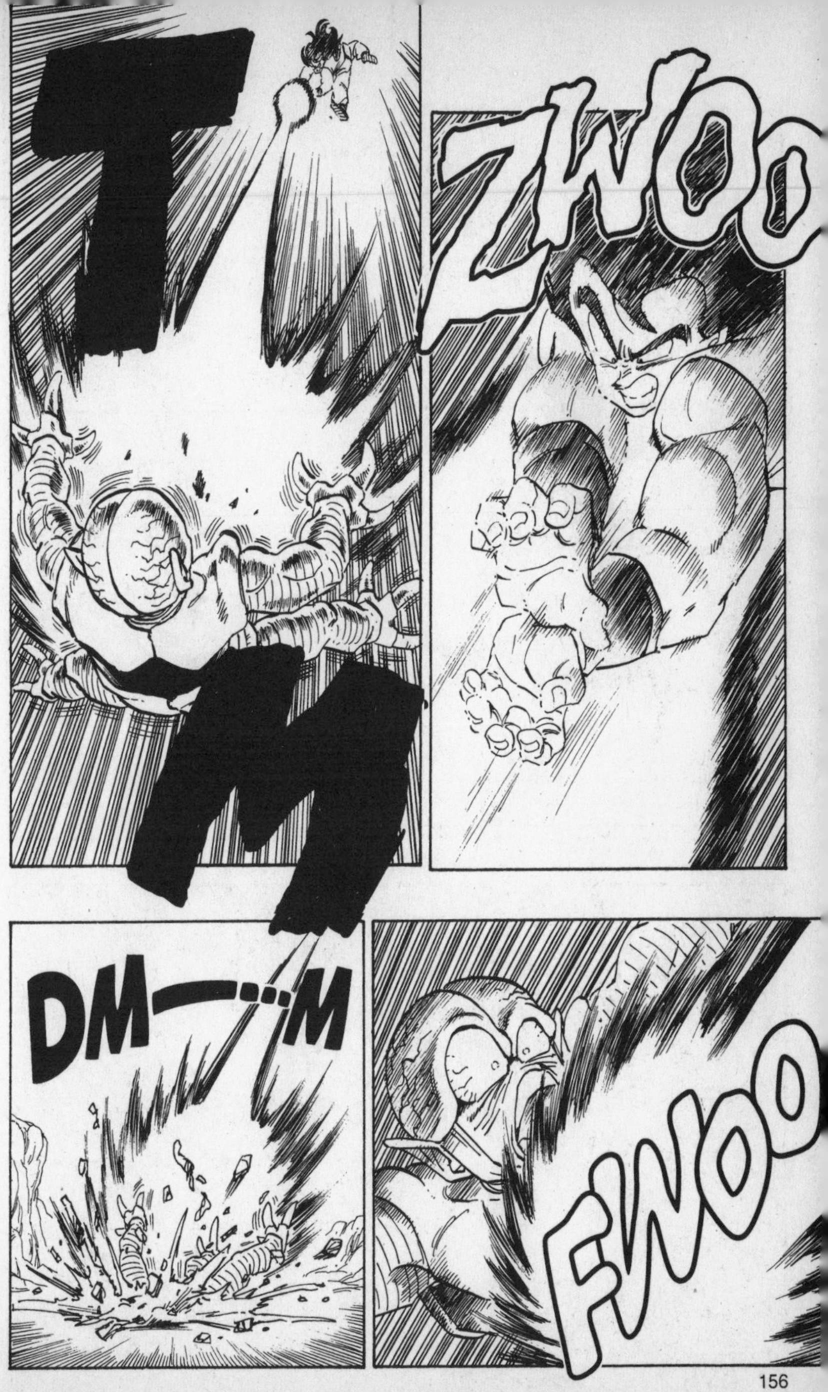
ZWOO
T
M
FWOO
DM—...M

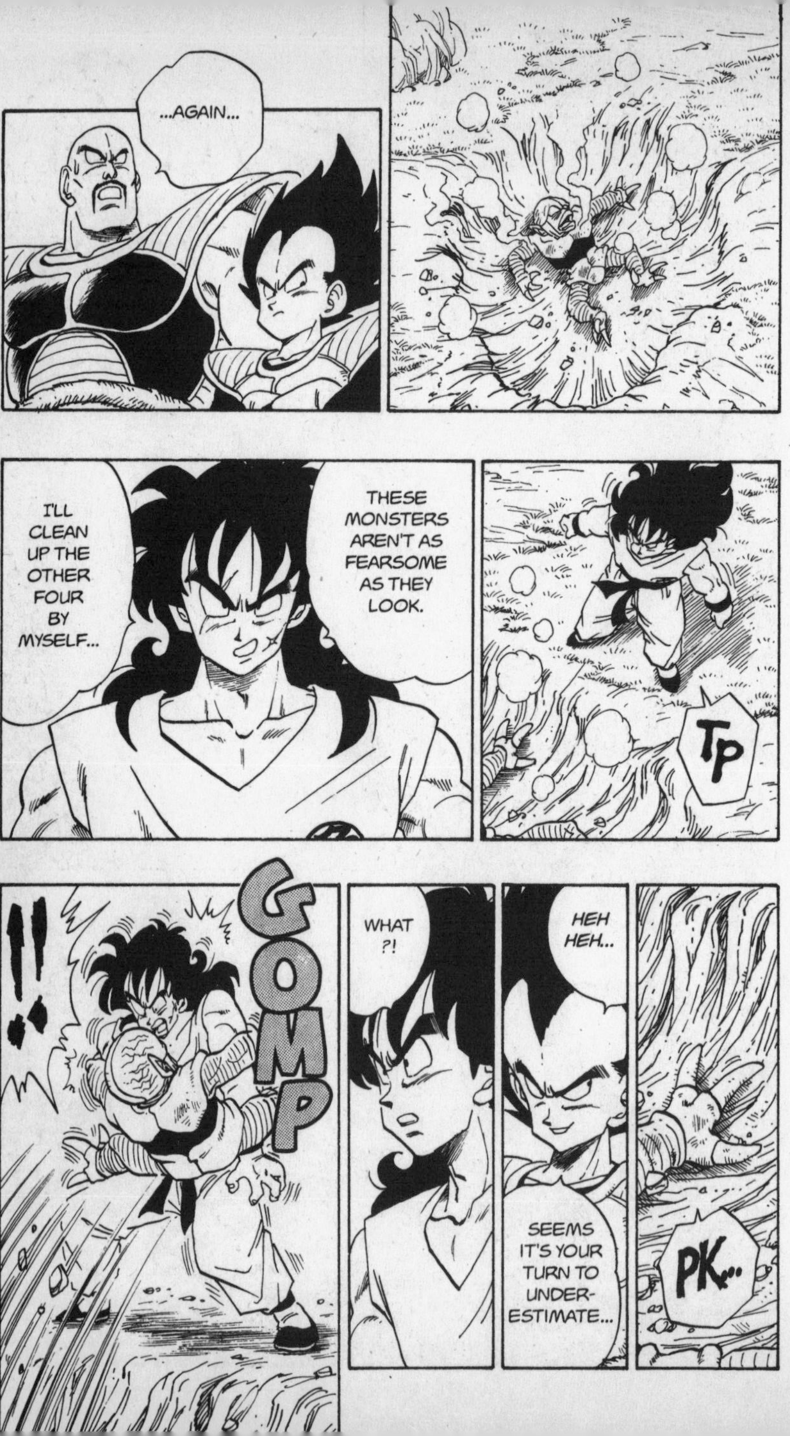
...AGAIN...
TP
THESE MONSTERS AREN'T AS FEARSOME AS THEY LOOK.
I'LL CLEAN UP THE OTHER FOUR BY MYSELF...
PK...
HEH HEH...
SEEMS IT'S YOUR TURN TO UNDER-ESTIMATE...
WHAT ?!
GOMP
!!

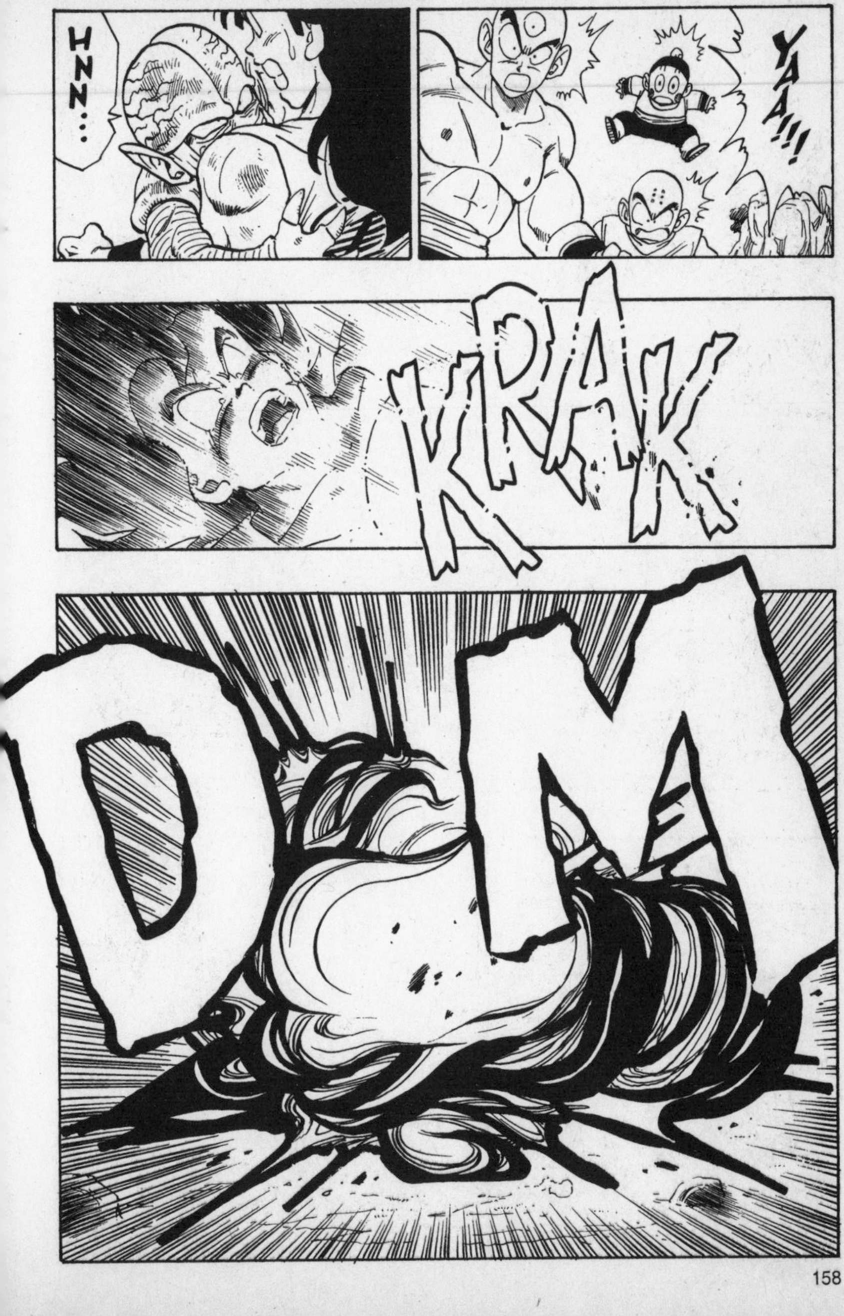
YAA!!!
HNN...
KRAK
DOM

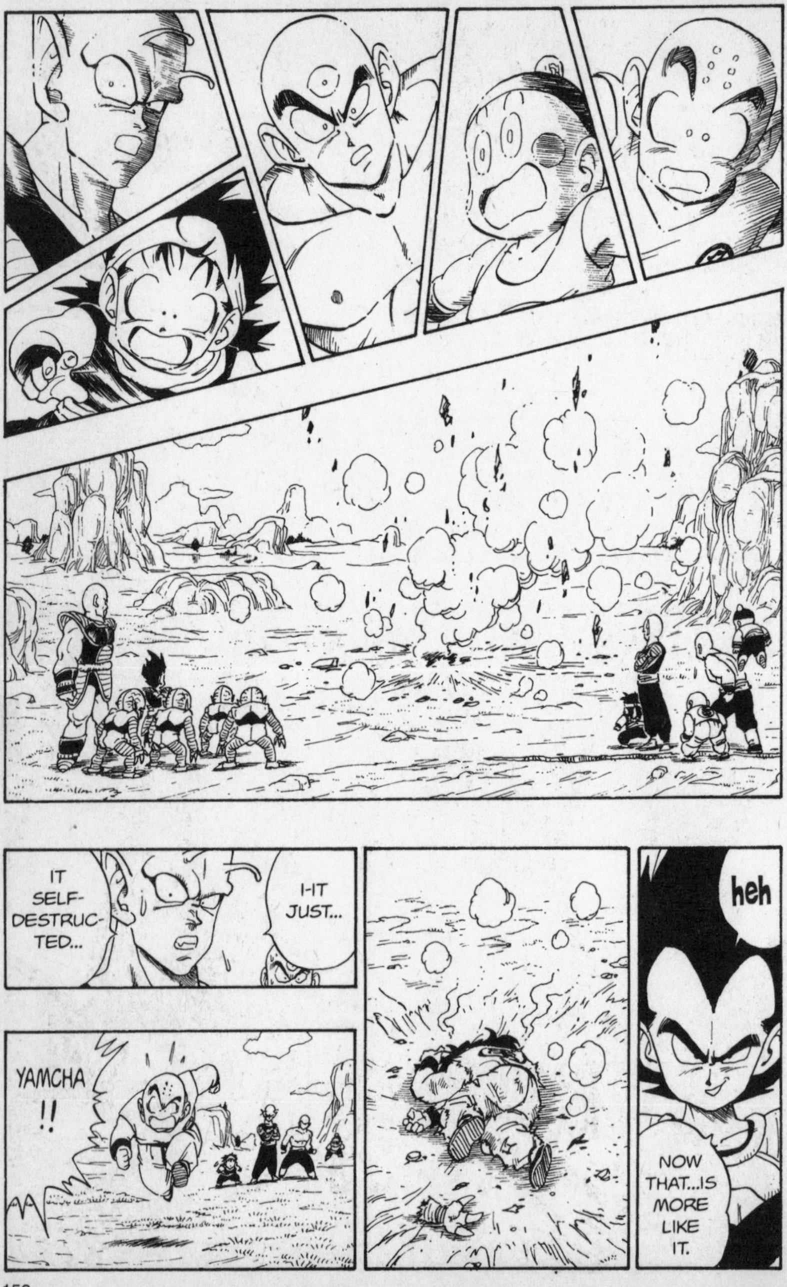
heh
NOW THAT...IS MORE LIKE IT.
I-IT JUST...
IT SELF-DESTRUCTED...
YAMCHA !!

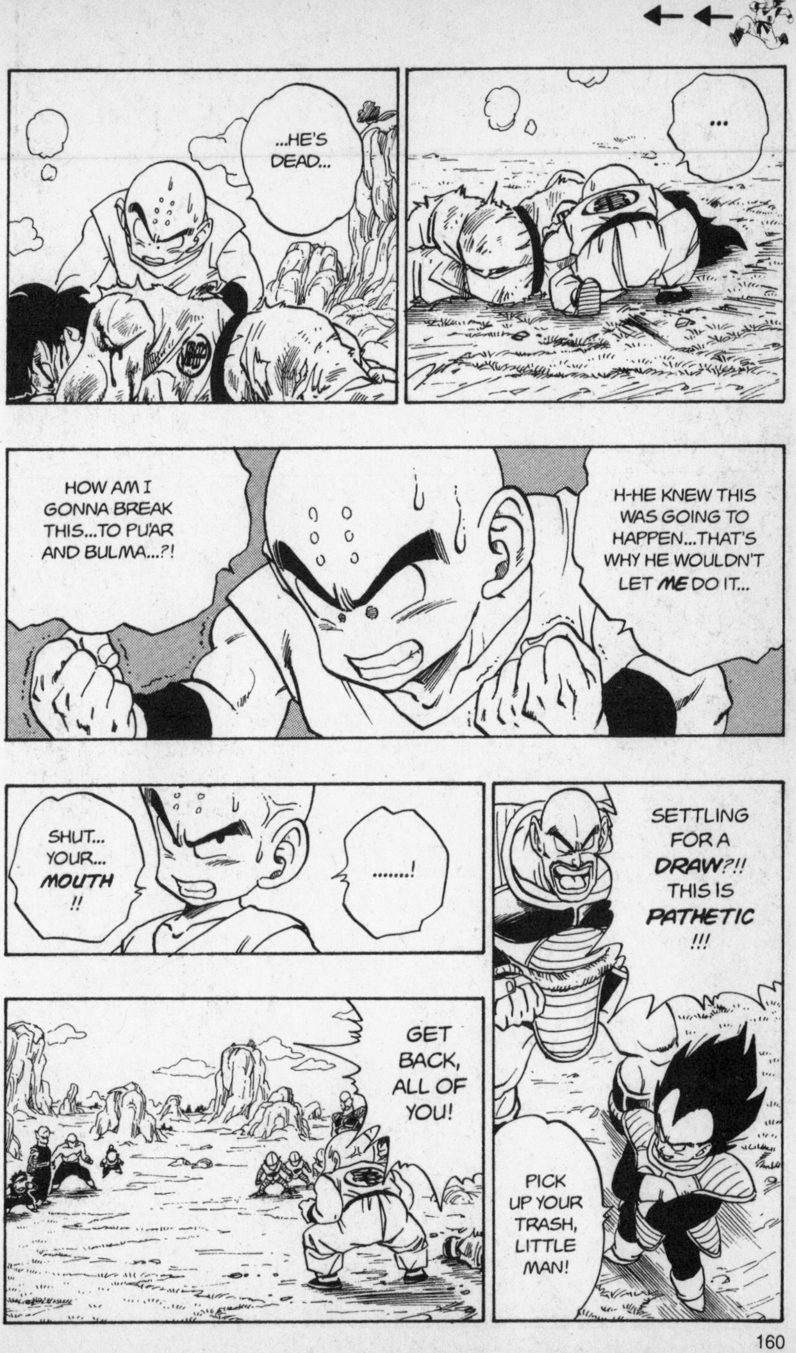
...
...HE'S DEAD...
H-HE KNEW THIS WAS GOING TO HAPPEN...THAT'S WHY HE WOULDN'T LET ME DO IT...
HOW AM I GONNA BREAK THIS...TO PU'AR AND BULMA...?!
SETTLING FOR A DRAW?!! THIS IS PATHETIC!!!
PICK UP YOUR TRASH, LITTLE MAN!
.......!
SHUT... YOUR... MOUTH!!
GET BACK, ALL OF YOU!

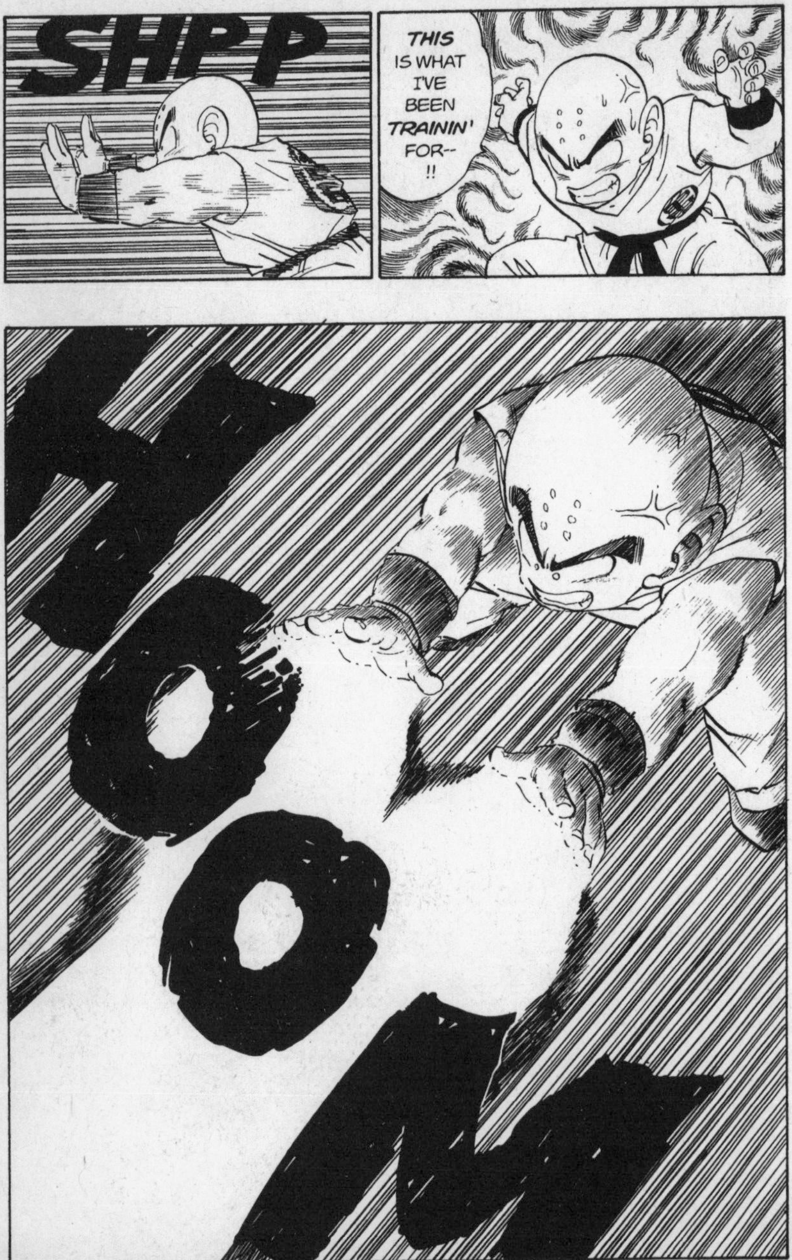
THIS IS WHAT I'VE BEEN TRAININ' FOR-- !!
SHPP

NEXT: PRELUDE to TERROR!

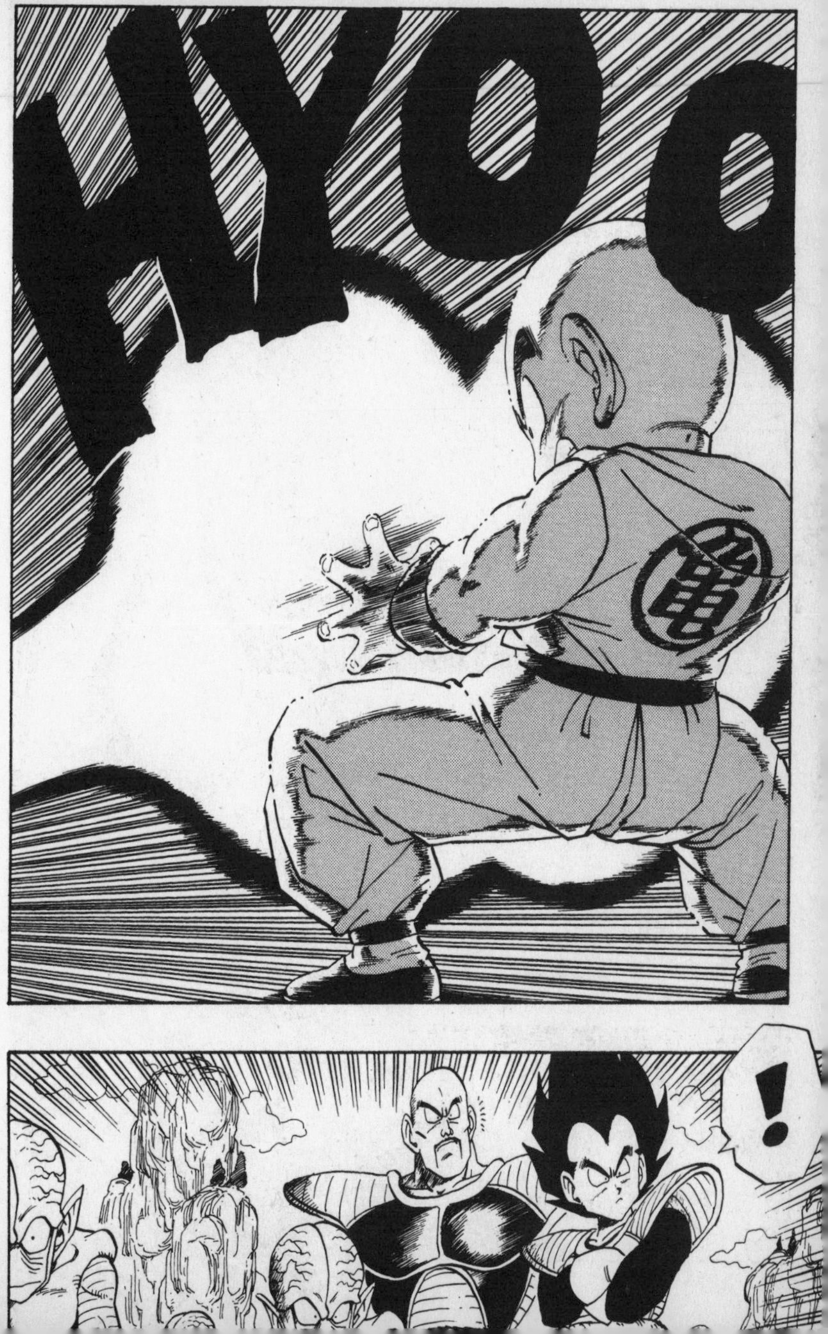
HYOO
!

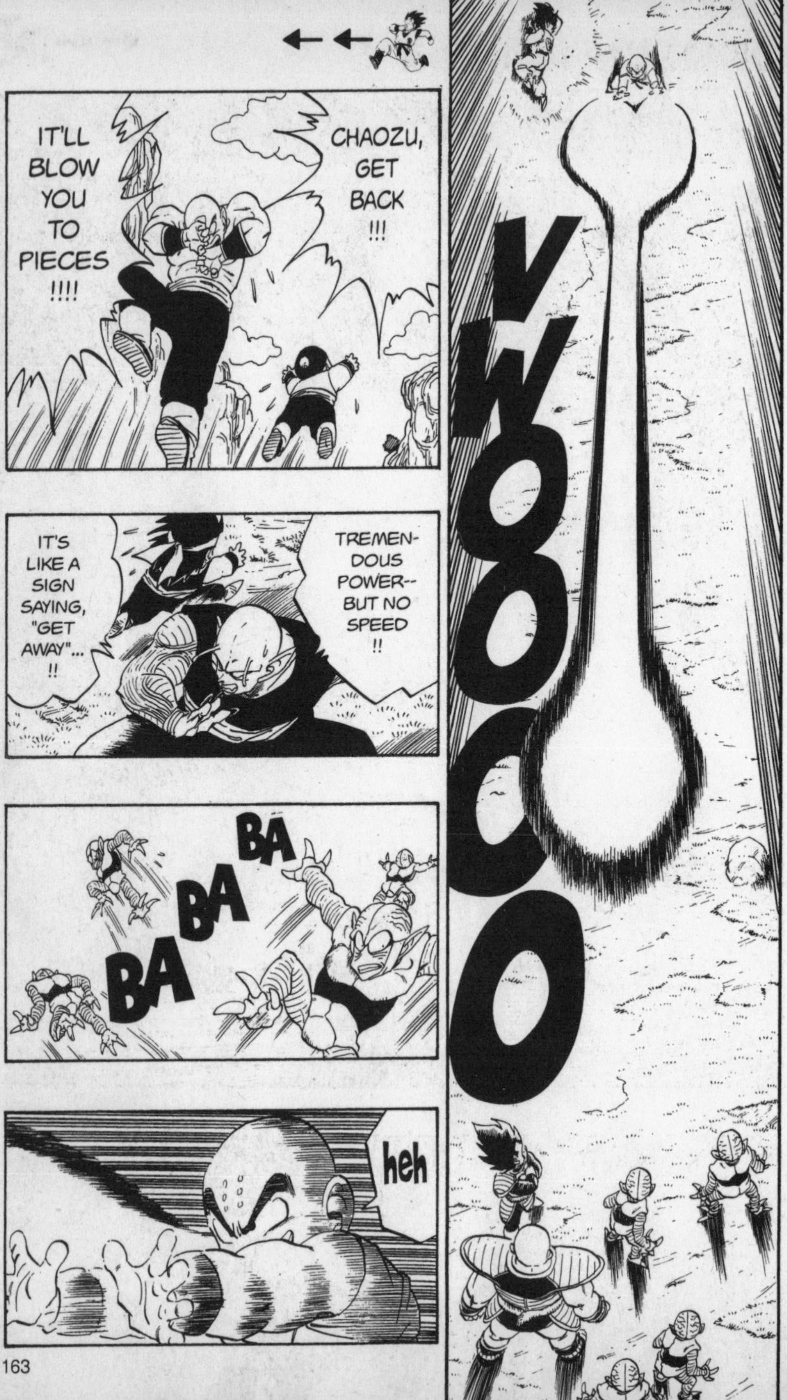
VWOOOO
CHAOZU, GET BACK !!!
IT'LL BLOW YOU TO PIECES !!!!
TREMENDOUS POWER-- BUT NO SPEED !!
IT'S LIKE A SIGN SAYING, "GET AWAY"... !!
BA BA BA BA
heh

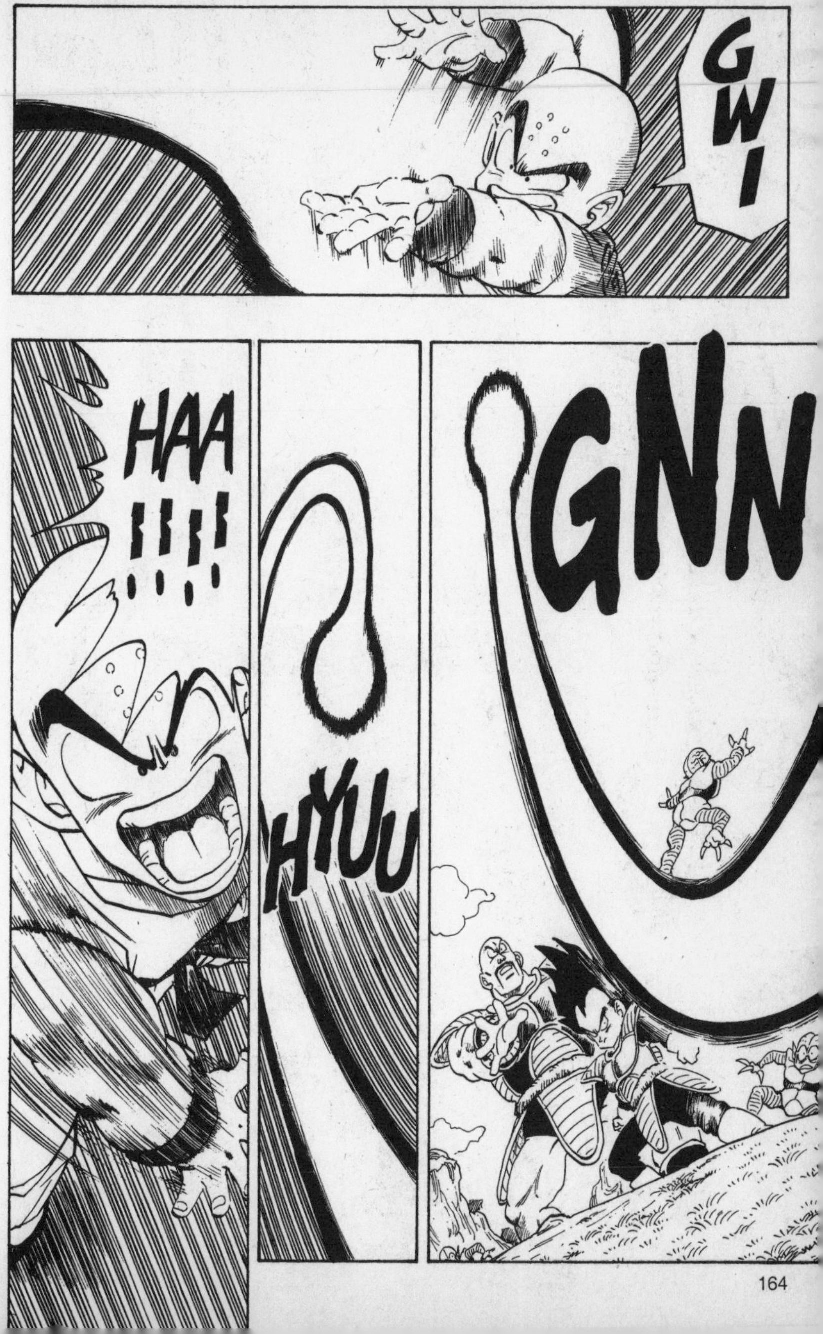
GWI
GNN
HYUU
HAA!!!!

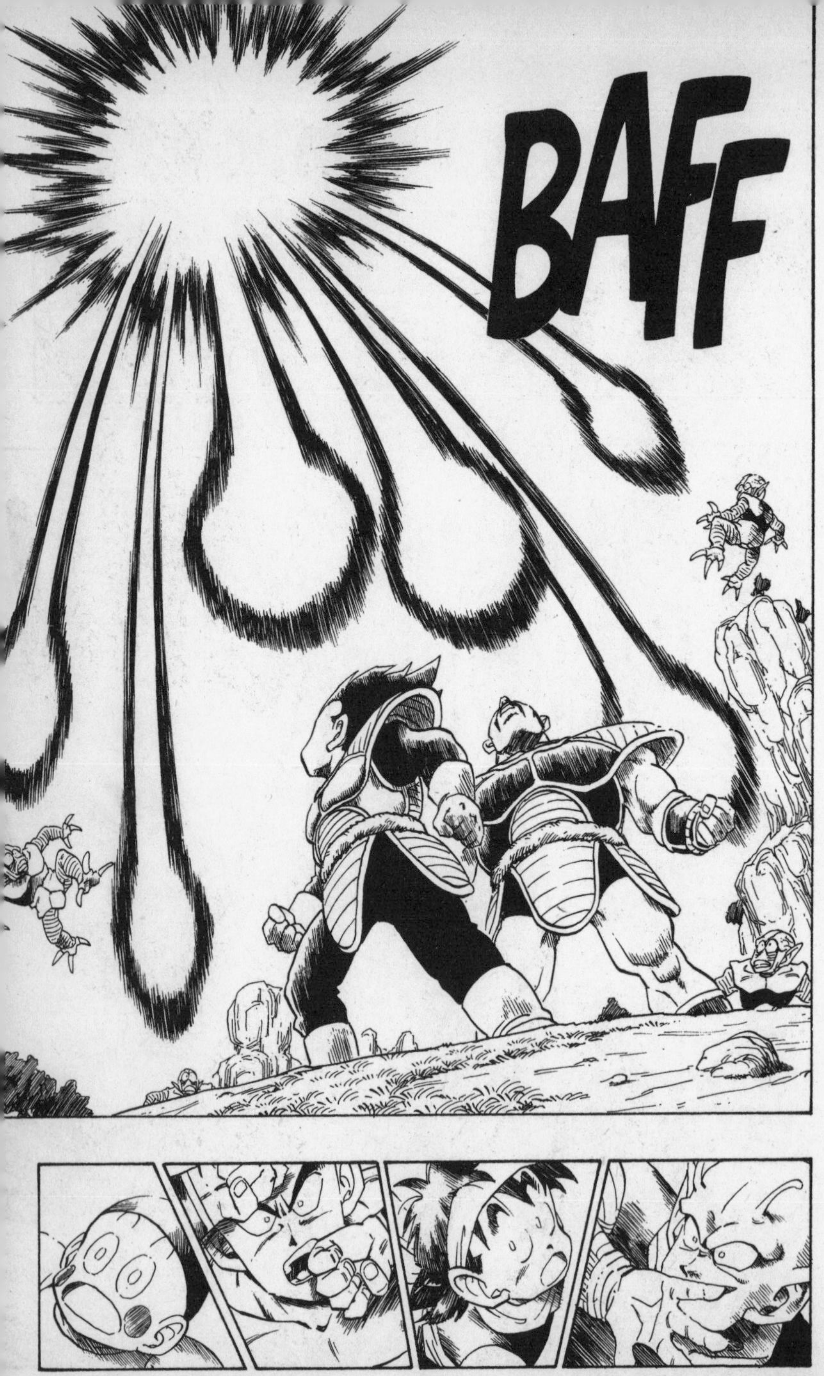
BAFF

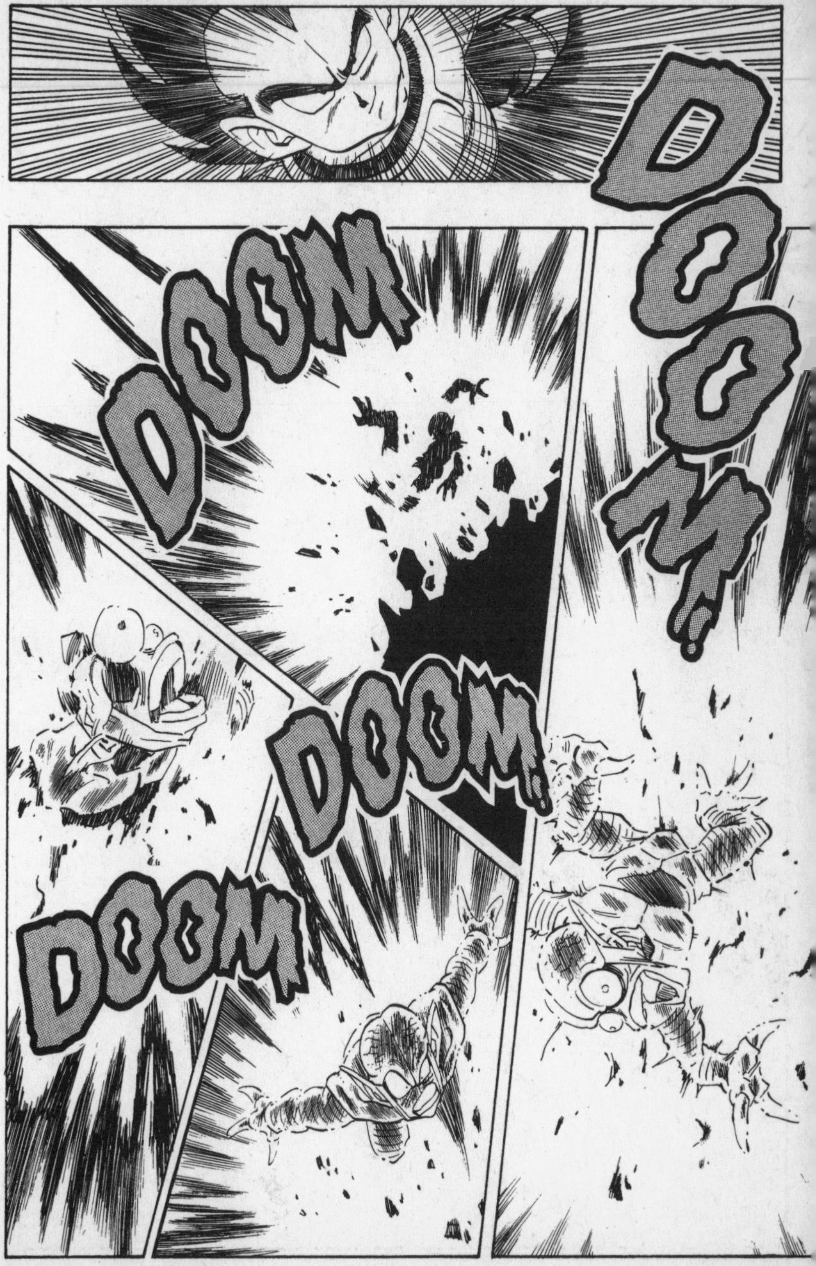
DOOM
DOOM
DOOM
DOOM

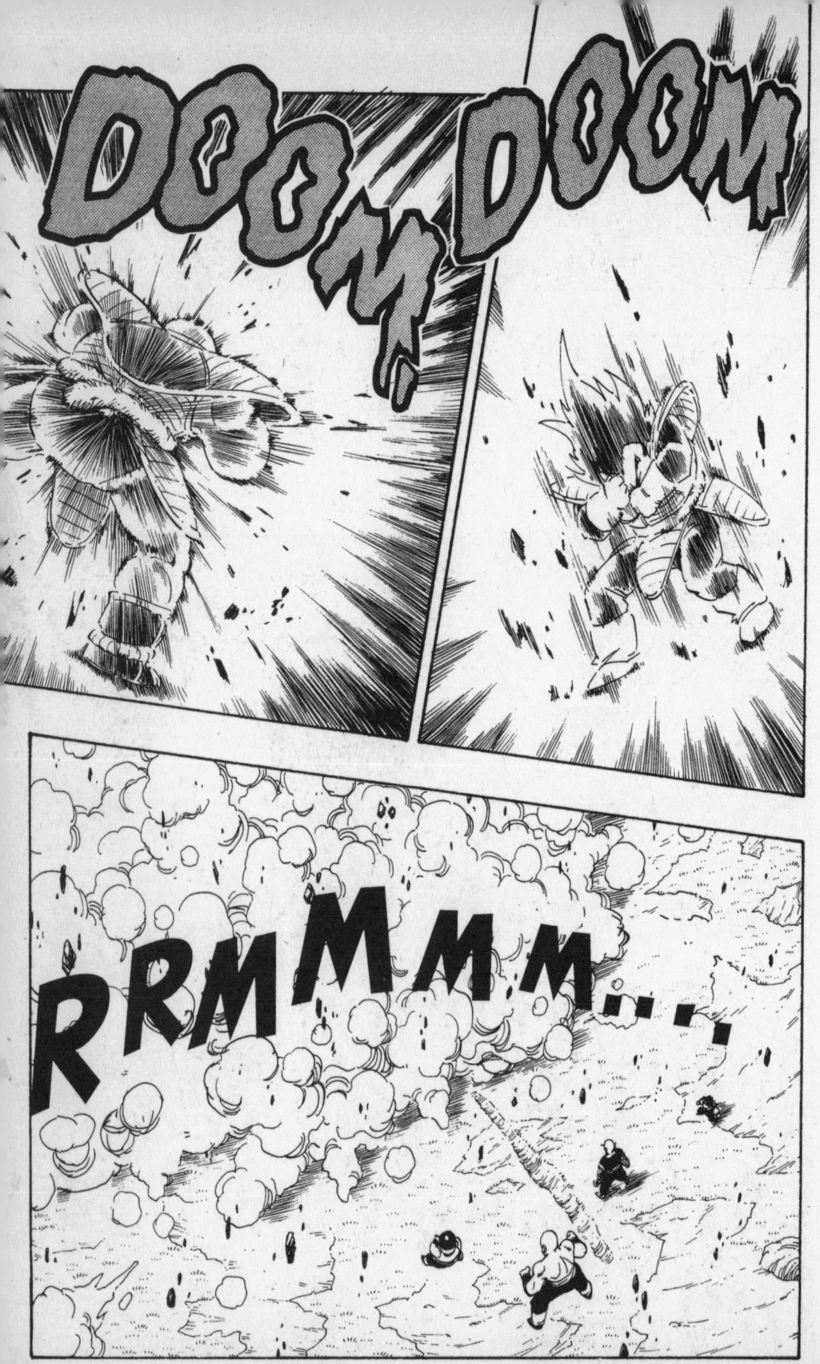
DOOM
DOOM
RRMMMM...

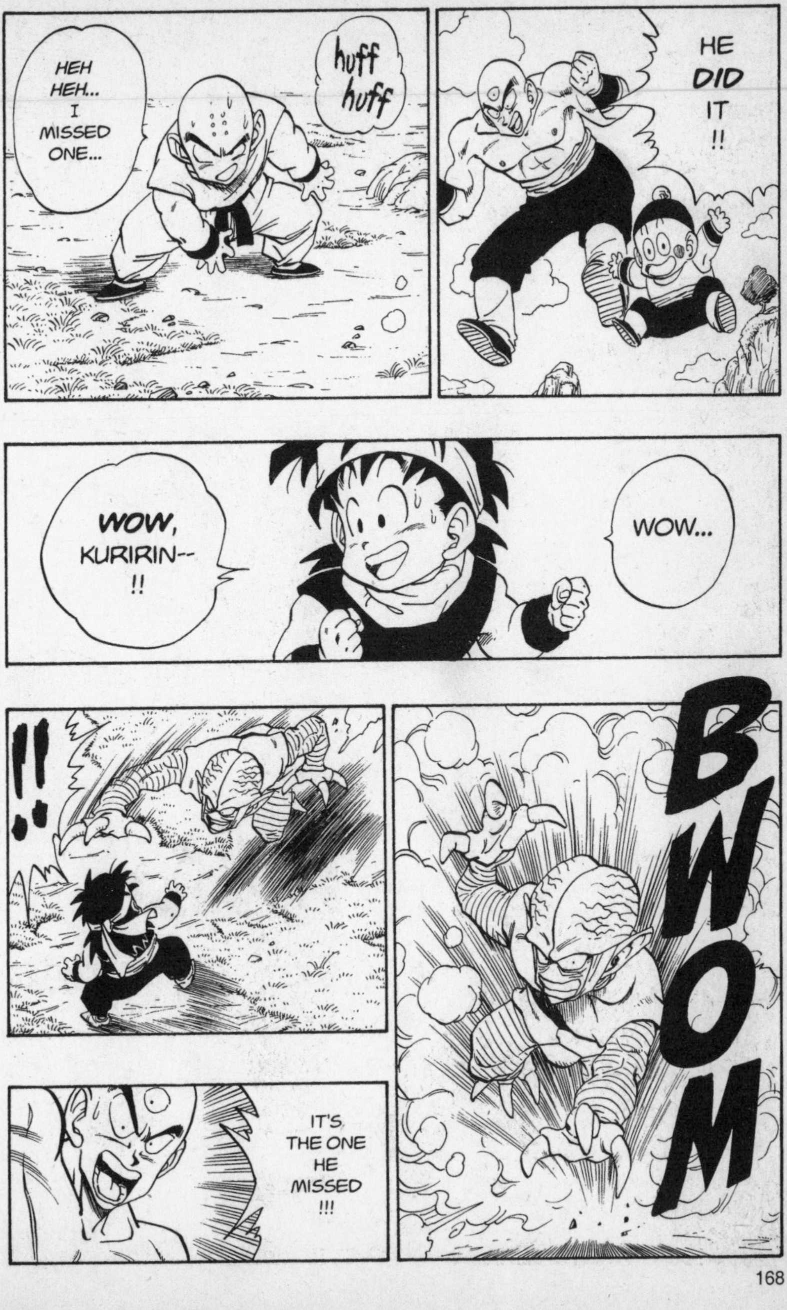
HE DID IT !!
huff huff
HEH HEH... I MISSED ONE...
WOW...
WOW, KURIRIN-- !!
BWOM
!!
IT'S THE ONE HE MISSED !!!

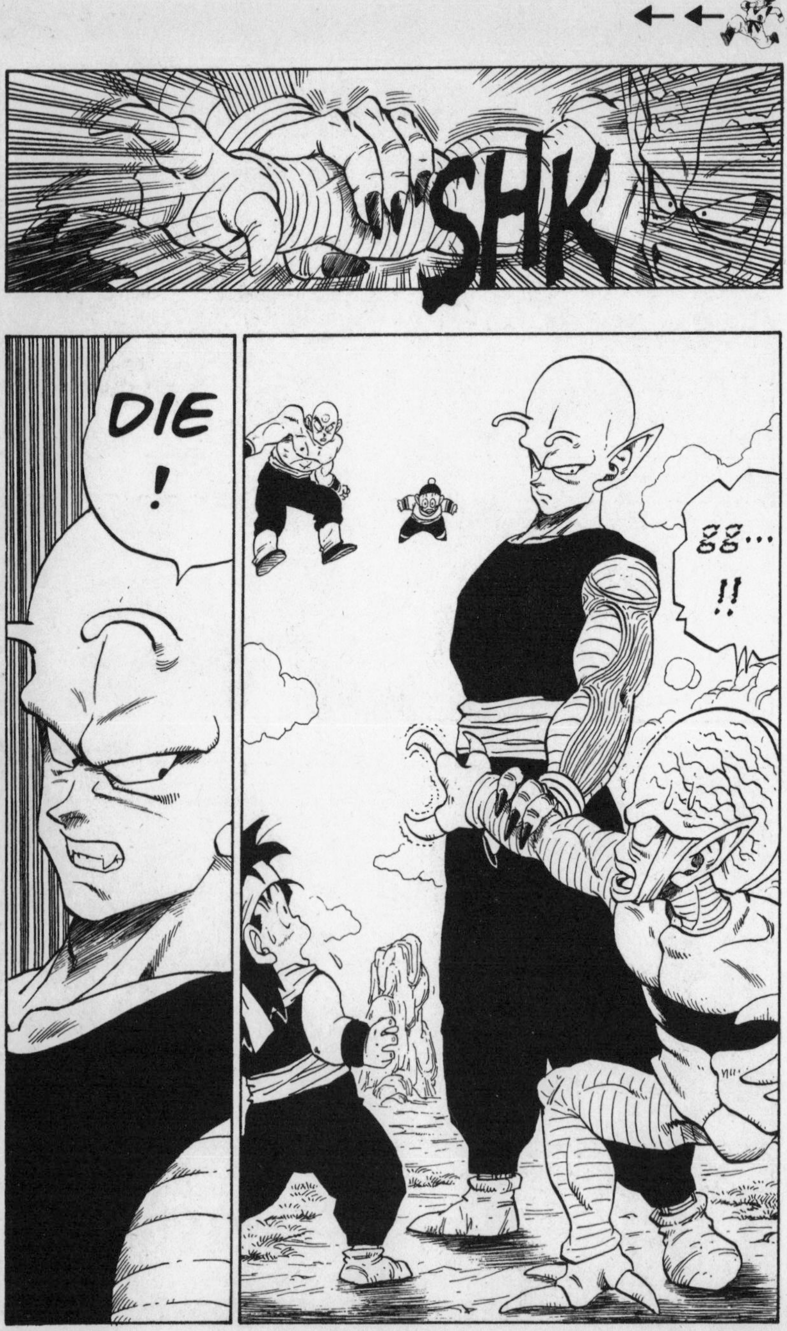
SHK
gg...
!!
DIE
!

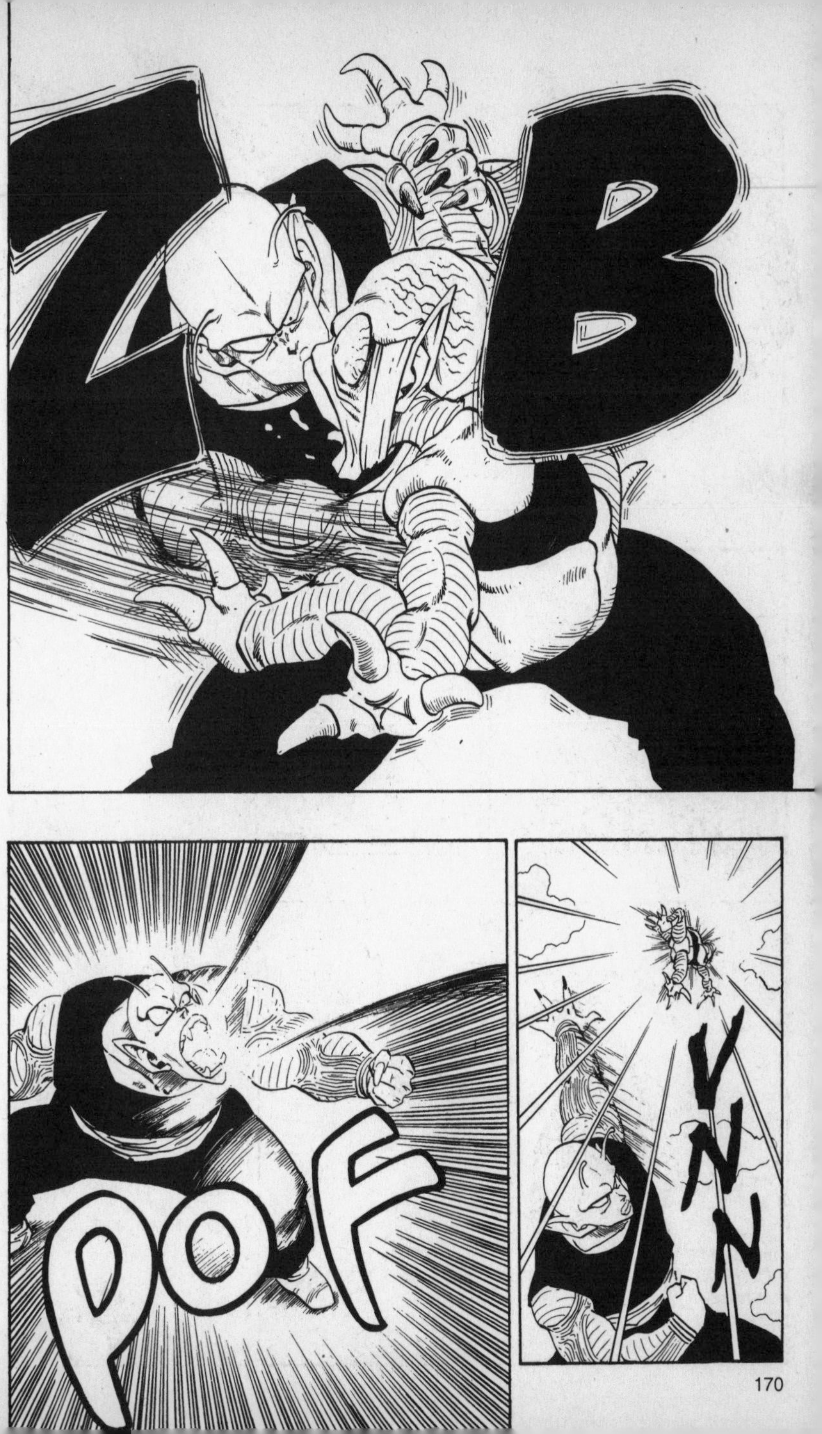
ZAB
VNN
POF

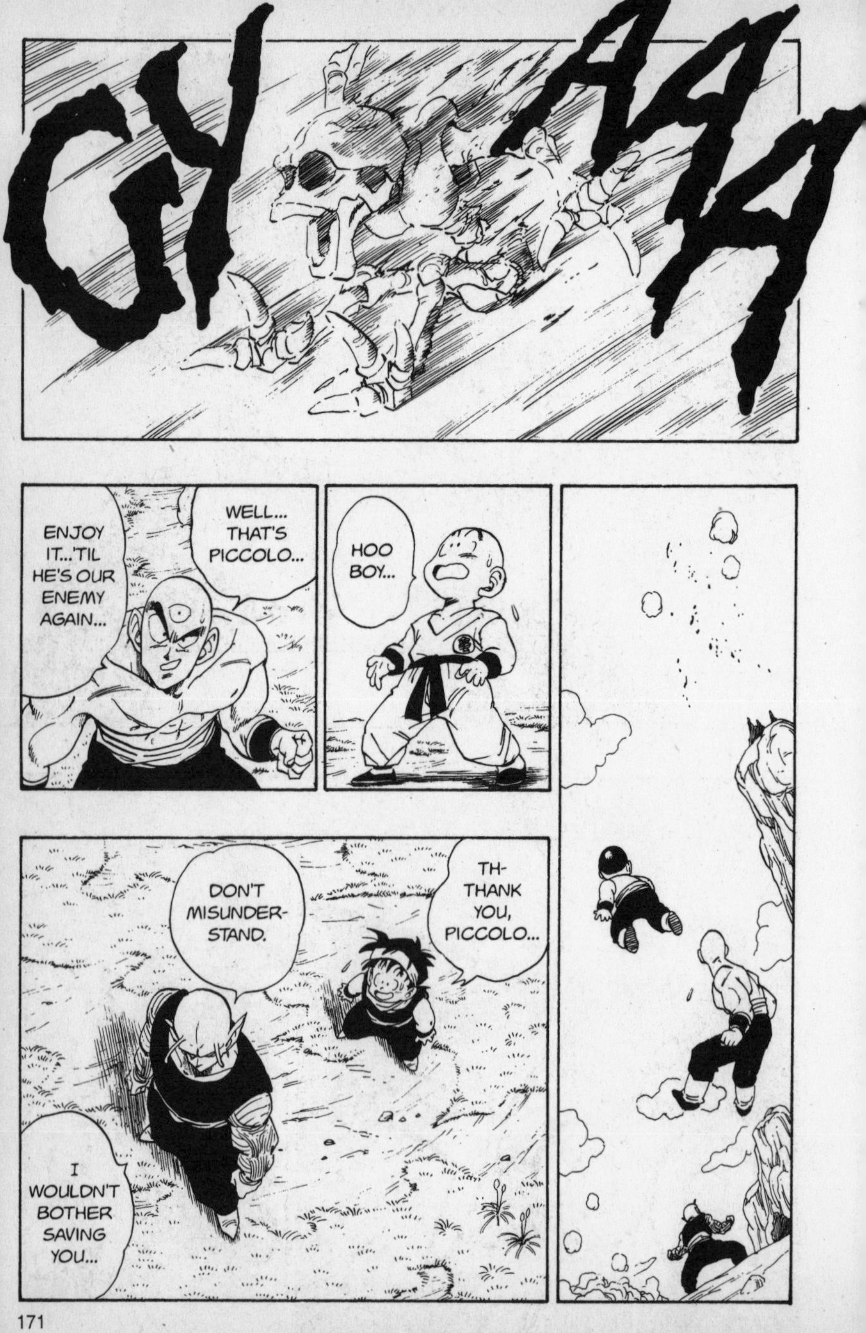
GYAAA
HOO BOY...
WELL... THAT'S PICCOLO...
ENJOY IT...'TIL HE'S OUR ENEMY AGAIN...
TH- THANK YOU, PICCOLO...
DON'T MISUNDERSTAND.
I WOULDN'T BOTHER SAVING YOU...

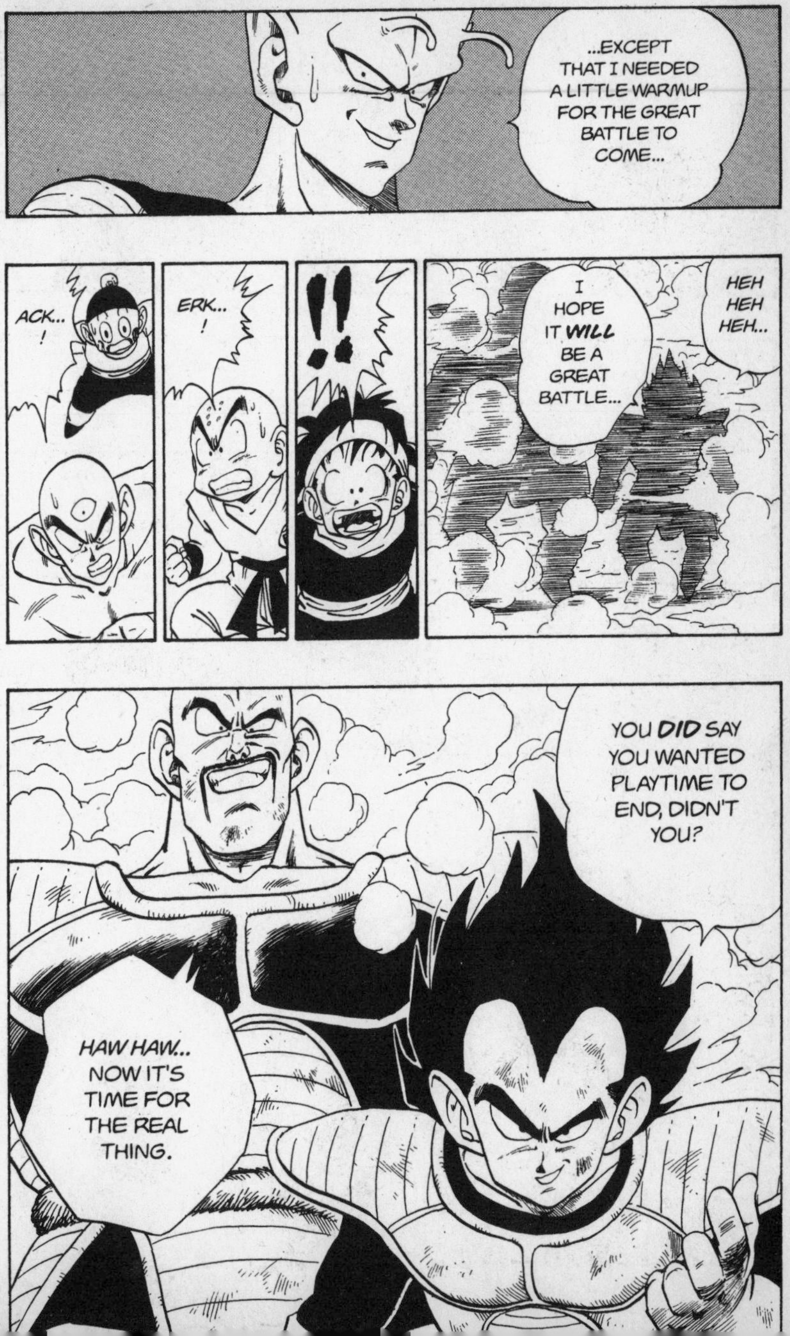
...EXCEPT THAT I NEEDED A LITTLE WARMUP FOR THE GREAT BATTLE TO COME...
HEH HEH HEH...
I HOPE IT WILL BE A GREAT BATTLE...
!!
ERK... !
ACK... !
YOU DID SAY YOU WANTED PLAYTIME TO END, DIDN'T YOU?
HAW HAW... NOW IT'S TIME FOR THE REAL THING.

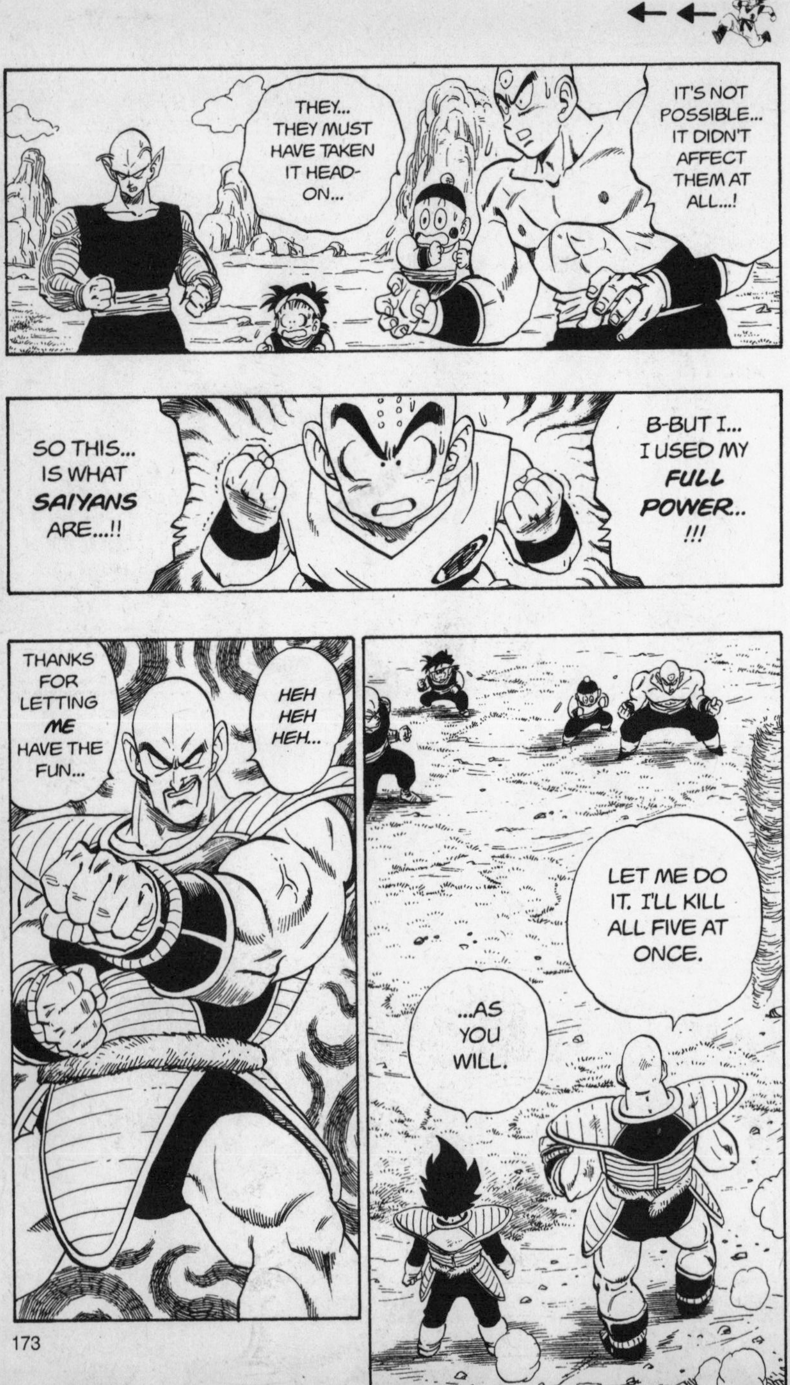
IT'S NOT POSSIBLE... IT DIDN'T AFFECT THEM AT ALL...!
THEY... THEY MUST HAVE TAKEN IT HEAD-ON...
B-BUT I... I USED MY FULL POWER.. !!!
SO THIS... IS WHAT SAIYANS ARE...!!
LET ME DO IT. I'LL KILL ALL FIVE AT ONCE.
...AS YOU WILL.
HEH HEH HEH...
THANKS FOR LETTING ME HAVE THE FUN...

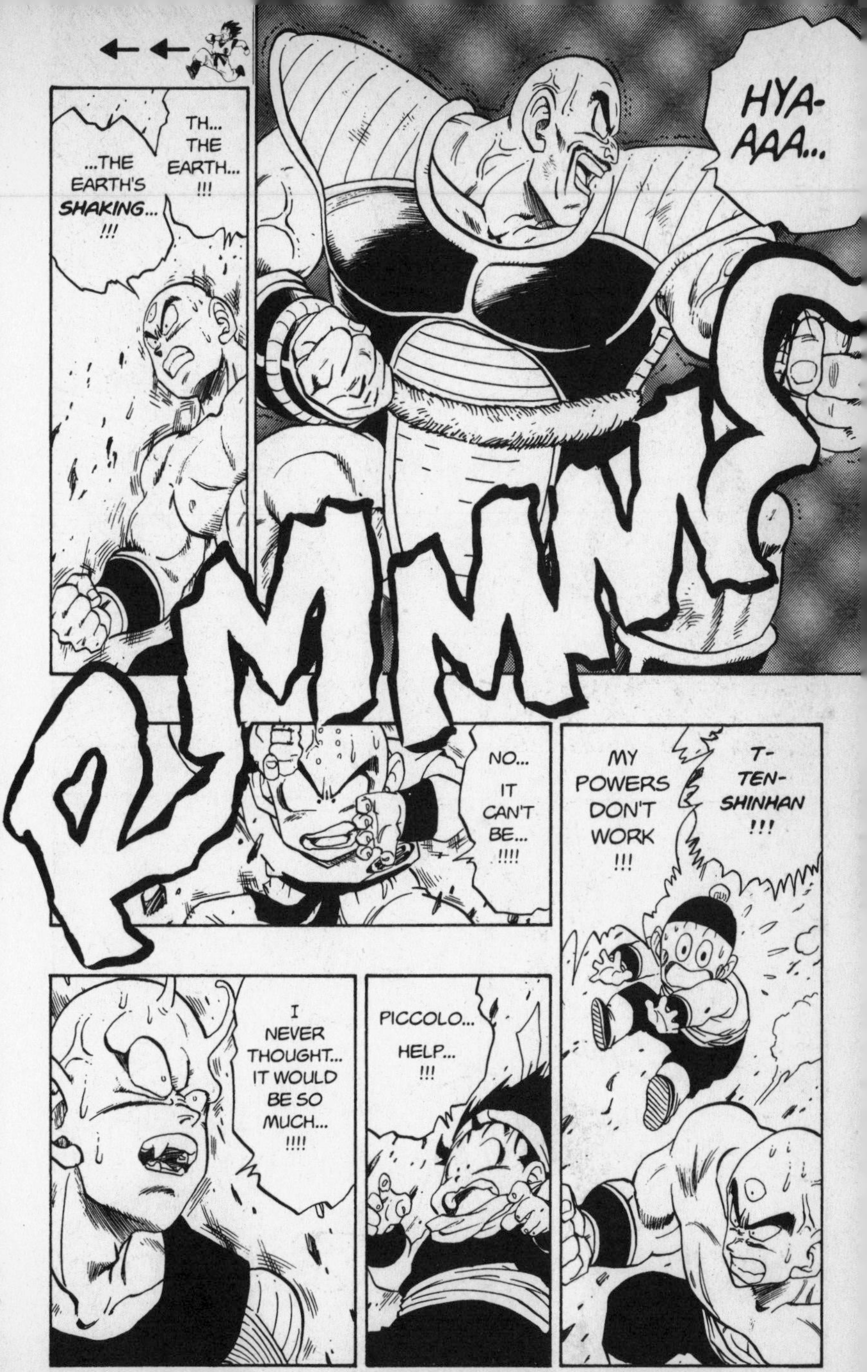
HYA-AAA...
TH... THE EARTH... !!!
...THE EARTH'S SHAKING... !!!
T- TEN-SHINHAN !!!
MY POWERS DON'T WORK !!!
NO... IT CAN'T BE... !!!!
PICCOLO... HELP... !!!
I NEVER THOUGHT... IT WOULD BE SO MUCH... !!!!

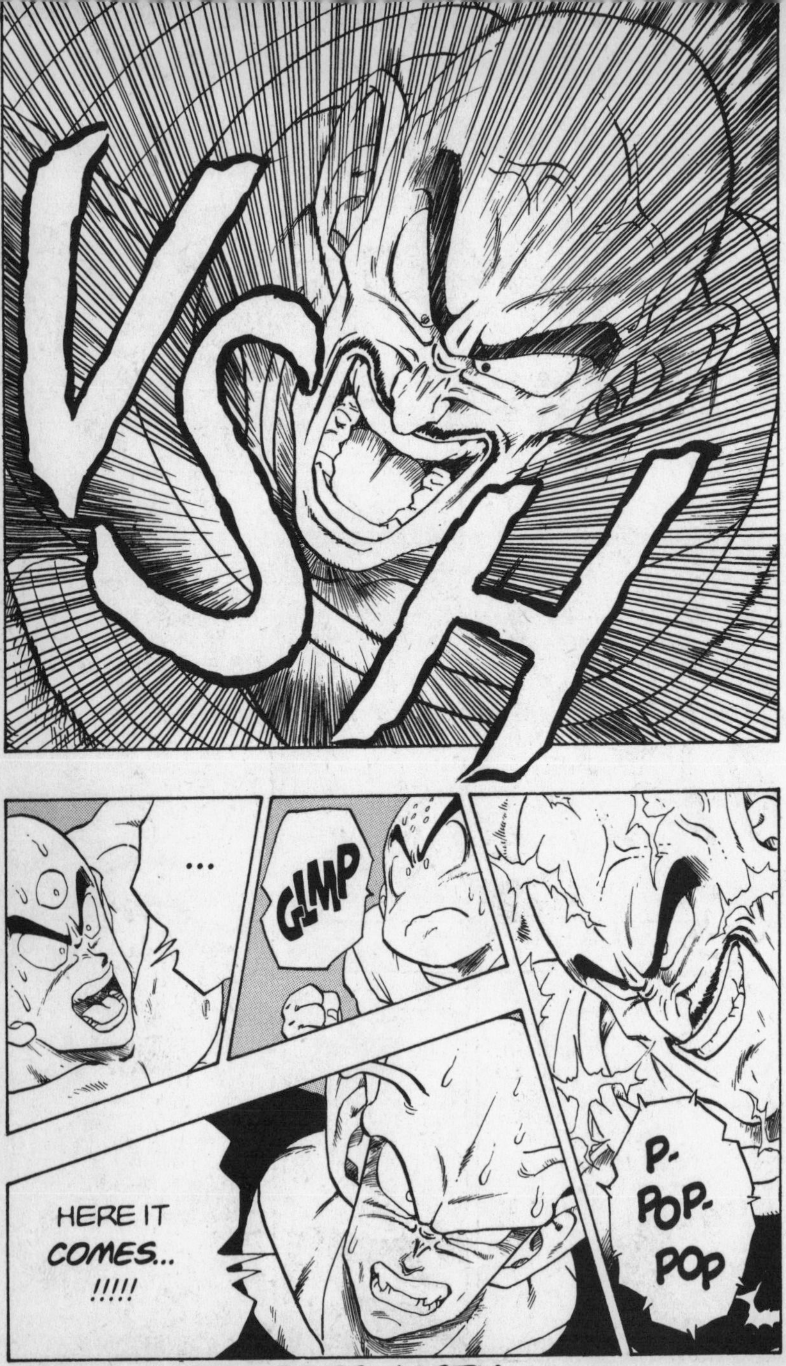
VSH
P-
POP-
POP
GLMP
...
HERE IT
COMES...
!!!!!

NEXT: NAPPA GETS NASTY

ドラゴンボール

DRAGON BALL

TITLE PAGE GALLERY

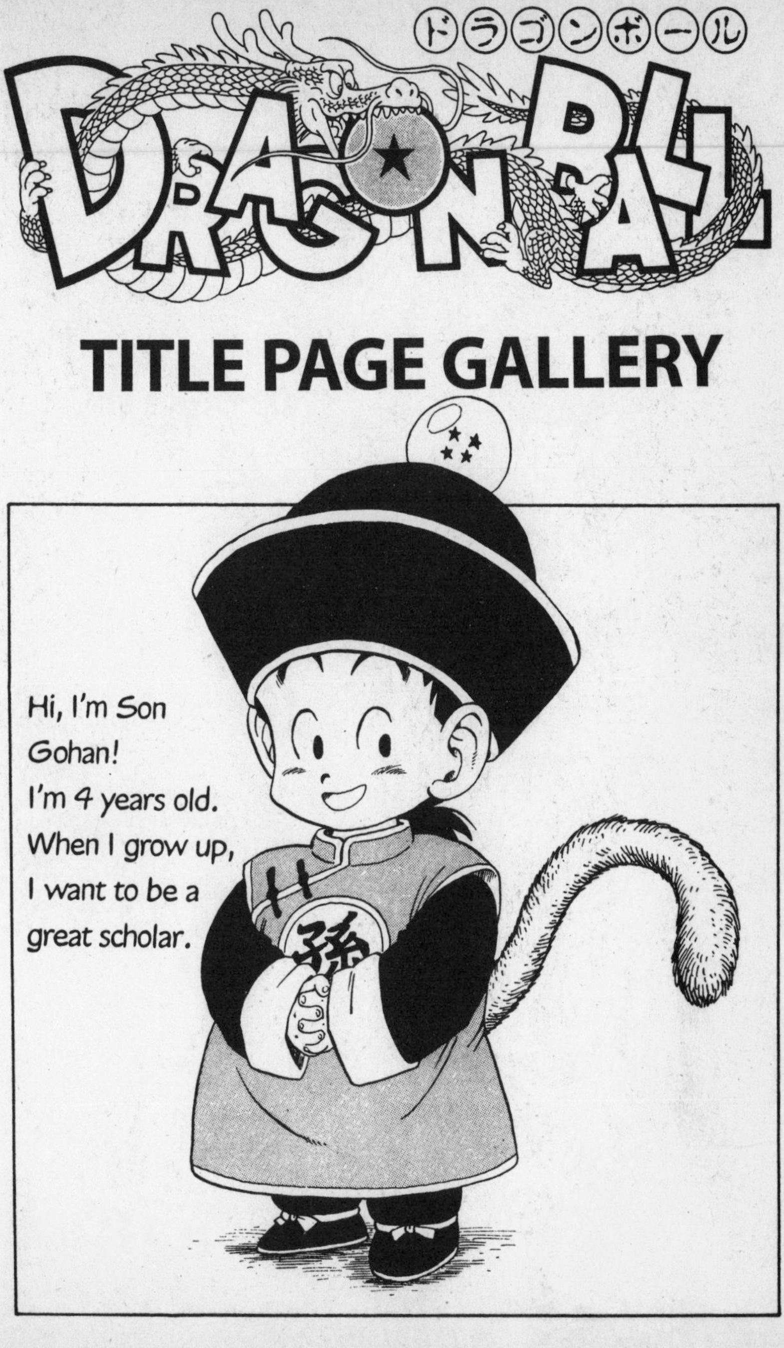
Hi, I'm Son Gohan!
I'm 4 years old.
When I grow up, I want to be a great scholar.
孫

DRAGON BALL

ドラゴンボール

Akira Toriyama

鳥山明

BIRD STUDIO

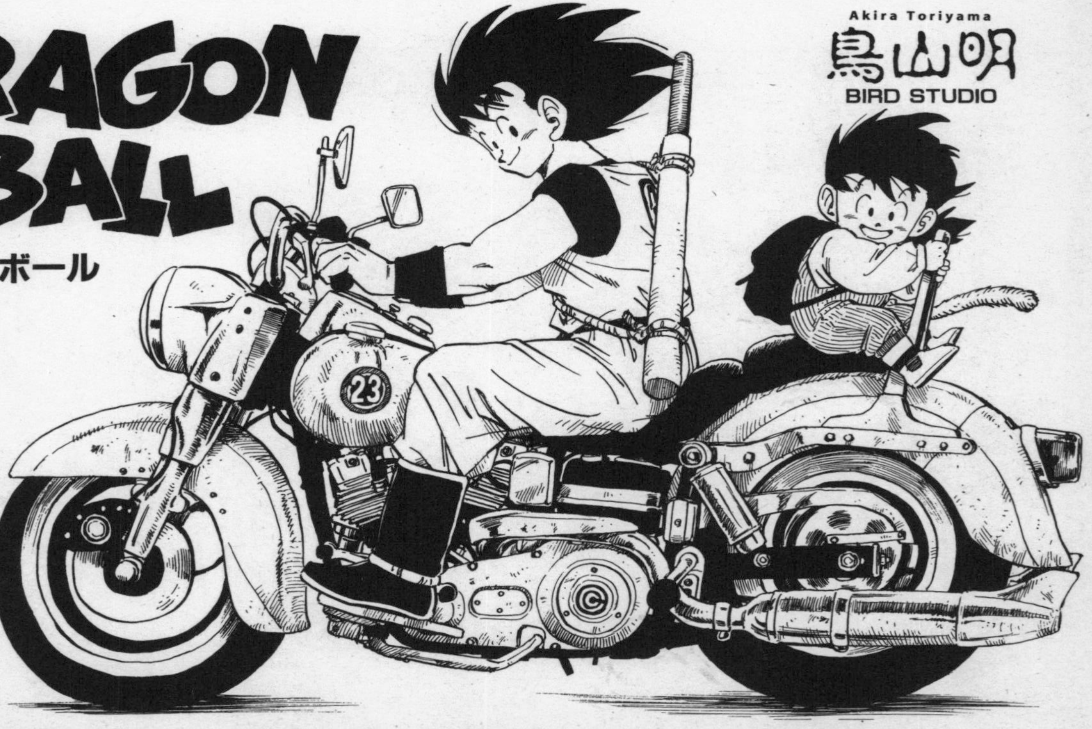

The Excitement Keeps Going… and Going…

DRAGON BALL

ドラゴンボール

Goku's Last Chance…Is Gohan!!?

STRIVE TO BE NO.1!

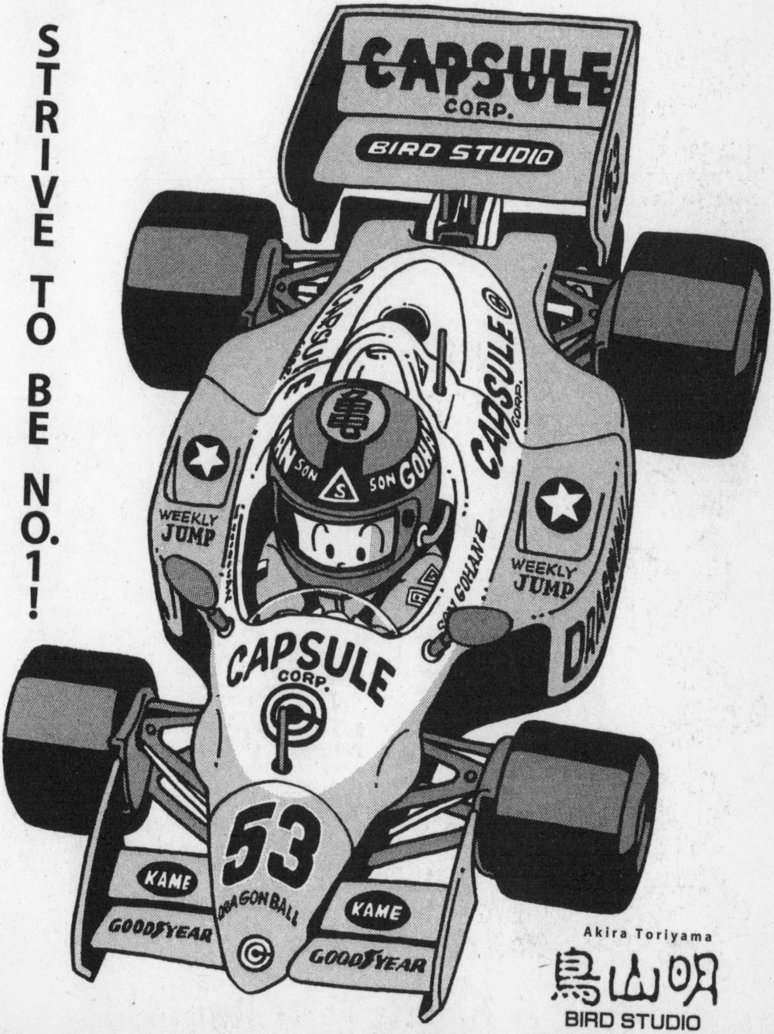
CAPSULE
CORP.
BIRD STUDIO
CAPSULE
CAPSULE
CORP.
CAPSULE
CORP.
SON
SON GOHAN
WEEKLY
JUMP
WEEKLY
JUMP
CAPSULE
CORP.
53
DRAGON BALL
KAME
KAME
GOODYEAR
GOODYEAR

Akira Toriyama
鳥山明
BIRD STUDIO

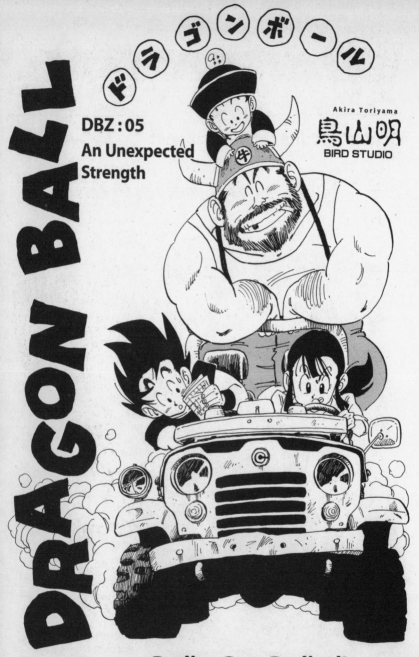

ドラゴンボール

DRAGON BALL

DBZ : 05

An Unexpected Strength

Akira Toriyama

鳥山明
BIRD STUDIO

Raditz Gets Radical!

ドラゴンボール

DRAGON BALL

DBZ:07 • Piccolo's Farewell to Arms!?

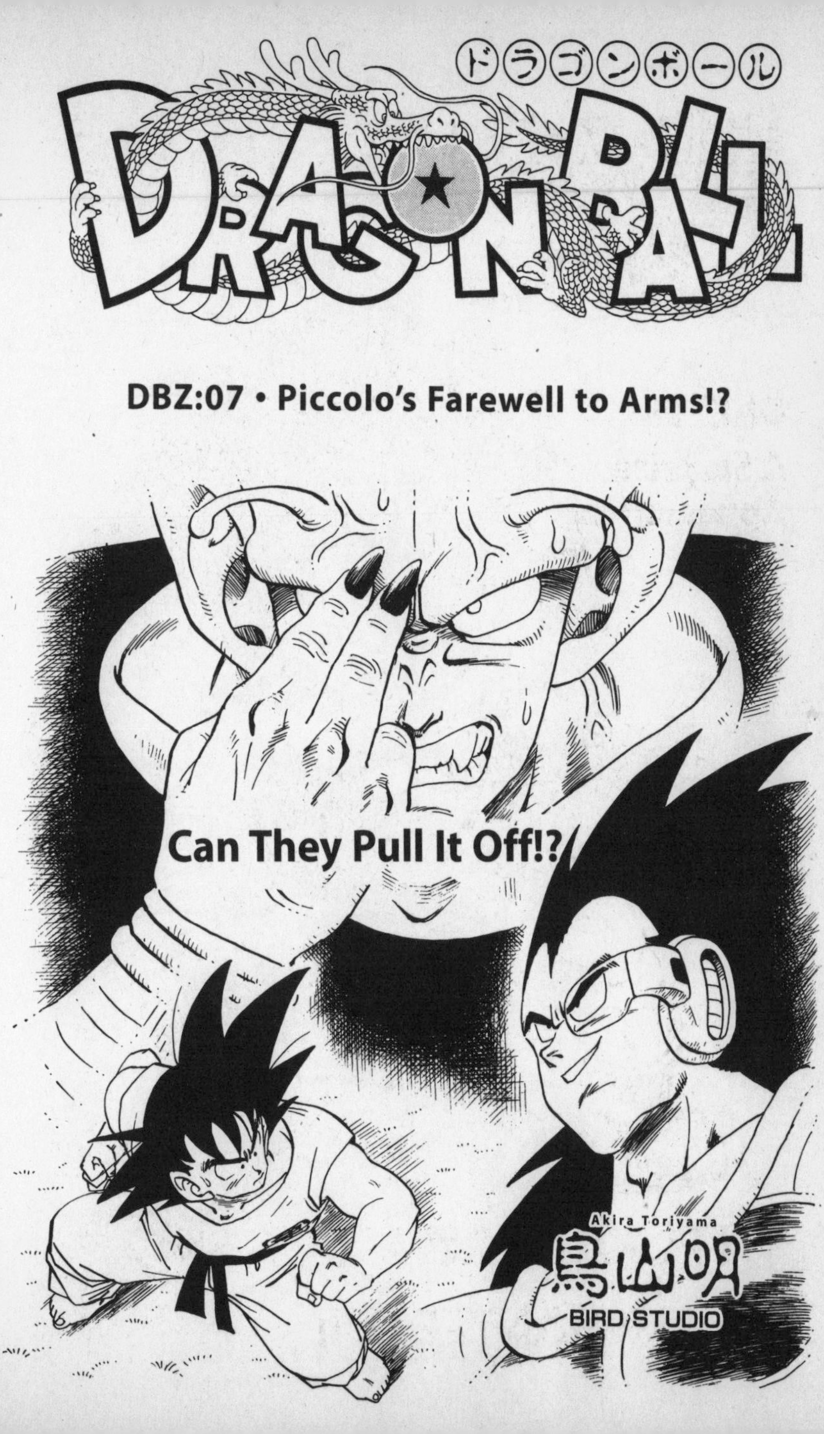

Can They Pull It Off!?
Akira Toriyama
鳥山明
BIRD STUDIO

DRAGON BALL

Akira Toriyama
鳥山明
BIRD STUDIO

DBZ : 08
A Surprise Appearance

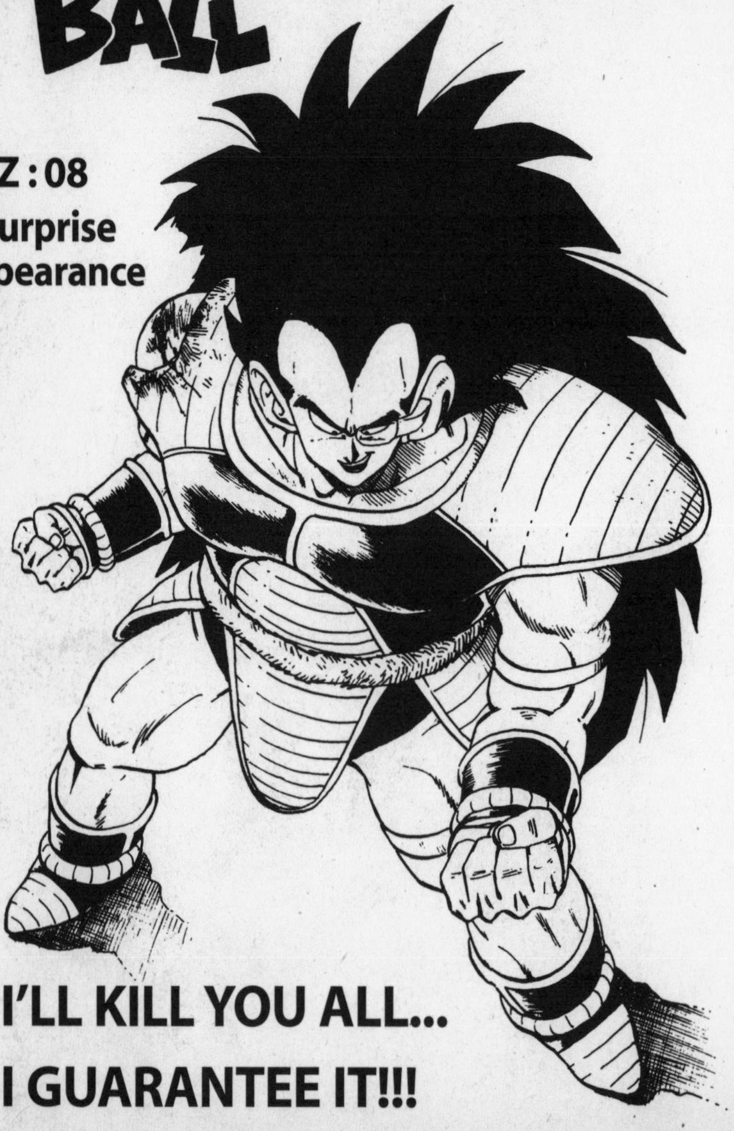

I'LL KILL YOU ALL...
I GUARANTEE IT!!!

DRAGON BALL

ドラゴンボール

DBZ:09 • Sayonara, Goku

Akira Toriyama
鳥山明
BIRD STUDIO

GONE... BUT NOT FORGOTTEN!

DRAGONBALL
Between Two Worlds

Akira Toriyama
鳥山明 BIRD STUDIO

THE FATEFUL YEAR BEGINS

ドラゴンボール

DRAGON BALL

DBZ:13
Son Gohan, the Iconsolable

Akira Toriyama
鳥山明
BIRD STUDIO

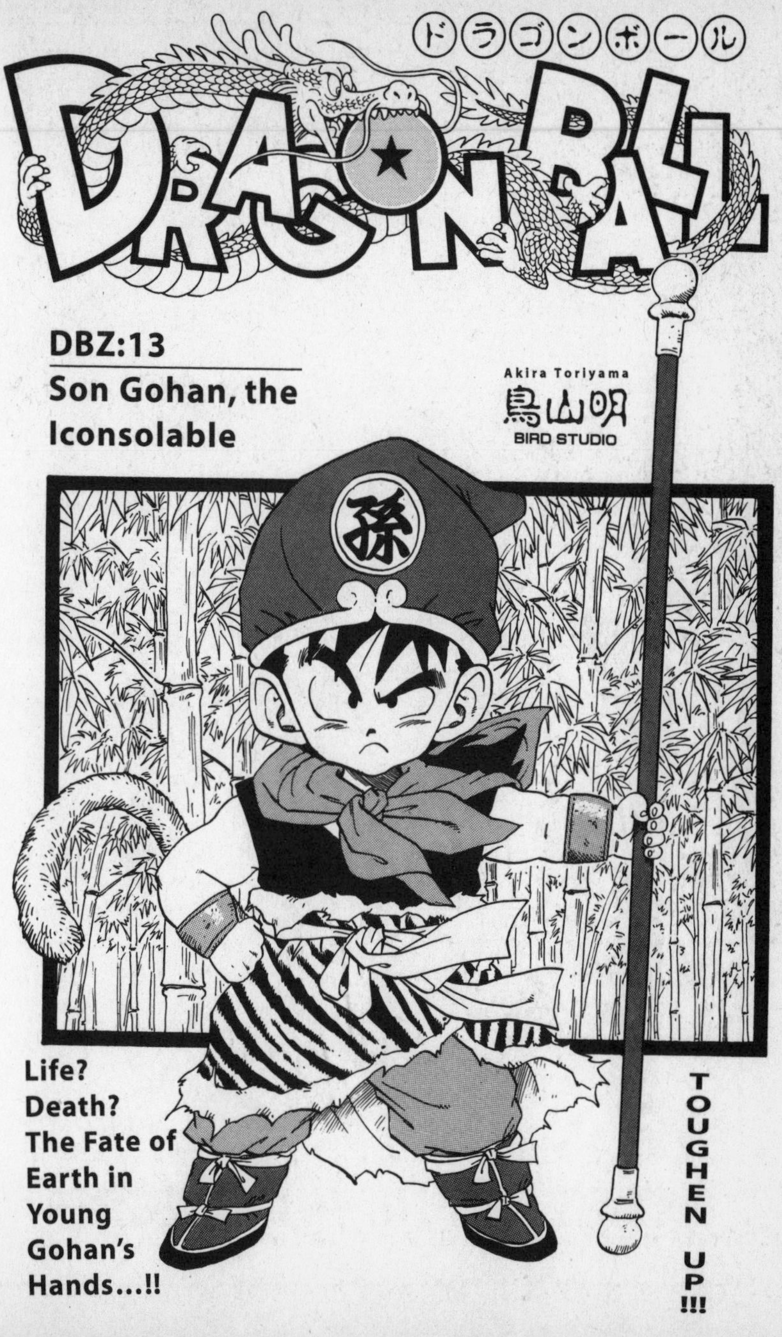

孫

Life? Death? The Fate of Earth in Young Gohan's Hands...!!

TOUGHEN UP!!!

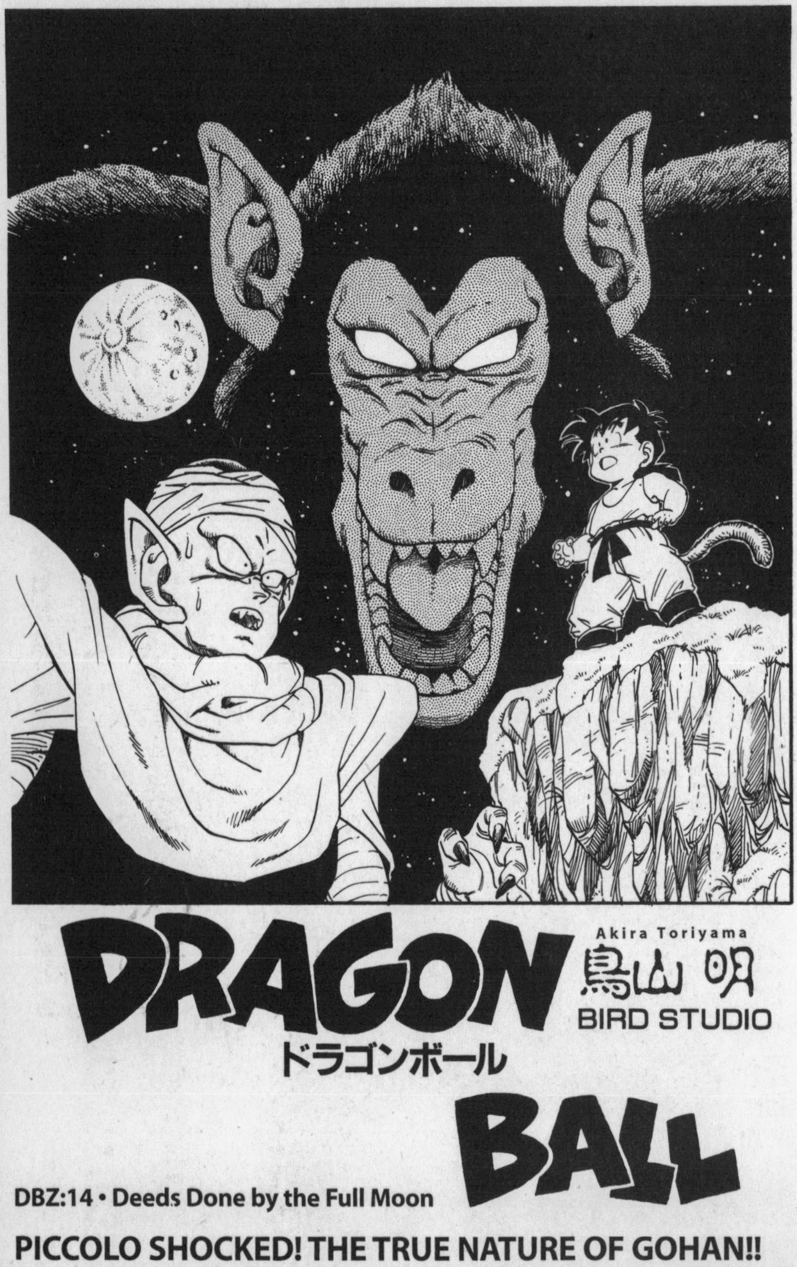

DRAGON BALL

ドラゴンボール

Akira Toriyama

鳥山 明

BIRD STUDIO

DBZ:14 • Deeds Done by the Full Moon

PICCOLO SHOCKED! THE TRUE NATURE OF GOHAN!!

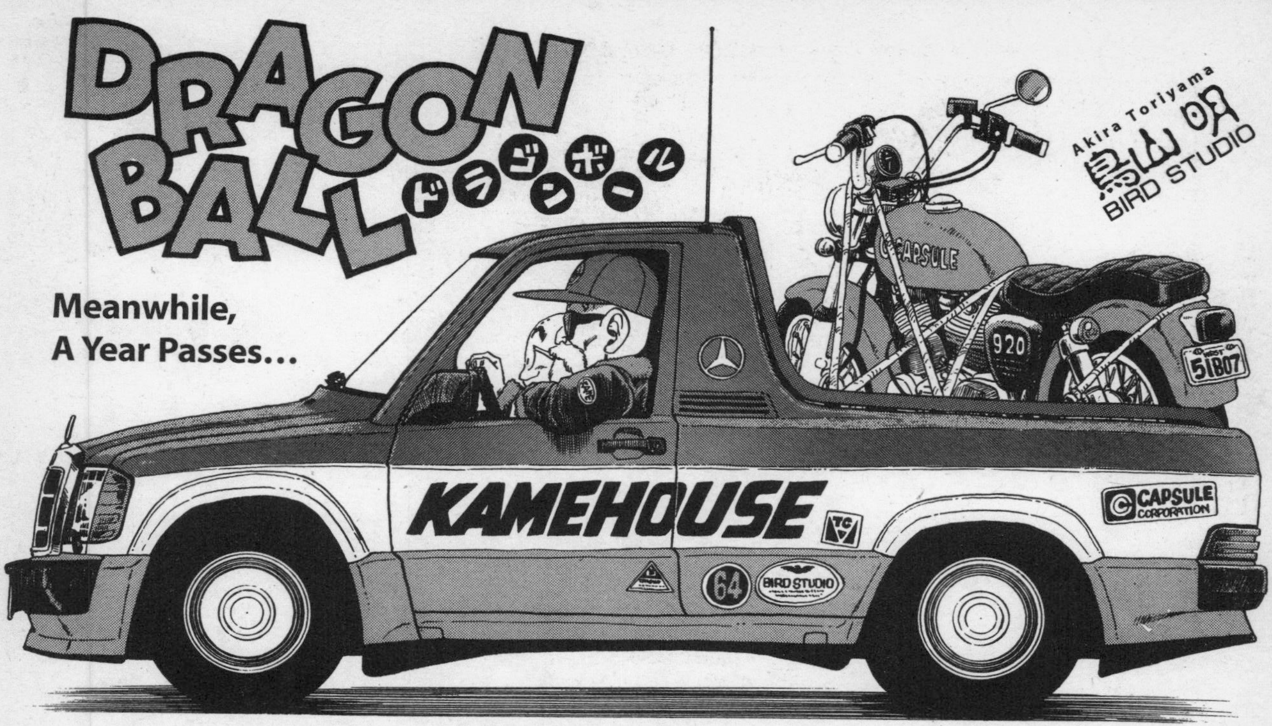
DRAGON BALL
ドラゴンボール
Meanwhile,
A Year Passes…
Akira Toriyama
鳥山明
BIRD STUDIO
KAMEHOUSE
CAPSULE CORPORATION
CAPSULE
920
51B07
64
BIRD STUDIO

Train Hard • Get Strong • Go Fast

On Heaven and Earth
Goku and Gohan's Training Begins!!!

TWO GENERATIONS • TWO KINDS OF TRAINING

AKIRA TORIYAMA 鳥山明 BIRD STUDIO

DRAGON BALL

ドラゴンボール

Akira Toriyama

鳥山明
BIRD STUDIO

DBZ:17 • The Hardest Time of His Death

MY TRAINING IS NOTHING TO LAUGH AT!